Medical Quality Management

Angelo P. Giardino
Lee Ann Riesenberg • Prathibha Varkey

Editors

Medical Quality Management

Theory and Practice

Third Edition

Editors
Angelo P. Giardino
Department of Pediatrics
University of Utah School of Medicine
Salt Lake City, UT, USA

Prathibha Varkey
Northeast Medical Group
Yale New Haven Health
Stratford, CT, USA

Lee Ann Riesenberg
Department of Anesthesiology
and Perioperative Medicine
University of Alabama at Birmingham
Birmingham, AL, USA

ISBN 978-3-030-48082-0   ISBN 978-3-030-48080-6   (eBook)
https://doi.org/10.1007/978-3-030-48080-6

This Springer imprint is published by the registered company Springer Nature Switzerland AG
The registered company address is: Gewerbestrasse 11, 6330 Cham, Switzerland

My work on this book is dedicate to Dr. Richard J. Baron, President and CEO of the American Board of Internal Medicine Foundation, who in the early 1990s, while we were both at Health Partners of Philadelphia, introduced me to the transformational work of Dr. Avedis Donabedian. Dr. Baron's encouragement and outstanding mentorship allowed me to build a strong foundation in Quality Improvement and he modeled how to strike a balance among a commitment to clinical care, the heart of a medical educator, and the stewardship of a healthcare administrator.

Angelo P. Giardino, MD, PhD, MPH, CMQ

I dedicate my work on this book to Dr. Donald M. Berwick, a passionate and tireless advocate for healthcare system improvement. Of his many accomplishments, I am particularly grateful for his leadership and innovation in launching the IHI Open School for Health Professions in 2008, which has provided a rich Quality and Patient Safety educational resource for countless healthcare students and professionals.

Lee Ann Riesenberg, PhD, MS, RN

I dedicate my work on this third edition of Medical Quality Management: Theory and Practice to all healthcare professionals who have committed to making positive change in improving healthcare and our systems.

Prathibha Varkey, MBBS, MPH, MHPE, MBA

Foreword

I have never been convinced that competition by itself will improve the efficiency or the effectiveness of care or even that it will reduce the cost of care....Health care is a sacred mission. It is a moral enterprise and a scientific enterprise, but not fundamentally a commercial one... Doctors and nurses are stewards of something precious. Their work is a kind of vocation rather than simply a job; commercial values don't really capture what they do for patients and for society as a whole.

—Avedis Donabedian, MD, MPH

The American College of Medical Quality continues to be a national leader in educating the medical community about both the science and the practice of medical quality management. The third edition of *Medical Quality Management: Theory and Practice* underscores the College's commitment to the shared vision of a safer, responsive healthcare system and provides many resources to readers to guide our collective journey. While much of the basics of medical quality management remain constant, it is essential that new and revised information be provided. Changes within the culture of medicine, technology, and new innovations in care management require that we acknowledge, inform, and educate healthcare professionals on the changing tide of medical quality management.

This third edition of the American College of Medical Quality's textbook is revised to include the latest information on quality improvement, measurement, and the many facets of medical quality that prove essential to the ever-evolving field of healthcare. Every chapter has been updated to impart the latest information on the specific areas that comprise the creation, improvement, and management of medical quality in every healthcare arena. "Data Analytics for the Improvement of Health Care Quality" and "Ethics and Quality Improvement" are new chapters in the third edition. The topic of ethics was previously covered in the chapter on quality improvement and the law; however, technological innovation and the use of electronic health records demands attention to potential ethical dilemmas afforded by the adoption and use of these means. With an expanded view of ethical considerations related to quality and patient safety, in addition to a thorough overview of the four pillars of ethics, this chapter seeks to uncover a myriad of evolving ethical issues.

Unfortunately, up-and-coming medical professionals do not always consider quality and quality improvement to be of great concern when first starting out on their career. I urge everyone, however, to make medical quality, safety, and quality improvement the foundation of your experience and "sacred mission" as a healthcare professional. I heartily encourage all healthcare professionals to read this book and utilize the concepts provided by the outstanding contributors who gave so generously of themselves to create this edition.

Paula J. Santrach, MD
Associate Professor, Laboratory Medicine and Pathology
Former Chief Quality Officer
Mayo Clinic

Book Abstract

This comprehensive medical textbook, *Medical Quality Management: Theory and Practice, Third Edition* is a compendium of the latest information on healthcare quality. This text provides knowledge about the theory and practical applications for each of the core areas that comprise the field of medical quality management as well as insight and essential briefings on the impact of new healthcare technologies and innovations on medical quality and improvement. The third edition provides significant new content related to medical quality management and quality improvement, a user-friendly format, and updated learning objectives.

Preface

I have looked in many places for the source of the commitment that would bring about such dedication to quality. I have seen it in professional values and traditions. It is implicit in the contract between the professions and society – a contract that confers privileges on the former in return for responsibilities toward the latter. I have wished to see it in each practitioner's need for the respect of colleagues and the gratitude of patients; in the quest for acceptance, for success, for the joy in virtuosity. Often, I have cast the commitment to quality in moral terms, preferring to see it as the ethical imperative that must govern the conduct of all caregivers.

—Avedis Donabedian, MD

The publication of the third edition of this textbook is a milestone for The American College of Medical Quality (ACMQ) as a leading organization in the training and skill building of quality improvement and patient safety professionals. ACMQ is a national organization of healthcare professionals who are interested in the advancement of medical quality and patient safety as a field of study and practice. Origins of ACMQ date back to 1973, when it was first called the American College of Utilization Review Physicians (ACURP). It is formally recognized by the American Medical Association and holds a seat in its House of Delegates.

A brief look back at the book's history is in order. In 2005, with a sizeable grant of $100,000 from Merck & Company, ACMQ produced the first edition titled *A Core Curriculum for Medical Quality Management*, edited by James Ziegenfuss, Jr., PhD, and Mark Lyles, MD, MBA. In 2009, a revised and updated second edition was edited by Prathibha Varkey, MBBS, MPH, MHPE, MBA, and was re-titled *Medical Quality Management: Theory and Practice*. And now, a revised and updated third edition with Dr. Varkey as Senior Editor joined by two additional ACMQ members as co-editors has been written.

In the Foreword to the second edition, Carolyn M. Clancy, MD, then the Director of the federal Agency for Healthcare Research and Quality, commended ACMQ and *Medical Quality Management: Theory and Practice* as follows:

> The American College of Medical Quality continues to be a national leader in educating the medical community about both the science and the practice of medical quality management. The new edition of this book underscores the College's commitment to our shared vision of a safer health care system and provides many resources to readers that will guide our journey.

The opening quote by the medical quality management icon, Avedis Donabedian, MD, casts the pursuit of quality and safety in healthcare as rooted in the values and traditions of the healthcare profession, the privileges enjoyed by those professionals that emanate from the responsibilities to the patient, and ultimately, as a moral imperative to do one's best for the patients whom we serve. ACMQ embraces these pursuits and offers a robust approach to learning the content at the foundation of medical quality management that its members adhere to — the values and traditions of which Donabedian speaks. This book, in its third edition, seeks to assist in that training and educational process.

We would like to acknowledge contributors from the second edition who made an indelible impression on the material presented herein and who were unable to participate in this third edition:

Harry Pigman, MD, MSHP
Quality Measurement

Lakshmi P. Chelluri, MD, MPH, CMQ
Patient Safety

Sharon Wilson, RN, BS, PMP
Patient Safety

Louis H. Diamond, MB, ChB, FACP
Health Informatics

Stephen T. Lawless, MD, MBA
Health Informatics

Arthur L. Pelberg, MD, MPA
Utilization Management

Thomas Biancaniello, MD, FACC
Organization Design and Management

James T. Ziegenfuss, Jr., PhD
Organization Design and Management

Mano S. Selvan, PhD
The Interface Between Quality Improvement, Law, and Medical Ethics

Jeffrey M. Zale, MD, MPH, CMQ
The Interface Between Quality Improvement, Law, and Medical Ethics

Salt Lake City, UT, USA   Angelo P. Giardino
Birmingham, AL, USA   Lee Ann Riesenberg
Stratford, CT, USA   Prathibha Varkey

About the Book

Medical Quality Management: Theory and Practice, Third Edition is written as a basic text to describe the key components of medical quality management (MQM). As such, this text has applicability for novices, committed students, and seasoned practitioners within the field. Each chapter has been designed for a review of the essential background, precepts, and exemplary practices within the topical area. A common format is followed within the chapters to provide structure to the authors' comments, including useful learning objectives, case studies, inter-chapter cross-references, and scholarly references. Each chapter seeks to reliably capture the essential elements that will allow a diligent reader to establish a practical fluency in the topic. As the editors, we are appreciative of the chapter authors who are all highly trained experts in their topical areas and who have summarized their extensive knowledge and experiences into exceptionally well-researched and written text. Individual chapters focus on the following core curriculum essentials.

Chapter 1 is a short introduction to the concept of medical quality management and its core components and objectives. It outlines the essential elements of a curriculum for teaching MQM and highlights the historical calls to integrate MQM training and implementation into the healthcare system.

Chapter 2 sets the tone and foundation for the book by highlighting the basic historical drivers of medical quality assurance and quality improvement by reviewing the major concepts and common applications of quality improvement (QI) methods and strategies, and by outlining the challenges and opportunities within the rapidly evolving field of medical quality management. The chapter opens the door to a sometimes complex field of quality measurement methods and systems, operational processes, and strategies.

Chapter 3 focuses on the history, types, characteristics, processes, and interpretations of quality measurements. This chapter provides a framework for understanding the basic components of quality measurement within direct care and policy-making settings, exemplified by illustrative case studies, and provides new information on the criteria for successful process measures, bundled measures, and balancing measures. The author effectively correlates the critical interface of quality measurement strategies and methods to areas highlighted in other chapters, especially medical informatics, utilization and quality management, patient safety, and health policy development.

Chapter 4 provides a detailed overview of the major patient safety concepts; specific, high profile medication errors and failures; and causal factors, including analysis methodologies and root cause analysis strategies. The chapter discusses perioperative complications and iatrogenic injuries, care transitions, bundles and patient safety collaboratives, techniques and tools for systematic patient safety enhancement (PSE), and future trends in patient safety measures. The authors also focus on attributes of high-reliability organizations and operational interventions for PSE and the national momentum towards substantive investments in patient safety promotion tracking and educational systems, representing a true megatrend in healthcare and a core area of focus in MQM.

Chapter 5 addresses updated developments and challenges within health informatics, a central component of MQM that has become a pivotal aspect of healthcare in the twenty-first century. The author concretely summarizes the major developments of medical informatics infrastructures, including health information exchange, data warehousing, coding classification systems, clinical decision support, data integrity, transparency, quality control and innovation, and analysis. A discussion of documentation modalities and updates to EHR information is also presented, in addition to a brief history of health informatics in the USA and current trends.

Chapter 6 is a new chapter produced for the third edition which addresses the growing sophistication of data analytics and its role in improving patient outcomes. This chapter summarizes the importance of mining big data and converting it to a useable form that coalesces technology and expertise in a manner that can be effectively applied to clinical and population health settings. The authors present timely information on the benefits of data analytics to healthcare systems and how accurate, precise data serve to measure healthcare value, discover areas in which quality improvement strategies could have a measurable impact, advance analytic maturity within an organization, and improve health outcomes.

Chapter 7 describes the essential processes, tasks, and common systems of utilization management (UM) and care coordination (CC). UM focuses upon prior authorization and concurrent and retrospective forms of utilization review to establish *medical necessity* of care. Medical necessity criteria, processes for determining the effectiveness and value of UM procedures (e.g., over- and underutilization markers), common organizational structures for UM activities, and accreditation standards and programs are also detailed. New sections in this chapter include a discussion of the role of UM in disease management, pay-for-performance programs, and models of care. This section is particularly important due to the current focus on the coordination of care models to make improvements in cost and quality. Care coordination focuses on the deliberate integration of personnel, providers, information, and resources to facilitate required patient care activities and the efficient delivery of healthcare services both within and across systems.

Chapter 8 focuses on organizational design and leadership in quality management. Most of the publications in these areas tend to be theoretical and descriptive rather than framed by the numbers and facts with which most health professionals are familiar. The discussions on quality management leadership, collaboration, strategic and operational planning, implementation, data analysis, and feedback are all presented clearly and—like all of the chapters—with an abundance of relevant references.

Chapter 9 presents the subject of economics and finance in relation to MQM and quality improvement with a detailed approach. They elaborate on major economic and business principles relevant to the future practice of MQM, including those related to accounting and finance, value and compensation in healthcare, organizational planning and psychology, project management, the development of business plans and financial statements, and sensitivity analyses. MQM professionals will need to make the business case for clinical services, framed by quality management objectives and outcomes metrics. The authors elegantly frame the lessons in this chapter, including several instructive case studies.

Chapter 10 focuses on key external QI activities, including accreditation, professional certification, and quality improvement education. It highlights major healthcare standards-setting and accreditation organizations, including medical specialty board certification, state professional licensing, and prominent national accreditation organizations such as the National Committee for Quality Assurance, Utilization Review Accreditation Commission, and the Joint Commission. The chapter discusses the Centers for Medicare and Medicaid Services' Center for Clinical Standards & Quality, the new Quality Payment Program, the CMS Five-Star Quality Rating System, and Accountable Care Organizations, and includes statistics from the 2016 Leapfrog Group Hospital Report. External QI resources serve to integrate the diverse number of utilization, quality, and risk management activities that frame clinical systems of care. The chapter includes a new focus on the importance of QI education for medical students and practicing physicians.

Chapter 11 addresses legal requirements, and the authors review several current, major national legal mechanisms for quality promotion such as the National Practitioner Data Bank, accreditation activities, peer review protections, the tort system, clinical practice guidelines, institutional review boards, and medical ethics programs. The chapter also provides thoughtful commentary about evolving trends aimed at improving the quality of healthcare service and delivery. Notable current movements that are evolving include how to handle apologies when a medical error has occurred, patient safety activities, and pay-for-performance initiatives.

Finally, Chapter 12 is also a new chapter for the third edition which provides an in-depth look at the prevailing values that affect quality ethics and the related clinical frameworks that guide decision-making and best practice in terms of patient safety and quality improvement efforts. The chapter also delves into ethics in research and describes effective, ethical, systematic investigation and, additionally, how research and quality improvement overlap in practice. Chapter themes also include a discussion of the Institutional Review Board and their review of quality improvement projects, as well as the foundational principles that guide the review and discussion of clinical dilemmas.

Contents

About the Editors

Angelo P. Giardino MD, PhD, MPH, CMQ, is the Wilma T. Gibson Presidential Professor and Chair of the Department of Pediatrics at the University of Utah School of Medicine. He also serves as the Chief Medical Officer at Intermountain Primary Children's Hospital in Salt Lake City, UT. Prior to arriving in Utah, Dr. Giardino served as Senior Vice President/Chief Quality Office at Texas Children's Hospital and was Professor of Pediatrics and Section Chief of Academic General Pediatrics at Baylor College of Medicine (BCM). He received his medical degree and doctorate in education from the University of Pennsylvania; completed his residency and fellowship training at The Children's Hospital of Philadelphia (CHOP); earned a Master's in Public Health from the University of Massachusetts, a Master's in Theology from Catholic Distance University (CDU), and a Master's in Public Affairs from the University of Texas Rio Grande Valley; and is a Certified Physician Executive (CPE) within the American Association for Physician Leadership. He completed the Patient Safety Certificate Program from the Quality Colloquium, is certified in medical quality (CMQ) as designated by the American Board of Medical Quality, and is a Distinguished Fellow of the American College of Medical Quality. He holds subspecialty certifications in Pediatrics and Child Abuse Pediatrics by the American Board of Pediatrics. He is a recipient of the Fulbright & Jaworski L. L. P. Faculty Excellence Award at BCM. Dr. Giardino serves as an Associate Editor for the 23rd edition of the classic *Rudolph's Textbook of Pediatrics*, is Co-Editor of the 4th edition of the *Medical Evaluation of Child Sexual Abuse* published by the American Academy of Pediatrics, and serves as the Co-Editor-in-Chief of the *Journal of Family Strengths*. Dr. Giardino serves on the Board of Directors of Prevent Child Abuse America, CDU, US Center for Safe Sport, and Intermountain Community Care Foundation.

Lee Ann Riesenberg PhD, MS, RN, CMQ, is Professor and Associate Director of Education, Anesthesiology, and Perioperative Medicine at the University of Alabama at Birmingham. Dr. Riesenberg works as a medical educator and conducts medical education and quality and patient safety outcomes research. Dr. Riesenberg has worked in medical education for 25 years, received numerous recognition awards for her dedication to medical education and quality improvement in graduate medical education, and serves on the editorial board of the American Journal of Medical Quality.

Prathibha Varkey MBBS, MPH, MHPE, MBA, is the CEO and President of the Yale New Haven Health Northeast Medical Group, home of about 1000 clinicians in CT, RI, and NYC. Dr. Varkey is a Professor of Medicine at the Yale School of Medicine and a Professor of Health Policy and Management at the Yale School of Public Health. Dr. Varkey is a past president of the American College of Medical Quality. Previously, Dr. Varkey served as the turnaround CEO of the Seton Clinical Enterprise in Austin, TX, and in various leadership roles at Mayo Clinic Rochester: Associate Chair of the Department of Medicine, Program Director of the Preventive Medicine Fellowship, Director of Quality at the Division of Preventive and Occupational Medicine, and Director of Quality at Mayo School of Graduate Medical Education and Mayo School of Continuing Medical Education.

Contributors

Julia Caldwell MD, MHA, CMQ, is an Assistant Professor of Anesthesiology, Pain, and Perioperative Medicine. She is board certified in anesthesiology, pain medicine, and medical quality. She is deeply passionate about resident education, pain medicine, and medical quality. Dr. Caldwell is an active leader on the educational and abstract committees within the American Medical College of Quality. She enjoys research as well as providing safe and quality care to her patients and the community

Kathleen F. Carberry RN, MPH, is the Outcomes Program Officer at the Value Institute for Health and Care at the University of Texas at Austin's Dell Medical School and McCombs School of Business where she teaches outcome measurement. She also engages with healthcare teams to implement outcome measurement strategies that drive the creation of high-value healthcare services. She is passionate about measuring the outcomes that matter most to patients and partnering with healthcare teams to create measurement systems that readily demonstrate improved outcomes for patients.

Nancy L. Davis PhD, is a Professor and Associate Dean of Faculty Development at the University of Kansas School of Medicine. She previously served as Director, Practice-Based Learning and Improvement, Association of American Medical Colleges; Executive Director, National Institute for Quality Improvement and Education; and Director, CME, American Academy of Family Physicians. She helped design the CME credit designation for clinical performance improvement. Dr. Davis earned a PhD in Adult and Continuing Education. She serves on the Editorial Board of the *American Journal of Medical Quality*, teaches, presents in national forums, and is widely published. She has been credentialed as a Certified Diabetes Educator, a Certified CME Professional, and a Certified Professional in Healthcare Quality.

Marc T. Edwards MD, MBA, has more than 30 years of healthcare management and consulting experience, including service as the senior physician executive in both teaching and community hospitals. He operated a federally listed and Connecticut-authorized Patient Safety Organization from 2010 to 2019. A native of Seattle, he graduated from the University of Washington. He earned his MD degree from the University of Colorado, trained in Family Medicine at Thomas Jefferson University Hospital, and completed an MBA at the University of Connecticut. He is a member of Phi Beta Kappa and maintains board certification in Family Medicine. He is an authority on best practices in clinical peer review having conducted four national studies and published 11 related scientific manuscripts. He relocated to Chapel Hill, NC, from Connecticut in 2017 and contributes to University of North Carolina School of Medicine as adjunct faculty.

Donald Fetterolf MD, MBA, FACP, is currently the Chief Medical Officer of MiMedx Group, Inc. Prior roles include EVP of Health Intelligence at Alere, Inc.; EVP of Matria Healthcare; Chief Medical Officer of Highmark, Inc.; and president of a multi-physician medical group practice. Dr. Fetterolf received undergraduate and medical degrees from the University of Pennsylvania and completed internal medicine training at the University of Pittsburgh, where he also received an MBA degree. He is Past President and a Distinguished Fellow of the American College of Medical Quality, and is Past Chairman of the American Board of Medical Quality. Dr. Fetterolf was the first recipient of the Brian Hayes Award of the Blue Cross Blue Shield Association and was awarded the 2006 Annual Disease Management Association of America Award for Outstanding Individual Leadership. He is a Fellow of the American College of Physicians and of the College of Physicians of Philadelphia.

Elizabeth A. Fracica MD, MPH, is in her first year of residency training at Johns Hopkins Hospital and completed her medical training at the Mayo Clinic School of Medicine. She has already contributed to federal and state-level healthcare delivery reform efforts through her work on the Maryland All Payer Model. She looks forward to pursuing a career in academic Neurology and healthcare reform.

Philip J. Fracica MD, MBA, FACP, is Chief Medical Officer at Bothwell Regional Health Center in Sedalia, Missouri. He also serves as Medical Director for Hospitalist Services. Dr. Fracica's experience includes 25 years as a Medical ICU Director at tertiary care academic medical centers. For the last 10 years he has served as Chief Medical Officer at institutions in Missouri, Texas, and Arizona.

Eileen R. Giardino PhD, RN, APRN, is an Associate Professor for the Department of Adult Health and Gerontological Nursing at Rush University College of Nursing and Adjunct Associate Professor in the Division of Health Systems and Community Based Care at the University of Utah College of Nursing. She earned a Bachelor of Science and PhD in Education from the University of Pennsylvania, and is certified as a family and adult nurse practitioner. Dr. Giardino teaches courses in quality improvement in the Doctor of Nursing Practice (DNP) program and works with doctoral students on their DNP scholarly projects, many of which are quality improvement initiatives at the clinical affiliates of DNP program.

Carrie Guttman MSN, BA, BS, RN, is the Nursing Lead and Quality Manager at Northeast Medical Group (NEMG) in Connecticut. She currently has oversight of nursing function at NEMG, quality improvement for all community-based sites, and clinical performance reporting. Her background includes gynecology oncology, hospital patient safety, and ambulatory clinical quality. Responsibilities include leading a quality collaborative that engages 30+ sites, managing a team of business analysts, and optimizing nursing practice across an organization that spans three states.

Linda Harrington PhD, DNP, RN-BC, CNS, CPHQ, CENP, UXC, CPHIMS, FHIMSS, is a Professor at Baylor College of Medicine where she teaches quality outcomes management, statistics, and informatics. She holds a DNP and post-master's certificate in informatics from Duke University, a PhD from Texas Woman's University, and is certified in healthcare quality and informatics. Linda serves as the Technology Today column editor for the American Association of Critical-Care Nurses' *Advanced Critical Care* and lead author of *Usability Evaluation Handbook for Electronic Health Records.*

Jennifer Hooks MBA, is Manager of Performance Improvement at the Medical University of South Carolina, where she is responsible for the deployment of Lean Six Sigma throughout the organization. She is an adjunct faculty member in MUSC College of Health Professions and College of Nursing where she teaches Lean Six Sigma methodology. Ms. Hooks is a retired Air Force Chief Master Sergeant and a certified Six Sigma Master Black Belt and also holds a LEAN Sensei Certification from Villanova University.

Antoine Kfuri MD, MPH, FACOG, currently serves as a senior medical director in the Clinical Analytics department at Inovalon. Dr. Kfuri is extensively involved in the clinical design, implementation, and improvement of Inovalon's portfolio of healthcare data analytics solutions, clinical data review tools, and clinical data integrity and quality oversight programs. Dr. Kfuri's medical expertise, coupled with his clinical experience and successful quality improvement programs and data analytics, foster effective patient-provider engagement and contribute to successful outcomes in areas of patient quality, utilization and cost management, and reporting. Prior experience includes clinical practice for more than 20 years and time as a consultant in Healthcare Management, leading to performance excellence awards. Dr. Kfuri is board certified by the American Board of Obstetrics & Gynecology. He is certified in both Health Policy and Health Finance & Management by the Johns Hopkins School of Public Health and holds an MPH in Health Management & Leadership from the Johns Hopkins School of Public Health. Dr. Kfuri is also a Senior Alumni Examiner and Team Leader for the prestigious Baldrige National

Performance Excellence Program (BPEP) and is a Senior Examiner and a Team Leader for the State of Maryland Performance Excellence Award Program (MPEA). He is also a senior fellow and Quality Judge in the Healthcare Division of the American Society of Quality (ASQ).

Michelle A. Lyn MD, FAAP, is an Associate Professor of Pediatrics at Baylor College of Medicine and the Medical Director of Care Management/Patient Flow at Texas Children's Hospital in Houston. She received her medical degree from the State University of New York at Buffalo School of Medicine and completed her residency in Pediatrics at Albert Einstein College of Medicine-Montefiore Medical Center in Bronx, New York. After serving an additional year as Chief Resident, she moved to Texas to complete her postgraduate fellowship in Pediatric Emergency Medicine at Baylor College of Medicine. Dr. Lyn holds board certifications in Pediatrics, Pediatric Emergency Medicine, and Child Abuse Pediatrics. Dr. Lyn is an administrator, educator, and clinician. She previously served as the Chief of Child Protection in the Section of Emergency Medicine. Dr. Lyn is the recipient of the Baylor College of Medicine Department of Pediatrics Award of General Excellence in Teaching and the Baylor College of Medicine Fulbright and Jaworski Excellence in Teaching Award. She is also the recipient of several Houston community awards including the Breakthrough Women Award from Texas Executive Women and The Houston Chronicle and the Unstoppable Leader Award from the Greater Houston Women Chamber of Commerce.

Charles G. Macias MD, MPH, is an Associate Professor of Pediatrics at Case Western Reserve University and serves as Vice Chair and Chief Quality Officer for University Hospitals Rainbow Babies and Children's Hospital. He is executive director of the national EMS for Children Innovation and Improvement Center, utilizing improvement science to help drive improved outcomes for ill or injured children in 58 states and territories. He chairs or co-chairs a number of quality improvement collaboratives, including the Improving Pediatric Sepsis Outcomes quality collaborative dedicated to decreasing mortality and morbidity from sepsis in greater than 50 hospitals. He was named HealthData Management's Clinical Visionary of the Year in 2014.

Robert McLean MD, MACP, is currently an Associate Clinical Professor of Medicine at the Yale School of Medicine. He has practiced internal medicine and rheumatology in New Haven since 1994. In 2013, he became chair of the Clinical Integration Steering Committee for Yale New Haven Health System and chair of the Quality & Performance Improvement Committee for Northeast Medical Group. In 2016, he became Medical Director for Clinical Quality at Northeast Medical Group. He served on the American College of Physicians' Medical Practice & Quality Committee from 2013 to 2017, and as Chairman from 2015 to 2017.

Perry Ann Reed MBA, MS, FACHE, is Executive Director of WakeMed Children's Hospital, where she oversees strategy formulation and execution, financial performance, and operational management. Previously, as Director of Ethics and Palliative Care at Texas Children's Hospital, she launched and led these two service lines. She holds an MBA in healthcare management from the University of Texas and an MS in Bioethics from Columbia University. Recent published chapters include "Law, Ethics and Clinical Judgment" in *Rudolf's Pediatrics* 23rd Edition. She and her husband John have four children.

Rahul K. Shah MD, MBA, FACS, FAAP, obtained a combined BA/MD from Boston University School of Medicine and completed his Otolaryngology residency at Tufts University, followed by a fellowship in Pediatric Otolaryngology at Children's Hospital Boston at Harvard University. After fellowship, he joined the faculty of Children's National Hospital, rising to the rank of Professor. He is recognized as a leader in patient safety and quality improvement and has chaired and serves on several national committees related to patient safety and quality improvement. He was the Executive Director of an international not-for-profit quality improvement initiative, the Global Tracheostomy Collaborative. He was the inaugural Associate Surgeon-in-Chief (Chief, Perioperative Services) within the Joseph E. Robert, Jr. Center for Surgical Care at Children's National Hospital and the Medical Director of Perioperative Services from 2011 to 2014. He served as President of the Medical Staff at Children's National Hospital from 2012 to 2014. In 2014, he was appointed the inaugural Vice-President, Chief Quality and Safety Officer for Children's National Health System. Under his leadership, Children's National has received numerous safety and quality distinctions and is a recognized leader in pediatric safety and quality.

David W. West MD, MMI, completed his pediatric residence at University of Virginia and then completed a fellowship in General Academic Pediatrics at Johns Hopkins University. He came to Nemours in 1989 and practiced as a primary care physician, consultative physician, and hospitalist. He subsequently served as the Medical Director of Primary Care for Nemours Children's Clinic in Delaware. In 1996, he was appointed Chief of Medical Informatics. In this role, he has overseen the deployment of a single integrated electronic health record for over 700 Nemours physicians practicing at two tertiary care children's hospitals and dozens of ambulatory locations across four states. He was board certified in medical informatics in 2016 after receiving his Master's degree in Medical Informatics from Northwestern University. He currently leads initiatives in precision medicine, patient engagement, and interoperability with external healthcare systems. Under his leadership, Nemours has successfully achieved Meaningful Use for both its Eligible Providers and Eligible Hospitals resulting in awards in excess of $20 million. In 2010 under Dr. West's guidance, Nemours earned the HIMSS Davies Organizational Award honoring Excellence in Health Information Technology. Both children's hospitals in the Nemours network, Alfred I DuPont Hospital for Children (Wilmington, DE) and Nemours Children's Hospital (Orlando, FL), have achieved Health Level 7 certification by HIMSS, indicating the highest level of health information technology integration for promoting improved healthcare quality and outcomes.

Chapter 1
Introduction

Angelo P. Giardino, Lee Ann Riesenberg, and Prathibha Varkey

Medical quality management (MQM) is elemental to clinical services and has been recognized as an area of medical specialization by the American Medical Association.

While many healthcare professionals have become engaged in MQM activities over the course of their clinical careers, only a few have received any formal training or orientation in the field during their undergraduate or postgraduate professional training. During their formative training, medical and nursing students and residents may become aware that some licensed professionals are involved in utilization review, quality improvement, and risk management activities; however, few are aware of the rich scientific base and health tradition that frames the field. In the foreword to the first edition of this book, Dr. George C. Martin offered a comment on the role of the American College of Medical Quality (ACMQ) in MQM, observing:

> The objectives of ACMQ's educational programs in medical quality management and clinical quality improvement are to: develop and disseminate a core body of knowledge; provide a forum for health care professionals, government agencies, and other regulatory bodies; take a leadership role in creating, sustaining, and applying a scientifically based infrastructure for the specialty; elevate the standards of medical schools and post-graduate education in quality management; and sponsor on-going research and evaluation [1].

Of note, in the introductory chapters for both the first and second editions, Dr. Alex Rodriguez points out the defining role that Avedis Donabedian had on shaping the content for the field of MQM (initially called clinical outcomes management) [2, 3].

A. P. Giardino (✉)
University of Utah School of Medicine, Salt Lake City, UT, USA

L. A. Riesenberg
Department of Anesthesiology and Perioperative Medicine,
University of Alabama at Birmingham, Birmingham, AL, USA

P. Varkey
Northeast Medical Group, Yale New Haven Health, Stratford, CT, USA

Specifically, in a 1986 Position Paper on the Future of American College of Utilization Review Physicians (ACURP), which would later become ACMQ, Donabedian outlined the following essentials for a core curriculum in what would come to be called MQM and which were listed in the first edition:

- *Clinical competence*: established training, experience, and certification in a clinical medical specialty, with a full understanding of relevant health ethics issues related to utilization and quality management
- *The healthcare system and health institutions*: requisite knowledge and experience in healthcare organizations' clinical services and administrative management
- *Performance review methods and systems*: understanding of clinical performance assessment methods, including facility in medical criteria formulation, professional consensus development skills, disease and case-mix classifications, measurements of health status, and patient satisfaction
- *Information systems*: competence in hardware and software applications for data design, collection, and assessment
- *Epidemiology and quantitative methods*: understanding of epidemiologic measurement principles and biostatistics that would allow appropriate data analysis of healthcare quality, costs, and risks
- *Organizational theory*: facility in implementing quality management programs in complex organizations
- *Adult education and organizational change*: understanding of principles and methods for instructing patients and practitioners in ways that result in effective clinical decisions and desired health outcomes
- *Healthcare law*: basic competence in understanding aspects of the law that impact health systems, including risk management functions
- *Institutional environmental health and safety*: knowledge of issues that would affect risks to quality of care in organized settings where clinical services are provided
- *Health economics*: understanding of essential principles and methods that are relevant to health cost structures, processes, and outcomes [2].

Rodriguez further clarified Donabedian's knack for seeing what the future would require of those in the healthcare quality and patient safety arena, stating:

> While Dr. Donabedian was surmising what knowledge and skills would most likely be needed in educational programs, it now appears prophetic that he forecast a core curriculum for a specialty that, at the time, was in its most formative stages. He believed market and professional demands would soon result in a number of undergraduate and post-graduate medical quality training programs, and that these demands would fuel the supply of health services research, scholarly publications, and training programs for the new specialty. Given the profound challenges already facing a health care system burgeoning with demand and supply financial pressures, legal and regulatory activity, technological innovations, and public expectations for quality, affordability, access, and safety, Donabedian thought that medical quality training programs would quickly expand across the United States and that in 20 years, "clinical outcomes management" would attract thousands of physicians into this new field of population health care [2].

In the foreword to the second edition of this work, Carolyn M. Clancy, MD, then the Director of the federal Agency for Healthcare Research and Quality, issues an additional call to action for those interested in MQM expertise to incorporate a focus on patient safety in addition to the typical quality improvement training and experience stating:

> Whether you have worked in quality improvement for 20 years or 20 days, I urge you to thoroughly educate yourself on patient safety. As public and private sector policies evolve, the reputation, clinical excellence, and financial success of your organization will depend greatly on patient safety outcomes [4].

In his last book, written as a call to action to those in medical quality management, Donabedian put the challenges confronting the MQM field in a clear and distinct focus:

> Some believe that quality in health care is too abstract and nebulous a concept to be precisely defined or objectively measured. It is said that a competent, experienced practitioner can almost intuitively recognize it, if it exists, and offer an equally intuitive measure of its magnitude. And it is similarly asserted that different persons differ in what they perceive quality to be, and how much of it there is. Consequently, some claim that there can be no definition or measure of quality that everyone will accept.
>
> While I agree with some of their views to some degree, I must wholeheartedly reject them. If it is true that quality is some ill-defined image in the eye of each beholder, it would be difficult to set it apart as a goal an individual or an organization can aspire to. Precisely at this point the quality assurance enterprise would crumble into nothingness ... I believe, on the contrary, that the concept of quality can be rather precisely defined, and that it is amenable to measurements accurate enough to be used as a basis for the effort to monitor and "assure" it. This is the conviction that I [we] must now justify [5].

We encourage you to embrace the confidence and optimism expressed by Donabedian about the future of MQM.

References

1. Martin G (2005) Foreword. In: American College of Medical Quality, Core curriculum for medical quality management. Jones and Bartlett Publishers, Sudbury
2. Rodriguez A (2005) Introduction. In: American College of Medical Quality, Core curriculum for medical quality management. Jones and Bartlett Publishers, Sudbury
3. Rodriguez A (2010) Introduction. In: Varkey P (ed) Medical quality management: theory and practice. Jones and Bartlett Publishers, Sudbury
4. Clancy C (2010) Foreword. In: Varkey P (ed) Medical quality management: theory and practice. Jones and Bartlett Publishers, Sudbury
5. Donabedian A (2003) The effectiveness of quality monitoring. In: Bashshur R (ed) An introduction to quality assurance in health care. Oxford Press, New York, pp 133–138

Chapter 2
Basics of Quality Improvement

Julia Caldwell and Prathibha Varkey

Executive Summary

The Institute of Medicine (IOM) defines quality of care as "the degree to which healthcare services for individuals and populations increase the likelihood of desired health outcomes and are consistent with current professional knowledge" [1]. According to the Agency for Healthcare Research and Quality (AHRQ), "Quality improvement (QI) is the framework we use to systematically improve the ways care is delivered to patients. Processes have characteristics that can be measured, analyzed, improved, and controlled" [2]. In today's healthcare field, an increasing focus is placed on medical errors, cost-effective medicine, public reporting, and pay for performance. As a result, payers and patients have turned to QI as a strategy and framework to address specific concerns within the current healthcare system. Crosby suggests that poor quality not only has a negative effect on patients but also squanders resources that could be used to treat other patients [3]. Therefore, internal QI is vital to the ability of a healthcare organization or practice to fulfill many goals including, but not limited to, maintaining the fiduciary relationship between the physician and the patient, enhancing medical care and care delivery, simplifying and streamlining procedures, reducing costs, increasing patient and provider satisfaction, and enhancing workplace morale and productivity. External QI is crucial for physician education, licensure and certification, benchmarking, accreditation, and health policy formulation.

J. Caldwell (✉)
American College of Medical Quality, Chicago, IL, USA

P. Varkey
Northeast Medical Group, Yale New Haven Health, Stratford, CT, USA

© American College of Medical Quality (ACMQ) 2021
A. P. Giardino et al. (eds.), *Medical Quality Management*,
https://doi.org/10.1007/978-3-030-48080-6_2

This chapter introduces quality management theories and practices that have evolved over the past 40 years and highlights some of the themes that have marked progress within the field. It also addresses the policies, philosophies, and processes that characterize the QI field today.

Learning Objectives

Upon completion of this chapter, readers should be able to:

- Describe the history of QI in the field of healthcare
- Describe the purpose and philosophy of QI
- Describe the tools, methods, and strategies for successful QI in healthcare
- List the key evidence-based QI initiatives that affect patient outcomes

The History of the Healthcare Quality Management Movement: Past to Present

In 1914, a surgeon named Ernest Codman developed one of the earliest initiatives in healthcare quality: challenging hospitals and physicians to take responsibility for the outcomes of their patients [4]. He called for a compilation and analysis of surgical outcomes and recorded pertinent data (patient case numbers, preoperative diagnoses, members of the operating team, procedures, and results) on pocket-sized cards which he then used to study outcomes.

Following Codman's early efforts, the next several decades focused primarily on evaluating poor outcomes and departures from standards, commonly referred to as quality assurance or quality control. This method focused on identifying deficient practitioners and mandating "improvements" (e.g., negative incentives, weeding out recalcitrant clinicians who refused to change). This narrow focus did not acknowledge the contribution of other organizational characteristics to QI such as leadership, resources, information systems, communication patterns among teams, or the patient's perception of quality.

In the 1960s, Avedis Donabedian created the structure, process, and outcome paradigm for assessing quality in healthcare [5]. This paradigm had such a profound influence that he is often thought of as the modern founder and leader of the quality field. His work influenced practitioners to identify various methods to enhance patient outcomes in the broad areas of structural, policy, and organizational changes as well as process change and patient preferences. These advances helped establish the systems approach to healthcare quality and its studies.

Quality as a business imperative evolved in the factory setting through specialization, mass production, and automation. In *Economic Control of Quality of Manufactured Product*, Shewhart points out that the goal should not be inspection and specifications but to minimize variation in processes and to focus on customer needs [6]. Influenced by his work with Shewhart, Deming recognized quality as a primary driver for business and communicated these methods to Japanese engineers and executives, which ultimately contributed to the tremendous successes in Japan in the 1950s and for years thereafter. Perhaps Deming's best-known contribution to American industry is a set of management principles that are applicable in large or small organizations and in any business sector [7]. Deming's 14 Points constituted a second conceptual development that both followed and extended the Donabedian model. Quality management was redefined as not just a technical, clinical exercise but also as an issue of culture and values, psychological climate, and leadership—it provided another model for the improvement process.

Deming's 14 Points for Management
1. Create constancy of purpose towards improvement. *Think long-term planning, not short-term reaction.*
2. Adopt the new philosophy. *Management as well as the workforce should actually adopt this philosophy.*
3. Cease dependence on inspection. *If variation is reduced, there is no need for inspection since defects (errors) will be reduced or eliminated.*
4. Move towards a single supplier for any one item. *Multiple suppliers mean variation.*
5. Improve constantly and forever. *Focus on continuous quality improvement.*
6. Institute training on the job. *Lack of training leads to variation among workers*
7. Institute leadership. *This draws the distinction between leadership, which focuses on vision and models, and supervision, which focuses on meeting specific deliverables.*
8. Drive out fear. *Management through fear is counterproductive and prevents workers from acting in the organization's best interests.*
9. Break down barriers between departments. *Eliminate silos. All departments are interdependent and become each other's customers in producing outputs.*
10. Eliminate slogans and exhortations for the workforce. *It is not people who make most mistakes—it is the process in which they are working.*
11. Eliminate management by objective. *Production targets encourage shortcuts and the delivery of poor-quality goods.*
12. Remove barriers to pride of workmanship. *This leads to increased worker satisfaction.*
13. Institute education and self-improvement.
14. The transformation is everyone's job.

In the 1980s and 1990s, the work of Crosby, Deming, and Juran became well known in manufacturing across the United States [3, 7, 8]. This work brought attention to systems design, process controls, and involvement of the entire workforce. Many executives who served on hospital and health system boards started using these concepts to push medical quality leaders to look beyond the boundaries of clinical quality assurance. The boards were encouraged to consider all aspects of the healthcare organization as targets for improvement—from leadership style and behavior to the presence of information system support and collaboration between departments and disciplines. Clinical quality management was now seen as part of total quality management (TQM), which emphasizes that all members of the team possess a thorough understanding of the process and the knowledge of specific tools to assess and improve processes [9]. *Continuous quality improvement* (CQI), an important part of TQM, emphasizes the opportunity for improvement through continuous effort in every aspect of the organization's operations.

The philosophy of TQM includes the following set of management principles:
CQI: a philosophy of continuously seeking improvement
Innovation: meeting customer needs in a whole new way
Quality into daily work life: integrating management principles into employee daily life
Strategic quality planning: the influence on long- and short-term planning [9]

Concurrently, during the 1980s and 1990s, various stakeholders (e.g., purchasers, regulators, patients, advocates) began to call for a more open examination of the quality of care. During these decades, healthcare professionals experienced a gradual erosion of autonomous quality control efforts. Accrediting bodies, such as the National Committee for Quality Assurance (NCQA) and the Joint Commission, as well as organizations like the National Quality Forum (NQF), became increasingly involved in the collection and assessment of quality data across the nation.

In 1998, Chassin and Galvin characterized the problems of overuse, underuse, and misuse in medicine [10]:

Overuse: The potential for harm from a health service exceeds the possible benefit.

Underuse: A health service that would have produced favorable outcomes was not provided.

Misuse: A preventable complication occurs with an appropriate service.

They also called attention to practice variation in medicine and to the suboptimal patient outcomes associated with this variation [10].

In 1999, Kohn, Corrigan, and Donaldson estimated that at least 75,000 people die from medical errors every year [11]. This number was revised in 2013 by an evidence-based estimate of patient deaths associated with hospital care, based on a weighted average of four studies, which suggested that greater than 400,000 people die from medical error related to hospital care annually [12]. Under the editorship of Kohn et al., the IOM published *To Err Is Human: Building a Safer Health System* [11]. This report identified the systems that must be developed to decrease the number of medical errors in the United States. In a second report, *Crossing the Quality Chasm: A New Health System for the 21st Century*, the IOM defined the state of the quality problem, offered recommendations for improvements, and outlined specific targets that would contribute to nationwide improvements [13] (see "Quality Measurement Framework" in Chap. 3).

During the 2000s and 2010s, quality improvement became increasingly important and an accepted practice in the medical field, utilizing accountability measures such as quality metrics designed to improve transparency in the payment for care, the delivery of care, and patient care overall [14]. Additional changes seen during this period included the use of big data and data analytics for quality improvement analysis as well as a shift in fee structure from fee-for-service toward value-based payment [15]. Also during this time, the development of formal quality leadership and management roles expanded to include offices such as chief quality officer, director of patient experience, and chief patient experience officer [16, 17].

The Purpose and Philosophy of Quality Management

The purpose and philosophy of quality management has evolved from an orientation toward policing (i.e., finding "bad apples" among primarily excellent physicians, nurses, and clinical teams) to a focus on the use of quality management as a tool for continuous development of high performance. Quality management can be thought of as having three aspects:

1. A means of accountability for the use of clinical and physical resources in the care of patients
2. An effort to continuously develop and improve the services provided to patients by care teams throughout the organization and the community
3. A mechanism to improve the clinical outcomes of patients as defined by the patient and the healthcare system

Because the focus of quality management has broadened, quality management programs currently tend to target both clinical and organizational structures and processes that lead to improved outcomes.

Modern quality management leaders are systems thinkers, attending to both operating- and strategic-level issues that concern quality. These quality management leaders put patients first, use data and information to examine and respond to problems, and rely on the participation of the entire workforce. They constantly seek changes that will co-produce improvement in a continuous cycle. Although outside regulators may check on the quality of care, the concerns of outsiders are dwarfed by the insiders' commitment to CQI of patient care systems and the outcomes they produce.

Case Study • • •
Using Continuous Quality Improvement to Decrease Mortality from Coronary Artery Bypass Graft Surgery

Using collaboration and CQI, the Northern New England Cardiovascular Disease Study Group, a voluntary regional consortium, achieved a 24% decline in mortality from coronary artery bypass graft (CABG) throughout the region [17]. This group included all cardiothoracic surgeons, interventional cardiologists, nurses, anesthesiologists, perfusionists, administrators, and scientists associated with the six medical centers in Maine, New Hampshire, and Vermont and one Massachusetts-based medical center that support CABG surgery and percutaneous coronary interventions. Training in CQI, benchmarking, and continued monitoring of outcomes allowed institutions to learn from one another. There were 293 fewer deaths (n = 575) than the 868 expected in the post-intervention period (mid-1991 through early 1992). Major improvements in hospital outcomes have occurred in relation to improving coronary stenting technology. Variability in practice patterns across the different practices was a major stimulus to enhance quality of care across all sites.

Implementing a Quality Improvement Project

Clinical QI aims to enhance implementation of evidence-based medicine into clinical practice and to inform quality measurement with evidence-based process measures linked to outcomes. Improvement projects often rise to the surface because of an adverse event or a patient or provider complaint, so there may not always be an opportunity to choose an improvement project. However, in instances when projects can be prioritized, reviewing potential improvement projects against the criteria depicted in Fig. 2.1 may help identify the best QI projects to undertake first. In general, one would prefer projects that fit in quadrants I or II and would avoid those with low impact.

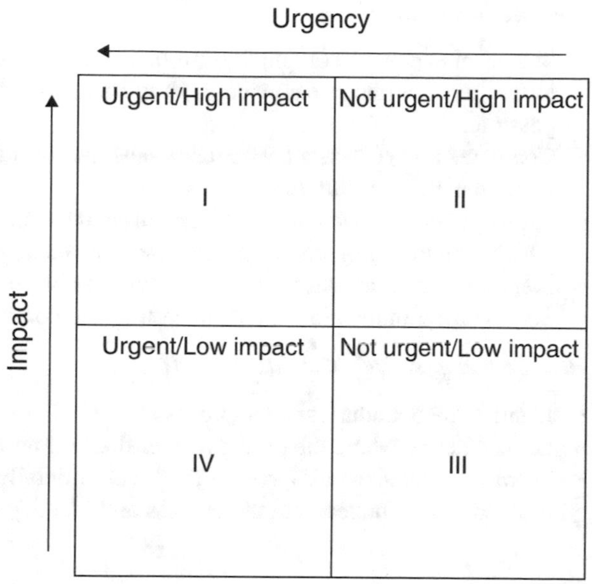

Fig. 2.1 Quadrant to help prioritize QI projects. From Bennett KE, Wichman R, Bentrock N et al. "Choosing a QI Project," Project Process Prioritization, Rochester, MN: Mayo Clinic Division of Engineering, September 1999; used with permission of Mayo Foundation for Medical Education and Research, all rights reserved

Urgency

	Urgent/High impact	Not urgent/High impact
Impact	I	II
	Urgent/Low impact	Not urgent/Low impact
	IV	III

Tools for Quality Improvement

Process Mapping

Regardless of the improvement methodology used, once a QI project is chosen, a systematic process is key to guiding project implementation. Process mapping is a fundamental, yet often overlooked, step that is crucial to understanding an existing clinical or system process. Process mapping involves studying the entire process through various techniques including photography or videotaping, observation ("fly on the wall"), interviewing, field notes, and role-play as necessary. The process map can then be depicted using flow charts.

Flow Charts

These charts allow for identification of the alignment of processes that must be followed in the QI project. They identify the beginning and the end of the process and how one part of the process is dependent on another. Figure 2.2 is an example of a flow chart.

Matrix for the Use of Flow Charts
What does this method do?

• Allows a team to identify the actual flow or sequence of events in a process.

Why use this method?

- Shows unexpected complexity, problem areas, redundancy, and unnecessary loops and reveals areas where simplification and standardization may be possible.
- Compares and contrasts the actual versus the ideal flow of a process to identify improvement opportunities.
- Allows a team to come to an agreement on the steps of the process and examine which activities may impact process performance.
- Identifies locations where additional data can be collected and researched.
- Serves as a training aid for understanding and completing the process.

How do you effectively use this method?

- Identify the boundaries of the process.
- Clearly define where the process under discussion begins and ends.
- Team members should agree on the level of detail they must show on the flow chart to clearly understand the process and identify problem areas.

Cause-and-Effect (Fishbone) Diagram

Another common tool used in QI projects is the cause-and-effect diagram, also referred to as a fishbone or Ishikawa diagram, which can be used to enhance the QI team's ability to map the full range of possible root contributors to the desired outcome. A fishbone diagram is a graphical representation of relationships among the fundamental variables on which the group will focus when initiating improvement action (see Fig. 2.3). The diagram is used to expand the group's purview and to begin to generate consensus on targets for action. It is commonly used to analyze sentinel events and is described in more detail in Chap. 4.

Brainstorming and Affinity Diagrams

The technique of storyboarding grew out of the film and cartoon industry; Disney Studios perfected it to an art form. In planning and organizational work, storyboarding is more properly called an affinity diagram. The process begins with brainstorming, during which every participant writes ideas about addressing a given issue on separate cards and mounts those cards on a large corkboard or similar display (the storyboard).

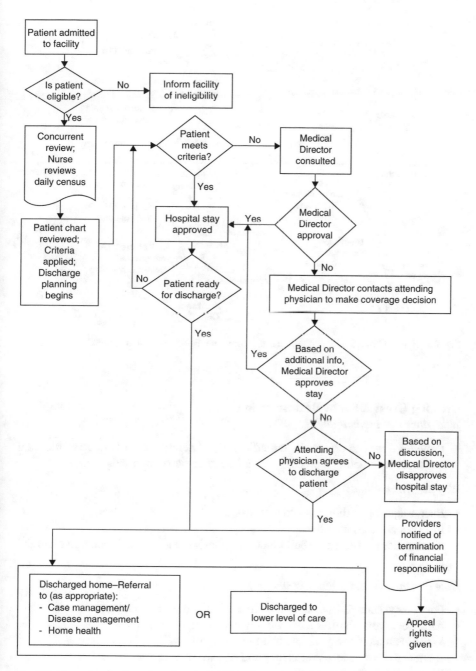

Fig. 2.2 Example of a flow chart for admission

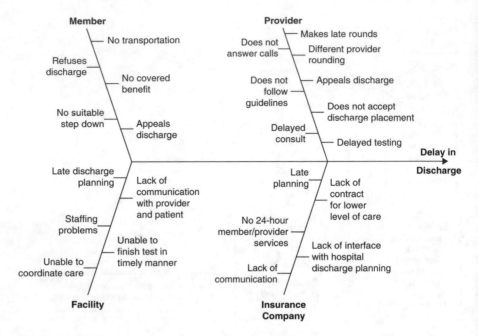

Fig. 2.3 Example of a fishbone diagram illustrating late discharge from a hospital

Creating Great Ideas by Brainstorming
What does this method do?

- Provides a way to creatively and efficiently generate a high volume of ideas on any topic by creating a process that is free of criticism and judgment.

Why use this method?

- Encourages open thinking and teamwork.
- Involves all team members.
- Allows team members to build on each other's creativity and maintain a unified goal.

How do you effectively use this method?

- For clarity, state the question to be discussed and write it down.
- Allow everyone to offer ideas without criticism!
- Write each idea down, visible to all team members.
- Review the list of ideas for clarity and discard duplicates.
- Participants may build on the ideas of others.

During the ensuing discussion, the ideas are grouped according to subject matter—hence the term affinity diagram. Further discussion enables the participants to
rearrange the groups into clusters and identify subject headings and causes, symptoms, impacts, or side effects of the original issue. The affinity diagram that results
from the brainstorming session is typically used at the beginning of a QI project or
process. If affinity diagramming occurs later in the process, when individuals or
group members are identifying actions for addressing immediate problems, the diagram will most likely contain alternatives that the group members have identified as
actions to take.

Gathering and Grouping Ideas in an Affinity Diagram
What does this method do?

- Allows a team to organize and summarize ideas after a brainstorming session to
  better understand the essence of a problem and possibly reach breakthrough
  solutions.

Why use this method?

- Encourages creativity by all team members at all phases of the process.
- Encourages creative connectivity of ideas and issues and allows breakthrough
  solutions to emerge naturally (even on long-standing issues).
- Encourages participant ownership of results.

How do you effectively use this method?

- Phrase the issue under discussion in a clear and complete sentence.
- Brainstorm at least 20 ideas and issues and record each on sticky notes.
- Sort ideas into related groups of five to ten ideas.
- Create a summary or header cards using the consensus for each group.

Pareto Chart

Once themes and clusters of potential causes of a lack of quality in an area of care
are noted, contributing factors must be identified. Without inspecting the data, managers may assume that all causes contribute equally to poor quality or that one or
more causes are most prominent. Pareto diagrams, often expressed as bar graphs,
help to show the relative contribution of various causes to the problem addressed
(see Chap. 4). Figure 2.4 presents a Pareto chart that was developed to help a provider group examine its late discharges from a hospital.

Using a Pareto Chart
What does this method do?

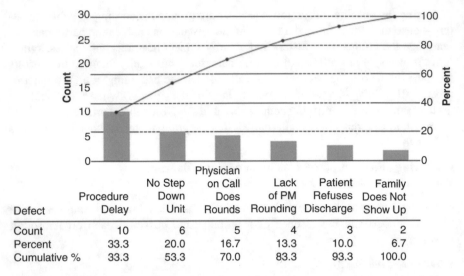

Defect	Procedure Delay	No Step Down Unit	Physician on Call Does Rounds	Lack of PM Rounding	Patient Refuses Discharge	Family Does Not Show Up
Count	10	6	5	4	3	2
Percent	33.3	20.0	16.7	13.3	10.0	6.7
Cumulative %	33.3	53.3	70.0	83.3	93.3	100.0

Fig. 2.4 Example of a Pareto chart to examine reasons for delayed discharge from a hospital

- Expends efforts on problems that offer the best possible improvement by showing their relative frequency or size in a descending bar graph.

Why use this method?

- Helps a team to focus on causes that will have the greatest impact if solved.
- Based on the Pareto principle: 20% of the sources cause 80% of any problem.
- Helps prevent "shifting the problem," i.e., the "solution" removes some causes but worsens others.

How do you effectively use this method?

- Decide which problem you want to know more about.
- Categorize the causes or problems that will be monitored, compared, and ranked by brainstorming or with existing data.
- Choose the most meaningful unit of measurement, such as frequency or cost.
- Choose the time period for the study.
- Collect the key data on each problem category either in "real time" or by reviewing historical data.
- Compare the relative frequency or cost of each problem category.
- List problem categories on the horizontal line and frequencies on the vertical line.
- Interpret the results: The tallest bars indicate the largest contributors to the overall problem.

Fig. 2.5 Example of a histogram showing the number of ER visits per day of the week

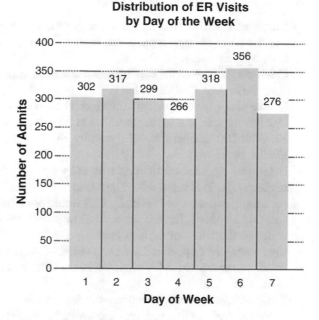

Distribution of ER Visits by Day of the Week

Histogram

The *histogram* can help elucidate the reasons for a variation by depicting the fro quency of each value of the quantitative variable (see Chap. 4). For example, the first step in understanding the reasons for variation in hospital discharge times is to choose a sample time span, perhaps a 2-week period, and to count the number of patients who were discharged each hour during that period. The values can then be graphed on a histogram (see Fig. 2.5).

Using a Histogram to Achieve Process Centering, Spread, and Shape
What does this method do?

- Aids in making decisions about a process or product that could be improved after examining the variation.

Why use this method?

- Displays measurement data in bar graph format, distributed in categories.
- Displays large amounts of data that are not easily interpreted in tabular form.
- Shows the relative frequency of occurrence of various data values.
- Depicts the centering, variation, and shape of the data for easy interpretation.
- Helps to indicate if the process has changed.
- Displays the variation in the process quite easily.

How do you effectively use this method?

- Gather and tabulate data on a process, product, or procedure (e.g., time, weight, size, frequency of occurrences, test scores, GPAs, pass/fail rates, number of days to complete a cycle).
- Calculate the rate of the data by subtracting the smallest number in the data set from the largest. Call this value R.
- Decide about how many bars (or classes) to display in the eventual histogram. Call this number K. This number should never be less than 4 and seldom exceeds 12. With 100 numbers, K = 7 generally works well. With 1000 pieces of data, K = 11 works well.
- Determine the fixed width of each class by dividing the range, R, by the number of classes, K. This value should be rounded to a "nice" number, generally a number ending in a zero. For example, 11.3 would not a "nice" number, but 10 would. Call this number I, for interval width. The use of "nice" numbers avoids strange scales on the x-axis of the histogram.
- Create a table of upper and lower class limits. Add the interval width to the first "nice" number less the lowest value in the data set to determine the upper limit of the first class.
- The first "nice" number becomes the lowest lower limit of the first class. The upper limit of the first becomes the lower limit of the second class. Adding the interval width (I) to the lower limit of the second class determines the upper limit for the second class. Repeat this process until the largest upper limit exceeds the largest data piece. You should have approximate classes or categories in total.
- Plot the frequency data on the histogram framework by drawing vertical bars for each class. The height of each bar represents the number.
- Note the frequency of values between the lower and upper limits of that particular class.
- Interpret the histogram for skew and clustering problems.

Bar Chart

A *bar chart* is similar to a histogram, except that the variable of interest is not a quantitative measure, such as discharge time, but rather a categorical variable, such as a department within the hospital. Bar charts are commonly used to illustrate comparisons, such as the number of patients discharged before or after 11:00 a.m. for each of several hospital services, and may help identify departments that require further attention. As with histograms, bar charts are especially useful for diagnosis and evaluation. A bar chart that displays the number of laboratory tests performed by a physician group by month is shown in Fig. 2.6.

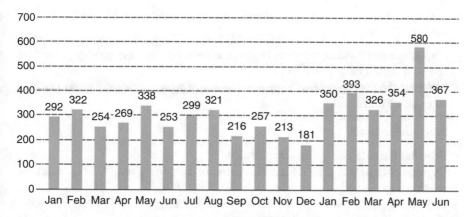

Fig. 2.6 Example of a bar chart showing number of lab tests performed by month

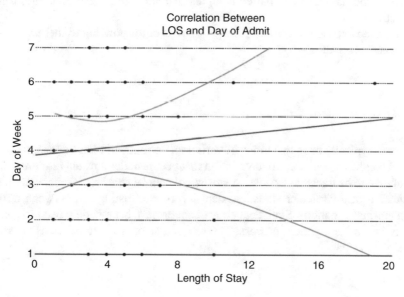

Fig. 2.7 Example of a scatter diagram showing correlation between length of stay and day of admission

Scatter Diagram

The *scatter diagram* in Fig. 2.7 shows the relationship between length of stay (LOS) and time of discharge and examines whether there is a pattern to this relationship; if so, the QI team could then investigate whether the pattern was controllable.

Using a Scatter Diagram to Measure Relationships Between Variables
What does this method do?

- Analyzes and identifies the possible relationship between the changes observed in two different measurements.
- Interpret the data to determine if any pattern or trend emerges, noting positive or negative correlation.

Why use this method?

- Provides the data to confirm a hypothesis.
- Depicts both visual and statistical means to test the strength of a potential relationship.
- Provides a good follow-up to a cause-and-effect diagram to determine if more than a consensus connection exists between causes and the effect.

How do you effectively use this method?

- Collect the data (50–100 paired samples of related data) and construct a data sheet.
- Draw the x-axis and the y-axis, and plot points corresponding to these measures for each observation.

Statistical Control Chart

Processes typically have two kinds of variation, normal variation that occurs under normal conditions and abnormal variation that occurs under unusual circumstances, and often can be traced to a cause. A *statistical control chart* represents continuous application of a particular statistical decision rule to distinguish between normal and abnormal variations. Statistical control charts have been widely used to control quality in the management process. The use of a statistical control chart is further explained in Chap. 3.

Methods for Quality Improvement

While there are several methods for quality improvement, we will focus on the three that are most commonly used in healthcare. Each has common elements and varies slightly for different settings, all eventually leading to testing and change. Principles from multiple different methodologies are used for the same project, making their differences less relevant and drawing on their commonalities and symbiosis (e.g., use of Sigma-Lean methodology) [18].

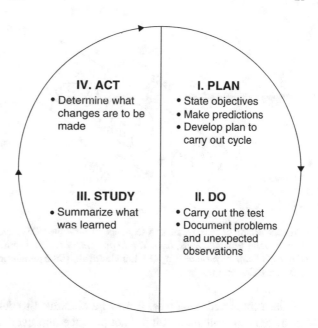

Fig. 2.8 The PDSA or Shewhart cycle. Republished with permission of John Wiley & Sons, from *The Improvement Guide: A Practical Approach to Enhancing Organizational Performance*, by G.J. Langley et al., 1996; permission conveyed through Copyright Clearance Center, Inc.

Plan, Do, Study, Act Methodology

The process of Plan, Do, Study, Act (PDSA) is also referred to as the Shewhart cycle. It involves a trial-and-learning methodology, whereby a hypothesis or suggested solution for improvement is made and tested on a small scale before any changes are made to the whole system [19]. The process entails a logical sequence of four repetitive steps, shown in Fig. 2.8.

During the Plan stage of the cycle, the areas in need of QI are identified. These can be high-cost, high-volume, high-risk areas or areas in which outcome results are not as good as the organization would like. During this part of the cycle, Nolan's three-question model [20] is often used to determine the aim for the project, establish measures, and select what changes should be made.

The first question in Nolan's model, "What are you trying to accomplish?", helps define the goal or aim of the project. The aim of the project should be time-specific and measurable. The second question, "How will you know a change is an improvement?", guides the selection of appropriate measurement tools and methodologies. The measures chosen should be quantifiable and should demonstrate if a specific change actually leads to an improvement. Finally, Nolan's third question, "What changes can you make that will result in an improvement?", generates improvement ideas. The changes that are most likely to result in improvement are chosen and tested through the PDSA cycle.

The Do part of the cycle entails implementation and documenting problems and unexpected observations. The Study portion of the cycle involves collecting data from the Do part of the cycle and then producing information from those data. The final stage of the cycle, Act, involves determining whether the intervention produced improved outcomes as reflected in the information. If the intervention did

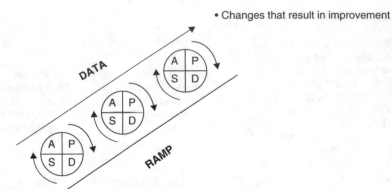

• Changes that result in improvement

Fig. 2.9 Ramp of improvement: a sequence of multiple PDSA cycles. Republished with permission of John Wiley & Sons, from *The Improvement Guide: A Practical Approach to Enhancing Organizational Performance*, by G.J. Langley et al., 1996; permission conveyed through Copyright Clearance Center, Inc.

produce improved outcomes, it may be continued to determine whether improvement can be maintained. If it did not produce improved outcomes, the cycle begins anew, and a new intervention is tried. The process is carried out over a course of small cycles, which eventually leads to exponential improvements, displayed in Fig. 2.9. The tools of data analysis and presentation described previously are used at one or more points in this problem-solving process.

Six Sigma

Sigma is the 18th letter of the Greek alphabet and the symbol for standard deviation. It is now utilized in service and healthcare organizations.

The aim of Six Sigma is to reach a level of quality that resides in the six standard deviations of average performance, resulting in an error rate of 0.0003% or about 3.4 defects per million opportunities; at this stage, the process is virtually error-free (99.9996%) [21].

Six Sigma uses data to identify quality problems, potential quality problems, and areas for improvement. The Six Sigma approach concentrates on customer-driven measures and acceptable quality and relies on data-driven process improvement. Six Sigma is achieved through a series of steps (akin to the PDSA cycle) identified as define, measure, analyze, improve, and control (DMAIC). Six Sigma is generally instituted by practitioners, known as Six Sigma Black Belts, who have been trained in the use of the proper analytic tools to address quality problems. A certified Black Belt understands and effectively employs DMAIC, demonstrates team leadership, understands team dynamics, and is able to assign team member roles and responsibilities appropriately.

The first step of the DMAIC model entails the definition of the problem, the project parameters, and the establishment of an improvement objective. In the second step, measure, the measurement of each of the process steps is conducted, and data is collected. In the third step, an analysis of the collected data is performed to test a hypothesis about key process factors. In the fourth step, the process is improved by conducting a pilot test. In the final step of the cycle, the process is controlled by implementing the process improvement and continuously working to monitor and sustain the process.

For Six Sigma efforts to be successful, senior management must support them. These efforts cut across operational lines, use the most talented people in the organization, and move them into new areas. The Six Sigma concept has become popular in healthcare organizations and is useful for processes that are repeated in large numbers (e.g., laboratory tests, radiological procedures).

Case Study • • •
Use of Six Sigma to Reduce Process Variations and Costs in Radiology

The Commonwealth Health Corporation (CHC) in Bowling Green, Kentucky, is a not-for-profit integrated delivery network that includes three medical centers and one extended care facility with over 2000 employees. Six Sigma was implemented within the Radiology Department in early 1998. Department members were trained in the Six Sigma approach, and participants achieved Green Belt status. At the completion of projects, Green Belts progressed to Black Belts and then to Master Black Belt status. As a result, the Radiology project reduced wait times for patients, generated faster turnaround times for radiology reports, and increased productivity. CHC's team managed to increase throughput by 25% while using fewer resources and decreasing costs per radiology procedure by 21.5%. In total, radiology cost per procedure decreased from $68.13 to $49.55 for over 100,000 procedures a year, resulting in a $1.65 million cumulative savings. In addition, errors in magnet resonance imaging (MRIs) decreased by 90% resulting in a cost savings of $800,000 within the 18-month period [22].

Lean

Lean methodology is used to accelerate the velocity and reduce the cost of any process by removing any type of activity that absorbs resources and yet creates no value (also known as muda) [23]. Perhaps the most noted and benchmarked "lean" organization is Toyota Manufacturing of Japan. Several healthcare systems have used Toyota's process (also called the Toyota Production System [TPS]) to improve healthcare quality in their organization [24].

One of the common terms used in Lean is Kaizen, a Japanese word meaning *good change* which refers to gradual and orderly, continuous improvement [25]. Kaizen is essentially a rapid, relatively low-cost, simple, team-based approach to improvement. A Kaizen Blitz or a Kaizen event is an intense process for introducing rapid change into a work unit or organization using the ideas, motivation, and energy of the people who do the work. The general principles and approaches behind Kaizen are very useful in healthcare quality improvement strategies. Kaizen is implemented through practices that help employees propose their own ideas and solutions to problems with the goal of striving for perfection through employee involvement, creating solutions for problems, and effectively sustaining results over time [26].

Lean thinking improves process outcomes by removing non-value-added processes including the waste of overproduction and underproduction (e.g., smoothing day-to-day variations in radiological procedures), waste of inventory (e.g., excess patient IV pumps in storage), waste of rework rejects (e.g., poorly done lab tests), waste of motion (e.g., repeating several steps to obtain clinical data from a medical record), waste of waiting (e.g., patients waiting for appointments), waste of processing (e.g., decreasing steps in the emergency department admission process), and waste of transporting (e.g., unnecessary transfer of patients between patient care units). In addition, lean processes line up value-creating steps in the best possible sequence in order to deliver services or products just as the customer needs them and in just the manner the customer requested. One of the most commonly used tools is called value stream mapping, whereby the process is depicted in a physical graph in order to identify wasted effort or steps that do not add value for the customer.

The three QI methods discussed in this chapter are summarized and compared in Table 2.1.

Table 2.1 Comparison of three improvement methodologies

	PDSA	Six Sigma	Lean
Process steps	Plan, do, study, act	Design, measure, analyze, improve, control	Eliminate non-value-laden steps, eliminate defects, reduce cycle time
Improvement focus	Rapid cycles of improvement toward identifying optimal process improvement	Eliminate defects, customer-centric	Enhanced efficiency, elimination of non-value activities, variance reduction, and reduced cycle time. Product "flows" when the customer wants and needs it
Ideal use	A target project is chosen for improvement; time and resources are limited	A target project is chosen for improvement and resources are available. The project consists of an activity that is repeated with high frequency	Process efficiency is the focus. Process can be clearly defined and is laden with non-value activities
Supports/tools for success	Environment for testing, prototyping, and piloting of ideas	Statistical process control charts, analytical tools, Six Sigma experts (i.e., black belts, green belts)	Value stream mapping, value analysis, Kaizen events

Commonly Used Quality Improvement Strategies

Most published literature suggests the use of multipronged approaches for successful QI as opposed to single interventions. Descriptions of commonly used QI strategies follow.

Academic Detailing

Academic detailing, also called *educational outreach*, employs trained providers (e.g., pharmacists, physicians) to conduct face-to-face visits to encourage adoption of a desired behavior pattern. Although academic detailing was originally conceived and proven effective as a one-on-one educational intervention, several studies have incorporated academic detailing principles in small group sessions. Academic detailing has been shown to be effective at enhancing provider knowledge and changing prescribing behaviors, although it has generally been proven ineffective at enhancing patient outcomes in a sustained fashion [27].

Opinion Leaders

Opinion leaders are members of the local system who are usually able to influence others, either on a broad range of issues or in a single area of acknowledged expertise. They do not always have leadership titles but generally have higher status among their peers and higher visibility. Peer feedback from local opinion leaders has been shown to have a modest effect on enhancing quality of care and has been used as part of multifaceted QI strategies in several institutions [28].

Audit and Feedback

This strategy entails the provision of a summary of the clinical performance of an individual provider, practice, or clinic to the respective entity. It is often done in conjunction with reports that contain anonymous performance rates of comparable clinics or providers. Based on the timeliness and type of feedback, this strategy has shown small-to-modest benefits in the improvement of targeted processes or outcomes, especially when combined with achievable benchmark feedback. In a study of diabetes patients by Kiefe et al., physicians were randomly assigned to receive either a chart review and physician-specific feedback or an identical intervention plus achievable benchmark feedback [28]. Odds ratios for patients of the achievable benchmark physicians versus comparison physicians were higher for influenza vaccination, foot examination, lipid control, and long-term glucose control measurement.

Reminder Systems

These interventions prompt providers to remember information relevant to a particular encounter, patient, or service. They are often effective when integrated into the workflow and are available at the point-of-care delivery. An example is the system of flagging charts of patients whose influenza vaccinations are due, which prompts the provider to remember and enhance the recommendation of influenza vaccination at the time of the visit.

Patient Education

Individual or group sessions to enhance patient self-management of disease were shown to have modest to large effects based on patient characteristics and conditions. These effects have been well studied, especially in the management of diabetes mellitus and chronic heart failure.

Case Management

Case management and disease management are described in detail in Chap. 7. They are well-studied QI strategies used to manage special populations who have specific diagnoses or who require high-cost or intensive services. These services are often centralized and involve the coordination of healthcare interventions and communication between members. This strategy has demonstrated a positive effect on enhancing quality of care for patients with chronic diseases.

Reengineering

Reengineering and process redesign consist of improving an existing process or system in such a way that allows expanded opportunities to be met or existing problems to be solved. This broadens the reach by allowing additional uses, generating lower costs, or delivering improvements in usability. Because of the nature of the process, this strategy has often yielded novel product or service innovations that go beyond the realm of improvement and result in the redesign of existing structures and processes. Examples are the use of telemedicine to enhance access to care in remote locations or convenient care clinics to enhance access and efficiency and to create new business models for healthcare service.

Incentives

This strategy is described in detail in Chap. 9. Financial incentives for achieving a certain percentage increase or target level of compliance with targeted processes of care have shown evidence of a positive relationship in the achievement of target goals. This concept has led to the current strategy of pay for performance. There is less evidence that negative incentives such as withholding of salary or year-end bonuses for not achieving target performance are an effective means of enhancing quality of care.

Quality Improvement Research

There is often confusion about whether a project is purely QI or research. In general, QI is used when changes need to be made to a local system for clinical management. In this case, the effects of rapid changes are studied using small samples and less rigorous documentation; this provides for rapid feedback to the system. A project is considered QI research if there is deviation from established good practices, the subjects are individual patients rather than systems or providers, randomization or blinding is conducted, the majority of the patients are not expected to benefit directly from the knowledge gained, and participants are subject to interventions that are not required in routine care.

There is limited understanding of the factors that truly make a QI project successful because systems changes often have multiple confounding factors, thus creating an urgent need for rigorous research in this area. It is especially important to know the costs of the intervention, any possible unintended "side effects" of the intervention, if the intervention contributed to improved patient outcomes in addition to improving the process, and if the overall effect of individual QI efforts actually enhances the quality of the entire system. As Perneger suggests, it is important to keep in mind that although quality improvement is the aim, not all change may be an improvement [29].

Study designs that may be useful in QI research include randomized controlled trials, controlled studies, pre- and post-intervention studies, as well as time series. Rigorous research designs become especially important when results are to be generalized or communicated externally and the impact of the change is potentially large.

Challenges to Successful Quality Improvement

Many organizations have encountered difficulties when implementing quality management. Barriers may be found in the organization's technology, structure, psychological climate, leadership, culture, and involvement in legal issues. A summary of each of these areas is given below.

Technology

Many organizations' quality managers have had to learn new quality management techniques while simultaneously building the information infrastructure needed to do the work. In many organizations, technologies designed for use in quality management are relatively new and require training and testing by the staff. Some technological innovations still await widespread diffusion due to a lack of necessary resources and change management necessary for implementation.

Structure

Some leaders have taken aggressive steps to put quality councils in place, recognize QI gains in public ways, and inject quality into performance requirements; however, these efforts are by no means widespread. How to structure the quality effort and how much visibility to give the quality initiative in the organizational structure are two barriers that often result in inaction.

Psychological Climate

The climate of the organization sometimes presents a barrier to two fundamental aspects of quality philosophy: openness to data sharing and teamwork. Quality management requires that the staff collect and analyze data and share the findings transparently in open meetings, yet the climate of some organizations is too closed for this type of exposure. In other organizations, teamwork is only an occasional proposition. Because QI depends on examining relationships and interdependencies across departmental boundaries and hierarchical levels, a lack of familiarity with this "boundaryless" movement may be a barrier.

Leadership

Just as leadership can support quality management, it can also obstruct it. Unless quality management has a clear and continuous commitment from the organization's leader, the quality effort is doomed. Frequently, the leader fails to adequately communicate the importance of the quality effort and its ongoing progress. The leader must constantly demonstrate visible support for the quality effort. Clinical and administrative staffs are keenly sensitive to any real or perceived wavering of support. As quality and value become more associated with payment by the Medicare Access and CHIP Reauthorization Act (MACRA) and the Medicare Incentive Payment System (MIPS), leadership will become more keenly focused on these topics.

Culture

In Deming's view, successful quality management requires building a supportive organizational culture [7]. Conversely, an organizational culture that has the following characteristics conflicts with the basic philosophy of quality management: decisions are made from the top down, the workforce is not empowered, communication tends to be closed (i.e., data are not openly shared), patients' interests are subservient to medical center objectives, errors bring blame-seeking and dismissal, and teamwork is thought to be unnecessary. Initiating quality efforts in a hostile environment is a doomed experiment. Unfortunately, many academic medical centers and large community institutions lack a history of a supportive culture for QI.

Legal Issues

An easy way to disable a quality program is to saddle it with legal implications. In such a climate, patients will not sign release forms, and the organization cannot legally ask for or disseminate information related to quality or safety. Because provider contracts do not specify that data can be requested, an organization's managers must be creative and innovative in moving these legal issues aside without harming the organization, its employees, and the patients who receive care.

Future Trends

The IOM reports heightened public and industry awareness of medical errors and quality issues in the healthcare system. Accrediting bodies and regulations have prompted healthcare institutions to enhance their QI and quality measurement initiatives to address these issues, resulting in a renewed interest in QI across the nation. Similarly, accrediting bodies of health profession education are increasingly interested in establishing competencies for upcoming graduates in the areas of QI and safety. This has resulted in a proliferation of curricula including the early involvement of trainees in QI efforts to enhance patient care.

Alternative Payment Models

In January 2015, the Department of Health and Human Services (HHS) tied 30% of payments in Medicare to alternate payment models (APMs) associated with quality or value. The aim is for almost all fee-for-service (FFS) payment to be tied to quality or value [30]. APMs include accountable care organizations (ACOs), bundled payments, and medical homes [30]. Additionally, recent changes made by the Medicare Access and CHIP Reauthorization Act (MACRA) (final ruling October 2016) yield incentives to providers participating in APMs. MACRA also combines incentives for providers participating in APMs and facilitating the new payment models, electronic health records (EHR), value-based payment, and current quality reporting into one system called the Merit-Based Incentive Payment System (MIPS) [30].

Accountable Care Organizations

Accountable Care Organizations (ACOs) were created under the Patient Protection and Affordable Care Act (PPACA) as a new payment model under Medicare. With ACOs, there will be pilot programs to extend the model to private payers and Medicaid. Proponents hope that ACOs will allow physicians, hospitals, and other clinicians and healthcare organizations to work together more effectively to both slow the growth of spending and enhance quality improvement [31]. The success of ACOs will depend in large part on whether the Centers for Medicare & Medicaid Services, doctors, private payers, and healthcare system leaders can work together to establish a tightly linked performance measurement and framework for evaluation. The goal of measurements and evaluations is to assure accountability to patients and payers and support rapid learning, timely correction of policy and organizational missteps, and broad dissemination of successful organizational and practice innovations [32].

Final Thoughts

Healthcare providers armed with knowledge of QI will be key to the success of such initiatives and shaping policy in this area, especially if they are supported by regulations that impose consequences to achieve compliance and accountability.

References

1. Harris-Wehling J (1990) Defining quality of care. In: Institute of Medicine, Medicare: a strategy for quality assurance: volume II sources and methods. National Academies Press, Washington, DC, p 5
2. Agency for Healthcare Research and Quality (2013) Module 4. approaches to quality improvement. In: Practice facilitation handbook. http://www.ahrq.gov/professionals/prevention-chronic-care/improve/system/pfhandbook/mod4.html. Accessed May 2013
3. Crosby PB (1979) Quality is free: the art of making quality certain. McGraw-Hill, New York
4. Codman EA (1914) The product of a hospital. Surg Gynecol Obstet 18:491–496

5. Donabedian A (1985) The methods and findings of quality assessment and monitoring, vols I, II, III. Health Administration Press, Ann Arbor
6. Shewhart W (1931) Economic control of quality of manufactured product. D. Van Nostrand Co, New York
7. Deming WE (1986) Out of the crisis. MIT Press, Cambridge
8. Juran J (1989) Juran on leadership for quality. Free Press, New York
9. Gustafson D, Hundt A (1995) Findings of innovation research applied to quality management principles for health care. Health Care Management Rev 20(2):16–33
10. Chassin M, Galvin R, National Roundtable on Health Care Quality (1998) The urgent need to improve health care quality. JAMA 280(11):1000–1005. https://doi.org/10.1001/jama.280.11.1000
11. Kohn L, Corrigan J, Donaldson M (eds) (1999) To err is human: building a safer health system. National Academies Press, Washington, DC
12. James J (2013) A new evidence based estimate of patient harms associated with hospital care. J Patient Saf 9(3):122–1128. https://doi.org/10.1097/PTS.0b013e3182948a69
13. Institute of Medicine (2001) Crossing the quality chasm: a new health system for the 21st century. National Academies Press, Washington, DC
14. Chassin M, Loeb J, Schmaltz S et al (2010) Accountability measures–using measurement to promote quality improvement. NEJM 363(7):683–688. https://doi.org/10.1056/NEJMsb1002320
15. Holland C, Foley K, Asher A (2015) Can big data bridge the chasm? Issues, opportunities and strategies for the evolving value-based health care system. Neurosurg Focus 39(6):E2. https://doi.org/10.3171/2015.9.FOCUS15497
16. Walsh K, Ettinger W, Klugman R (2009) Physician quality officer: a new model for engaging physicians in quality improvement. Am J Med Qual 24(4):295–301. https://doi.org/10.1177/1062860609336219
17. Malenka D, O'Connor G, Northern New England Cardiovascular Study Group (1995) A regional collaborative effort for CQI in cardiovascular disease. Jt Comm J Qual Improv 21(11):627–633
18. Antony J (2011) Six Sigma vs lean: some perspectives from leading academics and practitioners. Int J Prod Perform Manag 60(2):185–190. https://doi.org/10.1108/17410401111101494
19. Varkey P, Reller MK, Resar R (2007) The basics of quality improvement in healthcare. Mayo Clin Proc 82(6):735–739. https://doi.org/10.4065/82.6.735
20. Langley G, Moen R, Nolan K et al (1996) The improvement guide: a practical approach to enhancing organizational performance. Jossey-Bass, Hackensack
21. Goldstein M (2001) Six Sigma program success factors. Six Sigma Forum Magazine 1(1):36–45
22. Cherry J, Seshadri S (2000) Using statistics to reduce process variability and costs in radiology. Radiol Manage 8(1):42–45
23. Womack J, Jones D (1996) Lean thinking: banish waste and create wealth in your corporation. Simon and Schuster, New York
24. Young D (2002) Pittsburgh hospitals band together to reduce medication errors. Am J Health Syst Pharm 59(11):1014, 1016, 1026
25. Mazzocato M, Stenfors-Hayes T, Schwarz U et al (2016) Kaizen practice in healthcare: a qualitative analysis of hospital employees' suggestions for improvement. BMJ Open 6:e012256. https://doi.org/10.1136/bmjopen-2016-012256
26. Ahlstrom P (2004) Lean service operations: translating lean production principles to service operations. Int J Ser Technol Manag 5:545–564. https://doi.org/10.1504/IJSTM.2004.006284
27. Goldberg H, Wagner E, Fihn S et al (1998) A randomized controlled trial of CQI teams and academic detailing: can they alter compliance with guidelines? Jt Comm J Qual Improv 24(3):130–142
28. Kiefe C, Allison J, Williams O et al (2001) Improving quality improvement using achievable benchmarks for physician feedback: a randomized controlled trial. JAMA 285(22):2871–2879

29. Perneger T (2004) Why we need ethical oversight of quality improvement projects. Int J Qual Health Care 16(5):343–344. https://doi.org/10.1093/intghc/mzh075
30. Malinak J, Press M, Rajkumar R et al (2017) Principles for provider incentives in CMS's alternative payment models. Healthcare 5(1–2):9–11. https://doi.org/10.1016/j.hjdsi.2016.05.001
31. McClellan M, McKethan A, Lewis J et al (2010) A national strategy to put accountable care into practice. Health Aff 29(5):982–990. https://doi.org/10.1377/hlthaff.2010.0194
32. Shortell S, Casalino L, Fisher E (2010) How the Centers for Medicare & Medicaid innovation should test accountable care organizations. Health Aff 29(7):1293–1298

Additional Resources-Further Reading

Agency for Healthcare Research and Quality. http://www.ahrq.gov
American College of Medical Quality. http://www.acmq.org
American Health Quality Association. http://www.ahqa.org
Centers for Medicare and Medicare Services: Quality Measure and Quality Improvement. https://www.cms.gov/Medicare/Quality-Initiatives-Patient-Assessment-Instruments/MMS/Quality-Measure-and-Quality-Improvement-.html
Foundation for Health Care Quality. http://www.qualityhealth.org
Health Resources and Services Administration. https://www.hrsa.gov/
Institute for Healthcare Improvement. http://www.ihi.org
Kaiser Family Foundation. https://www.kff.org
National Academies of Science, Engineering, Medicine: Health and Medicine Division. Quality and Patient Safety. http://www.nationalacademies.org/hmd/Global/Topics/quality-patient-safety.aspx
National Association for Healthcare Quality. http://www.nahq.org
National Committee for Quality Assurance. http://www.ncqa.org
National Quality Forum. http://www.qualityforum.org
Quality and Safety in Healthcare. http://www.qhc.bmjjournals.com
RAND Health. http://www.rand.org/health
The Joint Commission. http://www.jointcommission.org
Utilization Review Accreditation Commission (URAC). http://www.urac.org

Chapter 3
Quality Measurement

Linda Harrington

Executive Summary

Quality measurement is a form of evaluation. It is fundamental for any attempt to improve the quality of healthcare. It is necessary for demonstrating current performance, setting goals, and validating achievement of those goals. Quality measurement doesn't have to be overly cumbersome, but it needs to be on target, measuring those things that matter, and make a difference in healthcare improvement.

The history of measurement of healthcare quality parallels the history of epidemiology and statistics in the late nineteenth and early twentieth centuries and is intertwined with the evolution of health services research in the late twentieth century. Quality measurement is now moving center stage in the twenty-first century as healthcare moves to a value-based system and the promises afforded through the massive amounts of electronic clinical data being accumulated. This chapter will focus on concepts necessary for the practical application of measurement in quality improvement (QI), highlighting challenges and opportunities related to the digital world.

Learning Objectives

Upon completion of this chapter, readers should be able to:

- Describe the historical evolution of the science of quality measurement
- Compare the characteristics of structure, process, and outcome measurements
- Construct appropriate measurements for QI projects
- Identify the necessary characteristics of quality measures, including reliability and validity

L. Harrington (✉)
Baylor College of Medicine, Houston, TX, USA

© American College of Medical Quality (ACMQ) 2021
A. P. Giardino et al. (eds.), *Medical Quality Management*,
https://doi.org/10.1007/978-3-030-48080-6_3

- Evaluate the success of QI projects
- Describe challenges and solutions associated with electronic data
- Identify upcoming trends in the science of quality measurement

Introduction

Measurement is very familiar to physicians. They routinely interact with different types of measurement in research, in practice, and increasingly in quality improvement. With all three types of measurement, discovery occurs when data are collected and analyzed.

Measurement is performed in research to discover new knowledge. Similarly, clinical measurement is done to determine a patient's wellness or illness. The goal of quality measurement is to discover the structures and/or processes of care that have a demonstrated relationship to positive health outcomes and are under the control of the healthcare system [1].

The objectives of healthcare quality measurement that have passed the test of time are to:

- Provide data to inform quality improvement efforts
- Inspect and certify that an organization or individual meets previously established standards
- Compare groups for a variety of purposes, including selective contracting by purchasers and choice of providers and practitioners by individuals
- Inform patients, families, and employees about the healthcare decisions and choices they face
- Identify and possibly eliminate substandard performers—those whose performance is so far below an acceptable level that immediate actions are needed
- Highlight, reward, and disseminate best practices
- Monitor and report information about changes in quality over time
- Address the health needs of communities [2]

Quality measures must be consistent in how they perform and valid in measuring what is intended to be measured. Measurement in research must be reliable and valid, otherwise threatening the internal validity of a study and as a result generalizability of the findings. Similarly, clinical measurement must be reliable and valid to accurately diagnose patients and evaluate progress.

Quality Measurement Framework

The most influential framework for guiding quality measurement development is from the Institute of Medicine [3] and focuses on the following six aims:

Safe: Avoid harm to patients from the care that is intended to help.

Effective: Provide services based on scientific knowledge to all who could benefit and refrain from providing services to those who aren't likely to benefit, avoiding underuse and misuse, respectively.

Patient-centered: Provide care that is respectful of and responsive to individual patient preferences, needs, and values, ensuring that patient values guide all clinical decisions.

Timely: Reduce wait times and sometimes harmful delays for both those who receive and those who give care.

Efficient: Avoid waste, including waste of equipment, supplies, ideas, and energy.

Equitable: Provide care that does not vary in quality because of personal characteristics such as gender, ethnicity, geographic location, and socioeconomic status [3, 4].

Desirable Characteristics of Quality Measurement

The Agency for Healthcare Research and Quality (AHRQ) has put forth the following as characteristics of effective quality measurement [5]:

Standardization: Quality measures are standardized at the national level, which means that all healthcare providers are reporting the same data in the same way.

Availability: Data will be available for most healthcare organizations being profiled.

Timeliness: The quality measure allows for results to be available by distribution of a report when it is most needed by consumers.

Experience: Use of the quality measure demonstrates that it measures actual performance, not shortcomings in information systems.

Stability: The quality measure is not scheduled to be eliminated or removed from a measurement data in exchange for a better measure.

Evaluability: Quality measures allow for the results to be evaluated as either better or worse than other results, in contrast to descriptive information that merely demonstrate differences. An example is complication rate, where a lower rate is always better.

Distinguishability: Quality measures reveal significant differences among healthcare organizations or other comparators.

Credibility: The quality measure is audited or does not require an audit.

Relevance: The quality measure should be relevant to consumers, providers, clinicians, payers, and policy-makers and should be of interest or value to the stakeholders and the project at hand.

Evidence-Based: Quality measures, especially those related to clinical issues, should be based on sound scientific evidence. Measures should clearly link structure or process to outcomes.

Reliability: Reliability is the degree to which the quality measure is free from random error. Measurement indicators and data collection techniques must be stable enough to justify the use of the collected information to make a judgment about quality. The same measurement process using the same data should produce the same results when repeated over time.

Validity: Validity of a quality measure refers to the degree to which the measure is associated with what it purports to measure. A key question to be answered is whether the measures selected to indicate the presence or the absence of quality actually represent quality in patient care.

Feasibility: Quality measures should be realistic and practical to collect and analyze. Measures that require too much time, money, or effort to collect may not be feasible to use.

History

The science of quality measurement is commonly recognized to have originated in the work of Florence Nightingale and her reports to the British parliament on mortality rates in British field hospitals during the Crimean War. Her early efforts to quantify healthcare were coupled with the birth of modern concepts of infection control, giving credence to the idea that measurement is needed for improvement [6].

Several decades later, Ernest Codman linked the interest in mortality to invasive procedures [7]. His exploration of postsurgical mortality can be considered the start of investigations into hospital outcomes. Codman is also credited with the notions that hospitals should have organized medical staffs and records of patient care—essentially the birth of structural measures.

The next major development in the measurement of quality occurred outside of healthcare in the interval between the World Wars. Walter Shewhart developed a branch of new statistics called statistical process control while working on the manufacture of telephones [8]. Perhaps his most important contribution was a change in the focus of measurement from the quality of products themselves to the steps required to produce those products. His other major contribution was a method to identify shifts in the manufacturing process that were statistically meaningful, a method that was simple enough to be implemented easily by individuals who did not have advanced scientific training. These shifts took the form of batches of product that differed significantly from other batches.

Arguably, the most influential contribution to measurement of healthcare quality occurred in the early 1960s when Donabedian began to explicitly differentiate the quality measures related to structure, process, and outcome [9]. The relative importance of process and outcome measures is still a subject of discussion in the contemporary literature, and Donabedian's general framework remains the dominant paradigm. Together, the three measures provide the best and most complete picture of quality.

In the last decade of the twentieth century, considerable efforts were made to implement approaches to quality measurement from industries outside of healthcare. One such approach is to apply measures of process and outcome to multiple domains of value across the organization. Kaplan and Norton originally advocated this approach in the information technology industry [10]. Batalden and Nelson brought it to healthcare in the very practical form of scorecards and dashboards [11]. Embedded in measurement tools is the understanding that the consideration of individual measures alone can be misleading, if not dangerous, because healthcare is a complex system subject to unintended consequences and that multiple perspectives (e.g., patient, provider, payer) must be considered in the design of a useful measurement system.

One of the most significant changes in quality measurement that has occurred in more recent history is the movement of healthcare from a volume-based model to a value-based model. Physicians are now being evaluated and reimbursed for quality, elevating the importance of quality measurement. The simultaneous implementation of electronic health records (EHRs) affords the opportunity to improve the collection and reporting of quality measures. Yet, significant challenges exist.

While EHRs have created improvements, such as electronic prescribing and increased access to patient records from any wired location, they have also created new challenges relevant to quality measurement, specifically the data [12]. EHR data are being degraded with preconfigured data entry aids such as documentation templates, macros, smart phrases, default text, copy-paste and copy-forward functionality [13], as well as overuse of alerts resulting in alert fatigue and overrides. These impact the characteristics and value of quality data.

Prior to EHR data, claims data were often used in quality improvement. In 2007, Tang et al. published a study funded by the Centers for Medicare & Medicaid Services comparing methodologies calculating quality measures based on administrative data, sometimes referred to as claims data, versus clinical data derived from EHRs [14]. The researchers sought to understand whether there was a significant difference in identifying patients with diabetes mellitus and associated quality measures between the more granular or detailed clinical data and claims data that are aggregated from clinical data. Using a random sample of 125 patient records, the researchers found 75% of diabetic patients were identified by manual review of the EHR, considered the gold standard at the time, compared to 97% of diabetics identified using queries of the EHR. As a result, there was a statistically significant difference in the quality measures for frequency of HbA1c testing (97% vs. 68%, $p < 0.001$), control of blood pressure (61% vs. 45%, $p = 0.05$), frequency of testing for urine protein (85% vs. 55%, $p < 0.001$), and frequency of eye exams for diabetic patients (62% vs. 41%, $p < 0.03$) [14].

It is important to note that claims data today are largely derived from EHR data. In fact, many healthcare professionals suggest that EHRs were designed first and foremost to capture data for the purposes of submitting claims. As such, claims data derived from EHRs are subject to the same issues of data quality mentioned previously. Thus, the quality of data used in QI is an ongoing challenge.

While organizations struggle to ensure the quality of data and thereby quality measurement, there is an ongoing increase in the number of quality measures expected of physicians that are inefficient and imbalanced [15]. There are measures that are duplicative, such as multiple measures for the same condition on follow-up care that use different time reporting requirements. Some quality measures overlap one another, such as diabetes composite measure and separate hemoglobin A1c measure. The ease in capturing some data and difficulty with other data has resulted in an overrepresentation and underrepresentation of measures. For example, there are several measures related to childhood immunizations and few related to chronic care. Given the evolution in quality measurement and the challenges being faced, there are some fundamental concepts in the types of quality measures that have sustained.

Types of Quality Measures

The gold standard for defining quality measurement remains Donabedian's three-element model of structure, process, and outcome [9].

Structural Measures

Structural measures relate to the ability of an organization to provide high-quality care associated with a healthcare setting, including its design, policies, and procedures. The underlying assumption is that healthcare organizations that have the necessary quantity and quality of human and material resources and other structural supports are best prepared to deliver quality healthcare. Examples of structural measures include the availability of appropriate equipment and supplies in a hospital setting and the education, certification, and experience of clinicians in an institution. Structure-focused measures often are easy to access. Healthcare organizations routinely maintain data on equipment and supply inventories, staffing, patient acuity, and staff qualifications.

Process Measures

Process measures are more often referred to today as *performance measures*. They are used to evaluate if appropriate actions were taken for an intended outcome and how well these actions were performed to achieve a given outcome. The underlying clinical assumption is that if the right things are done right, the best patient outcomes are more likely to occur [16]. An example of an evidence-based process measure to assess the quality of care for a patient with acute myocardial infarction is the proportion of patients admitted with this diagnosis (without beta-blocker contraindications) who received beta-blockers within 24 hours after hospital arrival.

Four criteria for successful process measures include the following:

- A strong evidence base demonstrating that the care process represented by the process measure leads to improved outcomes.
- The process measure accurately represents whether the evidence-based care process was provided.

- The measure addresses a process that has few intervening care processes that must occur before the improved outcome is realized.
- Deploying the process measure has little or no chance of introducing unintended adverse consequences.

Process measures that meet all four criteria are most likely to improve patient outcomes [17].

Example: Process Measure for Diabetes

> Percentage of patients whose hemoglobin A1c level was measured twice in the past year

Outcome Measures

Outcome measures seek to capture changes in the health status of patients following the provision of a set of healthcare processes and include the costs of delivering the processes. The patient is the primary focus, and outcome measures should describe the patient's condition, behavior, and response to or satisfaction with care. Outcomes traditionally are considered results that occur as a consequence of providing healthcare and cannot be measured until the episode of care is completed. Episodes of care may include hospitalizations, physician office visits, or care provided in post-acute care settings. For example, to assess the quality of care for patients with acute myocardial infarction admitted to a coronary care unit, the outcome measures may be related to incidence of reinfarction and patient satisfaction with the care received in the unit.

Outcome measures provide an indirect measure of the overall quality of an organization and can provide trending and benchmarking opportunities to demonstrate progress. On the other hand, outcomes can be influenced by factors that are not measured or are beyond the control of clinicians, such as genomics, case mix, and socioeconomic or environmental influences. As a general rule, the more structure and process variables a QI project employs, the greater the reliability of outcome measures [18].

Historically, quality measurement has focused primarily on outcomes. Today, structure and process measures provide important insights, illuminating which areas to address to improve outcomes. Structure and process provide direct measures of quality and thus yield more sensitive measures of quality, which can direct clinicians to the most effective ways to improve patient care. To be valid, however, structure and process must be empirically related to outcomes and be able to detect genuine differences in patient care. To maintain validity, they also must continually be reviewed and updated in accordance with current science (i.e., evidence).

Example: Outcome Measure for Diabetes

> Average hemoglobin A1c level for population of patients with diabetes in the past year

Bundled Measures

The Institute for Healthcare Improvement (IHI) developed the concept of "bundles" to assist healthcare providers in providing reliable care for patients undergoing specific treatments with known inherent risks [19]. A bundle is a package of interventions that must be applied for every patient every time. The power of bundles is related to the underlying evidence.

Example: Ventilator Bundle Measures

> *Process measure*: Percentage of intensive care patients on mechanical ventilation for whom all four of the ventilator bundle interventions are documented. *Outcome measure*: Number of ventilator-associated pneumonias per 1000 ventilator days.

Balancing Measures

Balancing measures are important for illustrating whether unintended consequences are introduced during quality improvement initiatives. For example, a balancing measure of hospital readmissions is important when the goal is to reduce length of stay. Another example of a balancing measure is the incidence of hyperglycemic episodes in intensive care when trying to reduce the number of hypoglycemic episodes.

Benchmarking

Quality improvement plans often include *benchmarking*, an effort to determine the current status of quality and compare it to the highest performers internal to an organization or external to the organization (e.g., comparing performance with competitors) [20]. An Achievable Benchmark of Care (ABC), as identified by Kiefe et al., is produced by benchmarks that (1) are measurable and attainable, (2) are based on the achievements of the highest performers, and (3) provide an appropriate number of cases for analysis [21].

Constructing a Measurement

Quality measures are constructed in several ways including proportions or percentages, ratios, means, medians, and counts [22]. The choice of measure depends on the goal trying to be achieved.

Proportion

Comparisons of quality measures within systems and across providers require standards for how quality measures are expressed. The generally accepted standard for the expression of quality measures involves a numerator and a denominator. The numerator describes the desired characteristics of care, and the denominator specifies the eligible sample. For example, in the treatment of heart failure patients, the numerator for one possible proven measure is the number of people who actually receive beta-blockers, and the denominator is the number of people who are eligible to receive beta-blockers. Together, the numerator and denominator provide a measure of insight into the quality of the treatment of heart failure with beta-blockers.

Ratio

Ratio measures are often structural measures denoting the capacity of a healthcare provider. Examples include the ratio of providers to patients, hospitalization per 10,000 residents of a targeted area, staff-to-patient ratio, or percent of heart failure patients tracked in a registry. Interpretation can be tricky as sometimes higher values are better, whereas at other times lower values are the goal.

Mean and Median

Means and medians are often used to measure processes. A commonly used example would be the median time an eligible patient arrives in the emergency department to the administration of fibrinolytic therapy. This measure captures timeliness of treatment when time is an important factor in the outcome of care. Like ratios, the interpretation of means and medians must be carefully examined as high values or low values may be good or bad depending on the context.

Count

Counts are quality measures often seen in surveillance such as the investigation of adverse outcomes. Examples include foreign body left in surgical patients or transfusion reactions. They cannot be used for comparison purposes across providers as they lack specification of the population.

Several factors should be considered when constructing a quality measure: the age of the persons included, the measurement period, the system or unit being examined, and whether the measure will be within a program of care, across an entire healthcare setting, or local, or national should be identified and taken into account [23].

Timing of Measurements

Baseline Measurement

Almost all quality improvement processes, projects, or programs begin with the measurement of quality in its current state, which is known as a *baseline measurement*. Baseline measurements use many types of quantitative and qualitative data as indicators and allow a supporting analysis and an eventual judgment to be made about the status of medical quality at that point in time.

In Table 3.1, a baseline assessment is shown for a group of patients with diabetes whose hemoglobin A1c levels were evaluated in Year 1. This evaluation was used to design a QI project and to determine the change in hemoglobin A1c levels after 1 year of intervention.

The drawback to baseline measures is that they provide snapshots of measured characteristics of structure, process, or outcomes at one point in time. Measurement at another time can only be interpreted as higher or as lower than baseline and does not indicate actual or sustained improvement. Measurement tools that allow for trending are discussed in the next section.

Table 3.1 Baseline assessment: hemoglobin A1c levels at baseline and after a 1-year intervention for patients with diabetes

Member interventions		
Applied program		
Stratification of diabetic population		
Special needs case management		
Outreach activities and education		
Referrals to employer program		
Provider interventions		
Contacted physician and coordinated information		
Sponsored a physician education program		
Member outcomes		
Improved diabetes control		
Lowered hemoglobin A1c		
Direct cost savings		
Reduced hospital readmission rate for diabetes		
	Hemoglobin A1c levels	
	Year 1	**Year 2**
N	212	212
Median	7.30%	7.10%
Average	7.62%	7.39%
% of patients with values <7.5%	54.7%	60.8%
% of patients with values >9.5%	16.5%	11.3%

Trending Measurements

Run Chart

A *run chart* is a quality tool used to identify trends by measuring changes in structure, processes, or outcomes over time. The run chart is created in an XY graph in which the x-axis represents time and the y-axis represents the aspect of the structure, process, or outcome being measured. A central line, if used, indicates the median of the data.

A *run* consists of consecutive points below or above the central line indicating a shift in the structure, process, or outcome measure being examined. A *trend* is a steady inclining or declining progression of data points representing a gradual change over time. Figure 3.1 provides an example of a run chart measuring length of stay over time.

This run chart shows a decreasing trend in length of stay, which suggests that interventions targeting a reduction in length of stay may be effective, assuming average daily census and patient acuity have remained similar over time. Run charts provide ready information on runs and trends in structure, process, and outcomes and are easy to construct and interpret. For more statistical power, control charts are preferred.

Control Chart

Control charts are most often used with process measures and are a more sensitive tool than run charts. The focus is on process variation. Additional features include a central line composed of the mean value of the data and upper control limits (UCL) and lower control limits (LCL) typically representing three standard deviations from the mean.

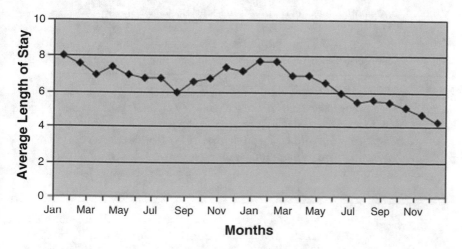

Fig. 3.1 Example of a run chart for average length of stay

A *statistical control chart* is a graph that represents the continuous application of a particular statistical decision rule to distinguish between normal and abnormal variations. Figure 3.2 shows a statistical control chart for the number of visits per day for a provider organization and covers each day. The threshold is the point at which intensive evaluation or action is taken.

Case Study • • •

Cardiac Services: Dartmouth-Hitchcock Medical Center

The cardiac services unit at Dartmouth is one of the pioneers in contemporary approaches to measurement and improvement of healthcare quality. In their work, measurement has been used as a central tool for tracking and improving care [24]. They have argued persuasively that measurement of clinical process and outcome must be controlled by the clinicians delivering care. Several key principles defined their approach.

Clinicians were involved in the design of a panel of measures that were both useful to them in their daily practice and useful to administrators and external stakeholders. This panel encompassed the entire process of care and contained a balanced set of cost and quality measures. Patient-centered measures (e.g., satisfaction, functional status) were incorporated along with other traditional measures of process and outcome (e.g., mortality, morbidity). Details concerning variations were presented, as were aggregate measures over time. In addition, current variation was evaluated against historical performance using statistical control charts.

Data for the project were obtained by chart abstraction in the perioperative period (i.e., at 3 weeks after surgery for satisfaction, at 6 months after surgery for functional status). Process variables were obtained in real time. The SF-36 indices of physical functioning, role functioning, bodily pain, and general health were used for the functional status measures. Among the measures of the surgical process were pump time, percent returning to pump, percent reexplored for bleeding, and internal mammary artery usage. Control charts were used with the surgical process data.

Control charts also were used for early detection of quality issues, allowing for near real-time correction. For example, the team was able to detect an increase in sternal wound infections by using a technique called a "successes between failures" chart to identify infrequent events and differentiate them from chance occurrences. This control chart allowed the team to decide if the increase in infections was due to random variation or a process shift. Because they used real-time data, they were able to quickly identify the process change related to this increase in infections and to correct it. Conventional methods usually result in delayed identification and more adverse events before solutions are found.

The results from this initiative are striking, although they cannot be attributed to measurement alone. Coronary artery bypass graft-related mortality dropped from 5.7% to 2.7% in a 2-year period; the average total intubation time decreased from 22 hours to 14 hours; and the number of patients discharged in fewer than 6 days increased from 20% to 40%.

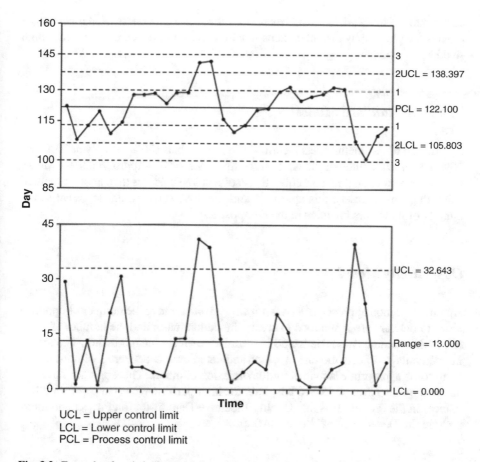

Fig. 3.2 Example of statistical control charts showing visits per day for a physician group

Interpreting Quality Measures

Appropriateness Model

There are many ways to interpret quality measures. The IHI advocates an "all-or-none" approach or *Appropriateness Model* to generate composite scores [22]. For example, if a patient with diabetes is expected to have a laboratory test, an eye exam, and a foot exam, failure to do any of these would result in failure of the composite measure of preventive diabetes care. The score reported reflects the proportion of patients who receive all the care recommended for them.

The AHRQ uses the Appropriateness Model to arrive at composite scores and to produce a comprehensive overview of the quality of care delivered in the United States. Composite measures based on this model are an increasingly large component of the report. AHRQ has chosen the Appropriateness Model because it reflects the philosophy that all citizens must receive all of the care that meets a high standard of evidence.

The 70% Standard Model

A variation of this method sets the threshold at less than 100%, usually at 70% (*the 70% Standard*). Although the all-or-none approach of the Appropriateness Model strives for perfection (and consequently results in lower scores than another method using the same dataset), this approach and the 70% standard are sensitive to the number of indicators included in the composite.

Opportunity Model

Another common approach is the *Opportunity Model* where the number of opportunities to deliver care is summed to create the denominator and the number of cases in which indicated care is delivered is summed to create the numerator. The resulting percentage reflects the rate at which indicated care is delivered without penalizing some appropriate activities for the omission of others. This approach has been adopted by the CMS to reward hospitals for high performance (via pay for performance) in the Premier Hospital Quality Incentive Demonstration Project and internally in the Department of Veterans Affairs.

Program Evaluation

Program evaluation is necessary to measure the overall success of QI programs or projects and is usually conducted using two methods: formative evaluations and summative evaluations.

Formative Evaluations

Formative evaluations involve routine examination of data on program activities and provide ongoing feedback about components of the program that work and those that require intervention. *Dashboards* and *scorecards* are tools used in formative evaluations to track and trend quality improvement activities on a monthly basis. They highlight key quality improvement initiatives and identify successful progress, thereby allowing for timely intervention as necessary. For example, the use of a dashboard for critical care may report monthly compliance with a ventilator-associated pneumonia bundle.

Summative Evaluations

Summative evaluations are more formal and occur less often than formative evaluations, typically annually. Their focus is on measuring and determining the outcome or the effectiveness of the quality improvement program. The information evaluated is used to make decisions about the program, such as the need for more resources or education or perhaps better communication.

Effective program evaluations, whether formative or summative, are those that provide actionable information to program participants and management. Synthesis and use of information gleaned from program evaluations promote the continuous development of the quality improvement program.

One aspect of program evaluation that should not be overlooked is the ongoing assessment of the costs of quality measurement [25]. These include both direct costs associated with quality measurement operations and variable costs related to specific measures. Understanding the costs of quality measurement enables organizations to prioritize measures, understand the magnitude of costs, and ideally spur innovation in cost-effective quality measurement.

Quality Measurement in the Digital Age

Innovations in the digital age will continue to change quality data, measurement, and analyses. Data are largely digitized, albeit with an abundance of manual data entry, especially as it pertains to EHRs. Types of quality measures, specifically Donabedian's three-element model of structure, process, and outcome, will conceptually continue but will evolve operationally as they become more technologically based [26].

Quality measurement will become increasingly applied in real time, affording more rapid analyses and improvement. This will be enabled by the expanding use of sensors and data captured electronically [27]. Advances in analytics will afford faster and more powerful analyses of digitized data that are big, dark, and deep [28].

Big Data

Big data refers to "data whose scale, diversity, and complexity require new architecture, techniques, algorithms, and analytics to manage it and extract value and hidden knowledge from it" [29]. The goal of big data is to gain new insights and improve decision-making [30].

Big data involves what is commonly referred to as the 4Vs, i.e., volume, variety, velocity, and veracity [31]. Volume is defined as the vast amount of data generated every second. How much data constitutes big data is currently undefined. Variety refers to the range of data types and sources. This can include structured and unstructured text, images, numbers, and signals such as those from sensors. Velocity is defined as the speed at which data are generated. Lastly, veracity is the accuracy and reliability of data [31].

Dark Data

Dark data include all the unstructured data gathered in healthcare. These include text, images, audio recordings, as well as signals for wearable sensors, biometric data, retinal scans, and more. Dark data represents 80% of all data generated and is predicted to increase to 93% by 2020 [32]. Advances in computing power allow for increasing use of dark or unstructured healthcare data.

Deep Data

Deep data involve large amounts of data collected per patient [33]. These data provide a more complex view of patients. Value is derived through the time stamp and context of the deep data.

EHRs today do not offer big, dark, or deep data. While they have volume, EHRs lack the variety and velocity, slowed largely by manual data entry. Veracity is also an issue [34, 35]. Big data in healthcare will be uncovered with the addition to EHR data of genomic data and patient-generated data that is not episodic interactions with the current delivery system but instead involves lifestyle data. It is not until healthcare moves away from transactional data to a more dimensional, non-transactional data model will we receive better information on performance and better support for decision-making and quality improvement.

Future Trends

We believe that quality measurement as a science will be the future [36]. A convergence of factors supports the need for increased rigor in quality measurement, including ongoing issues in the delivery of quality patient care, pay for performance, and growing consumer awareness. The desire to improve the rigor of measurement parallels the need to improve quality and safety in patient care. Timely acquisition and analysis of sound data through the increasing use of information systems and the use of reliable and valid measurement tools are essential. Rigorous quality measurement promotes the generalizability of findings in quality improvement initiatives, expanding their usefulness to the larger patient population.

CMS's pay-for-performance reimbursement strategy uses quality measurement to reward providers and practitioners for complying with evidence-based standards for providing patient care. By rewarding quality, the hope is that compliance with new efficacious treatments will increase and clinical outcomes will improve. Chapter 9 will provide more details on CMS's pay-for-performance strategies.

We believe that in addition to payers, consumers will drive improvements in quality measurement. Consumers are increasingly interested in healthcare delivery, especially as they assume greater responsibility for the cost of care, through increasingly higher premiums, deductibles, and co-pays and become more active in monitoring their own health through telehealth, mHealth (mobile health), and other approaches.

Anything can be measured. How well something is measured is another issue. The caveat to the adage "Any data are better than no data" is the reality that bad data are worse than no data [37]. Bad data misclassify physicians and hospitals, provide misinformation to healthcare consumers, and waste time and resources.

The goal is to measure quality by focusing on the right structure, process, and outcome measures that are relevant, meaningful, important, evidence-based, reliable, valid, and feasible. Improving the quality of data being input into EHRs while increasing automation of data capture is critical to more timely analyses, prevention, and earlier intervention.

Lastly, increasing reporting requirements from multiple agencies has resulted in quality measurement becoming untamed [38]. According to Don Berwick, we need to reduce excessive measurement by 50% [38]. The goal is clear—make quality measurement meaningful.

Acknowledgments Harry Pigman, MD, MSHP, for his key contributions to the prior edition of this work.

References

1. Agency for Healthcare Research and Quality (2012) Understanding quality measurement.. https://www.ahrq.gov/professionals/quality-patient-safety/quality-resources/tools/chtoolbx/understand/index.html. Accessed 15 May 2018
2. Advisory Commission on Health Consumer Protection and Quality in the Health Care Industry (1998) Quality first: better health care for all Americans. U.S. Government Printing Office, Washington D.C.
3. Institute of Medicine (IOM) (2001) Crossing the quality chasm: a new health system for the 21st century. National Academy Press, Washington D.C
4. Donabedian A (1989) The end results of health care: Ernest Codman's contribution to quality assessment and beyond. Milbank Qtrly 67(2):233–256
5. Agency for Healthcare Research and Quality (2015) Key questions when choosing health care quality measures.. https://www.ahrq.gov/professionals/quality-patient-safety/talkingquality/create/gather/index.html. Accessed 15 May 2018
6. Scobie S, Thomson R, McNeil J et al (2006) Measurement of the safety and quality of health care. MJA 184(suppl 10):S51–S55
7. Codman EA (1990) The end result idea and the product of a hospital: a commentary. Arch Pathol Lab Med 114(11):1105
8. Shewart W (1981) Economic control of quality of manufactured product. American Society for Quality, Milwaukee
9. Donabedian A (1980) Explorations in quality assessment and monitoring. In: The definition of quality and approaches to its assessment, vol 1. Health Administration Press, Chicago

10. Kaplan R, Norton D (1996) The balanced scorecard: translating strategy into action. Harvard Business School Press, Boston
11. Nelson E, Mohr J, Batalden P et al (1996) Improving health care part 1: the clinical value compass. Jt Comm J Qual Improv 22(4):243–258
12. Hochman M (2018) Electronic health records: a "quadruple win," a "quadruple failure," or simply a time for reboot. J Gen Intern Med 33(4):397–399. https://doi.org/10.1007/s11606-018-4337-6
13. Harrington L (2017) Copy-forward in electronic health records: lipstick on a pig. Jt Comm J Qual Patient Saf 43:371–374
14. Tang P, Ralston M, Arrigotti M et al (2007) Comparison of methodologies for calculating quality measures based on administrative versus clinical data from electronic health record system: implications for performance measures. J Am Med Inform Assoc 14:10–15
15. Schuster M, Onorato S, Meltzer D (2017) Measuring the cost of quality measurement: a missing link in quality strategy. JAMA 318(13):1219–1220
16. Ranson S, Maulik S, Nash D (2005) The healthcare quality book: vision, strategy and tools. Health Administration Press, Chicago
17. Chassin M, Loeb J, Schmaltz S et al (2010) Accountability measures–using measurement to promote quality improvement. NEJM 363(7):683–688
18. Mant J (2001) Process versus outcome indicators in the assessment of quality in health care. Intl J Qual Health Care 13(6):475–480
19. Institute for Healthcare Improvement (2017) What is a Bundle?. http://www.ihi.org/resources/Pages/ImprovementStories/WhatIsaBundle.aspx. Accessed 17 Jan 2017
20. Mohr J, Mahoney C, Nelson E et al (1996) Improving health care, part 3: clinical benchmarking for best patient care. Jt Com J Qual Improv 22(9):599–616
21. Kiefe C, Weissman N, Allison J et al (1998) Identifying achievable benchmarks of care: concepts and methodology. Int J Qual Health Care 10(5):443–447
22. Nolan T, Berwick D (2006) All-or-none measurement raises the bar on performance. JAMA 295(10):1168–1170
23. Agency for Healthcare Research and Quality (2017) Evaluation of the AHRQ QI program. https://www.ahrq.gov/research/findings/final-reports/qualityindicators/chapter4.html
24. Nugent W, Schultz W, Plume S et al (1994) Design an instrument panel to monitor and improve coronary artery bypass grafting. JCOM 1(2):57–64
25. Schuster M, Onorato S, Meltzer D (2017) Measuring the cost of quality measurement: a missing link in quality strategy. JAMA 318(13):1219–1220
26. Donabedian A (1996) Evaluating the quality of medical care. Milbank Qrtly 44:166–206
27. Aitken M (2018) The growing value of digital health: evidence and impact on human health and the healthcare system. IQVIA Institute for Human Data Science, In. https://www.iqvia.com/institute/reports/the-growing-value-of-digital-health
28. Harrington L (2017) New data of the digital age: big, dark and deep. AACN Adv Crit Care 28(3):239–242
29. Smitha T, Kumar V (2013) Applications of big data in data mining. Int J Emerging Technol Adv Eng 3(7):390–393. http://www.ijetae.com/files/Volume3Issue7/IJETAE_0713_65.pdf
30. Demchenko Y, Ngo C, Membrey P (2013) Architecture framework and components for the big data ecosystem. Universiteit van Amsterdam System and Network Engineering Group. http://uazone.org/demch/worksinprogress/sne-2013-02-techreport-bdaf-draft02.pdf
31. Sicular S (2013) Gartner's big data definition consists of three parts, not to be confused with three "V"s. Forbes Magazine, In. https://www.forbes.com/sites/gartnergroup/2013/03/27/gartners-big-data-definition-consists-of-three-parts-not-to-be-confused-with-three-vs/#5459367642f6
32. Trice A (2015) The future of cognitive computing. The IBM cloud blog, In. https://www.ibm.com/blogs/bluemix/2015/11/future-of-cognitive-computing/. Accessed 15 May 2018
33. Poucke S, Thomeer M, Heath J et al (2016) Are randomized controlled trials the (g)old standard? From clinical intelligence to prescriptive analytics. J Med Internet Res 18(7):e185. https://doi.org/10.2196/jmir.5549

34. Valikodath N, Newman-Casey PA, Lee P et al (2017) Agreement of ocular symptom reporting between patient-reported outcomes and medical records. JAMA Ophthalmol 135(3):225–231. https://doi.org/10.1001/jamaophthalmol.2016.5551
35. Echaiz J, Cass C, Henderson J et al (2015) Low correlation between self-report and medical record documentation of urinary tract infection symptoms. Am J Infect Control 43(9):983–986
36. Harrington L, White S (2008) Interview with a quality leader: Mark Chassin, new president of the Joint Commission. J Healthc Qual 30(1):25–29
37. Shahian D, Mormand S, Friedberg M et al (2016) Rating the raters: the inconsistent quality of health care performance measurement. Ann Surg 264:36–38
38. Stempniak M (2015) Don Berwick offers health care 9 steps to end era of 'complex incentives' and 'excessive measurement'. In: Hospitals & Health Networks.. http://www.hhnmag.com/articles/6798-don-berwick-offers-health-care-9-steps-to-transform-health-care. Accessed 21 Feb 2017

Chapter 4
Patient Safety

Philip J. Fracica and Elizabeth A. Fracica

Executive Summary

The Institute of Medicine (IOM) report *To Err Is Human* brought to the forefront the issue of medical errors and the resulting risks to patient safety and preventable adverse events [1]. Recognition that high-reliability organizations (HROs) such as aviation and the nuclear power industry improved safety by focusing on organizational processes led to a closer examination of organizational issues in healthcare. Today, there is more of a focus to create a transparent culture that addresses safety from an organizational perspective.

There are a number of tools, systems, methodologies, resources, and patient safety products used to guide the implementation of safe practices. Analytic tools can provide powerful insight into the causes of a poor outcome. Understanding the causes of errors and failures is important; using that understanding to change the process is critical to improvement. Designing systems that make it difficult for people to make mistakes, and easy for them to do the right thing, is often referred to as "hard wiring" for reduced risk. There are several standard strategies that consistently improve the safety and reliability of processes, including those listed below, to be discussed in detail in this chapter:

- Reduced reliance on memory with automation, algorithms, and easily accessible references
- Simplification through reduction of unnecessary process steps and hand-offs
- Standardization to reduce variation

P. J. Fracica (✉)
Bothwell Regional Health Center, Sedalia, MO, USA

E. A. Fracica
Johns Hopkins Hospital, Baltimore, MD, USA

© American College of Medical Quality (ACMQ) 2021
A. P. Giardino et al. (eds.), *Medical Quality Management*,
https://doi.org/10.1007/978-3-030-48080-6_4

- Use of constraints to eliminate undesired behavior and forcing functions to assure desired behavior
- Careful and appropriate use of protocols and checklists
- Improved access to information at the point of care
- Reduced reliance on vigilance through automation, alarms, and scheduled monitoring
- Cautious use of automation to avoid introduction of new errors, to avoid staff complacency, and to maintain individual responsibility

Learning Objectives

Upon completion of this chapter, readers should be able to:

- Describe the history and development of patient safety initiatives
- Discuss a systems approach to the prevention of errors
- Describe the different types of errors that pose risks to patient safety
- Identify issues in organizational culture than can affect error reporting
- Describe processes to identify and analyze errors
- Explain how teamwork and crew resource management can improve patient safety

History

From the time of Hippocrates, the primary goal of medicine has been to improve the health of individuals, or at least to "do no harm." In the nineteenth century, physicians recognized that infections could be acquired at the hospital, and Semmelweis proposed handwashing prior to patient contact to decrease puerperal fever [2]. Unfortunately, 150 years after Semmelweis's proposal, handwashing is still not universal. In the early twentieth century, Codman listed errors due to deficiencies in technical knowledge, surgical judgment, diagnostic skills, and equipment as causes for unsuccessful treatments [3]. Schimmel studied adverse events in a group of hospitalized patients in 1964 and reported that 20% of patients admitted to medical wards suffered an adverse event and that 6.6% of the adverse events were fatal [4]. Since Schimmel's initial report, there have been multiple studies reporting an adverse event rate of 2–4% of hospital admissions [5]. In 1994, Lucian Leape brought a new perspective on errors in medicine by focusing on the psychology of error and human performance, arguing that fundamental change would be needed to reduce errors [5]. This was followed by an Institute of Medicine report focusing on the issue of the quality of healthcare [6]. Media attention to high-profile adverse events cases raised awareness of safety issues in the healthcare system, prompting the landmark IOM report on medical errors and patient safety, *To Err is Human* [1].

Anesthesia is the epitome of success in patient safety efforts to reduce medical errors. The field's focus on detecting adverse events and prevention of harm has led to a decrease in the number of anesthesia-related deaths from 3.7/10,000 anesthetics to 1–2/200,000 in ASA I or II patients [7], reaching the levels achieved by HROs such as aviation.

In the past decade, there has been continued and increasing attention focused on improving the quality of healthcare outcomes and patient safety. Although significant progress has been made since the publication of *To Err is Human*, a 2015 report by the National Patient Safety Foundation found that the degree of improvement has been rather limited and that patients continue to experience significant harm from the healthcare system [8]. The report noted that the challenge of improving healthcare safety is a considerably more complex challenge than was previously understood.

Error as a Systems Issue

Systematic studies of organizational accidents have led to an understanding that errors do not occur as isolated events but are shaped by the nature of the organization in which they occur. This insight has led to a deeper understanding of how organizations act as complex adaptive systems and how system factors can contribute to errors. The metaphor of a sword or spear has been used to describe the dichotomy between the work itself and the processes that support that work, with the term "sharp end" serving as a label for the direct action elements of work and "blunt end" serving as a convenient term for the support functions of work. In his book, *Human Error*, British Psychologist James Reason defines an unsafe act as "an error or a violation committed in the presence of a potential hazard" [9]. Unsafe acts can be direct hazards or can act to weaken existing defenses. These errors, referred to as *active failures*, occur at the sharp end. When accidents occur, active failures are often identified and blame commonly assigned to one or more individuals at the sharp end. This focus on the sharp end has been described as the "person approach" because it emphasizes assigning blame to individuals. A problem with this approach is that active failures are virtually never intentional and are usually not random occurrences.

Errors tend to fall into recurrent patterns. A focus on individual culpability for error can divert attention away from a systems approach to uncover the cause of the error. Investigations of errors which identify an active failure by an individual as the principal or sole cause of an error with harm often fail to identify the full range of failures that contributed to the adverse outcome. Active failures of individuals are commonly symptoms of overlooked, deeper *latent conditions*.

Latent Conditions

Examples of latent conditions include poor supervision and training, poor design of work tasks, inadequate staffing levels, impractical and unworkable processes, inadequate tools, and poorly designed and implemented automated systems. Each of these latent conditions can contribute to an increased frequency of active failures as well as weaken the barriers that protect patients from harm. Latent conditions can be thought of as scattered holes within these protective barriers, or layers of defense, like a series of slices of Swiss cheese [10] (see Fig. 4.1). Latent conditions are represented by existing holes in layers. Active failures can be represented as new holes that are created. Harm results when an occasional hazard travels along a "golden trajectory" along which the holes in the slices all line up, allowing the hazard to make its way through all of the safeguards and result in an accident. This is a useful conceptual model because it makes it easy to see how the frequency of hazards in conjunction with the number and adequacy of the layers of defense interact to produce an accident. It is accepted that most accidents occur when an unlikely combination of multiple failures, each insignificant alone, combine to create the necessary circumstances to allow a disaster to occur.

Many levels contribute to the healthcare system, and each provides a frame of reference within which to identify latent factors that can contribute to patient harm.

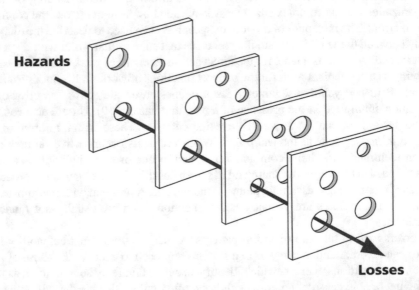

Fig. 4.1 The Swiss cheese model of hazards, defenses, barriers, and accident trajectories that produce harm. Republished from Wikimedia Commons, https://commons.wikimedia.org/wiki/File:Swiss_cheese_model_of_accident_causation.png, under the Creative Commons Attribution-Share Alike 3.0 Unported (CC BY-SA 3.0) license: https://creativecommons.org/licenses/by-sa/3.0/deed.en

Active Failures

The study of active failures reveals that the majority do not occur due to negligence or disregard [11]. Most healthcare errors are made by individuals who are competent and well intentioned. Active failures can be viewed as the failure to achieve a desired outcome that occurs when the wrong plan is selected or when the right plan is poorly executed.

Active failures are classified in terms of the type of cognitive activity involved and intentionality. James Reason proposed the Generic Error Modeling System (GEMS) of classification of errors which categorizes in terms of three common types of cognitive activities: skill-based, rule-based, and knowledge-based activity [9].

Skill-Based Activity

Skill-based activity is characterized as a familiar task, performed by an experienced individual. It is rapid, automatic, and effortless and requires little conscious feed back. Obtaining and recording vital signs, dispensing medication, and stocking supplies by experienced individuals are examples of healthcare skill-based activities. Active failures of skill-based activities can also be described as *failures of execution*. The individual intends to perform the correct activity but unconsciously deviates from the intended task. Anyone who has planned to make an unfamiliar stop on the trip home from work only to proceed directly home has personally experienced a skill-based activity failure.

Slips, lapses, omissions, duplications, and confusion are examples of errors of skill-based activity. When tasks fall into predictable patterns, then routine and habit are important contributors to success. However, when circumstances require some deviation from routine and attention wavers, individuals naturally revert to a familiar habit. For example, if it is routine to administer a cephalosporin antibiotic as surgical prophylaxis for a particular procedure, it would be expected that the antibiotic might be unintentionally administered to a patient undergoing the procedure despite a known cephalosporin allergy.

Rule-Based Activity

Rule-based activity can be accomplished by breaking the task up into a group of "if-then" rules. Mistakes in this category are errors that involve a wrong intention or plan and are the cause of active failures of rule- and knowledge-based activities. The wrong plan may be selected because a bad rule is being used, a good rule is being misapplied, or other relevant rules are being ignored.

Often complex processes, such as the development of a diagnostic and therapeutic plan, are reduced to the application of appropriate rules and result in mistakes based on rule-based activity failure. For example, the use of routine empiric therapy for community-acquired pneumonia for a patient with significant immune compromise would represent a rule-based mistake. As medical knowledge advances and more protocols and algorithms are validated, many knowledge-based activities have, and will, become rule-based activities. Computerized "expert systems" that apply intricate systems of interacting rules and algorithms to manage difficult clinical situations may further blur the distinction between rule-based and knowledge-based activities in the future.

Knowledge-Based Activity

Knowledge-based activity occurs with a novel task. It tends to be slower, requiring conscious thought, mental effort, and awareness. Knowledge-based activities are those where the intended outcome cannot be achieved by the mere application of rules. Failure to establish the correct diagnosis and therapy in a challenging case is an example of the failure of a knowledge-based activity. Errors in knowledge based activities are referred to as mistakes.

Human Factors as a Cause of Errors

Inherent limitations to human performance, referred to as *human factors*, contribute to the occurrence of errors. Understanding human factors is essential to effectively identify the root causes of errors and facilitate the design of systems that are error resistant. Strategies to reduce failures of skill-based activity include work flow design that reduces interruption and distractions, the use of checklists, conscious pauses, forcing functions, and automation. Human factors are important determinants of skill-based errors and also influence more complex knowledge-based problem-solving activities. For example, consider confirmation bias and the tendency to favor solutions that have been initially identified in lieu of potentially better solutions and to selectively filter data to reinforce a chosen course.

Once a physician arrives at a tentative diagnosis (even if incorrect), there is a tendency to emphasize information that supports the diagnosis and minimize conflicting data. In order to avoid confirmation bias, it is better for two individuals to independently make a calculation or observation and compare results rather than for one individual to "check" the result of another. The problem of diagnostic error has been identified as a significant patient safety challenge that is heavily influenced by human factors affecting cognitive performance.

Fatigue

Although physicians have traditionally worked prolonged hours, the impact of sleep deprivation on medical errors received more attention after the death of Libby Zion [12, 13].

Case Study • • •
Death of Libby Zion

Libby Zion was an 18-year-old woman admitted to a New York hospital with fever and agitation, who died within eight hours. Her father, journalist Sidney Zion, suggested that inadequate supervision of house staff, high workload, and long hours led to errors in her care that resulted in her death. As a result of this incident, the Bell Commission was formed to review the practices and suggest changes. Although the commission reported that both supervision and work hours were a concern, the issue of work hours received more publicity. As a result, the state of New York mandated changes in resident work hours in 1989. The limitation on work hours was adopted by the Accreditation Council on Graduate Medical Education (ACGME) in 2003.

These changes were controversial within the medical profession for a number of reasons: the need for increased hand-offs, which itself could cause additional errors; the lack of convincing data to support the perception that longer shifts adversely impact patient care; and the concern about loss of professionalism. However, most training programs voluntarily implemented the changes due to the threat of losing accreditation and the possibility of government legislation. Research investigating the effects of these changes has indicated improvement in resident well-being with a lesser defined impact on clinical outcomes. Particularly in medical-surgical specialties, there is evidence that reduced training hours may adversely affect experience and educational outcomes [14].

Healthcare workers are exposed to multiple factors that put them at increased risk for developing fatigue. These include nonstandard schedules (shift work and night shifts), interaction with and responsibility for acutely ill patients, need for continuous vigilance, work-related stress and physical fatigue, and inadequate rest and sleep.

Sleep loss and disruption of circadian rhythm has been shown to affect performance; Dawson reported that the performance of an individual without sleep for 24 h is similar to one with a blood alcohol level of 0.1% [15]. Sleep loss and fatigue can result in depression, anger, anxiety, irritability, and decreased psychomotor function. Sleep loss results in nano-naps, where the individual falls asleep for a few seconds at a time without realizing it [16]. These brief lapses increase the potential to make an error.

Shift work increases the risk of fatigue because of inadequate rest between shifts and decreased ability of the body to adjust to changes in shift between day and night. The two most vulnerable periods of the day are mid-afternoon (around 3 p.m.) and early morning (around 3 a.m.). Nursing shifts longer than 12 h and work weeks longer than 40 h are risk factors for fatigue and increased errors [17, 18]. The effects of fatigue become cumulative if the rest periods are inadequate, resulting in the development of chronic fatigue. Multiple interventions have been implemented in the past few years to address fatigue in healthcare workers, particularly among physicians in training. The interventions include limiting the number of duty hours and altering schedules to allow for adequate rest between on-call hours, providing nap periods during the shift, the strategic use of stimulants, avoiding scheduled double shifts for nurses, providing bright lighting, supporting the development of healthy sleep habits, standardizing processes, and simplifying tasks [17]. More study is needed regarding the effectiveness of interventions to decrease fatigue and medical errors.

Alarms

Alarms are designed to be tools that monitor patients for the development of serious problems and then communicate the concern to healthcare providers who can evaluate and address the problem. Unfortunately, alarm systems are not perfect and, like most diagnostic tests, are plagued with the opposing problems of false negative and false positive results. An alarm may fail by not activating when a serious condition occurs. Conversely, alarms may repeatedly be triggered when patients are not actually in danger. Staff can become desensitized to a repeated "false alarm" and may either ignore the alarm or even deactivate the alarm function and as a result, may fail to respond to the occurrence of a serious event [19].

Medication Errors

Modern pharmacologic agents are potent modulators of physiologic processes. If used optimally, these actions can produce significant improvements in patient morbidity and mortality; however, failures of the medication system can produce significant harm. A *medication error* is any error occurring in the medication use process. It is important to define relevant terms to comprehend the patient safety implications of the medication system: an *adverse drug event* (ADE) is an unexpected or dangerous reaction to medication. Some adverse drug events are the result of medication errors and have also been referred to as *preventable adverse drug events*. Due to individual variability, accurately predicting the consequences of the use of any medication is impossible. For example, allergic reactions in patients not known to have drug sensitivity and idiosyncratic drug reactions can occur unpredictably [20]. The term adverse drug reaction is synonymous with non-preventable adverse drug event. Medication errors can be categorized by the process that has failed [21].

Prescribing Errors   *Prescribing errors* involve the assessment of the patient, clinical decision making, drug choice, dosing interval and duration of therapy, documentation of the decision, and generation of an order or prescription. Although prescribing is the responsibility of the physician or non-physician advanced practitioner, prescribing errors can result from system problems such as failure to provide relevant information about previously identified drug allergies. Information failures, including lack of knowledge about the drugs and lack of information about the patients, are a major system cause of medication errors. Prescribing errors may include failure to prescribe beneficial therapy, prescription of an ineffective medication, failure to dose appropriately, failure to consider interactions with other medications and foods, comorbid medical conditions, and significance of known hypersensitivity. Prescribing errors can also occur due to poor documentation or communication of the drug order. Illegibility and the use of potentially ambiguous abbreviations are common causes of medication error at the prescribing step. Prescribing errors may be identified by pharmacy staff, nursing staff, or other members of the care team, and interventions can be taken to avert an adverse event.

Transcription Errors   *Transcription errors* occur in the hospital environment when the physician's medication order in the patient chart is incorporated into the Medication Administration Record used to manage and document the administration process. Transcription errors can occur when a written physician order is incorrectly transcribed into the pharmacy record system The transcription process usually involves communication of the written medication order to the pharmacy. Communication of the order can occur through the physical delivery of a copy of the order by courier or pneumatic tube system or electronic communication through the use of telephone, fax, or digital scanning technology. Once received, the order is transcribed into the pharmacy information system and incorporated into the Medication Administration Record provided to nursing staff. A transcribing error may represent a failure in both prescribing and transcribing. The generation of an unclear drug order is the prescribing error, and the failure to identify or to clarify the ambiguous order represents a transcribing error. The risk of transcription error is even higher when the initial order is verbal or provided by telephone.

Dispensing Errors   *Dispensing errors* include errors related to medication mixing or formulation, transfer of medication from stock supply to patient containers, double-checking, labeling, and other documentation. The dispensing process is usually performed by pharmacy staff. In the hospital environment, dispensing errors occur when the pharmacy staff dispenses drugs that differ in some way from the transcribed order. Dispensing errors may result due to confusion over drugs that may have similar names or appearance (look-alike and sound-alike medications).

Administration Errors *Administration errors* involve the actual introduction of the drug in the patient. The drug may be administered by nursing staff or other caregivers or may be self-administered by the patient. Administration usually includes verification of the order or instructions, preparation or measuring of the dose, and actual administration via the proper route in the proper fashion. Administration errors include omitted doses, duplicated doses, incorrect time of administration, administration of medications that were not ordered, administration of incorrect quantity, and administration by an incorrect route. Drugs administered by intravenous infusion carry the additional risk of inappropriate infusion rate.

Monitoring Errors *Monitoring errors* involve the assessment of the intended therapeutic effect and the identification of unintended adverse consequences. The monitoring may be done by the patient or by healthcare professionals. In either case, feedback must be provided to the prescribing practitioner and documented so that the therapy can be optimized. Monitoring errors include failure to recognize that the expected benefit has not occurred and failure to identify drug-induced adverse effects.

Medication Errors in the Ambulatory Setting Medication errors in the ambulatory setting may also occur when patients do not understand medication indication, dosage schedule, proper administration, duration of therapy, and potential adverse effects. Low health literacy and poor patient education are significant contributing factors. As outpatient visits between patients and providers often occur weeks to months apart, patients and their caregivers are increasingly accountable for managing their own medications. Polypharmacy or the prescribing of many medications also places a large burden on patients, especially among the elderly population.

Outpatient dispensing errors occur when the medication given to the patient by the pharmacy differs from the written prescription.

Measurement of Medication Errors It has been difficult to arrive at an authoritative determination of the prevalence and significance of medication errors and ADEs. Wide variation in measurements can occur depending upon the type of methods used to detect and record these occurrences. Staff may be encouraged to self-report medication errors using manual reporting forms or incident reports. Direct observation of drug administration, with comparison to the written physician order, provides accurate, and much higher, measurements of medication error rates. The direct observation method is often impractical, as it is resource intensive and dependent upon the availability of trained observers.

There is a similar variation in the reporting of ADEs. Self-reporting by staff produces relatively low rates. Review of randomly chosen hospital medical records by expert reviewers trained to identify adverse drug events generally produces the highest measured rates; however, the resources required for chart extraction limits the extent to which this method is employed. The use of trigger tools to prescreen charts for exhaustive review has been shown to be effective and efficient [22].

The most common inpatient medication errors occur in prescribing and medication administration. Prescribing error incidences of 15 to 1400 errors per 1000 hospital admissions have been reported. Prescribing errors can also be recorded in terms of errors per 1000 orders, with a range of 0.5 to 50 errors per 1000 hospital medication orders. Reported incidences of administration errors range from 3% to 11% of doses. Considering the number of medication doses that patients typically receive during a hospital admission, it is apparent that most hospitalized patients are likely to experience one or more medication errors over the course of their stay. Medication administration errors in nursing home populations have been found to be about twice as frequent as the hospital inpatient rates [23].

Fortunately, many medication errors do not result in measurable harm to patients. The reported incidences for preventable ADEs range from 1 to 2 events per 100 hospital admissions or 3 to 6 events per 1000 patient days. Medication errors account for between 25% and 50% of all ADEs in the inpatient setting, excluding patients in nursing homes. Ordering errors and administration errors are consistently the most frequent causes of preventable ADEs, collectively accounting for about three quarters of the total [21].

A comparison of the frequency of inpatient medication errors within each of the medication processes, along with care team member responsibility for each type of error, is reflected in Table 4.1.

Specific High-Profile Medication Errors

While it is important to avoid medication errors at all times, there are some particularly high-risk situations which deserve specific mention.

Hypoglycemia While adequate control of blood glucose is an important goal of therapy and is associated with improved clinical outcomes, hypoglycemia is a significant and dangerous complication of diabetes therapy. Hypoglycemia can result in seizures, permanent neurologic injury, and death [24].

Opioids Opioid drugs are tools to treat severe pain which must be used with great care. These medications can significantly depress central nervous system functions,

Table 4.1 Comparison of medication error frequency and responsibility in the inpatient setting

Process	Frequency	Physician	Pharmacy	Nurse
Prescribing	+++	+++	+	+
Transcribing	+	+	+++	−
Dispensing	+	−	+++	−
Administration	+++	−	−	+++
Monitoring	+	+	−	+++

+++ = Highest rate of frequency/responsibility
+ = Lower rate of frequency/responsibility
− = Typically not responsible for this type of error

most notably the respiratory drive, with the resulting risk of fatal respiratory suppression, severe anoxia, and death. This can occur either in the hospital or outpatient setting. Comorbid conditions such as advanced chronic obstructive lung disease with hypercarbia and obstructive sleep apnea, as well as negative interaction with benzodiazepine sedative agents, result in a particularly high risk of respiratory suppression.

Chemotherapy Drugs Chemotherapeutic agents create a particular risk due to several factors. These drugs are inherently toxic, and effective therapy often involves the delivery of a carefully calculated dosage intended to optimize the balance of maximizing the antineoplastic effect while avoiding serious systemic toxicity. Because there are a large number of chemotherapy drugs, which are easily confused, and they are administered at a patient-specific, calculated custom doses, it is harder for staff to identify inadvertent overdosing. The use of staff specifically trained in the use of these drugs combined with standardized dosing protocols can help ensure the safe use of these medications.

Strategies to Prevent Medication Errors

Systems Interventions The routine inclusion of an indication for the drug order is an important safeguard against order misinterpretation. This practice can prevent pharmacy staff from misinterpreting a poorly legible drug name. It can also help pharmacy staff to recognize when a physician has confused two drugs and ordered the wrong one through a slip, lapse, or poor knowledge about the medication. Providing an indication could conceivably have the unintended consequence of additional physician calls when drug use for an off-label indication is misinterpreted as an ordering error. As safeguards such as this become more robust, the chances increase that legitimate interventions will be intercepted or delayed. The appropriate "tuning" of safeguards to optimize safety without undue compromise of efficiency is likely to remain a major challenge for the foreseeable future.

Particular caution in the labeling, storing, and handling of drugs that either look alike or sound alike can also help prevent mix-ups throughout the entire process. Labeling of drugs with "tall man" lettering, which capitalizes key portions of similar sounding drug names to make it easier to distinguish between the two medications, is an example of a safety measure intended to reduce confusion between medications. This is a useful safety intervention to reduce dispensing errors [25].

The development of standardized drug formulary lists reduces the number of medications used in a healthcare organization. This standardization makes it easier for staff to become familiar with the available drugs, making everyone involved in the transcription of orders or the dispensing of drugs less prone to error. The potential benefits of a standardized formulary can be further leveraged through the use of standardized medication management protocols and order sets (e.g., weight-based heparin protocols or standardized insulin protocols). However, there are potential safety issues that must be addressed when discharging patients whose medication was switched in case the formularies of the ambulatory drug plan are different or a generic is used that is a different color or shape.

The use of standardized concentrations for intravenous infusions can reduce errors in dispensing and administration [23].

The consistent use of effective patient communication strategies, including the teach-back method and other health literacy best practices, may improve patient self-efficacy and protect the safety of patients in the ambulatory setting. The patient's functional and cognitive status should also be assessed, as appropriate, to determine the level of additional assistance the patient will need to follow medication instructions successfully. The use of clear and standardized dosage information, usage instructions, and the simplification of label content can reduce errors, especially among patients with low literacy levels.

Patients often see multiple providers in multiple settings of care. Poor care transitions represent a significant source of medication errors due to the lack of electronic health record interoperability and lapses in communication regarding medication changes across settings of care. Care transitions should be optimized to ensure patients have a clear point of contact with a healthcare provider to ask follow-up questions about a medication or discuss alternative options if cost, transportation, insurance coverage, or other barriers prevent patients from filling a prescription. Strategies to address patient communication need across the care continuum provide important safety nets for patients in the ambulatory setting.

As powerful as many of the individual safeguards are, they provide even greater benefit when used together.

Medication Reconciliation Medication reconciliation is a process that enables the review and documentation of the most complete and accurate list of medications a patient is taking. Accurate medication reconciliation can help prevent ordering errors of omission, may uncover likely drug interactions (prescribed, herbal, and over-the-counter medications), and prevent the duplication of medications. The availability of relevant patient-specific information (such as age, renal, and hepatic function) and drug information as the order is being written can also prevent errors.

Computerized Physician Order Entry Computerized physician order entry (CPOE) allows practitioners to generate medication orders or prescriptions through a computer system. (More details are available in Chap. 5, Medical Informatics.) In addition to addressing problems of legibility and miscommunication, the automated system contains relevant patient data and has the ability to generate real-time alerts to the practitioner as the order is being written. Although CPOE holds promise for reducing or eliminating many current errors [23], this technology represents a major redesign of a complex process and, as such, may well introduce new failure modes as it reduces or eliminates specific known errors.

Potential problems with CPOE systems include the difficulty in appropriately tuning the sensitivity of the alerts. If alerts are generated even when there is a low risk of an order causing harm, then the system will have a high sensitivity (miss very few ordering errors) but will have a poor specificity (generate many false alarms). If too many alerts are generated, practitioners can become conditioned to the alerts and, as a result, may ignore or override them. There is an increasing appreciation that, while CPOE can be effective in reducing some types of ordering errors, there is potential for the introduction of new errors into the system. Specific ordering errors that have been identified with CPOE include inadvertent prescribing for the wrong patient due to confusion among several CPOE displays, failure or delay in the cancellation of prior medications when new orders are placed, inappropriate low dosing, and the interruption of medically necessary treatment due to the automated cancellation of orders.

Automated Pharmacy Systems Automated systems similar to CPOE are currently used by pharmacists during the transcription or dispensing phases. The pharmacist notifies the physician when a potential ordering error has been detected. A central part of the dispensing process involves the physical movement of the drug from a storage area into a packaging designed for administration. For outpatient medications, dispensing may involve counting out pills from a large container into a pill bottle meant to contain a supply for a prescribed number of days. For hospital patients, it may involve placing the proper medications into a drawer or a medication cart or accomplished through the use of an automated drug dispensing unit (which must be periodically correctly restocked by the pharmacy). For intravenously administered medications, the mixing of the drug infusion is a critical part of the dispensing process. The use of premixed solutions and standardization of the concentration of infused drugs helps to reduce errors.

The development of automated robotic devices to dispense medication from pharmacy stock and automated equipment to formulate complex infusion mixtures are revolutionizing dispensing processes. Some of the more advanced robotic dispensing systems include motorized robotic transport carts carrying drugs to resupply automated dispensing units. An important requirement for automated dispensing systems is an ability to label individual drug doses in a manner that can be easily recognized by the system, such as optical barcoding. Because pharmaceutical manufacturers have failed to incorporate standardized barcode identification into their drug packaging, additional automated equipment is required to repackage unit doses of drugs with barcode identifiers to facilitate the automation of the medication administration system.

Redundancy for Safety The administration process is the source of a relatively large number of medication errors that are difficult to detect or intercept. These errors can include the administration of the wrong drug or wrong dose at the wrong time, an omission or duplication of scheduled doses, or a patient may be misidentified and receive medications intended for another patient. Some high-risk medications are routinely double-checked by a second nurse before administration. However, this type of safeguard is particularly vulnerable to the slips and lapses that humans inevitably manifest, as the double-checking process requires prolonged attention and concentration.

Forcing Functions   The design of technology to prevent unsafe modes of operation is referred to as *forcing functions*. A good example of this method of risk reduction is infusion technology. Drugs administered by intravenous infusion carry additional risks. If the drug is infused too rapidly, an overdose will occur. Errors in calculating infusion rates from drug concentration are well described, particularly with drugs dosed by patient weight. Because infusion pumps remain continuously at the bedside, errors have occurred when patients inadvertently alter the pump settings. Safeguards against infusion pump medication administration errors include limitations on the amount of drug contained within the reservoir and the incorporation of safety features into the design of infusion pumps. Standard infusion pump safety features include "no free-flow" designs and locking mechanisms to prevent unauthorized tampering. Newer safety features include smart pump technology.

Smart pumps contain microprocessors programmed with upper dose limits for infused drugs. When the infusion is attached to the pump, the nurse is required to indicate the drug and the concentration. If the pump is set for an infusion rate greater than the upper safety limit for that drug, an alert will be triggered, and the pump will not deliver the excessive rate. Forcing functions incorporated into the design of tubing systems have been successful in reducing the risk of inadvertent administration by the wrong route (intravenous instead of via enteral tube or intrathecal instead of intravenous).

Patient Empowerment   Patients and their families can provide an important safeguard at the medication administration phase by asking questions about any medication they are receiving and the reason it is being given. They should also be encouraged to fully disclose all medications, supplements, and over-the-counter medications. Patient involvement is essential to safeguard against allergic reactions and inadvertent omissions of chronic maintenance medications, which should not be interrupted.

Common Risks to Patient Safety

Invasive Procedures

Surgical operations and other invasive medical procedures have many risks. Many of the risks are influenced by the specialized skills of the operator or the procedure team and are inherently difficult to safeguard against with generic risk reduction strategies. General risk factors apply across a wide range of *invasive procedures*. One of the most basic safety factors involves verification to prevent wrong-site surgery. This process ensures that the correct patient is about to undergo the correct procedure on the correct site and that the correct equipment (including implants) is available. The use of a pre-procedure "time out" to complete a checklist to verify each of these elements is an important safety step. Best practice is to have a well-developed script that the surgeon, anesthesiologist, and nurse all utilize. These improvements are based on the aviation model of crew resource management and can help reduce errors in the hierarchical operating room environment [26]. This systematic pre-procedure checklist approach has been formalized as the "Universal Protocol" which was adopted as a requirement by The Joint Commission as a National Patient Safety Goal to prevent wrong site, wrong procedure, and wrong person surgery.

Patient management by anesthesiologists is highly standardized and includes some of the most robust safety engineering found in healthcare [7]. Many minor invasive procedures involve minimal or moderate sedation and local anesthesia and do not routinely require the presence of an anesthesia specialist. Oversedation during procedures or post-procedure recovery can lead to respiratory compromise. The use of sedation protocols and post-procedure care protocols developed in collaboration with anesthesia specialists can help reduce this risk.

Some operative procedures require prophylactic antibiotic administration that must be timed to coincide with the surgical incision to optimally protect against wound infection. Standardized processes for incorporating the antibiotic administration into the operating room workflow help avoid errors of omission. Other safety risks associated with surgical procedures include the risk of retained surgical equipment, and the risk of transfusion reaction if blood delivered to the operating room is brought to the wrong patient. For invasive procedures such as thoracentesis, paracentesis, organ biopsies, and central venous catheter insertion, the use of diagnostic imaging such as ultrasonography can help reduce complications.

Fire safety is also important in the operating room and other procedural areas where oxygen, combustible materials, and energy sources such as high-intensity illumination, lasers, and cautery devices are combined.

Perioperative Complications and Iatrogenic Injuries

Deep Vein Thrombosis and Pulmonary Embolism Extended immobilization, trauma, cancer, genetic abnormalities of the clotting system, and other factors increase risk of venous thromboembolism. Because a patient's disease state may also place them at increased risk of bleeding, patients should be assessed for the risk of thromboembolism and bleeding prior to the initiation of venous thromboembolism prophylaxis. Prophylaxis with heparin or related drug is recommended unless the risk of bleeding outweighs the potential benefits. Sequential compression devices may also lower risk of developing venous thromboembolism and may be used when pharmacologic therapy is contraindicated.

Abdominopelvic Laceration and Puncture Though the increased use of laparoscopy has dramatically improved safety and the recovery time associated with abdominopelvic surgery, accidental puncture or lacerations of the bowel, bladder, and major vascular structures represent significant patient safety concerns. Timely recognition of iatrogenic injury and the use of surgical techniques and instruments designed to minimize injuries are crucial in the reduction of postoperative morbidity and mortality.

Postoperative Wound Dehiscence Postoperative wound dehiscence is associated with an increased length of stay, herniation, the need for additional surgery, and a higher risk of mortality. Identification of preoperative risk factors (such as nutritional status), timely administration of antibiotics to prevent surgical site infection, and postoperative wound assessment are encouraged.

Iatrogenic Pneumothorax This serious complication may arise following procedures involving structures adjacent to the lung or pleural space such as central venous catheter insertion or feeding tube placement. Iatrogenic Pneumothorax is associated with an increased length of stay, higher hospital charges, and excess mortality. The use of real-time ultrasound guidance has been shown to decrease the risk of pneumothorax associated with internal jugular venous catheter placement.

Postoperative Acute Kidney Injury Adequate hydration and goal-directed fluid management, avoidance of nephrotoxic drugs, and the use of appropriate renal dosing are encouraged to prevent acute kidney injury. Risk factors such as older age, diabetes, and a lower estimated glomerular filtration rate should be considered.

Perioperative Hemorrhage or Hematoma While one of the key goals of surgical procedures is to achieve appropriate intraoperative hemostasis, even with optimal technique, significant bleeding can occasionally occur. A key challenge is timely recognition of this potentially devastating complication. Failure to recognize a perioperative hemorrhage or hematoma can allow an inconvenient complication to progress to a life-threatening event. Careful monitoring of vital signs, urine output, peripheral perfusion, and the surgical site can reduce this risk. Appropriate clinical management often includes transfusion therapy in combination with additional, varying interventions based on the location and size of the bleed.

It is important to evaluate and correct abnormalities in hemostasis and to differentiate bleeding due to coagulopathy, which is treated by correction of the clotting abnormality, from bleeding due to a technical surgical issue. Significant persistent bleeding not due to coagulopathy will often require a repeat surgical procedure to identify and definitively treat the source of hemorrhage. In selective cases, interventional radiology may be useful in identifying the origin and nature of the bleeding.

Postoperative Respiratory Failure Pneumonia, aspiration, acute respiratory distress syndrome (ARDS), pulmonary emboli, opioid overdose, inadequate reversal of paralytics, and other complications may lead to postoperative respiratory failure. Failure to adequately assess the magnitude of preoperative respiratory impairment and adequately optimize preoperative respiratory function can also be contributing factors. Careful monitoring of respiratory status, consideration of the patient's disease state, and appropriate medication use are important to the prevention of this rare but life-threatening complication.

Postoperative Cardiac Complications Cardiac ischemia, myocardial infarction, and acute exacerbation of heart failure can occur in the postoperative setting and are often related to unmanaged or unknown risk factors. Ischemia and cardiac injury can result from demand ischemia in which acute factors related to the stress of surgery increase myocardial perfusion demand which exceeds the capacity of a chronically limited coronary blood flow. This risk can be reduced by appropriate assessment of cardiac risk factors before surgery and avoiding significant perioperative hypotension and anemia. Patients who are receiving long-term beta-blocker therapy should be identified and provisions made to maintain beta blockade during the perioperative period. It is generally not useful to initiate beta-blocker therapy on an immediate preoperative basis.

Infections

Hospital-acquired infections (HAI) have received increased attention due to devastating consequences related to cost, morbidity, and mortality. The Centers for Medicare and Medicaid Services (CMS) and other payers have begun to refuse reimbursement for additional care resulting from treatment for an infection not present on admission [27]. Consistent, mindful adherence to basic infection control principles, usually referred to as *universal precautions*, is a critical protective strategy that too often fails. A key part of universal precautions is hand hygiene. Handwashing is one of the most effective means of reducing the spread of harmful microorganisms. One of the challenges of handwashing is the time needed for effective washing and the accessibility of sinks for washing. Appropriate hand hygiene should occur upon entering and leaving every patient encounter.

The use of alcohol-based skin cleansers, often located at the doorway, provides a highly effective, efficient, and convenient method of hand hygiene. For patients with certain particularly dangerous types of infections, isolation and the use of disposable gowns and gloves in addition to hand decontamination can help limit patient-to-patient spread. It is important to remember that any physical objects such as pens, documents, or medical equipment that come into contact with the patient can also transmit infections and should be decontaminated or sequestered. Close attention to maintenance of normal range blood glucose levels has been shown to be an effective intervention to reduce the incidence of multiple types of HAIs.

Site-Specific Infection Prevention

Postoperative Surgical Wound Infections Appropriate surgical site preparation through the use of hair clippers rather than shavers and the use of chlorhexidine-based cleansing agents has been shown to be important [28–31]. The appropriate timing and selection of prophylactic antibiotic therapy also reduces infections.

Central Venous Catheter Infections Effective interventions to decrease the incidence of central venous catheter infections include the use of chlorhexidine-based skin cleansers, the use of sterile technique and full barrier precautions, the selection of the subclavian insertion site over femoral or internal jugular sites, the use of chlorhexidine-containing insertion site dressings, and the use of antimicrobial bonded catheter technology [32].

Urinary Tract Infection Avoidance of unnecessary or prolonged use of indwelling bladder catheters is the most important method of reducing urinary infections. Effective strategies to reduce urinary catheter use include physician reminders to discontinue or reevaluate the need for continued catheter use and incorporating a defined, limited duration (stop order) into the initial catheter order as well as nurse-initiated catheter removal protocols.

Resistant Organisms The emergence of virulent pathogens, which are resistant to multiple antimicrobial agents, is a major threat. Specific organisms of concern include methicillin-resistant *Staphylococcus aureus* (MRSA), vancomycin-resistant enterococcus (VRE), gram-negative organisms producing the extended-spectrum beta-lactamase (ESBL) resistance factor, and other multiple drug-resistant strains of gram-negative infections such as *Pseudomonas* and *Acinetobacter*. Because patients can be asymptomatic carriers of resistant organisms, some healthcare organizations are employing active surveillance procedures in which cultures are routinely obtained at scheduled intervals to promote earlier identification of resistant organisms. Beyond isolation measures, the careful management of antibiotic use is an important intervention to limit the development of these types of infections.

It is important to manage antimicrobial formularies carefully and implement mechanisms to monitor and control the appropriate use of selected antibiotics that promote the development of resistance. Close cooperation among medical staff, infection control, pharmacy, and clinical microbiology professionals is essential for the development of effective institutional control measures. The importance of this type of multidisciplinary, systematic scrutiny of antimicrobial therapy has resulted in the requirement for formal antimicrobial stewardship activities as a 2017 Joint Commission standard based upon recommendations from the CDC and CMS.

Ventilator-Associated Events

Due to methodological difficulties with the use of chest radiographs to establish the presence of pneumonia in ventilated patients, the Centers for Disease Control and Prevention (CDC) has introduced a new taxonomy. The term *ventilator-associated event* includes ventilator-associated conditions (worsening of oxygenation without evidence of infection), infection-related ventilator associated complications (which adds temperature abnormality or white blood cell indications of infection with the initiation of new antimicrobial therapy to worsening oxygenation), and ventilator-associated pneumonia (which further adds purulent secretions or positive respiratory cultures). Important interventions shown to reduce the incidence of ventilator-associated events include minimizing the duration of intubation, maintaining effective oral hygiene (including the use of chlorhexidine), elevating the head of the bed by at least 30°, minimizing the opening of the ventilator circuit, avoiding prolonged uninterrupted sedation, and using endotracheal tube designs which allow the continuous removal of subglottic secretions.

Patient Falls

Falls, with resultant injury, represent a significant risk for adverse patient outcomes. Unfortunately, some falls result in serious injuries such as hip fracture, subdural hematoma, or intracranial hemorrhage. One of the best general prevention strategies is an effective assessment designed to recognize patients at risk for falls [33]. Risk factors intrinsic to the patient include altered mental status, reduced vision, musculoskeletal disease, history of previous falls, and presence of acute and chronic illness. Extrinsic risk factors are those present in the patient's environment and include sedating medications, elevated beds, an absence of grab rails, ill-fitting footwear, poor illumination, unstable flooring, and inadequate assistive devices. Once the risk has been identified, appropriate patient-specific measures should be implemented to reduce the risk. These can include modifications to the patient's environment, patient education, and adequate assistance and supervision, in some cases including the use of sitters.

Pressure (Decubitus) Ulcers

Pressure ulcers occur when tissue is compressed between bony prominences and external surfaces for sufficient duration to cause tissue necrosis. Ulcers commonly occur in soft tissue overlying the sacrum, ischial tuberosities, the thoracic spine, and heels. Pressure ulcers may require extensive surgical interventions and can lead to systemic infection, sepsis, and death. Due to serious sequelae, prevention, early diagnosis, and interventions are key management strategies. Common risk factors include immobility, inactivity, nutritional compromise, fecal and urinary incontinence, and impaired ability to perceive or to respond to sensations of soft tissue discomfort.

Several validated risk assessment tools have been developed (e.g., the Braden Scale [34], Norton Scale [35], and Gosnell Scale [36]). It is important that patients be adequately assessed for the risk of ulcer development, as well as the actual presence of ulcers. Preventive strategies include optimization of skin care, pressure reduction through the use of cushioning, and frequent repositioning. In patients at risk for pressure ulcers, particular care must be taken to avoid friction injury or abrasion during repositioning. Reversible causes of fecal and urinary incontinence should be evaluated and treated. If the incontinence cannot be prevented, absorbent materials designed to transfer moisture away from the skin surface should be used. Continued education of health professionals, patients, and families is also an important preventive strategy [37].

Patient Safety Tools

Tools for Data Acquisition

Safety Surveys

Safety culture assessment tools are used for developing and evaluating safety improvement interventions in healthcare organizations and provide a metric by which implicitly shared understandings about the expectation of how things are done are made available. A number of national organizations (e.g., the Leapfrog Group, the National Quality Forum (NQF), the American Medical Association, and the American Hospital Association) have designed or promoted various survey tools. One of the most commonly used hospital surveys is the Agency for Healthcare Research and Quality (AHRQ) Hospital Survey on Patient Safety Culture [38]. A key advantage of using these tools is that a nationwide sharing of data can provide local and national benchmarks for comparison. Similar culture surveys have been customized to address specific populations or healthcare settings, such as surgical areas of a hospital, nursing homes, nurses, and nursing assistants.

Error Reporting

The reporting of errors or unexpected negative events provides a critical data source. Every error that is recognized and examined provides an opportunity to learn from the error and become more resilient. Classification of events into various categories can help organizations keep track of events and determine what type of action plan is appropriate. *Preventable adverse events* are acts of omission or commission resulting in harm to the patient. *Close calls* or *near misses* are events or situations that could have resulted in an adverse event but did not. *Sentinel events* are unexpected occurrences involving death, serious physical or psychological injury, or risk thereof and can be considered to be the subset of adverse events containing the most serious occurrences. The reporting of such events, either through a mandatory or voluntary reporting system, provides critical data necessary to understand the risk and motivate effective action to reduce the risk [39].

Incident reporting is a common formalized method of reporting the actions of oneself or others in the healthcare environment [40]. Such systems may use simple paper forms with checkboxes and areas for recording event characteristics or more sophisticated networked computer-based applications that interface directly with data systems. Incident reporting is an important means of capturing information on errors and adverse events. Some states have established formal incident reporting structures, which allow statewide benchmarking [40]. In organizations with a punitive culture, staff may be reluctant to generate reports that could create negative consequences for themselves or colleagues. For this reason, incident reporting systems are likely to underestimate actual numbers of incidents. Underreporting makes it difficult to establish clear benchmarks and standards of practice because reports are influenced both by the frequency of occurrence of events and by the willingness of staff to report those events. As a result, organizations that are likely becoming safer may observe an increase in reported events as they develop systems to reduce risk.

Self-Reporting Systems

Self-reporting systems, a subset of incident reporting, are often unique to an individual organization or an organizational system. The intent is to gather and aggregate data that can be used to create safety alerts and tips, to identify and showcase best practices, and to highlight trends. Self-reporting systems that are unique to an organization lack an in-depth common language that can hinder learning and minimize comparative data for benchmarking.

Record Review

Record review has long been a primary tool for morbidity and mortality committees to identify contributory factors, which indicate areas for improvement and prevention. Gathering information helps to develop a collective picture of a practice that can identify the outlier or unusual event during a particular procedure/process. Targeted record reviews aimed at sentinel events, high-rate incidences, or other trigger events yield important epidemiological information. Screening charts for the presence of several markers for adverse events can be used to trigger a more thorough review of the records. For example, the administration of the drug naloxone, which reverses or antagonizes the effects of opiate analgesic agents, can be considered a marker for opiate overmedication. A review of 20 charts of patients who received naloxone is likely to yield a much higher incidence of opiate over-medication than a random sample of 20 charts. The Institute for Healthcare Improvement (IHI) has developed a standardized trigger tool to identify records that are more likely to contain adverse events or errors [22].

The increasing use of electronic health records offers the potential for an auto-mated review of records for the presence of triggers. This is particularly exciting because it can address attention to a case while the patient is being actively treated during the same care encounter. When a patient is noted to have a pattern suggestive of an adverse event, a timely, focused review may help to identify the problem and avert a negative outcome.

Case Study • • •
An Innovative Event Recognition System

Many institutions utilize Medical Emergency Teams (MET) (also known as Rapid Response Teams) to manage acute patient decompensation. The University of Pittsburgh Medical Center (UPMC) has used feedback from MET interventions to detect medical errors [41]. UPMC initiated a review of MET responses performed by a group led by senior medical staff and admin-istration in order to identify medical errors and address the cause of errors. Approximately one-third of the MET responses involved errors (both diag-nostic and treatment errors). The information from the review was provided to the unit managers and staff for inspection and subsequent suggestions for improvement. The proposed changes to address identified issues were pre-sented at the hospital-wide Patient Safety Committee meeting for approval. The MET review resulted in interventions to decrease the misplacement of feeding tubes and improved management of hyperglycemia, resulting in bet-ter glycemic control and a decrease in hypoglycemic episodes [41]. The medi-cal director and nursing leadership provided support and coordinated the implementation of interventions with individual departments.

Situation Monitoring

Situation monitoring of error events, also known as *direct observation*, is the pro-cess of actively scanning and assessing routine healthcare standards of practice delivery (e.g., handwashing or medication administration). Monitoring situational elements provides an understanding of event errors in real time and helps to main-tain functional awareness of practices. The observation of clinical events performed by different practitioners can also lead to the development of more standardized approaches to care.

There is an increasing emphasis on required reporting. In *To Err Is Human*, the IOM called for a nationwide mandatory reporting system that would provide for the collection of standardized information about adverse events that result in death or serious harm [1]. To date, there is no national reporting requirement. However, as of 2015, 28 states and the District of Columbia have established adverse event reporting systems [42]. All state licensed hospitals are mandated to comply with specific requirements to ensure that minimum health, safety, and quality standards are maintained.

Proponents of *public reporting* believe it will help accelerate the pace of improvement throughout the healthcare industry and provide individuals with the information needed to make informed decisions about their own care and protect themselves against adverse medical events. The recommended list of standardized reportable events described by the National Quality Forum (NQF) includes "adverse events that are unambiguous, largely preventable, and serious, as well as adverse, indicative of a problem in a healthcare setting's safety systems, or important for public credibility or accountability" [42]. The use of data for internal performance improvement and the safe practice of medicine are supported by all.

Analytic Tools

Retrospective Event Analysis

Critical or sentinel events have been identified as particularly concerning. Most organizations have processes for performing a rigorous, detailed analysis of such events in order to prevent recurrence. A prerequisite to solving and eliminating a problem is finding the root cause. *Critical event analysis* or *root cause analysis* (RCA) is a practical problem-solving tool used to define the problem, to identify the cause(s) (often at multiple levels), and to create solutions.

The tools used as part of the RCA process can be grouped into several categories: data collection, event understanding, possible cause analysis, cause and effect, and pattern recognition. Reliable data is an essential foundation for a successful RCA. Data collection supports and substantiates analysis.

Brainstorming Brainstorming is used to generate multiple ideas, which are then evaluated to reach consensus over the significance of these possible causes as a contributing factor to the event. Scoring mechanisms can provide a more structured framework to determine the relative importance of the potential causes identified through brainstorming. The US Department of Veterans Affairs (VA) *Safety Assessment Code* (SAC) matrix, developed by the VA in partnership with AHRQ and the National Center for Patient Safety, is an easy-to-use method for analyzing the key factors of severity and probability of adverse events and near misses or close calls [43].

Pareto Charts *Pareto charts* can help to identify dominant causes among the possibilities when quantitative data exist as to the frequency of the various causes. Visual diagrams help identify patterns, dominant causes, relationships between two causes, or other variables. *Histograms* and *scatter diagrams* or *affinity charts* can help identify these patterns.

Fishbone Diagrams *Fishbone diagrams* are another important RCA tool, invented by Dr. Kaoru Ishikawa, to determine the root causes of an event. A fishbone diagram provides a systematic way of looking at the effect (major problem, e.g., error or near miss) and the possible cause or origin of the major problem at the head of the diagram.

Other methods used to facilitate cause-and-effect analysis include matrix diagramming (to arrange pieces of information according to certain aspects) and the "Five Whys" (used in brainstorming to delve more deeply into causal relationships). The latter method involves asking the question "Why?" in reference to the initial event and repeating it four more times in response to each answer. Each repetition of the question can uncover a deeper level of contributing factors.

Prospective Event Analysis

An effective method of prospective event analysis is *failure mode and effects analysis* (FMEA). FMEA was developed as an engineering design tool for the aerospace industry in the mid-1960s, specifically looking at safety issues, and has since become a key tool for improving safety in many industries, including healthcare. FMEA is a systematic method of identifying potential failures, effects, and risks within a process with the intent of preventing problems before they occur. This method requires careful analysis of the current process at a fairly detailed level, using input from individuals who are experienced in the day-to-day practical operations.

Any means by which the process can fail is a failure mode. Each possible failure mode has a potential effect on an associated, relative risk. The relative risk of a failure, and its effect, is determined by three factors: severity (the consequence of the failure), occurrence (the probability or frequency of the particular mode of failure), and detection (the probability of the failure being detected before harm occurs). By multiplying the severity, occurrence, and severity subscores, a composite risk profile number (RPN) can be determined for each possible failure mode. This method allows the calculation of an overall process risk score and allows prioritization of the relative importance of any particular step in the overall process. Finally, it allows an organization to model the reduction in overall risk as changes in high-risk elements of the process are implemented. This tool may also be referred to as a *proactive risk assessment*.

Disclosure of Errors

The increased focus on errors and their disclosure to patients and families has a profound impact on healthcare workers. Successful strategies to address the impact on house staff (i.e., interns, residents, fellows) include accepting responsibility, constructive changes in practice, advice about avoiding recurrence, and provision of emotional support [44, 45].

Healthcare workers—physicians in particular—are reluctant to discuss errors with patients and families or peers for a variety of reasons, including the difficulty in defining errors, complex emotional reactions (e.g., anger, guilt, shame, embarrassment), a loss of the sense of autonomy, individual responsibility, loss of self-esteem, concern about perception of peers and patients, perceived lack of feedback and support from the organization, and concerns over financial and legal liability. The disclosure of error is sometimes partial or misleading because of the perceived uncertainty about the relationship between the error, the harm, and the natural progression of the disease.

Interviews with patients and families reveal a concern about a lack of disclosure of errors. Patients and families suggest that describing the mistake (explaining what happened), apologizing, and outlining steps that will be taken to minimize recurrence, in addition to compensation, when appropriate, would address the issue of disclosure. In spite of the healthcare workers' concerns about family-patient perception, surveys show that disclosure could improve relationships with patients [40, 45–48]. Reports of disclosure programs, implemented by the University of Michigan and the VA hospital in Lexington, did not show an increase in malpractice costs [48, 49]. The impact of widespread use of these programs on litigation and malpractice is not clear.

Prevention of Errors

An understanding of the limitations of human factors as well as common types of healthcare adverse events has allowed for a systematic effort to implement changes in the healthcare system that have helped to reduce risk and improve safety. The IOM has provided useful publications to help reduce errors in healthcare [50, 51].

Systems Approach

Leaders play a large role in creating and nurturing the *culture of safety* which is an essential requirement for high-reliability healthcare organizations. By partnering with staff, healthcare leadership can create a workplace environment that minimizes latent factors which often serve to generate errors. A culture of safety challenges leaders to look beyond assigning blame to an individual and instead address underlying system problems.

Organizations with a positive safety culture are characterized by communications founded on mutual trust, shared perceptions of the importance of safety, and confidence in the efficacy of established preventive measures. Key measurements of safety performance should be systematically recorded, monitored, and openly discussed so that the organization can track progressive improvements in safety.

In a culture of safety, the reporting of errors and near misses is rewarded and viewed as an important contribution that helps identify and improve unreliable processes. The use of nonpunitive reporting policies for self-reported errors helps encourage open communication about latent conditions. Individuals are accountable not only to accomplish tasks successfully but to report failures and identify conditions that promote failure. This type of approach has been described by the label of "Just Culture" which provides organizations consistent and constructive methods and procedures for dealing with error accountability and is a best practice for promoting a culture of safety. Standardized rituals that help promote safety can be incorporated into routine clinical unit workflow to create opportunities for staff to consider and discuss potential safety problems. Patients should be empowered with knowledge and information so that they can participate in their own care and support efforts designed to safeguard them from harm.

Healthcare leaders should become familiar with the topic of patient safety and frequently discuss the subject in communications with staff, physicians, patients, the public, and organization governing board members. Members of the senior administrative team should periodically visit frontline staff in patient care areas and support services to discuss safety concerns and conduct.

Leaders should promote organizational transparency and openness. Formal disclosure policies can help reinforce the message of transparency and openness about errors. The free flow of information that comes with openness and transparency also helps build *learning organizations* [51]. Learning organizations that continually grow and improve incorporate information from internal and external sources.

Leaders must view safety consciousness as a major strategic priority. Resource allocation, reward systems, and organizational policies must align to reinforce the importance of safety. Key measurements of safety performance should be systematically recorded, monitored, and openly discussed so that the organization can track progressive improvements in safety.

The critical importance of healthcare leaders' active engagement with patient safety has been formally recognized by the American College of Healthcare

Executives (ACHE) which has issued a policy statement addressing "The Healthcare Executive's Role in Ensuring Quality and Patient Safety" [52].

Case Study • • •
Culture of Safety

Sentara Health system, a six-hospital integrated healthcare system in southeastern Virginia, achieved a 46% reduction in the incidence of serious adverse events after implementing a system-wide patient safety initiative. The commitment of senior leadership was key to the program's success. Key components included integration of patient safety concerns into the development of strategic priorities, staff incentives, human resource policies, and resource allocation. Fifty percent of the organization's employee incentive gain-sharing program was based on safety and quality measures [53]. Both hospital staff and medical staff were involved in the process. Operational leaders were given responsibility for implementing the program.

The program utilized training in behavior-based expectations. All staff members were expected to demonstrate the following: pay attention to detail, communicate clearly, have a questioning attitude, hand off effectively, and never leave your wingman [54]. Organization leaders were expected to demonstrate accountability, promote safety, and provide continuous reinforcement of the commitment to safety. Medical staff were to utilize physician-to-physician communication for consultations and designate a physician responsible for coordinating the care for each patient.

Operational Interventions to Prevent Error

An understanding of the human factors that lead to active failures can help healthcare organizations design resilient systems that provide safeguards against slips, lapses, and mistakes. The use of information technology to automate repetitive, skill-based tasks is an increasingly important innovation used to reduce errors. A revolutionary redesign of healthcare workflow processes has evolved as information technology devices have become integrated with point-of-care administration.

Forcing functions are an important protection against slips in action. Forcing functions constrain behavior by either forcing individuals to consciously consider a suspect action or make certain types of actions impossible. An example of a simple forcing function is a computer alert message that requires positive confirmation before files are deleted, or potentially dangerous files are accessed. Forcing functions can easily be incorporated into automated systems as an element of design and are compelling tools used to adapt and customize processes and behaviors in the clinical setting, providing warnings, alerts, or text box notifications that must be addressed.

Heralded as an important quality improvement measure, forcing functions can also be used in clinical settings to either prompt a healthcare specialist to consider a predetermined cause of action such as verifying the need for a specific test or procedure in terms of clinical decision support, be used as an educational instrument, or utilized in high-risk intervention protocols. Electronic programming is not the only means of utilizing forcing functions methodology. Forcing functions can also be initiated through material or procedural methods whereby healthcare professionals are constrained in terms of equipment, tools, or processes.

Excessive use of some forcing functions can actually increase the risk of errors. If staff members are continuously faced with a stream of cautions concerning low-risk possibilities, the alerts may gradually become ignored. Careful attention must be paid to ensure that workarounds are not employed to avoid what some resistant to changes may see as a hindrance to efficiency. The use of aids such as checklists, redundant double-checking, reminders, and automated prompting systems help prevent skill-based slips and lapses.

Case Study • • •
Forcing Functions

Improper positions of central venous catheters can result in positioning the catheter tip within the right atrium. This presents a risk of catheter erosion through the thin atrial wall with resulting potentially lethal cardiac tamponade. After observing two cases of fatal cardiac tamponade due to this problem, the Los Angeles County Department of Health Services identified that a significant percentage of central venous catheters in their facilities were being advanced too far. They noted evidence in medical literature that identified a reduced risk of this problem when 16 cm length catheters were used. The standard catheter length for their facilities was changed from 20 cm to 16 cm, resolving the problem with catheter malpositioning. The switch to the shorter catheters was a forcing function, which prevented the problem of over insertion. An added, and unforeseen, benefit was a significant reduction in the number—and the cost—of repeat chest radiographs that had been used to adjust the position of the longer catheters.

Decision Support Systems

Healthcare organizations function under extreme variations of activity and stress. Emergency departments are subject to particularly chaotic swings in activity and acuity due to open access to the community and rapid turnover times. Within minutes, emergency departments can transition from being almost empty with no serious cases to large numbers of patients waiting to be seen, while the staff tries to manage several life-threatening conditions simultaneously. Healthcare organizations have defined various operating states that require different types of support and resources. When certain threshold triggering conditions are met, the organization can implement standardized preconceived contingency plans. This strategy can be employed by clinical units that might transition between condition green, condition yellow, and condition red, with each operating state triggering different levels of staffing, resources, and operating procedures. This creates a safer, more reliable system by turning the problem of what to do under peak demand conditions from a knowledge-based task where solutions are worked out "on the fly" to a rule-based task. The activation of specialized response teams to deal with high-risk events such as cardiac arrest and major trauma is another example of how healthcare organizations can dynamically reorient resources to effectively meet emergent needs.

Reduction in variation through the use of standardized protocols and order sets is a powerful strategy to reduce errors. As information system technology becomes more sophisticated, more complex rules will likely be developed. The technology to provide health professionals with knowledge and person-specific information to enhance decision-making and workflow is referred to as clinical *decision support systems* [55]. Examples include computerized alerts and reminders, clinical guidelines, condition-specific order sets, focused data reports, diagnostic support, and easily accessed relevant reference material. The increasing power and sophistication of information technology offers the promise of combining the benefits of standardized rules while avoiding the risk of oversimplification of complex situations.

Teamwork and Crew Resource Management

Missed communication and miscommunication are the most common causes of sentinel events analyzed by the Joint Commission [56]. Teamwork provides a defense against error by individuals through the use of monitoring and double-checking. *Crew Resource Management* (CRM), a formal tool used in aviation to improve safety, focuses on how human factors interact with stressful environments [26, 57, 58]. The components of CRM are situational awareness, problem identification, decision-making, workload distribution, time management, and conflict resolution. The goals of CRM are error avoidance, prevention of progression of an error, and mitigating the harm from the error. Team training provides a shared understanding of the task and goals and improves communication between team members with differing expertise.

In the past few years, there has been an increased emphasis on adopting CRM principles in medical settings. CRM or Medical Team Training (MTT) programs for emergency medicine, operating room, and intensive care unit (ICU) staff have been introduced to improve communication and teamwork [54, 58]. Although CRM training is reported to change attitudes in medical settings, more studies are needed on the appropriate format for implementing CRM principles and the impact on adverse events. Strategies & Tools to Enhance Performance & Patient Safety (STEPPS) is another multicomponent program, designed by the US Department of

Defense, which aims to improve teamwork through mutual support, leadership, situation monitoring, and communication [59].

An approach that has been successfully used to improve communication in teams and access providers is to standardize the format for communication between staff and physicians through use of the SBAR tool [60]:

- Situation: description of clinical situation
- Background: clinical history and context
- Assessment: description of the possible problems
- Recommendation: description of possible solutions

It is also critically important to effectively communicate at the point of handoff or transition in care. As the responsibility for the patient is transferred from one individual to another, there is a heightened risk that disruptions will occur. This risk can be mitigated by organizing workflow to minimize the frequency of transition and through the development of effective handoff communication [60].

Care Transitions

Similarly, care transitions should be optimized to ensure patient information is communicated to providers across settings of care and that patients have appropriate access to follow-up care. Due to limited interoperability of electronic health record systems across settings of care, the availability of a discharge summary at the first discharge visit is often low, leaving patients vulnerable to errors. All relevant information should be transferred from one entity to the next to avoid gaps or the discontinuity of care. Clear accountability for ensuring effective care coordination across providers and settings of care is necessary to avoid delays in treatment and adverse events.

High-Reliability Organizations (HROs)

High-reliability organizations (HROs) are routinely exposed to unexpected high-risk events, yet they achieve lower than expected occurrences of failure or accidents [61]. Classic examples of HROs include air traffic and electrical power grid control systems, nuclear power plants, and aircraft carriers. Diverse types of HROs display certain common cultural attributes and institutional capabilities. There are five key concepts at the core of HROs: preoccupation with failure, reluctance to simplify, sensitivity to operations, deference to expertise, and resilience [62].

Preoccupation with Failure Preoccupation with failure is an important attribute of HROs. This preoccupation involves constant vigilance and a commitment to compulsively and rigorously focus on the potential for any and all failures, large or small, regardless of whether actual harm occurred. This vigilance is manifested by an organization's ability to identify and report errors, investigate errors, and implement effective measures to prevent recurrence. Poor outcomes rarely occur without warning, and, in the vast majority of cases, the failure or error that ultimately led to disaster was known within the organization but tolerated because it was unlikely to cause "real problems."

Ironically, organizations with very high standards for success and performance may be culturally incompatible with a preoccupation with failure. The temptation of the organization that values high performance is to view individuals who display a concern over small failures as "naysayers" who are standing in the way of success. Senior leaders may create a "shoot the messenger" culture where they end up being buffered from the reality of what is going on in the organization. Preoccupation with failure also requires a measurement culture that continuously monitors key processes and includes feedback mechanisms to identify and to correct deficiencies. When errors are identified, they should be investigated to pinpoint the active human failures and latent system conditions that contributed to the errors.

Reluctance to Simplify A reluctance to simplify is another characteristic of HROs, which are commonly good at simplifying complexity in order to maintain a focus on areas of high priority and key performance drivers. Unfortunately, complex interactive systems are not easily reduced to simple rules. Oversimplification generates operational practices that may work very well in most cases but fail spectacularly when the uncommon complication occurs. Organizations that resist simplification are less likely to experience these types of adverse events.

Sensitivity to Operations HROs also demonstrate sensitivity to operations. The latent conditions that create the "Swiss cheese holes" in system safeguards are frequently well known to those at the organization's sharp end. To the extent that managers are removed from day-to-day operations, or even worse, actively discourage feedback from frontline staff, these latent conditions may go uncorrected. HROs have organizational cultures that (1) promote understanding of frontline operational issues and open communication of operations problems throughout the organization and (2) are committed to correcting operational problems as they are discovered.

Deference to Expertise Deference to expertise, another attribute of HROs, can be viewed as a part of sensitivity to operations. Deference to expertise refers to the practice of pushing decisions down to the level of the individual most knowledgeable about the process involved, regardless of their position of authority within the organizational hierarchy. A practical example would be involving clerical staff in a redesign of a patient scheduling process.

Resilience HROs also share the quality of *resilience*, which refers to the ability of an organization to effectively respond to unanticipated threats and to recover from disruptive events. Standardized, well-thought-out policies and procedures generally promote safety. However, HROs recognize when hazards are not being successfully addressed by existing procedures. This ability to identify and adapt to novel situations and crises is a critical attribute of HROs and requires an ability to optimize standardization while maintaining an ability to respond to challenges that require new solutions. This has been referred to as "constrained innovation" or "adaptive rule-breaking."

Bundled Interventions and Patient Safety Collaboratives

Bundles and Patient Safety Collaboratives have emerged as important tools in driving rapid, system-wide improvements in healthcare delivery through maximizing consistent adoption of evidence-based practices for all patients and creating learning communities. A "bundle" or evidence-based care bundle is a standard set of elements of care or processes that, when consistently implemented together, have been shown to improve patient safety outcomes, yet are often not performed uniformly. Bundles can be a powerful tool to ensure best practices are delivered consistently for every patient, every time. Bundles rapidly came into use across thousands of hospitals through the Institute for Healthcare Improvement's "5 Million Lives" Campaign which included the Central Line Bundle, the Ventilator-Associated Pneumonia Bundle, and the Surgical Site Infections Bundle among other initiatives [63]. The use of bundles has now spread internationally through the "Surviving Sepsis" Campaign.

Patient Safety Collaboratives are system-level initiatives that unify multiple stakeholders around specific, shared goals for improvements in patient safety and outcomes through consistent implementation of best-practices, similar to bundles. Examples include the Missouri Center for Patient Safety's coordination of the AHRQ-funded CUSP/Stop CAUTI Collaborative, [64] which began in 2011. The Comprehensive Unit-Based Safety Program (CUSP) is an educational model designed to teach bedside caregivers specific methods and tools to promote the consistent use of practices to reduce the incidence of hospital-acquired infections. The collaborative aimed to reduce catheter-associated urinary tract infections (CAUTI) by 25% by 2012. Missouri hospitals exceeded this goal by achieving a 30% reduction in CAUTIs by the end of the demonstration period. Another example includes the California Perinatal and Maternal Quality Care Collaboratives (CPQCC and CMQCC) [65] which aimed to reduce preventable maternal morbidity and mortality, improve perinatal outcomes, and promote equitable maternity care in California.

Future Trends

The topic of patient safety is a crucial focus of the healthcare industry. Technological advances serve to facilitate the elimination of error and adverse events and grant the full disclosure of errors to patients and the healthcare system.

In addition to increasing scrutiny and transparency of event reporting, there will likely be an increase in insurers' refusals to pay for care resulting from adverse events and complications.

This incorporation of patient safety and health outcomes into the healthcare payment system has been referred to as value-based purchasing (VBP). VBP refers to a wide array of strategies and payment programs that link financial incentives to performance on quality metrics. Value-based payment programs have been increasingly adopted by government and commercial payers alike over the past decade to standardize the adoption of best practices, encourage innovation, moderate excessive cost growth, and improve patient safety. Examples of VBP models include pay for performance (P4P), accountable care organizations (ACOs), and bundled payment programs.

Making patient care safer by reducing harm caused in the delivery of care was outlined as a key priority in the Department of Health and Human Service's 2011 National Strategy for Quality Improvement in Healthcare. The 2010 Patient Protection and Affordability Act significantly expanded value-based purchasing programs, which represent a powerful tool to align and accelerate progress in patient safety across the delivery system. Key examples of government payer VBP programs include the Hospital Readmission Reduction Program, the Hospital Value-Based Purchasing Program, and the Hospital-Acquired Condition (HAC) Reduction Program. As of 2014, hospitals in the lowest performing quartile on patient safety and quality metrics measured in the HAC Reduction Program (e.g., surgical site infection rates) received reduced Medicare payments.

Recently, federal payer value-based payment programs have been expanded to include healthcare providers through the Quality Payment Program under the 2015 Medicare Reauthorization and CHIP Reauthorization Act (MACRA). Performance on quality measures under the Medicare Incentive Payment System (MIPS) or participation in an Advanced Alternative Payment Model became tied to physician Medicare reimbursement starting in 2017. Many of the MIPS quality measures are directly linked to patient safety, for example, "Medication reconciliation" and "Performing a fall risk assessment." While VBP has been predominately driven by government payers, over 40 private sector pay-for-performance programs exist [66]. Early adopters of VBP models include the California Pay for Performance Program (a program founded in 2001, which bases physician incentives on improving quality performance) and the Alternative Quality Contract through Blue Cross Blue Shield of Massachusetts. Though value-based payment programs traditionally focused on hospitals and providers, CMS has begun developing and implementing value-based purchasing programs across healthcare settings including home health agencies, skilled nursing facilities, ambulatory surgical centers, and specialty hospitals. VBP will likely play an increasing role in healthcare reimbursement across all settings of healthcare delivery.

Recent technological advances have enabled the rapid growth of high fidelity clinical simulation. This is a promising new area that can not only improve the skills of individuals but is also very beneficial for team training. This technology is rapidly becoming a mandatory component of training in areas such as Anesthesiology and Surgery. It is likely that this field will continue to gain more importance with the maturation of technologies such as virtual reality and augmented reality simulation and haptic or force feedback functionality which adds a tactile component to the simulation.

References

1. Kohn LT, Corrigan JM, Donaldson M (1999) To err is human, Institute of Medicine (IOM) report. National Academy of Sciences, Washington, DC
2. Nuland SB (2003) The doctors' plague: germs, childbed fever, and the strange story of ignac. W.W. Norton & Co, New York/London
3. Mallon WJ (2000) Ernest Amory codman: the end result of a life in medicine. W.B. Saunders, Philadelphia
4. Schimmel EM (2003) The hazards of hospitalization. Qual Saf Health Care 12:58–64
5. Leape LL (1994) Error in medicine. JAMA 272:1851–1857
6. Chassin MR, Galvin RW (1998) The urgent need to improve health care quality. Institute of Medicine National Roundtable on Health Care Quality. JAMA 280:1000–1005
7. Pierce EC Jr (1996) 40 years behind the mask: safety revisited. The 34th Rovenstine lecture. Anesthesiology 84:965–975
8. National Patient Safety Foundation (2015) Free from harm: accelerating patient safety improvement fifteen years after to err is human. National Patient Safety Foundation, Boston
9. Reason J (1990) Human error. Cambridge University Press, Cambridge
10. Reason J (2000) Human error: models and management. BMJ 320(7237):768–770
11. Vincent C (2003) Understanding and responding to adverse events. NEJM 348:1051–1056
12. Lerner BH (2006) A case that shook medicine. How one man's rage over his daughter's death sped reform of doctor training. In: Washington Post. http://www.washingtonpost.com/wp-dyn/content/article/2006/11/24/AR2006112400985_pf.html. Accessed 28 Dec 2007
13. Asch DA, Parker RM (1988) The Libby Zion case. One step forward or two steps backward? NEJM 318(12):771–775
14. Fletcher KE, Reed DA, Arora VM (2011) Patient safety, resident education and resident well-being following implementation of the 2003 ACGME duty hour rules. J Gen Intern Med 26(8):907–919
15. Dawson D, Reid K (1997) Fatigue, alcohol, and performance impairment. Nature 388:235
16. Gregory P, Edsell M (2013) Fatigue and the anaesthetist. Continuing Education in Anaesthesia. Crit Care Pain 14(1):18–22
17. Parshuram CS (2006) The impact of fatigue on patient safety. Pediatr Clin 53(6):1135–1153
18. Gaba DM, Howard SK (2002) Fatigue among clinicians and the safety of patients. NEJM 347(16):1249–1255
19. Joint Commission (2013) Medical device alarm safety in hospitals. Sentinel Event Alert Issue 50. https://www.jointcommission.org/assets/1/18/SEA_50_alarms_4_5_13_FINAL1.PDF
20. Leape L, Bates D, Cullen D et al (1995) Systems analysis of adverse drug events. JAMA 274:35–43. https://doi.org/10.1001/jama.1995.03530010049034

21. Bates D, Cullen D, Laird N et al (1995) Incidence of adverse drug events and potential adverse drug events: implications for prevention. JAMA 274:29–34
22. Rozich J, Haraden C, Resar R (2003) Adverse drug event trigger tool: a practical methodology for measuring medication related harm. Qual Saf Health Care 12:194–200
23. Aspden P, Wolcott J, Bootman J et al (eds) (2007) Preventing medication errors. National Academies Press, Washington, DC
24. Dinardo M, Naschese M, Korytkowski M et al (2006) The medical emergency team and rapid response system: finding, treating, and preventing hypoglycemia. Jt Comm J Qual Saf 32(10):591–595
25. Institute for Safe Medication Practices (2016) Look-alike drug names with recommended tall man letters. https://www.ismp.org/recommendations/tall-man-letters-list
26. Healy G, Barker J, Madonna G (2006) Error reduction through team leadership: applying aviation's CRM model in the OR. Bull Amer Coll Surg 91:10–15
27. U.S. Centers for Medicare and Medicaid Services (2007) FY 2008 inpatient prospective payment system proposed rule: improving the quality of hospital care.. https://www.cms.gov/newsroom/fact-sheets/fy-2008-inpatient-prospective-payment-system-proposed-rule-improving-quality-hospital-care. Accessed 1 July 2008
28. Ko W, Lazenby W, Zelano J et al (1992) Effects of shaving methods and intraoperative irrigation on suppurative mediastinitis after bypass operations. Ann Thorac Surg 53(2):301–305
29. Balthazar E, Colt J, Nichols R (1982) Preoperative hair removal: a random prospective study of shaving versus clipping. South Med J 75(7):799–801
30. Lefebvre A, Saliou P, Lucet JC et al (2015) Preoperative hair removal and surgical site infections: network meta-analysis of randomized controlled trials. J Hosp Infec 91(2):100–108. https://doi.org/10.1016/j.jhin.2015.06.020
31. Fletcher N, Sofianos D, Berkes MB et al (2007) Current concepts review: prevention of perioperative infection. J Bone Joint Surg 89:1605–1618
32. Veenstra DL, Saint S, Saha S et al (1999) Efficacy of antiseptic-impregnated central venous catheters in preventing catheter-related bloodstream infection: a meta-analysis. JAMA 281:261–267
33. American Geriatrics Society, British Geriatrics Society, and American Academy of Orthopaedic Surgeons Panel on Falls Prevention (2001) Guideline for the prevention of falls in older persons. J Am Geriatr Assoc 49(5):664–672
34. Bergstrom N, Braden BJ, Laguzza A et al (1987) The Braden scale for predicting pressure sore risk. Nurs Res 36(4):205–210
35. Hodge J, Mounter J, Gardner G et al (1980) Clinical trial of the Norton scale in acute care settings. Aust J Adv Nurs 8(1):39–46
36. Gosnell D (1989) Pressure sore risk assessment: a critique, part I: the Gosnell Scale. Decubitis 2(3):32–39
37. Sullivan N, Schoelles K (2013) Preventing in-facility pressure ulcers as a patient safety strategy: a systematic review. Ann Intern Med 158(5):410–416
38. Agency for Healthcare Research and Quality (2013) Hospital survey on patient safety culture. https://www.ahrq.gov/sops/surveys/hospital/index.html
39. Vincent C (2007) Incident reporting and patient safety. BMJ 334(7584):51. https://doi.org/10.1136/bmj.39071.441609.80
40. Leape L (2002) Reporting of adverse events. NEJM 347:1633–1638
41. Braithwaite R, DeVita M, Mahidhara R et al (2004) Use of medical emergency team (MET) responses to detect medical errors. Qual Saf Health Care 13:255–259
42. Hanlon C, Sheedy K, Kniffin T et al (2015) 2014 guide to state adverse event reporting systems. National Academy for State Health Policy, Washington D.C. https://nashp.org/wp-content/uploads/2015/02/2014_Guide_to_State_Adverse_Event_Reporting_Systems.pdf
43. U.S. Department of Veterans Affairs (2015) Safety Assessment Code (SAC) matrix. In: VA National Center for Patient Safety. https://www.patientsafety.va.gov/professionals/publications/matrix.asp?_ga=2.218383066.2141382797.1552852589-915450714.1552852589
44. Wu A, Folkman S, McPhee S et al (1991) Do house officers learn from their mistakes? JAMA 265(16):2089–2094. https://doi.org/10.1001/jama.1991.03460160067031

45. Gallagher R, Levinson W (2005) Disclosing harmful medical errors to patients: a time for professional action. Arch Intern Med 165:1819–1824
46. Gallagher T, Waterman A, Ebers A et al (2003) Patients' and physicians' attitudes regarding the disclosure of medical errors. JAMA 289(8):1001–1007. https://doi.org/10.1001/jama.289.8.1001
47. Witman A, Park D, Hardin SB (1996) How do patients want physicians to handle mistakes? A survey of internal medicine patients in an academic setting. Arch Intern Med 156:2565–2569
48. Gallagher T, Studdert D, Levinson W (2007) Disclosing harmful medical errors to patients. NEJM 356:2713–2719
49. Kraman S, Hamm G (1999) Risk management: honesty may be the best policy. Ann Intern Med 131:963–967
50. Reason J (1997) Managing the risks of organizational accidents, 1st edn. Ashgate Publishing Company, Burlington
51. Senge P (2006) The fifth discipline: the art & practice of the learning organization. Doubleday, New York
52. American College of Healthcare Executives (2009) The healthcare executive's role in ensuring quality and patient safety. Healthc Exec 24(2):88
53. McCarthy D, Klein S (2011) Sentara Healthcare: making patient safety an enduring organizational value. In: The Commonwealth Fund. https://www.commonwealthfund.org/publications/case-study/2011/mar/sentara-healthcare-making-patient-safety-enduring-organizational
54. Grogan E, Stiles R, France D et al (2004) The impact of aviation-based teamwork training on the attitudes of health-care professionals. J Am Coll Surg 199:843–848
55. Office of the National Coordinator for Health Information Technology (2018) Clinical decision support. https://www.healthit.gov/policy-researchers-implementers/clinical-decision-support-cds
56. Healthcare Benchmarks and Quality Improvement (2002) Poor communication is common cause of errors. Healthcare Benchmarks Qual Improv 1(2):18–19
57. Dunn E, Mills P, Neiely J et al (2007) Medical team training: applying crew resource management in the Veterans Health Administration. Jt Comm J Qual Patient Saf 33:317–325
58. Oriol M (2006) Crew resource management: applications in healthcare organizations. J Nurs Adm 36(9).402–406
59. Agency for Healthcare Research and Quality (2015) About TeamSTEPPS. https://www.ahrq.gov/teamstepps/about-teamstepps/index.html
60. Leonard M, Graham S, Bonacum D (2004) The human factor: the critical importance of effective teamwork and communication in providing safe care. Qual Saf Health Care 13(suppl 1):185–190
61. Weick K, Sutcliffe K (2007) Managing the unexpected: resilient performance in an age of uncertainty, 2nd edn. Jossey-Bass, San Francisco
62. Hines S, Luna K, Lofthus J et al (2008) Becoming a high reliability organization: operational advice for hospital leaders (Prepared by the Lewin Group under Contract No. 290–04-0011) AHRQ Publication No. 08–0022. Agency for Healthcare Research and Quality, Rockville, MD
63. McCannon C, Hackbarth A, Griffin F (2007) Miles to go: an introduction to the 5 million lives campaign. Jt Comm J Qual Patient Saf 33(8):477–484
64. Fakih M, George C, Edson B et al (2013) Implementing a national program to reduce catheter-associated urinary tract infection: a quality improvement collaboration of state hospital associations, academic medical centers, professional societies, and governmental agencies. Infect Control Hosp Epidemiol 34(10):1048–1054
65. Main E, Oshiro B, Chagolla B et al (2010) Elimination of non-medically indicated (elective) deliveries before 39 weeks gestational age, California Maternal Quality Care Collaborative Toolkit to Transform Maternity Care. (Developed under contract #08–85012 with the California Department of Public Health; Maternal, Child and Adolescent Health Division)
66. James J (2012) Health policy brief: pay-for-performance. Health Affairs Oct:1–6. http://www.healthaffairs.org/healthpolicybriefs/brief.php?brief_id=78

Additional Resources-Further Readings

Healthcare Quality Organizations that Include Patient Safety Information:

The Agency for Healthcare Research and Quality (AHRQ) is the federal organization tasked with responsibility for improving the quality, safety, efficiency, and effectiveness of healthcare for all Americans and is an excellent resource for patient safety information. http://www.ahrq.gov

The Institute for Healthcare Improvement (IHI) is dedicated to the task of improving the quality of the healthcare system. Reduction of harm and error is an important part of the IHI's mission. http://www.ihi.org

The Institute for Safe Medication Practices (ISMP) is an excellent resource for information about safety in the medication system and pharmacy practice. http://www.ismp.org

The Joint Commission (TJC) provides assistance in the form of requirements for accredited healthcare organizations including annual National Patient Safety Goals. https://www.jointcommission.org/topics/patient_safety.aspx

Specific Sources of Current Patient Safety Information

AHRQ Evidence-Based Practice Centers. https://www.ahrq.gov/research/findings/evidence-based-reports/centers/index.html

American Journal of Medical Quality. https://journals.sagepub.com/home/ajm

American Medical Association Patient Safety. http://www.ama-assn.org/ama/pub/category/12582.html

Cohen M (2007) Medication errors, 2nd edn. American Pharmacists Association, Washington

Dekker S (2011) Patient safety: a human factors approach. CRC Press, Boca Raton

The Joint Commission Journal on Quality and Patient Safety. https://www.jcrinc.com/the-joint-commission-journal-on-quality-and-patient-safety/

Journal of Patient Safety. https://journals.lww.com/journalpatientsafety/pages/default.aspx

Morath JM, Turnbull JE (2004) To do no harm: ensuring patient safety in health care organizations, 1st edition. Jossey-Bass, San Francisco

The National Patient Safety Foundation. http://www.npsf.org/

Shekelle P, Wachter R, Pronovost P (eds) (2013) Making health care safer II: an updated critical analysis of the evidence for patient safety practices. Agency for Healthcare Research and Quality, Rockville, MD.

Vincent C (2010) Patient safety, 2nd edition. Blackwell Publishing Ltd., Oxford.

Wachter R (2012) Understanding patient safety. McGraw-Hill, New York.

Chapter 5
Health Informatics

David W. West

Executive Summary

As defined by the US National Library of Medicine, health informatics is "the inter-disciplinary study of the design, development, adoption, and application of information technology (IT) based innovations in healthcare services delivery, management, and planning" [1]. It has emerged as a growing field of study as healthcare delivery is largely dependent on an exchange of information between both the patient and the healthcare professional and among the healthcare professionals themselves. Effective information exchange relies on an information infrastructure that has the patient medical record at its root. The infrastructure is often supplemented by additional components, including, but not limited to, computerized practitioner order entry (CPOE), clinical decision support at the point of care, performance management systems, and health information exchange (HIE) with disparate healthcare systems. All these components support individual patient management and the overall administration of patient populations.

Technology has enhanced healthcare quality and quality measurement in various ways. An early major achievement was an electronic medium allowing multiple users to access medical records simultaneously as opposed to having to rely on duplicated "shadow" charts with varying levels of completeness and consistency. Another achievement has been shortening the latency between new evidence of best practice in literature and the incorporation of that evidence into practice; previously, this latency could be as long as 17 years [2, 3]. Electronically generating and disseminating practice performance information to practitioners can speed provider behavioral change, and quality improvement can be accomplished in a more timely manner.

D. W. West (✉)
Nemours Children's Health System, Wilmington, DE, USA

Thomas Jefferson University, Philadelphia, PA, USA

© American College of Medical Quality (ACMQ) 2021
A. P. Giardino et al. (eds.), *Medical Quality Management*,
https://doi.org/10.1007/978-3-030-48080-6_5

Technology has enabled data aggregation on a scale not possible with traditional medical record systems. So-called big data affords the opportunity to detect previously imperceptible patterns in healthcare outcomes that can drive decision-making. Health plans and policy makers can harness big data for measuring quality and improvements in healthcare over time.

The study of health informatics would be incomplete without acknowledging the unintended consequences technology can have on healthcare practices. Selection bias, alert fatigue, cloning, note bloat, and an increased potential for privacy breach are some of the undesirable effects observed. However, applying a disciplined process of observation, analysis, and system redesign can reduce "technology-induced" errors.

This chapter provides an overview of health informatics necessary for an executive in charge of quality management.

Learning Objectives

Upon completion of this chapter, the reader should be able to:

- Describe the fundamental tenets of health informatics
- Discuss the electronic health record (EHR) and its impact on safety and quality
- Describe the principles, components, and pitfalls of EHRs and decision support systems
- Describe the national initiatives driving the development of health information technology
- Identify the basics of the US coding classification systems

History: The Evolution of Health Informatics in the United States

In the National Academy of Medicine (previously named Institute of Medicine) report *Crossing the Quality Chasm,* [3] there was a clear imperative to develop health information infrastructure in the United States to support quality and safety. The report noted that in the absence of a national commitment to build a national health information infrastructure, the progress of quality improvement would be painfully slow. Appointed in 2004, David Brailer led the Office of the National Coordinator for Healthcare Information Technology (ONCHIT), a new office created within the Department of Health and Human Services by executive order of President Bush. The ONCHIT created the US National Health Information Network (NHIN), which has now been renamed the eHealth Exchange. The eHealth Exchange, managed by a non-profit industry coalition called Sequoia Project (formerly HealtheWay), provides a web service-based series of specifications designed to securely exchange healthcare-related data. The framework has four overarching goals: inform clinical practice, interconnect clinicians, personalize care, and improve population health.

Health informatics and health information technology have grown rapidly in response to the American Recovery and Reinvestment Act (ARRA) stimulus package initiated in 2009. Large capital requirements to implement an EHR were one of the most significant barriers to adoption. As a result, the Meaningful Use (MU) program that resulted from the 2009 Health Information Technology for Economic and Clinical Health (HITECH) Act defrayed costs to healthcare entities that provide a significant proportion of their services to Medicare or Medicaid recipients. In addition to requiring a "certified" EHR application to qualify for funding, MU also stipulated a variety of functional requirements as part of the implementation process to support initiatives in patient engagement, interoperability, and quality. Eligible hospitals and providers could receive separate funding with somewhat different requirements for each group.

Another historical trend for health informatics has been the increasing application of technology to support new paradigms of delivering healthcare services, particularly in telemedicine. Initial efforts to implement telemedicine as a means to provide direct patient healthcare on a remote basis began in the 1990s, but the high cost and low quality of the available technology at the time hampered these efforts. Network bandwidth struggled to sustain reliable performance in video connections, and the size and complexity of the required equipment was substantial. Additional barriers included a lack of reimbursement models for remote care through video and the supporting technology to facilitate remote examination. Dr. Clement McDonald insightfully predicted what the path forward was in 1998: "The advantage could well tip to video links when video phones become ubiquitous" [4]. With 2015 data indicating that 187.5 million people in the United States own smartphones, [5] the technical investment required to make video links is declining rapidly. Supplemental applications to enhance video interactions are becoming more numerous, and insurers are gradually recognizing and reimbursing telemedicine visits. A brief history of health informatics in the United States is shown in Table 5.1.

Health Informatics Objectives

A fundamental tenet of health informatics is that effective interaction between technology and people can lead to higher-quality care for both the individual patient and populations at large. Technology alone, without human-derived clinical insight, often fails to deliver desired outcomes. Similarly, clinical experience and insight without information technology can lead to clinical decisions inconsistent with the current evidence of best practice, often due to the previously noted translational lags.

Inaccessibility of patient data, both within a healthcare organization and between healthcare organizations, can also challenge providers. An emerging health informatics objective is to bring the best, most relevant information about a clinical

Table 5.1 Recent history of health informatics in the United States

Date	Key event/milestone
1959	Robert Ledley publishes "Reasoning Foundations of Medical Diagnosis" (with Lee B. Lusted) and "Digital Electronic Computers in Biomedical Science" in *Science*
1965	The National Library of Medicine begins using MEDLINE as a means for easily retrieving scholarly articles
1966–1967	MUMPS (Massachusetts General Hospital Utility Multi-Programming System), also known as "M," developed as a general-purpose computer programming language for use in healthcare-related information systems
1972	Homer R. Warner founded the first Department of Biomedical Informatics in the United States at the University of Utah
1999	IOM publishes *To Err is Human: Building a Safer Health System* highlighting the importance of evaluating systems as the primary source of errors leading to diminished patient safety
2001	IOM publishes *Crossing the Quality Chasm: A New Health System for the 21st Century*, which dedicates an entire chapter to the necessary role of information technology in the redesign of healthcare delivery systems
2004	First mention of health information technology in state-of-the-union address by George W. Bush: "By computerizing health records, we can avoid dangerous medical mistakes, reduce costs, and improve care." David Brailer is appointed to lead the new Office of the National Coordinator of Healthcare Technology (ONCHIT)
2009	The Health Information Technology for Economic and Clinical Health Act (HITECH), enacted under Title XIII of the American Recovery and Reinvestment Act (ARRA), provided $25 billion in funding to subsidize adoption of electronic health records nationally under the provisions of "meaningful use" as outlined by ONCHIT. Through the Meaningful Use program, adoption of electronic health records is tied to adjustments in Medicare payments. It also includes the National Health Information Network aimed at promoting interoperability and health information exchange between healthcare systems
2010	The Direct Project launched as a part of the Nationwide Health Information Network, creating a simple, secure, scalable, standards-based way for participants to send authenticated, encrypted health information directly to known, trusted recipients over the Internet
2014	HL7 publishes Fast Healthcare Interoperability Resources for exchanging EHR data in a simpler modular format for easier consumption

decision to the time and place that decision-making happens. The sources of relevant information can be broad, but there are two general types: *information specific to the patient* and *information specific to populations that share clinical features with the patient*. Health information exchange (HIE) promotes the availability of the former, while clinical decision support (CDS) promotes the latter. Both the HIE and CDS will be discussed in more detail later in this chapter. It is worth noting that though HIE traditionally applies to the effective and timely exchange of patient information between disparate healthcare organizations, in a broader context, it also applies to the direct interaction between the patient and healthcare provider through a variety of vehicles that might be synchronous or asynchronous. "Synchronous" usually refers to time or place such that the patient and care provider are interacting simultaneously (time) or in the same geographic location (place).

Beyond individual patient decision-making, another core health informatics objective is to convert health information into knowledge that can improve population outcomes. The National Institutes of Health (NIH)-funded National Center for Biomedical Computing has created the "i2b2" Center (Informatics for Integrating Biology at the Bedside). Their mission is developing "a scalable informatics framework that will enable clinical researchers to use existing clinical data for discovery research and, when combined with IRB-approved genomic data, facilitate the design of targeted therapies for individual patients with diseases having genetic origins" [6]. Numerous other collaborative initiatives have emerged in the advent of electronic health records to share electronically stored patient data in a de-identified manner between healthcare organizations. The growing combination of increasingly diverse datasets in healthcare and health-related domains has been dubbed *big data* [7, 8]. The totality of data related to patient healthcare and well-being includes:

- Clinical data that is patient specific such as notes, monitor feeds, orders, test results, insurance claims, and other administrative data
- Health research information including journal content, open research protocols, and public health alerts
- Information from outside the traditional healthcare domain such as social media posts, blogs, and Twitter feeds

Health Informatics Core Values

As the breadth of innovation related to health information continues to expand, the inherent values sought by applied health informatics and health information technology innovations have remained relatively constant. These values are primarily oriented around primary stakeholder types as listed in Table 5.2.

System Usability

Usability for healthcare applications, particularly EHRs, has long been an area of focus for improvement. Compared to other industries such as aviation, nuclear power, automobiles, and consumer software, medical care is especially complex, so achieving usability is challenging.

Table 5.2 Health informatics core values and primary stakeholders

Core value	Primary stakeholder type
System usability	User
Transparency	Consumer/reader
Data integrity	Population/public health
Quality	Healthcare organizations

In one particular framework, the components of task, user, representation, and function (TURF) determine the usability of an EHR system [9]. This framework strives to assess how useful, usable, and satisfying a system is for intended users by asking them to perform a certain sequence of assessments as seen in Fig. 5.1. The dimensions and measures of usability under TURF are described in Table 5.3.

Transparency

Medical information is expanding rapidly in both the breadth of academic research and in the depth of data available about individual patients. Genetic data, continuous bedside-monitoring modalities, and home-monitoring modalities are some of the areas that have significantly increased the amount of data managed in a healthcare system. The tabular methods for displaying data, which are similar to the traditional presentations from paper health records, are increasingly inefficient and difficult to navigate in the visual frame of an electronic monitor. However, though the electronic monitor lacks in expandability, it excels in parsing, drill-down, and cascading capability, allowing a new dimension in information display. The ability to parse information automatically has made it easier to share information with a wider array of caregivers while maintaining compliance with regulations regarding privacy. The opportunities for creating a better value proposition through the graphical and dynamic display of patient information, as discussed by Powsner and Tufte, remain largely untapped by health information technology vendors [10].

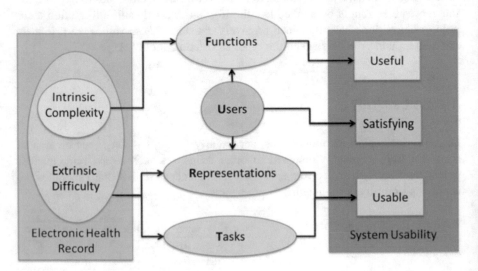

Fig. 5.1 TURF framework for EHR usability. Reprinted from *Journal of Biomedical Informatics,* 44(6), J. Zhang and M.F. Walji, "TURF: Toward a unified framework of EHR usability," p. 1058. Copyright 2011, with permission from Elsevier

Table 5.3 Dimensions and measures of usability under TURF

Usability dimension	Descriptions	Representative measures
Useful	A system is useful if it supports the work domain where the users accomplish the goals for their work, independent of how the system is implemented	Across-model Domain Function Saturation: percentage of domain functions in the EHR vs. all domain functions in the work domain
		Within-model Domain Function Saturation: percentage of domain functions over all functions (domain and non-domain) in the EHR
Usable	A system is usable if it is easy to learn, easy to use, and error-tolerant	Learnability
		Number of trials to reach a certain performance level
		Number of items that need to be memorized
		Number of sequences of steps that need to be memorized
		Efficiency
		Time on task
		Task steps
		Task success
		Mental effort
		Error prevention and recovery
		Error occurrence rate
		Error recovery rate
Satisfying	A system is satisfying to use if the users have good subjective impression of how useful, usable, and likable the system is	Various ratings through survey, interview, and other instruments

Reprinted from *Journal of Biomedical Informatics, 44*(6), J. Zhang and M.F. Walji, "TURF: Toward a unified framework of EHR usability," p. 1057, ©2011, with permission from Elsevier

Data Integrity

The large number and diversity of data imports into a healthcare system supporting a wide array of clinical specialties leads to continuous pressure to either duplicate or introduce ambiguity into existing data concepts. For example, the use of "glucose" as a data label in a data stream would have significant ambiguity without further context. Similarly, creating a unique blood pressure capture tool for a particular clinic could duplicate already existing standard concepts and impair the ability to aggregate like data. Diminished data integrity could reduce the validity of data queries that strive to extract knowledge from data warehouses in healthcare systems. The promotion of national data standards has improved the capability for disparate healthcare organizations to share patient data without a loss of data integrity. Managing information in a complex healthcare system in a way that does not compromise data integrity is a significant value proposition to health informatics.

Quality

When regarding any innovation in health information technology its impact on quality must be assessed rigorously. While the literature has shown that the implementation of EHRs has had a positive impact on healthcare quality, there is also evidence of unintended consequences and adverse outcomes. While EHRs offer significant new capabilities to support quality, the complexity of implementation and the usability issue previously discussed have created barriers to achieving their full promise for improved quality. This will be discussed further later in this chapter.

Electronic Health Records

The primary subject of study and development in the field of health informatics for decades has been EHRs. Many of the early manifestations were simple storage and organization vehicles. This is consistent with one of the early objectives: solve the problem of singular access to the paper chart. Singular access was especially problematic for larger, more complex healthcare organizations. The need for multiple clinicians to have the primary chart simultaneously made it virtually impossible to meet all demands in a timely manner. Local chart copies were frequently maintained ("shadow charts") to mitigate the challenges of having to make decisions without the primary medical record. Shadow charts had their own inherent risks such as incompleteness or the addition of unique information not found in the primary medical record. EHR storage granted parallel access to multiple authorized users simultaneously, significantly reducing the incentive to manage shadow charts.

A second early objective for EHRs was resolving the issue of handwriting legibility. Illegible handwriting has confounded communication in paper charts, with, at times, particularly adverse implications on medication management. Illegibility causing confusion in medication selection, dosing, and frequency leading to adverse outcomes, including death, has been well documented [11, 12]. EHRs have largely resolved errors caused by illegibility, though other sources of error have emerged and are discussed later in this chapter.

While EHRs have significantly evolved with increasing scope, specialization, and integration since the early stages, the core functionalities continue to be documentation, order entry/communication, and data retrieval/access. An important and increasingly significant addition to these core functionalities has been clinical decision support, discussed later in this chapter. Some of the ideal specifications of an EHR are listed in Table 5.4.

As EHRs became more sophisticated, adoption increased steadily and significantly from 2006 to 2015, aided in part by the national Meaningful Use program administered by the Office of the National Coordinator for Health Information Technology [13, 14]. Physician practices lagged behind hospitals as a whole for basic EHR adoption, though many practices have implemented specific EHR

Table 5.4 Ideal specifications of an EHR

Expectation	Definition
Patient-centered	Provides an electronic documentation of all patient events, both episodic and recurrent
Longitudinal	Serves as a single source of all information for the patient, trended from conception to death
Networked	Allows data availability on a just-in-time basis for all care providers who are directly working with the patient
Queryable	Allows data views that accommodate the needs of unique users without creating data exposure and noise
Data standard enabled	If combined with a data warehouse, the data collected from multiple EHRs and applications provide a means to determine best practice, appropriate guidelines for care, and population health improvements

functionality. Regional and practice-sized variations currently exist in terms of larger practices having higher adoption rates than smaller ones.

Documentation

Recording patient events in the medical record for later reference has been a core function of the medical record since its inception. In the transition from pen-and-ink to electronic tools, a variety of documentation modalities emerged to allow care providers to work as efficiently as possible. This is important as experience tells us that patients present in a wide range of scenarios from highly predictable to highly variable, so the most efficient modality must also vary accordingly. Where patient assessment and treatment planning are more predictable, documentation using templates can be highly effective, affording both speed and discrete capture of concepts in a comprehensive manner. Where patient assessment and treatment planning are more variable, structured templates are less effective, requiring greater time to complete documentation and carrying the potential for omitted or erroneously entered important clinical data. A summary of common note documentation modalities is seen in Table 5.5. The modalities described are not mutually exclusive and can be combined to create the best solution. Healthcare organizations may choose to offer only a subset of these modalities.

In addition to note documentation models, table formats capture a significant amount of patient data. This is analogous to the traditional "bedside flowsheet," so-named because it typically resided on a clipboard outside the patient's room. With these data becoming electronic, accuracy and efficiency have improved. Patient monitor data has the potential to feed directly into the EHR, thus avoiding transcription errors. To keep monitor artifacts (such as patient movement) from distorting the data, clinician validation is usually required before logging the data on a permanent basis.

Table 5.5 EHR documentation modalities for physicians

Modality	Definition
Handwritten documentation	This modality has become relatively obsolete in the era of EHRs but may continue to be a component to an organization's downtime strategy. Handwritten documentation is typically scanned as soon as possible once the EHR system is again operational
Typing without template	Typing speed can vary significantly among providers and completeness of documentation may be compromised. This method does not easily store granular clinical concepts
Dictation into and transcription from a stored voice file	Dictation is a conventional method of documentation that predates the use of the EHR. There is a time lag between dictation and the transcription appearing in the medical record. This method is usually associated with ongoing costs per transcription
Entry into a structured template, selecting from pre-populated choices	This modality can efficiently capture granular clinical concepts, but becomes unwieldy when the clinical case includes too many variables or results in additional, unanticipated variables
Voice-activated dictation with real-time computer-generated transcription	This modality allows immediate access to the documentation. If reliability of transcription is high, it can be very efficient and allows freedom of expression by the healthcare provider
Use of scribes to document based on verbal instruction from care provider	Scribes afford the convenience of not only recording draft documentation, but also entering pended orders per the verbal instruction of the healthcare provider in the exam room. Entries made by the scribe must be proofed carefully prior to providing the documentation to the healthcare provider for authentication

Electronic data captured bedside can take the form of constrained data entry, which is when entries are defined by a range or list of choices. Data captured in a controlled manner can display graphically and be used to contribute to patient risk assessment.

Order Entry/Communication

Electronic order entry allows orders to be instantly available to all stakeholders, eliminating the lag time for transcribing and couriering orders. Computerized physician order entry (CPOE) has created the opportunity to provide clinical decision support at the moment order entry occurs. When CPOE is supplemented with bar coding at transition points in order execution, the opportunities for error are reduced. In medication management, this process is referred to as a component of closed-loop medication management (CLMM), where bar coding occurs at both the dispensing phase and the administration phase of execution. Bar coding at these transition points seeks to enforce the "five rights" of medication administration: the *right* drug to the *right* patient in the *right* dose by the *right* route at the *right* time. It is important to examine these transitional workflows carefully for efficiency. If they are cumbersome or difficult, there will be an incentive for staff to develop workarounds that negate the effectiveness of the closed-loop medication process. Adherence to the five rights is not a guarantee that medication errors will not occur.

EHRs also provide a vehicle for patient-related communication, allowing easy reference and convenience. Communications are either recorded as permanent entries in the medical record or treated as more transient communications ultimately purged from the EHR depending on regulations and policies of the hosting healthcare organization.

Retrieval/Access

Though simple access and retrieval of medical record data has existed in EHRs from their origins, there are dimensions of data retrieval that continue to develop. For instance, an EHR displaying the same view to all users would have limited usability for the wide breadth of clinical and non-clinical users. EHRs thus can display summarized views of a medical record that are adapted for the particular type of user logged into the system. In addition, aggregate views of populations of interest (registries) are available to help efficiently identify opportunities for improved outcomes.

Another area of development for data retrieval and access is health information exchange (HIE) between healthcare organizations.

Health Information Exchange

As described at the chapter's beginning, quality healthcare is fundamentally dependent on effective HIE. Both patient-provider and provider-provider exchange within a given healthcare system have improved significantly with health information technology. However, the efficiency of HIE between healthcare systems has significantly lagged. This represents a significant opportunity for efficiency and quality improvement that has not been fully realized. The Office of the National Coordinator for Health Information Technology (ONC) put a particular focus on this deficiency as it developed requirements for later stages of the Meaningful Use (MU) program. The attention to this unrealized opportunity has narrowed the scope of the term HIE to usually refer to exchanges between healthcare systems.

Transitions of care are a primary triggering event for HIE. Traditional methods relying on signed release of information, printing, and faxing have proved problematic from the perspective of timeliness and resource requirements, leading to delays in care. HIE was significantly enhanced with the launch of the Direct Project in 2010 which provided a secure framework for exchanging patient medical records [15]. The Direct Project defined specifications to ensure the security of exchanged records, but it did not define the standard content of exchanged information. Standardizing the structure and content of exchanged patient information has emerged from a joint effort by HL7 International and ASTM called the Continuity of Care Document (CCD) [16]. CCD is an implementation guide for sharing patient summary data as a Continuity of Care Record (CCR), and it establishes a rich set of templates representing the typical sections of a summary record. These same templates for vital signs, family history, plan of care, etc. can then be used in other document types, establishing interoperability across a wide range of clinical use cases.

Healthcare organizations can exchange information with different levels of *interoperability* representing increasing levels of sophistication.

Foundational

This allows data exchange from one information technology system to another for the purpose of patient care. It does not require that the receiving information technology system be able to interpret the data.

Structural

This is an intermediate level of uniform movement of healthcare data from one system to another such that the clinical or operational purpose and meaning of the data is preserved and unaltered. Structural interoperability defines the syntax of the data exchange. It ensures that data exchanges between information technology systems can be interpreted at the data field level. This means the information is parsed with data labels provided to transmit meaning. This further allows the receiving system to reorganize information to enhance visualization and comparison with other information in the EHR.

Semantic

This provides interoperability at the highest level, which is the ability of two or more systems or elements to exchange information and use the information exchanged [17]. Semantic interoperability takes advantage of both the structuring of the data exchange and the codification of the data, including vocabulary, so that the receiving information technology systems can interpret the data. This level of introperability supports the electronic exchange of patient summary information among caregivers and other authorized parties via potentially disparate EHR systems and other systems to improve quality, safety, efficiency, and efficacy of healthcare delivery. The goal of achieving semantic interoperability and its reliance on codification in exchanged data has reinforced the need for national standards for coding systems. Table 5.6 lists some of the major coding systems in use in the United States.

Table 5.6 Medical coding classification systems

System	Description
International Classification of Diseases (ICD)	The healthcare system in the United States uses the International Classification of Diseases, Version 10 (ICD-10), formulated and maintained by the World Health Organization (WHO). The National Center of Health Statistics (NCHS) and Center for Medicare and Medicaid Services (CMS) manage the system and modify it as needed to meet the particular needs of the nation's evolving healthcare system [18]. It provides codification for diagnoses (ICD-10-CM) and hospital-based procedures (ICD-10-PCS)
Current Procedural Terminology (CPT)	Developed under the auspices of the American Medical Association (AMA), the Current Procedural Terminology (CPT) system classifies clinical procedures and services performed by physicians. Accreditation organizations, payers for administrative, financial, and analytical purposes, and researchers for outcomes studies, public health initiatives, and health services research also utilize the CPT system
Systematized Nomenclature of Medicine (SNOMED)	Used in numerous countries, the Systematized Nomenclature of Medicine (SNOMED) represents a broad array of healthcare concepts [19]. SNOMED CT was created for indexing the entire medical record including signs and symptoms, diagnoses, and procedures. Adopted worldwide, it is the standard for indexing medical records information. SNOMED CT is also a valuable resource for disease management, health services research, outcomes research, and quality improvement analyses. It is promoted as a system through which detailed clinical information can be shared across specialties, sites of care, and various information system platforms
Unified Medical Language System (UMLS)	Developed by the National Library of Medicine, the Unified Medical Language System (UMLS) provides an electronic link between clinical vocabularies and medical literature from disparate sources [20]. The goal is to develop a means whereby a wide variety of application programs can overcome retrieval problems caused by differences in terminology and the scattering of relevant information across many databases. For example, UMLS eases the linkage between computer-based patient records, bibliographic databases, factual databases, and expert systems. The National Library of Medicine distributes annual editions, free of charge under a license agreement, and encourages feedback, which promotes expansion of the database
RxNorm	RxNorm is a US-specific terminology system that contains all medications available on the US market. It is part of UMLS terminology and maintained by the National Library of Medicine. "RxNorm provides normalized names for clinical drugs and links its name to many of the drug vocabularies commonly used…By providing links between these vocabularies, RxNorm can mediate messages between systems not using the same software and vocabulary." [21]
Logical Observation Identifiers, Names, and Codes (LOINC)	The development of the Logical Observation Identifiers, Names, and Codes (LOINC) system originally focused on a public use set of codes and names for electronic reporting of laboratory test results. Expanded to encompass a database of names, synonyms, and codes, it can also capture clinical measurements such as EKG data. LOINC data are available from the Regenstrief Institute [22]. Content is continually expanding to include more direct patient measurements and clinical observations

(continued)

Table 5.6 (continued)

System	Description
Diagnosis-Related Groups (DRGs)	Diagnosis-related groups (DRG) serve to categorize patients into one of hundreds of groups by diagnosis, major surgical procedure, age, sex, and presence of a complication or comorbidity. DRGs are homogeneous groupings with respect to hospital charges and length of stay, and are best known for their use in Medicare hospital payments. These groupings also prove useful for comparative hospital cost and efficiency studies
All Patient Refined Diagnosis-Related Groups (APR-DRGs)	This methodology uses the DRG case-mix schema with diagnosis-based severity levels to account for a patient's level of illness. Although the underlying DRG structure is resource-based, clinical judgment and empirical testing are used in designing and validating the severity levels

A later development in the evolution of HIE has been the development of the Fast Healthcare Interoperability Resources (FHIR, pronounced "fire"). HL7 published the first draft of FHIR in 2014 as a collection of data elements and formats, called resources [23], combined with an application-programming interface (API) for EHR exchange. It strives to simplify the complex nature of document exchange by significantly parsing the exchanged elements into more basic and modular components.

Clinical Decision Support

A key objective of health informatics is to provide critical information to bolster informed decision-making. EHRs have had integrated clinical decision support (CDS) from early in their evolution. CDS is a manifestation of the health informatics core belief that the combination of technology and human expertise can provide higher-quality care than either alone. For example, one report cited significant errors that could have affected patient care that resulted from sign-out data elements (weight, medications, allergies) being omitted. Introduction of an EHR-based sign-out sheet eliminated the errors [24]. Also, EHR-based clinicians were significantly more likely to address a variety of routine healthcare maintenance topics including diet, identification of psychosocial issues, smoking, lead risk assessment, exposure to domestic or community violence, guns in the home, behavioral or social developmental milestones, infant sleep position, breastfeeding, poison control, and child safety [25].

Though perhaps best known for its most conspicuous manifestations, such as pop-up alerts and hard stops, CDS uses a much broader array of tools:

Links to Expert Systems

In one of its simplest forms, CDS presents convenient links to useful expert sites that describe evidence-based best practice or clinical protocols. Clinicians elect to use these links only when desired, saving time when working knowledge is sufficient.

Documentation

Documentation templates are another simple form of CDS used to promote consistency in clinical data collection. Templates can become inefficient, however, when configured to include all the facets of documentation required for billing or when built to anticipate all clinical variables.

Orders

A large body of CDS focuses on the order creation process. CPOE and structured order entry reinforce the complete composition of orders, facilitating accurate execution by the individual/system responding to the order. However, structured order entry has the potential to increase the time it takes to complete an order entry. Composing order sentences, which are complete orders with all structured elements completed by default, can improve the efficiency of order entry. Order sentences enable single order selection with reduced, if any, further entry needed. Another order-related form of CDS is order sets, which aggregate structured orders into a single selectable item aimed at a specified clinical presentation. Order sets promote consistency of care yet allow clinicians to adapt according to specific patient needs. Complex protocols with large numbers of orders that can guide or direct care over a span of days or longer are sometimes referred to as care plans.

Medication Management

About 6% of medication orders have an error, and 19% of those represent a potential adverse drug event (ADE) [26]. Medication errors have therefore received considerable attention in the health information technology arena. Investigation into medication errors often seeks to determine the most proximal source of error: *Did the error originate in the ordering, dispensing, or administration phase?* For these purposes, we will refer to the sequence of these phases as the *medication loop*.

To provide CDS in the ordering phase, EHRs often interface with an expert system that provides and maintains the data regarding recommended drug dosing thresholds. It also provides information about drug-allergy, drug-drug, drug-disease, drug-pregnancy, and drug-lactation interactions. Additionally, there is the ability to configure the EHR to detect duplications of therapy or specific medications.

Pharmacogenomics is an emerging, new CDS area applied to the order phase of medication management. This field recognizes that there are genetically based phenotypic variants of drug metabolism that, if known, would significantly alter the choice and/or dosage of particular medications. Phenotypes, described as high and low metabolizers, would need dosage alterations to achieve therapeutic effect and avoid toxicity. Other phenotypes may render a medication completely ineffective or toxic and require a different regimen. A full discussion of pharmacogenomics is beyond the scope of this chapter; however, the goals of CDS in applying pharmacogenomics can be summarized as follows:

- Advise when genetic information should be captured to inform selection and dosing of medications
- Store genotype and phenotype information in a granular fashion so that it can be effectively applied to CDS
- Prevent duplication of testing once the genotype is known
- Provide the information not only to the clinician who requested the gene testing but also to future clinicians who order any medication affected by the phenotype

These goals reflect facets of *precision medicine*, wherein therapy is guided by individual patient traits to supplement population-based studies. The opportunity to apply gene data to medication decision making will likely create a new genre of third-party expert systems so that each healthcare organization does not have to create and manage the rules based on the growing knowledge in this area.

An additional ordering phase feature in ambulatory practice is *e-prescribing*, which is the electronic transmission of the medication order to the outpatient pharmacy. This is similar to what occurs for inpatient medication orders at EHR-enabled healthcare organizations that have utilized electronic transmission for much longer. E-prescribing has improved reliability and timeliness of delivery, but the recipient pharmacy must be specified when the prescription is created. This is a new element to the standard prescription workflow. This factor combined with the need for an electronic device has slowed the adoption of e-prescribing for many years. There was a significant increase in e-prescribing rates in 2008 when Medicare started an incentive program with financial rewards for using e-prescribing [27]. The FDA further enhanced e-prescribing in 2009 by approving technical requirements permitting controlled substance prescriptions to be electronically transmitted to outpatient pharmacies. E-prescribing controlled substances (EPCS) relies on *dual-factor authentication* which is typically something the prescriber *knows* (e.g., personal identification number or password) and something the prescriber *has* (e.g., token device that generates temporary passwords that are only valid for a brief window of time). A third factor, something the prescriber *is* (e.g., fingerprint or facial mapping), is used rarely.

The *dispensing phase* of the medication loop can occur in the pharmacy or at the point of care. In the hospital pharmacy, the EHR will present the medication order for electronic review by a pharmacist. The order is then verified before it is released to the pharmacy technician for preparation. Some hospitals deploy medication-dispensing robots to mitigate human error in medication selection and preparation, though the costs are often prohibitive for smaller hospital settings. Another technological alternative to mitigating human dispensing error is barcoding. Barcoding connects the original order to the selected product and provides an alert if there is a mismatch. This is particularly important when the product needs to be mixed or otherwise formulated such that the manufacturer's bar code is not available at the administration phase for further verification.

For dispensing at the point of care, automated dispensing cabinets (ADCs) have largely replaced simple floor stock. ADCs offer efficient access to ordered medications but still require pharmacist verification before dispensing the medication. ADCs also limit the selection by opening only the drawer or cabinet consistent with the order.

The *administration phase* has incorporated CDS in the form of an electronic medication administration record (MAR) which helps detect violations of the five rights (see EHR section on order entry above for definition). Barcoding, at the point of medication administration, allows the ability to detect errors before they reach the patient more robust. However, CDS at the administration phase can be confounded if documentation in the MAR is cumbersome. Burdensome MAR documentation will drive users to adopt workarounds to remain efficient, such as barcoding after administering medication [28].

Clinical Alert

This is the most conspicuous form of CDS. A variety of workflow actions generate clinical alerts, including opening the patient's EHR, writing/signing an order, signing documentation, etc. These alerts identify potential errors of both omission and commission. Published studies report the value of decision support through the use of reminders and forced data entry [29, 30]. However, usability and quality can be competing concerns in the deployment of clinical alerts.

As described above, when deploying a CDS system, there is a wide array of tools from which to choose. When selecting the best tool, there are important principles that should guide selection and implementation to avoid wasted effort and bypassed/overridden guidance. Several important principles are highlighted below:

- Speed is everything.
- Anticipate needs and deliver in real time. If an action is recommended, then allow the action to be executed from the alert. Simply describing what is needed increases the risk of overriding the alert without action.
- Simple interventions work best. Overly complex corrections are likely to be ignored (this is a corollary to "speed is everything").
- Ask for additional information only when needed. This is particularly true when the additional information requested is uniquely sourced from the physician (i.e., it could not be easily provided by someone else).
- Monitor impact, get feedback, and respond. Clinical alerts should evolve and improve.
- Manage and maintain your knowledge-based systems. Clinical alerts should be reviewed periodically to ensure that they remain relevant and necessary [31].

Unintended Consequences

The literature supports the fact that healthcare quality has improved after the implementation of EHRs with integrated CPOE and CDS [32]. However, there is a need for caution during implementation and long-term management so that there is not a disruption of workflow in ways that actually impair care delivery. CPOE technology is still evolving and requires ongoing assessment of systems integration and human-machine interface effects—both predictable and unpredictable—on patient care and clinical outcomes. One early study demonstrated that mortality could increase if clinical workflows and efficiency are not carefully considered [33]. CPOE, even with the features that help reduce medication errors, can be implemented in ways that conversely foster medication errors [34]. Medical errors and adverse outcomes attributed to the interaction between users and health information technology are referred to as *technology-induced errors*. Over time, health information technology has improved to mitigate many technology-based errors. However, there are persistent challenges with EHRs that have adversely influenced user experience and clinical quality:

Selecting vs. Writing Orders

Structured order entry has improved the completeness and clarity of electronically transmitted physician orders. However, the paradigm change from writing orders de novo on a blank order sheet to selecting items from a menu has introduced new forms of technology-induced errors. When order look-ups are performed, and desired orders do not appear at or close to the top, clinicians may inadvertently select the top item, especially if system changes are introduced that change the sequence of selections after users become accustomed to a particular look-up response. For medication ordering, mixing dose unit buttons between flat dosing (e.g., mg, ml) and weight-based dosing (e.g., mg/kg) can create inadvertent dosing errors. This highlights the importance of dose range checking to alert the ordering clinician to the possibility that a dosing error has occurred. The following section describes the pitfalls of over-reliance on clinical alerts to prevent errors.

Alert Fatigue

The volume of clinical alerts generated by an EHR with CPOE and integrated CDS typically is high. This phenomenon is brought about by the belief that warning clinicians when they are potentially making a mistake will alter behavior and prevent an adverse event or improve compliance with evidence-based best practice. However, experience has shown clinical alerting that is too frequent or has a high false-positive rate can cause *alert fatigue*. This can cause appropriate alerts to potential hazards to be overlooked or bypassed. Healthcare organizations experience diminished quality when alerts are not actively reviewed and managed. Alert occurrences and resulting actions in the EHR are stored routinely in the healthcare organization's data warehouse, which provides a data-rich opportunity to evaluate and modulate alerts to more desirable effect.

Copy-Paste/Cloning Patient Notes

EHRs offer a wide array of content-importing technologies (CIT) that permit efficient inclusion of already captured patient data or standardized templates into a patient note. The use of Windows-derived Copy (Ctrl-C) and Paste (Ctrl-V) functionality in particular to replicate large bodies of text (*copy-paste*) or entire notes (*cloning*) has elicited the occurrence of significant adverse events. This list summarizes the risks associated with CIT:

- Inaccurate recording of patient symptoms and clinical course
- Perpetuation of errors in medication and allergy lists
- Incorrect insertion of data from other parts of record
- Repetition of expired or irrelevant clinical information
- Excessively long, bloated notes distracting the reader from key, essential facts and/or data
- Use of inappropriate template for condition or visit type
- Inconsistency of documentation
- Diagnostic bias [35]

The lack of appropriate review and update of pasted information contributes to diagnostic errors that have led to unplanned readmissions [36]. From a regulatory standpoint, the increased prevalence of cloned documentation has been noted by the Center for Medicare and Medicaid Services (CMS). One Medicare contractor stated, "Cloned documentation will be considered a misrepresentation of the medical necessity requirement for coverage of services due to the lack of specific individual information for each unique patient. Identification of this type of documentation will lead to denial of services for lack of medical necessity and the recoupment of all overpayments made" [37].

Note Bloat

When clinicians handwrote their notes, there was greater efficiency in recording less—perhaps calling out the specific abnormal test result(s) or patient monitoring information. When clinicians use CIT tools, there is often greater efficiency in recording more information due to the utilities that import all of the labs and monitoring data. Combined with the copy-paste behaviors discussed above, this efficiency has caused the size of patient notes to expand dramatically. From a usability perspective, clinicians have greater difficulty extracting the accurate and concise patient history due to the volume of replicated and imported information, sometimes with obvious inconsistencies. This phenomenon is referred to as *note bloat* [38]. This pronounced bulk of information is partially attributable to the systems of healthcare reimbursement that tend to increase payment with increasing amounts of documentation. It also derives from the inefficient presentation of patient data while creating notes such that users find it easier to import the data for review rather than navigating directly to primary data. This increases the risk that non-imported data go unnoticed.

Privacy

Enabled by data warehouses, extracting data on large populations of patients has become more efficient by orders of magnitude. This capacity has enabled the significant potential of big data discussed throughout this chapter. However, this capacity has created the capability for many *super-users* in the health information technology community to have broad and deep access to the contents of vast storehouses of information. Super-users can be database or network administrators, or even application support. Health informaticists can also be considered super-users if they are provided this type of direct access to the data warehouse. To prevent massive breaches of personal health information (PHI), information security has taken a much higher profile at healthcare organizations. Despite these efforts, breaches in excess of 10 million patient records have been reported in a single month [39]. A significant driver of these breaches is the black market value of medical records, which is reportedly ten times higher than credit cards [40].

Data Warehousing

Healthcare systems are striving to align with achieving the Institute for Healthcare Improvement's (IHI) *Triple Aim* objective, which has these three core elements:

- Improve the patient experience of care (including quality and satisfaction)
- Improve the health of populations
- Reduce the per capita cost of healthcare [41]

Data warehousing becomes a critical component of the health information technology infrastructure when trying to achieve the Triple Aim [41]. A data warehouse provides complete and accurate information from across an entire organization and sometimes from beyond those boundaries. The approach to data warehousing, similar to EHRs, has evolved significantly.

Enterprise Model

The enterprise model approach relies on a determination of all of the data elements anyone would ever need to use for data analysis, including safety and patient satisfaction data. Designers make lasting decisions about the data model in the beginning without being able to plan for changes in the short- or long-term. They structure the database accordingly, a process that can take months or even years to complete.

The enterprise model is difficult to sustain in the healthcare analytics domain. New healthcare information affecting standard care processes is generated in healthcare literature at a rapid rate, and it is difficult to predict where new modeling will be necessary and whether that model will be consistent with the existing data models of the enterprise data warehouse. It is a costly process to update these models, and it can risk an erosion of data integrity if not done carefully. Designers of an enterprise model incorporate both existing and anticipated data elements into their model to avoid costly redesign later but this can lead to the creation of never-used data elements that add to the bulk of the enterprise data warehouse without associated value. The amount of time required to create a robust enterprise data warehouse can be so great that the original drivers for its creation become obsolete; the healthcare organization must see this model as a long-term commitment.

Independent Data Marts

In contrast to a large, all-encompassing enterprise data warehouse model, the independent data mart focuses on a discrete operational segment of the healthcare enterprise. Data are channeled from their primary health information technology systems into the data mart serving that segment. For instance, a data mart might focus on a chronic condition, such as diabetes, that is highly prevalent in the healthcare organization's clinical care. Source data systems are channeled into the data mart dedicated to the management of those patients, providing valuable information about their care and management. The data mart may also focus on an operational center, such as revenue cycle.

To some extent, the data mart is a microcosm of the larger, more expansive enterprise data warehouse, but since it is smaller and less complex, it can take less time to develop and revise. Data marts, however, are challenging when they become numerous. In this model, each of the healthcare organization's primary data-capture systems will be compelled to feed each data mart separately, a repetitious and sometimes costly endeavor. Granularity of data may be sacrificed for efficiency and performance, limiting its future analytic value.

Late-Binding Architecture

Both enterprise data warehouses and independent data marts take data from primary data collection systems (e.g., EHRs, patient-monitoring systems, ancillary information systems, employee management systems, financial ledger systems, etc.) and direct them to end-use cases for analysis. This direct connection between primary systems and end-use cases is referred to as *early binding,* and, as discussed earlier, it can create difficulty when developing alternative use cases for the same data, especially if the primary data source is constrained by its primary function. *Late-binding* architecture is a model wherein the primary data sources do not directly connect to their end-use cases. Instead, the data are fed directly into the data warehouse, preserving all of the native granularity. There is very little transformation of data in this primary extract, and the data are considered unbound since they have not been connected to their end-use case. When an analytic use-case arises, the source data for that activity comes from the tables that emulate the source data systems but offer much greater flexibility in transformation and manipulation. This increased flexibility has given rise to the term data-mining, wherein relationships not originally anticipated become more easily detectable and investigated for validity. Late-binding architecture has therefore grown in popularity as a less constrained way to manage a data warehouse.

Patient Portals

Consumerism, or the degree to which patients are taking an active role in healthcare decision-making, is another significant trend in the field of healthcare. A full discussion of consumerism is beyond the scope of this chapter, but patient portals as a manifestation of this trend are worth mentioning due to their contribution to transparency, a core value in health informatics.

In an effort to promote patient-centered care, many healthcare organizations have made EHR data available directly to patients through portals. Active medication lists, test results, visit notes, and problem lists are among the common data elements shared in the early phases of portal development.

While information sharing via patient portals is growing rapidly [42], the majority of Americans still do not utilize portals [43]. There is a growing effort to enhance the value proposition of patient portals by sharing practitioner progress notes and reducing the challenges and costs of having to fill out release of information forms to gain access. A consortium of healthcare professionals created the OpenNotes Collaborative to promote direct access to doctors' notes and overcome some of the concerns about unnecessary patient anxiety and confusion generated by notes written using medical terminology [44]. Other value propositions will likely develop as patient portals become more interactive and user-friendly.

In addition to allowing the patient to access data, many portals allow the patient to communicate with the healthcare provider in terms of making, confirming, or canceling appointments; making prescription refill requests; or asking questions. In this way, patients participate as a direct source of medical record information on a remote basis apart from the traditional visit to the healthcare organization. Personal healthcare devices have created opportunities for "solicited" data feedback wherein the healthcare provider requests a stream of information after the healthcare visit. For example, electronic transmission of weights from a scale in the patient's home to the healthcare provider has shown to be an effective means of managing chronic heart failure [45].

It is worth noting that the growth of healthcare devices marketed directly to consumers has created a large body of "unsolicited" healthcare data collected by patients to help them manage their own health. How these "unsolicited" forms of data can effectively integrate into a healthcare organization's EHR via telemedicine and patient portals is an area needing further research.

Future Trends

The field of health informatics continues to evolve rapidly through innovative health information technology devices and clinical applications. There are also major trends in the healthcare industry that will significantly influence the application of health informatics to patient care.

Telemedicine

Health information technology has created new opportunities to provide direct healthcare without having the healthcare provider and the patient in the same place at the same time ("synchronous" in time and place). These settings allow patients to overcome some of the barriers to healthcare related to time and travel. The term *telemedicine* covers a wide array of clinical use cases.

Remote Interpretation

Telemedicine also describes a clinical scenario where diagnostic studies are stored digitally and forwarded to a provider at another facility or healthcare organization for interpretation. This permits access to specialized expertise, needed only in rare cases, for a much larger population without having to duplicate resources. A neuropathologist or neuroradiologist, for instance, can serve multiple organizations without having to travel. This model typically requires licensing in multiple states but allows patients access to the highest levels of expertise for their diagnostic studies.

Home Monitoring

Many tools in healthcare gather information between encounters to help reach a clinical diagnosis or assess the impact of a treatment plan. Glucose readings for diabetics, peak flows for asthmatics, daily weights for patients with chronic congestive heart failure, and blood pressure readings for hypertensive patients are just some examples of the information requested from patients to help with their management. However, the practitioner often did not receive these data until the next encounter or until sporadically transmitted by the patient. Healthcare technology now allows this monitoring information to be passively acquired (no extra effort required of the patient) on a real-time basis. For a given condition, a steady stream of information can be immediately available to the practitioner for review at any time. Even medication administration devices like pill bottles and inhalers can be "digitized" to monitor compliance and unexpected need for rescue medications without having to rely on patient memory.

Remote Clinic Visit

Medical specialists tend to aggregate around population centers as they need access to a larger population to generate a sufficient caseload. This can create a barrier to specialty services for patients in remote, less populated areas. Healthcare facilities close to the patient can video conference with a specialist's healthcare facility, removing geographical barriers to care. At the local healthcare facility, adjunct staff can assist with the visit as needed. Local devices, such as digital otoscopes, digital stethoscopes, and portable ultrasound devices, can be available to transmit digital images or sound to assist with the remote assessment. An EHR networked between the sites can facilitate documentation and make information available for the visit. Even without a shared EHR, health information exchange between two healthcare systems can facilitate an effective clinical visit. However, not all clinical presentations can be managed with telemedicine. Clinical assessment of some presentations would be inadequate without a physical examination. Research to determine which clinical conditions have the potential to be managed effectively with telemedicine tools, for all or part of the care plan, is ongoing.

Remote House Call

The concept of the remote house call is an extension of the remote clinic visit model. With handheld devices, specialists can see patients wherever they happen to be. This type of telemedicine is available in the home, school, or work setting as necessary. Trained adjunct healthcare staff are usually not available in this case, and adjunct devices are unlikely to be available, so health information is limited to that gathered via history and through the handheld device's camera. Therefore, applicable clinical presentations managed in these scenarios are a bit more limited than the remote clinic visit model. However, the ability to extend video into the patient's home setting may allow the practitioner to observe environmental, cultural, or social factors that may not have been evident if the patient had traveled to the healthcare facility.

Despite these limitations, this modality is gaining popularity, especially for patient initiated "on-demand" services. The market for patients seeking medical advice without having to travel to a healthcare facility is growing. Practitioner discipline is required to determine when the remote house call will not be adequate and require referral to a healthcare facility. In addition to "on-demand" services, providers can use the remote house call for scheduled follow-ups where only inspection and verbal history are necessary to establish that the patient's clinical course is on track.

Genomics and Precision Medicine

Increased genetic information collection has significantly enhanced the potential for using that information for patient care. Pharmacogenomics, previously described in this chapter, is one example of using genetic data for patient care but can be expensive. Costs for individual gene assays and large-scale individual genome determinations are rapidly falling; as a result, other types of predictors and care-plan modifications can be enabled. Cancer and coronary artery disease, two leading causes of mortality in the United States, are conditions for which screening for genetic predispositions is available, facilitating effective early intervention.

Effectively integrating this knowledge into a broad clinical decision support system is a core component of *precision medicine*. The NIH defines precision medicine as "an emerging approach for disease treatment and prevention that takes into account individual variability in genes, environment, and lifestyle for each person" [46]. This approach will allow doctors and researchers to predict with a higher degree of accuracy which treatment and prevention strategies for a particular disease will work in narrower groups of people. This is in contrast to a one-size-fits-all approach in which disease treatment and prevention strategies are developed for the average person with little consideration for the differences between individuals.

Value-Based Contracting vs. Volume-Based Reimbursement

Motivated by the desire to contain healthcare costs that have persistently grown faster than inflation for decades, there is a continued trend toward increased financial risk-sharing by healthcare organizations to promote health outcomes rather than just pay for service. Dating back to the early twentieth century, risk-sharing programs are not new but have had difficulty commanding a significant market share. However, both CMS and state governments are increasingly leveraging programs that promote value-based contracting where more service will not create more revenue. This will drive healthcare organizations toward sophisticated population health management at a fixed cost where prevention and early intervention will be rewarded. Robust healthcare analytics will be a necessary component of the information architecture if healthcare organizations are to succeed.

Natural Language Processing

The percentage of electronic and structured data held in healthcare systems has been increasing with the adoption of EHR systems. However, unstructured data remains a significant component to organizational data warehouses in healthcare. These are typically free-text expressions in either clinician-patient encounters or diagnostic test interpretations.

A significant development in the field of computer science has been the ability for computers to extract discrete concepts from free text using natural language processing (NLP). While the accuracy of NLP has not achieved sufficient reliability for independent case management or CDS for an individual patient, it has been used in clinical research studies to classify findings in large populations from a data warehouse without having to read and code charts manually. It therefore has the potential to heighten the capacity to extract meaningful information from data warehouses that store these large unstructured values.

Personal Health Records

The personal health record (PHR) has been a concept in health informatics since early in its development as a field of study. The ONC defines the PHR as an electronic application used by patients to maintain and manage their health information in a private, secure, and confidential environment. The features of a PHR that distinguish it from EHRs and patient portals are as follows:

- Managed by patients
- Can include information from a variety of sources, including healthcare providers and patients themselves
- Can help patients securely and confidentially store and monitor health information, such as diet plans or data from home monitoring systems, as well as patient contact information, diagnosis lists, medication lists, allergy lists, immunization histories, and much more
- Separate from, and do not replace, the legal record of any healthcare provider
- Distinct from portals that simply allow patients to view provider information or communicate with providers

The adoption rate of PHRs has been significantly limited, largely due to the effort required by patients to maintain them, especially when seen by multiple healthcare organizations. PHR applications have been unable, so far, to easily exchange and reconcile information between different healthcare organizations. Recent innovations may improve the usability of PHRs and increase adoption:

- The growing use of data standards in EHRs could enhance interoperability with PHRs.
- The growing use of telemedicine as a direct-to-consumer service will further decentralize health data storage and increase the sophistication of HIE using the PHR as a conduit.
- The growing use of cloud computing could be a vehicle for highly mobile storage of data.

Cloud Computing

Health information technology and EHRs have been associated with a continually growing demand for data storage. The emergence of cloud computing as a vehicle to securely store segments of a patient's medical record outside of the internal storage infrastructure of a healthcare organization will increase the demand for seamless health information integration outside of individual healthcare providers. This will likely create an avenue for increasing patients' control over their own healthcare data. Cloud computing also brings a super-computing power to healthcare as demonstrated by the application of IBM Watson to clinical care for individual patients.

References

1. Healthcare Information and Management Systems Society (2019) Health informatics defined. https://www.himss.org/health-informatics-defined
2. Morris ZS, Wooding S, Grant J (2011) The answer is 17 years, what is the question: understanding time lags in translational research. J R Soc Med 104(12):510–520. https://doi.org/10.1258/jrsm.2011.110180
3. Institute of Medicine Committee on Quality of Health Care in America (2001) Crossing the quality chasm: a new health system for the 21st century. National Academies Press, Washington, DC
4. McDonald CJ (1998) Perspective: need for standards in health information. Health Aff 17(6):44–46
5. Comscore, Inc. (2015) Comscore reports March 2015 U.S. smartphone subscriber market share. http://www.comscore.com/Insights/Market-Rankings/comScore-Reports-March-2015-US-Smartphone-Subscriber-Market-Share. Accessed 2 Dec 2016
6. i2b2 tranSMART Foundation (2019) Our history. https://transmartfoundation.org/our-history
7. Raghupathi W, Raghupathi V (2014) Big data analytics in healthcare: promise and potential. Health Inf Sci Syst 2:3. https://doi.org/10.1186/2047-2501-2-3

8. Frost & Sullivan White Paper (2012) Drowning in big data? reducing information technology complexities and costs for healthcare organizations. http://www.emc.com/collateral/analyst-reports/frost-sullivan-reducing-information-technology-complexities-ar.pdf

9. Zhang J, Walji M (2011) TURF: toward a unified framework of EHR usability. J Biomed Inform 44(6):1056–1067. https://doi.org/10.1016/j.jbi.2011.08.005

10. Powsner SM, Tufte ER (1994) Graphical summary of patient status. Lancet 344(8919):386–389. https://doi.org/10.1016/S0140-6736(94)91406-0

11. Devine EB, Hansen RN, Wilson-Norton JL et al (2010) The impact of computerized provider order entry on medication errors in a multispecialty group practice. JAMIA 17(1):78–84. https://doi.org/10.1197/jamia.M3285

12. Sokol DK, Hettige S (2006) Poor handwriting remains a significant problem in medicine. J R Soc Med 99(12):645–646

13. Office of the National Coordinator for Health Information Technology (2016) Adoption of electronic health record systems among U.S. non-federal acute care hospitals: 2008–2015. https://dashboard.healthit.gov/evaluations/data-briefs/non-federal-acute-care-hospital-ehr-adoption-2008-2015.php. Accessed 22 Jan 2017

14. Hsiao CJ, Hing E (2014) Use and characteristics of electronic health record systems among office-based physician practices: United States, 2001–2013, NCHS data brief, no 143. National Center for Health Statistics, Hyattsville

15. Office of the National Coordinator for Health Information Technology (n.d.) The Direct Project. https://www.healthit.gov/sites/default/files/pdf/fact-sheets/the-direct-project.pdf. Accessed 22 Jan 2017

16. HL7 International (2019) HL7/ASTM implementation guide for CDA® R2 -Continuity of Care Document (CCD®) Release 1. https://www.hl7.org/implement/standards/product_brief.cfm?product_id=6. Accessed 22 Jan 2017

17. Healthcare Information & Management Systems Society (HIMSS) (2010) HIMSS dictionary of healthcare information technology terms, acronyms and organizations, 2nd edn. HIMSS, Chicago

18. Centers for Disease Control and Prevention (2015) Classification of diseases, functioning, and disability. In: National Center for Health Statistics. https://www.cdc.gov/nchs/icd/index.htm

19. SNOMED International (2019) SNOMED CT 5-Step briefing. http://www.snomed.org/snomed-ct/five-step-briefing

20. U.S. Department of Health & Human Services (2019) Unified medical language system (UMLS). In: U.S. National Library of Medicine. https://www.nlm.nih.gov/research/umls/

21. U.S. Department of Health & Human Services (2019) RxNorm. In: U.S. National Library of Medicine. https://www.nlm.nih.gov/research/umls/rxnorm/

22. Regenstrief Institute (2019) LOINC. https://www.regenstrief.org/resources/loinc/

23. HL7 International (2018) FHIR overview. https://www.hl7.org/fhir/overview.html

24. Frank G, Lawless ST, Steinberg TH (2005) Improving physician communication through an automated, integrated sign-out system. J Healthc Inf Manag 19(4):68–74

25. Adams WG, Mann AM, Bauchner H (2003) Use of an electronic medical record improves the quality of urban pediatric primary care. Pediatrics 111(3):626–632

26. Kaushal R, Bates DW, Landrigan C et al (2001) Medication errors and adverse drug events in pediatric inpatients. JAMA 285(16):2114–2120

27. Joseph SB, Sow MJ, Furukawa MF et al (2013) E-prescribing adoption and use increased substantially following the start of a federal incentive program. Health Aff 32(7):1221–1227. https://doi.org/10.1377/hlthaff.2012.1197

28. Hein A, Onzenoort A, Plas AGK et al (2008) Factors influencing bar-code verification by nurses during medication administration in a Dutch hospital. Am J Health-Syst Pharm 65:644–648

29. Balas EA, Weingarten S, Garb CT et al (2000) Improving preventive care by prompting physicians. Arch Intern Med 160(3):301–308. https://doi.org/10-1001/pubs. Arch Intern Med.-ISSN-0003-9926-160-3-ioi90092

30. Morris AH (2003) Treatment algorithms and protocolized care. Curr Opin Crit Care 9(3):236–240

31. Bates DW, Kuperman GJ, Wang S et al (2003) Ten commandments for effective clinical decision support: making the practice of evidence-based medicine a reality. JAMIA 10(6):523–530. https://doi.org/10.1197/jamia.M1370
32. Menachemi N, Collum TH (2011) Benefits and drawbacks of electronic health record systems. Risk Manag Healthc Policy 4:47–55. https://doi.org/10.2147/RMHP.S12985
33. Han YY, Carcillo JA, Venkataraman ST et al (2005) Unexpected increased mortality after implementation of a commercially sold computerized physician order entry system. Pediatrics 116:1506–1512
34. Koppel R, Metlay JP, Cohen A et al (2005) Role of computerized physician order entry systems in facilitating medication errors. JAMA 293(10):1197–1203. https://doi.org/10.1001/jama.293.10.1197
35. Weis JM, Levy PC (2014) Copy, paste, and cloned notes in electronic health records. Chest 145(3):632–638. https://doi.org/10.1378/chest.13-0886
36. Singh H, Giardina T, Meyer A et al (2013) Types and origins of diagnostic errors in primary care settings. JAMA Intern Med 173(6):418–425. https://doi.org/10.1001/jamainternmed.2013.2777
37. National Government Services (2019) Cloned documentation could result in Medicare denials for payment. In: Policy Education Topics. https://ngsmedicare.com/ngs/portal/ngsmedicare/newngs/home-lob/pages/policy-education/documentation/. Accessed 14 Jan 2017
38. Versel N (2013) 'Note bloat' putting patients at risk. In: Healthcare IT News. http://www.healthcareitnews.com/news/note-bloat-putting-patients-risk. Accessed 22 Jan 2017
39. McCarthy J (2016) 11 million patient record breaches make June worst month for information security in 2016. In: Healthcare IT News. http://m.healthcareitnews.com/news/11-million-patient-record-breaches-make-june-worst-month-information-security-2016. Accessed 14 Jan 2017
40. Humer C, Finkle J (2014) Your medical record is worth more to hackers than your credit card. In: Reuters Technology News. http://www.reuters.com/article/us-cybersecurity-hospitals-idUSKCN0HJ21I20140924
41. Evans RS, Lloyd JF, Pierce LA (2012) Clinical use of an enterprise data warehouse. In: AMIA Annual Symposium Proceedings, pp. 189–198
42. Irizarry T, DeVito DA, Curran C (2015) Patient portals and patient engagement: a state of the science review. J Med Internet Res 17(6):e148. https://doi.org/10.2196/jmir.4255
43. Pennic F (2014) 64% of Americans do not use online patient portals. In: HIT Consultant. http://hitconsultant.net/2014/12/16/64-of-americans-do-not-use-online-patient-portals/. Accessed 16 Dec 2014
44. OpenNotes (n.d.) FAQs. https://www.opennotes.org/tools-resources/for-patients/patient-faqs/
45. Kvedar J, Coye M, Everett W (2014) Connected health: a review of technologies and strategies to improve patient care with telemedicine and telehealth. Health Aff 33(2):194–199. https://doi.org/10.1377/hlthaff.2013.0992
46. Genetics Home Reference (2015) What is precision medicine? In: U.S. National Library of Medicine. https://ghr.nlm.nih.gov/primer/precisionmedicine/definition. Accessed 15 Jan 2017

Additional Resources: Further Reading

Agency for Healthcare Research and Quality (AHRQ) (n.d.) Health information technology. https://healthit.ahrq.gov/
Office of the National Coordinator for Health Information Technology (2018) Health Information Security & Privacy Collaboration (HISPC). https://www.healthit.gov/policy-researchers-implementers/health-information-security-privacy-collaboration-hispc
American National Standards Institute (n.d.) Health Information Technology Standards Panel (HITSP). http://www.hitsp.org

Health Resources and Service Administration (HRSA) (n.d.) Data portal. https://data.hrsa.gov/
    hdw/tools/dataportal.aspx
National Institute of Standards and Technology (NIST) (n.d.) Health. https://www.nist.gov/topics/
    health
National Quality Forum (2007) CEO survival guide to personal health records. National Quality
    Forum, Washington, DC

Health Information Technology Standards (Abbreviated List)

LOINC – Laboratory testing coding: https://loinc.org/downloads/loinc-table/
SNOMED CT3 – Clinical text coding (within EHR): http://www.snomed.org/snomed-ct/
    get-snomed
UMLS – Overall Coded Medical Language: https://www.nlm.nih.gov/research/umls/
ICD-10 – Diagnosis/Procedure Coding (hospitals): https://www.who.int/health-topics/
    international-classification-of-diseases
Continuity of Care Record (CCR) – Snapshot of patient for next caregiver: https://www.astm.org/
    Standards/E2369.htm
Clinical Document Architecture (CDA) – Discharge summaries and progress noted: http://www.
    hl7.org/implement/standards/
NCPDP – Pharmacy: https://www.ncpdp.org/Standards-Development/Standards-Information
DICOM – Radiology images: https://www.dicomstandard.org/current/

Chapter 6
Data Analytics for the Improvement of Healthcare Quality

Charles G. Macias and Kathleen E. Carberry

Executive Summary

Today's healthcare environment demands an expanded scope and sophistication of data collection from a variety of electronic health records to mobile and wearable devices. But there remains an untapped potential to maximize existing analytics systems to measure and improve healthcare quality at the individual and the population level. Organizations must support cross-functional teams comprised of clinical, operational, and financial expertise with a data governance structure to support their functions. This demands more than strategy; it requires a cultural change. This transformation demands that macro system strategy and micro system implementation accept data and analytics as a tool for learning rather than a tool for punitive reform. We present several cases illustrating how data can be harnessed to improve healthcare quality: this includes the development of clinical decision support tools to improve sepsis outcomes and the use of registries to benchmark outcomes across institutions. We also explain how the timely delivery of high-quality data can be streamlined to enable clinicians to drive improvement. The challenges of measuring healthcare value with the current information systems in healthcare are also described.

C. G. Macias (✉)
Case Western Reserve University, Cleveland, OH, USA

K. E. Carberry
University of Texas, Austin, TX, USA

© American College of Medical Quality (ACMQ) 2021
A. P. Giardino et al. (eds.), *Medical Quality Management*,
https://doi.org/10.1007/978-3-030-48080-6_6

Learning Objectives

Upon completion of this chapter, readers should be able to

- Describe the current landscape of data analytics in healthcare
- Discuss the differences between the stages of analytic maturity
- Discuss the key strategic elements needed to advance analytics in healthcare
- Discuss how advanced analytics can be applied to clinical and population health settings as well as the measurement of healthcare value
- Describe the difference between accuracy and precision of data

Current Analytics Landscape in Healthcare

Strategies for measurement, including the collection and utilization of healthcare data, vary widely. Ideally, technology can enable improvement work by creating timely access to, and the transformation of, data. Unfortunately, fragmented and proprietary data collection mechanisms and policies that limit data sharing create barriers to the effective use of technology in healthcare. Fragmentation in data exists both at the patient level and at the system level. Electronic health records (EHRs) are linked to the site of care such that one patient can have numerous elements of healthcare data related to their own health across several prehospital systems, hospitals, practitioners, and alternative care delivery venues. Efforts to bridge some of these practice silos have included the use of administrative data sets, particularly, billing and claims data; however, medical claims and billing information offer limited utility in the construction of robust clinical data models and decision support tools [1].

To accelerate the adoption of technology as a tool to drive healthcare improvement and stimulate the facile use of healthcare data, the federal government invested billions of dollars to fuel the implementation of EHRs (e.g., the American Recovery and Reinvestment Act of 2009) [2]. Unfortunately, despite a 2005 Rand report forecasting an $80 billion dollar savings in healthcare expenditures annually from the adoption of health information technology (HIT), costs have continued to grow. Failures of such initiatives have been attributed to a number of factors including sluggish adoption of HIT systems, poor interoperability of systems with limited ease of use, and a failure of providers and infrastructures to reengineer their care processes to reap the full benefit of HIT [3]. Some systems have managed to integrate data across their systems to drive improvement work (e.g., Kaiser Permanente); however, this has been accomplished by functioning as both the provider and payer, which is not possible in many other health system arrangements.

Advancing Data Analytics Maturity

Health informatics is "the interdisciplinary study of the design, development, adoption and application of IT-based innovations in healthcare services delivery, management, and planning." [4] Healthcare systems benefit when health informatics is applied and data is converted to useable information with timely delivery. This transformation requires technology and expertise as well as a strategy to coalesce both toward the aim of improving patient outcomes.

In the world of informatics, data use increases in sophistication from simple data gathering and reporting, as can be done from a patient EHR report at the bedside, to aggregating and analyzing data in populations for themes (data analytics), predicting events or patients at risk (predictive analytics), or linking health observation with health knowledge to influence clinical decisions (prescriptive analytics or clinical decision support). Incorporating clinical decision support capabilities into practice can improve workflow through ease of documentation, provide alert information at the point of care, and improve the cognitive understanding of the clinician [5, 6]. An organization's move toward leveraging technology and analytics to improve outcomes moves along a continuum of maturity. Typically, organizations begin with using static data in the form of reports and then move toward using simple analytic tools to manipulate data to gain insights (data analytics stage). Then, more advanced statistical algorithms are applied to data that allow organizations to predict outcomes and apply early interventions (predictive and prescriptive analytic stages) [7–9]. These stages of analytic maturity are illustrated in Fig. 6.1. The speed at which organizations move through the stages can vary, and often, in any given organization, there may be pockets of advanced maturity while the organization as a whole is less developed.

A multipronged approach must be in place to achieve value from advancing analytics. The first prong is having the right expertise such as informaticists and data analysts and tightly coupling the two so as to design efficient and defined data analytic tools as part of technology implementation. The second prong is to create strategies to manage significant organizational change that comes with increasing technological capability and desire for data. The third prong is an effective approach to data governance.

An institution or practice's hardware and software and data management processes are critical to its capability of advancing along the continuum from data reporting to prescriptive analytics. Many EHRs are developing analytics platforms that embed some of these capabilities into their existing workflows; however, robust analytics must still overcome gaps in delivering transformed data to the provider. EHRs and other information systems are costly to implement and maintain. Furthermore, beyond the hardware and software to collect the data, there is a requirement for human investment. Data within the most spectacular system is worthless if not interpreted and applied appropriately. Thus, the evolution of informatics from data reporting to sophisticated analytics requires collaborative teams to drive improvement strategies. Our experience suggests that optimal team members

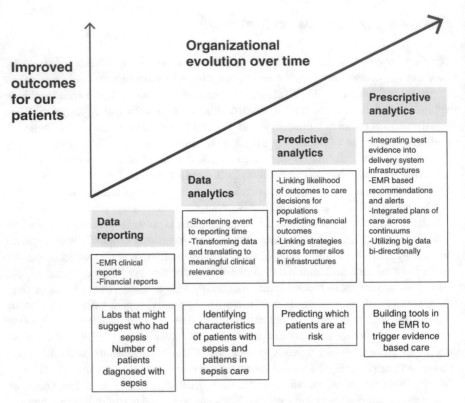

Fig. 6.1 The stages of analytic maturity in the healthcare enterprise can be illustrated on a growth continuum. Reprinted from *Clinical Pediatric Emergency Medicine, 18*(2), C.G. Macias, J.N. Loveless, et al., "Delivering Value Through Evidence-based Practice", p. 95, Copyright 2017, with permission from Elsevier

include experts in evidence-based medicine, EHR and clinical data specialists, and data architects in addition to outcomes analysts, healthcare providers, and operational leaders. The size and level of expertise of such a team depend on the problem to be addressed, but all domains are necessary. Redesigning workflow is critical to maximize the investment in HIT, analytics, and decision support. This requires a cultural change driven by leadership understanding and participating in the transformation of healthcare that analytics can drive [5].

With the widespread use of EHRs in today's healthcare environment, data is expected at the bedside when technology provides it for a single patient. However, the vast growth of available data has given rise to the concept of *big data*. Big data represent large volumes of high-velocity, complex data that require advanced techniques and technologies to capture, store, distribute, manage, and analyze them [10]. The benefit of analyzing such data is not limited to the operational needs of healthcare systems. Outputs of analytics can be delivered to the bedside through visualization tools, thus benefitting prehospital providers, single-physician offices, hospitals, and hospital networks [10, 11].

As healthcare systems respond to the availability of massive amounts of data and progress through the stages of analytic maturity, the culture of an organization must embrace the value of data to drive improved outcomes of care. Overcoming a cultural resistance to the uses and *truth* of data is critical and requires a nonpunitive environment for demonstrating successes and failures based upon data and the analytics. Don Berwick has described the journey of data acceptance in four stages [12]:

Stage One: "The data are wrong."

Questions about adjustments, hidden variables, sampling, poor input information, and other weaknesses in the validity and reliability of the transformed data will exist. Thus, there is a tendency to default to a belief that the data do not reflect reality. However, while no data set is ever perfect, in general, most are good enough to act upon.

Stage Two: "The data are right, but it's not a problem."

While people and teams may believe in the integrity of the data, they will point to natural variation as the cause and the justification for inaction. There is an acceptance that the status quo is sufficient.

Stage Three: "The data are right; it's a problem, but it's not my problem."

At this stage, stakeholders recognize there is a problem but are not engaged in driving a solution, expecting that *others* or *the system* are responsible for taking action.

Stage Four: "The data are right; it's a problem, and it's my problem."

All levels of acceptance of the validity of the data, the importance of the problem, and the personal or team responsibility for correcting the problem are achieved at this level. This is the stage where stakeholders engage in action as the problem is *my burden*.

Once the relationship to data transparency, accountability, and action is firmly established, the work of engaging in a culture focused on quality improvement (QI) can be accelerated. However, an understanding that data delivery is not the same as analytics takes cultural change. It shifts stakeholders from a paradigm of asking for the solution (a data report) to asking the question of *what problem are we trying to solve* in order to develop the needed analytics. Criteria have been developed to evaluate such a change in a health system's analytic culture. Most criteria take into account characteristics as defined within six domains:

- *Data sources*: Scope and number of data sources feeding into an organization's analytics.
- *Data quality*: Minimal to consistent accuracy and integrity of data.
- *Data currency*: Timeliness of data and frequency of its use.
- *Analytic features*: Sophistication of data from reporting to predictive modeling and workflow integration.

- *User profiles*: Nature and breadth of users from analysts to multiple skilled everyday users.
- *Adoption profiles*: Organizational sophistication from report users to a performance management culture [13].

In addition to the expertise and culture change required to advance a health system toward analytic maturity, a nimble and effective data governance strategy must be applied. Data governance is the foundation for any health system that strives to use data to improve care. It is critical to assuring the effective uses of data within an organization and between partner entities. At its most foundational, data governance ensures that data is of the highest quality and easily accessible. In its more advanced applications, it ensures that there is a strategy behind increasing data content for use. Data governance allows organizations to implement best practices, pool analytics, standardize metrics, provide clinical decision support, and optimize the EHR and data warehousing. Data governance must be iterative to accommodate new evidence discovery, growing amounts of data, evolving personal technologies, and a shifting payment landscape [14].

Ownership and privacy of healthcare data create additional hurdles to the sharing of data for quality improvement purposes. Most organizations are comfortable with the uses of their own data for quality improvement when all sources remain internal. However, the use of data across multiple entities (health plan, hospital, clinic, and primary care physician office) can create legal challenges to utilizing data for improvement purposes and add delays to achieving the optimal integration of systems. Collaboration with legal counsel is critical to ensuring that standards are in place to protect the privacy of data while allowing robust usage within the healthcare system.

Data Analytics to Support Population Health Strategies

Strategies that drive sophistication in analytics allow an organization to engage in accelerated practices to improve care across the health spectrum. In an era of evolving healthcare reform (payment reform and delivery system reform) population health has become critical, and big data and data analytics are essential to engaging in and measuring effective care delivery [15]. Population health is a term that reflects the health of patients across continuums of care with a goal of improving health outcomes. Delivering improved outcomes for populations of patients requires partnerships with disciplines outside of traditional care delivery teams, including professionals in public health, advocacy, policy, and research. The focus of population health improvement activities may span geography (e.g., a region), a condition (e.g., children with a chronic condition such as asthma), a payer (e.g., patients in an accountable care organization or within a health plan), or any characteristic that would link accountability for outcomes for that group of patients. Population management is a concept in which a common condition or other linking element may drive the practitioner to create and implement prevention or care strategies and promote health for groups of patients [15].

As achieving improved health outcomes extends beyond the simple delivery of healthcare to ameliorate an acute illness or injury, the definition of population health expands to become the art and science of preventing disease, prolonging life, and promoting health through recognized efforts and informed choices of society, organizations, public and private communities, and individuals. Engaging in population health means expanding the reach (and the obligation) of the clinician from bedside care alone to a goal of assuring the health of the patient, including helping the patient and family overcome barriers to accessing and coordinating care [15].

In order to improve outcomes of care, the clinician and system must identify and mitigate the effects of social determinants of health and engage the patient and family in their own health management and disease and injury prevention. Social determinants of health may include education level, economic stability, social and community contexts, neighborhood and physical environments, and other such factors that are not within the locus of control of the clinician unless actively attempting to work in concert with other aspects of the healthcare system. As examples, childhood obesity, asthma, and dental caries are not only prevalent in children in the United States child population but have a reciprocal interaction with family dysfunction and school stress, necessitating that a provider addresses these social determinants in order to achieve improved outcomes of care [15].

Data analytics are necessary to quantify demographic information for populations and understand opportunities for improvements and demand robust analytics to create attribution models for understanding the potential areas in which quality improvement interventions may have potential impact. Bedside data reporting and simple EHR reports are insufficient to drive quality improvement across entire populations [14].

As payers and governments move toward value-based payment models (models that reward high-quality outcomes rather than provide fee-for-service), providers and healthcare systems are faced with external pressures to engage in population management to meet the demands of payers. The impact to the provider may be thought of in four domains of healthcare transformation within population health: *business models* (facilities and services as an infrastructure for a system), *clinical integration* (provision of care across a continuum), *technology* (EHRs and the systems of hardware and analytics that support care delivery), and *payment models* (innovative payment models that reward good outcomes or penalize poor outcomes). All of these components require data to identify opportunities for improvement and assess the impact of interventions [15].

Achievement of improvement in quality and satisfaction and reducing per capita costs through population health inherently require a measurement system capable of rapidly collecting and managing the storage and transformation of data analytics to drive advances in population health management. For example, sophisticated data analytics would allow users to derive prediction models to understand and subsequently intervene in population health issues such as readmission rates for children with diabetes through dietary counseling or home visits. Data in that setting can be utilized to understand the nuances in the population to effectively and efficiently deliver the right care to the right patient at the right time to optimize patient outcomes.

Use Cases for Data Analytics in Quality Improvement

Case Study • • •
Using Advanced Data Analytics to Improve the Outcomes of Patients with Sepsis

Sepsis is a potentially life-threatening complication of an infection in the blood and occurs when chemicals released into the bloodstream to fight the infection trigger an inflammatory response throughout the body. Worldwide, pediatric sepsis, or septic shock, is a leading cause of death in children. Some best practices have been identified to provide more timely recognition and management of sepsis. This includes timeliness of intravenous fluid resuscitation and antibiotics [16].

In our experience, initial efforts at improving processes were initially unsuccessful when data systems—which at the time were in disparate electronic systems and databases housed in the emergency department (ED), the pediatric intensive care unit (PICU), the EHR, and in billing and coding data—were utilized to retrieve valuable information on processes and outcomes. Piecemeal data was challenging to link, and without outcomes data (mortality rates clearly attributable to septic shock), clinicians were not convinced that there was a significant problem to be solved. Eventually, these disparate data sources had to be manually linked to pull data that was reliable and valid. Once the integrity of the data could be assured, clinicians and administrators engaged in improvement efforts. Our mortality rates for cases of septic shock mirrored what has emerged as national rates (about 3%–12%) depending on the unit and underlying condition of the patient.

Once the analytics could produce visualizations of the scope of the problem, ED and PICU members united to create a quality improvement team that was focused on rapid cycle process improvement to drive quicker recognition (diagnosis) and more timely and efficient management with fluids, antibiotics, and when necessary, vasoactive drug therapies. Utilizing risk stratification approaches, the team identified a number of comorbidities and vital sign abnormalities that could define patients with lower and higher levels of risk. A predictive model to identify those patients at high risk for septic shock was created within a computerized triage system alarm (a form of clinical decision support). System changes were enacted that would allow recruitment of additional nursing, respiratory therapy, and pharmacy personnel and physician clinicians when a patient was identified by the trigger tool (see Fig. 6.2). The tool is the third iteration of a best practice alert generated from predictive analytics data utilizing 4 years of data on patients evaluated for sepsis or potential sepsis [17].

Fluids were administered via syringe (rather than pump) to improve time to fluid bolus. Standardized laboratory studies and antibiotics were prioritized within an evidence-based guideline to reduce unwanted variation in care. Frequent measurement and interventions were documented in a standardized graphical flowsheet to facilitate interpretation of physiologic responses to therapy (see Fig. 6.3). When compared to process measures before the intervention, time from triage to first bolus decreased, as did time to third bolus and time to first antibiotics.

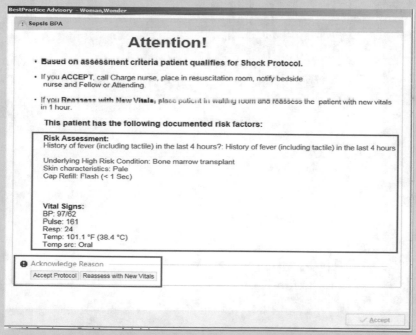

Fig. 6.2 Clinical decision tool alert identifying a patient at high risk for septic shock. Used with permission from Andrea T. Cruz, MD, Texas Children's Hospital

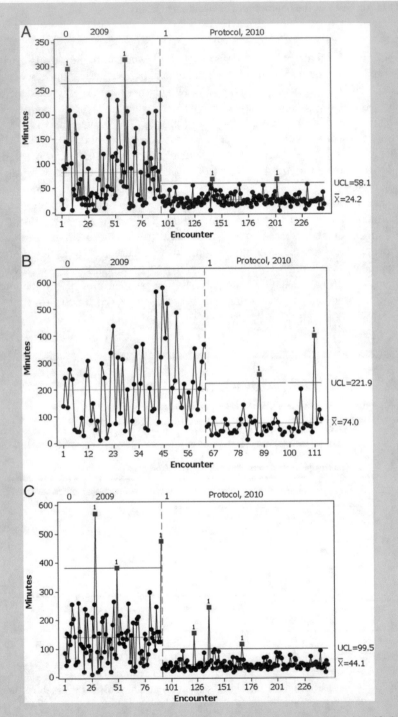

Fig. 6.3 Statistical process control charts of (a) time to first bolus for children identified at triage, (b) time to third bolus for children identified at triage, and (c) time to first antibiotic for children identified at triage. From A.T. Cruz, A.M. Perry, et al. "Implementation of goal-directed therapy for children with suspected sepsis in the emergency department." Reproduced with permission from *Pediatrics*, Vol. 127(3), pages e758–66, Copyright 2011 by the AAP

Delivering Data for Local Quality Improvement Activities

One of the biggest barriers to clinicians and healthcare administrators engaging in quality improvement work is having access to high-quality data. High-quality data is defined not only as valid and reliable data but timely data as well. With the implementation of EHRs and data warehousing, unprecedented amounts of data are available in modern healthcare systems. However, the ability to readily access these data presents another challenge. Several dependencies must be met before high-quality data is made available. Data have to be complete, which means that the source systems must capture the data requested. Data need to be valid, which involves the cataloging of data fields and tables in such a manner that a source of truth can be identified for the various data types, and those delivering the data must have knowledge of the valid data fields and tables. Finally, the process of delivering data in a timely manner requires the development of an intuitive and nimble process for requestors as well as clearly delineated expectations of those completing the requests. The process must also take into account compliance and legal requirements as well as meeting best practices for cybersecurity. All of these dependencies should be considered in the context of a data maturation process to inform data governance strategies and help manage the expectations of data requestors. In other words, not every data point requested will be available initially. Expanding data content and assuring data validity occurs over time. Having high-quality data requires an institutional investment in resources as well as an institutional commitment to the development of an evolving data governance strategy [18].

In our experience, the initial installation of an enterprise data warehouse (EDW) included finding and accessing core data content from our clinical, financial, human resource, and patient satisfaction source systems. It also included an initial attempt at cataloging the content made available in the EDW. Having addressed two of the three dependencies to producing high-quality data, the next step was to improve the final dependency–timeliness of delivery. To address this, we developed a standardized data request process for the workforce. The previous request process was cumbersome and often resulted in a request that would seem to get lost in a black hole with the information services team.

The solution was to streamline the request process by asking fewer and more relevant questions initially, providing transparency to the approval steps required prior to delivering data, and ultimately linking these steps to the organization-wide ticketing system which is necessary for tracking and following-up on requests. Another key improvement to our process was the creation of a triage team to review incoming requests and assign them appropriately, while accounting for prior subject matter knowledge or knowledge of existing data repositories that can be used to fulfill requests. In addition to members from the information services team, the triage team includes members from the quality and finance teams to help review requests and provide additional subject matter expertise. This allowed a deeper understanding of the problem being solved and a better solution than the data report which the requestor, who may not have an in depth understanding of data, sought.

A critical and necessary step that was added to our new data request process was a data training module. This training is mandatory and required as part of the approval process before a data request can be completed. This also represented the first step in a system-wide approach to improving data literacy, which is a growing responsibility of any organization providing data to its workforce. Although it is not new for a healthcare organization to be communicating about protecting privacy and following regulations that govern patient information, providing this information within the data request workflow provides context to the regulations and also creates a more direct connection point between the requestors and their responsibilities with data once it is delivered. The entire process was codified in our policy and procedure manual.

Measuring Healthcare Value

With the shift in healthcare payment models from fee-for-service to value-based payment (lower costs for better outcomes), there is an increasing need to measure both outcomes and costs with a more holistic view that encompasses the perspectives of the provider (both institutional and physician), payer, and ultimately the patient. With the exception of a few health systems, historically, quality improvement strategies primarily focused on measuring improved clinical processes and outcomes at the provider level—either institutional (e.g., hospital or clinic) or sole practitioner. Over time, it has become increasingly evident that measuring the financial impact of improvement activities is important and necessary to demonstrate positive contributions to the operating margin that quality improvement can make. Measuring value requires the ability to measure the outcomes of healthcare delivery, the costs of delivering that care, and the impact to the payer and patient. This requires increasing knowledge of the measurement and data systems for all parties tied to the value equation.

When attempting to measure value, a critical issue to address is the legal aspect of sharing data between payers and providers. This hurdle can be overcome with one-time data use agreements or more comprehensive legal arrangements like the organized healthcare arrangement described under rules that allow for the seamless exchange of data across different entities within the same health system for either operational or quality improvement purposes.

Our organization recently embarked on a 12-month value-based payment pilot between our hospital, a physician services organization, and a health plan (insurance company) to understand and learn the nuances of value-based payment contracts. The health plan was the administrator of the program. The goal of the program was to achieve value for health plan members diagnosed with appendicitis who had an appendectomy. Quality metrics and financial targets were agreed upon at the outset of the program. A patient experience component was also added in the form of a measurement-only goal to understand the feasibility of using the existing patient satisfaction metrics in a value-based payment program. The quality and financial targets were derived from studying a comprehensive data set created by joining data from the health plan and the hospital. Ultimately, pace toward the quality and financial goals was measured using the health plan claims data, and not the clinical data. Another distinguishing feature of the program was the definition of the appendectomy episode. The appendectomy care cycle started 7 days before diagnosis and ended 30 days after the appendectomy operation. This had important implications for measurement as the unit of measure was not the individual patient encounter but the entire episode of care.

Undertaking this pilot elucidated the practical challenges of measuring value in the contemporary healthcare setting using the current data systems available. It also brought to light the limitations of our current units of measurement in healthcare that have implications for analyzing value and understanding performance. For example, merging the claims and clinical data sets necessitated routine reconciliation of the member identification number and the patient's medical record number. While a patient's medical record number in the provider system stays the same, the same patient can have several member identification numbers because of changes in enrollment status. Another challenge was the protracted intervals between performance reports. This was due, in part, to delays in claims processing that resulted in 3-month lag times to receive claims data and, in part, to the time required to manually merge the claims and clinical data together. This type of lag time hinders the clinical team's ability to refine intervention strategies efficiently, if needed, and also translated into the untimely reporting of performance toward goals considering the program was only 12 months in duration.

Measurement at the hospital also presented challenges. Clinical process and outcome metrics were available in a relatively automated fashion, but measuring the cost of caring for a patient with appendicitis who subsequently had an appendectomy proved to be difficult. Generally speaking, costs incurred by a provider are measured by the business unit incurring the costs and not by the disease process that is necessitating the care delivery. In an attempt to understand the costs of the appendectomy episode, we employed a time-driven activity-based costing methodology. This allowed us to study the costs of care based on time spent and costs incurred at key milestones in the patient care continuum [18].

Measuring patient experience presented a similar challenge for a similar reason. Currently, patient experience is measured by location of care and, again, not by disease, so measuring the experience of our patients undergoing an appendectomy had to be done differently using billing codes. While feasible, the analysis of patient experience data for the appendectomy patients did not show much difference from all patients encountering our system (i.e., the dissatisfiers for the appendectomy population were similar to the dissatisfiers for the whole population).

These lessons illustrate the complexity of data analytics and the skills and technology that must be grown by organizations to enter into sophisticated value-based payment programs if those programs are to drive meaningful quality improvement.

Participation in Quality Improvement Activity Beyond the Local Institution

Local quality improvement work often extends beyond the confines of the local institution to leverage best practices of other facilities and to create robust data repositories for clinical research. This is achieved through participation in either multicenter patient registries or quality collaboratives. As is the case with all issues of data transfer as described earlier, regulatory requirements must be met prior to participation. Methods to address these regulations vary from institution to institution. Most often, participation is governed either through clinical research mechanisms and obtaining local institutional review board (IRB) approval or business associate and data use agreements. Some institutions require both.

A considerable obstacle to participating in these multicenter quality improvement efforts is the burden of data collection at the local level and subsequent submission to the outside, hosting organization. This is most often a manual process of extracting data from the medical record (paper or electronic) and transferring that data into a centralized data repository maintained by the host institution. Most often, participants are given access to data entry portals where data are manually submitted. In such scenarios, local participants have limited access to their own raw data for analysis. Sometimes data is simply submitted via encrypted simple spreadsheet files – a method that gives pause to any cybersecurity enforcer. There are a few organizations that have established systems whereby local participants can load data actively at their site, and then data is harvested by the national organization through mechanisms programmed within local software. This allows the local participant to have access to their raw data at any time.

Another potentially frustrating aspect of participating in multicenter QI efforts is the limited control by the participant over the metrics that are established by the multicenter group for reporting. The desired data to be reported is dictated by an outside entity which means that there is not necessarily consistency or alignment with metrics that may be tracked at the local level. Or, as is most often the case, there are nuances in the definition of the populations, processes, and outcomes being measured. Typically, a committee establishes the data elements, and metrics required for reporting and influence is gained only by being a member of that committee. Considering that the resources required to participate in QI activity are committed at the local institutional level, there is little consideration for the feasibility of data gathering when new measures are added to the existing compendium of measures. This culminates in an ever-increasing burden of reporting that rests with the provider participant [19, 20]. As the number of registries and QI collaboratives continues to grow, providers and their organizations will have to decide what they can support and consider the potential and realized return they are getting on their local investment.

Both consumers and payers are demanding more information about performance of both hospitals and individual providers [21]. While most multicenter QI efforts are currently considered voluntary, there is an increasing expectation that hospitals participate, and their participation is accounted for through hospital ranking systems such as US News and World Report Best Hospital Rankings. While much of what is in the public domain currently for publicly reported data is based on Medicare claims information, some professional societies have worked with payers to establish clinical data registries as *sources of truth* for their outcomes reporting [22].

For all the reasons cited previously, the number of data fields being requested is increasing, while the demand for transparency of quality and outcomes data is also increasing. Therefore, it seems logical that, in the era of big data and with the onset of the EHR, there would be more seamless mechanisms to move data from one electronic system to another to decrease the manual burden of data collection and ensure the validity and reliability of the data being reported from each participating site. Although there has been some progress made with EHR vendors and professional societies to create mechanisms for data retrieval within the EHR, there have been no major breakthroughs. Locally, we have developed strategies to extract data from the EHR and push them to data registries that are locally maintained and subsequently harvested at a national level. There remains a significant manual component to this process to map the fields from one data system to the appropriate field in another system.

Accuracy and Precision of Data

When embarking on any endeavor to measure quality, costs, or value, one must consider the concepts of accuracy and precision. Mathematically and statistically speaking, accuracy refers to how close the data reflects the true value of what is being measured, while precision reflects the exactness of that measurement. Consider the target in Fig. 6.4.

The center dot represents the true value of what is being measured. The first target represents a measurement that is precise, but not accurate. The repeated

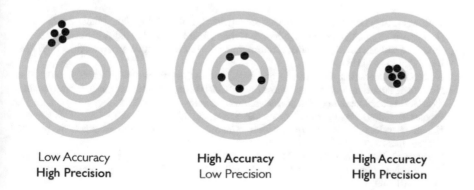

Low Accuracy   High Accuracy   High Accuracy
High Precision   Low Precision   High Precision

Fig. 6.4 An illustration of the difference between precision and accuracy

measurements, while near each other, are not near the true value. The second target shows a measurement that has high accuracy but low precision. The repeated measurements are not near each other, but they are near the true value. The third target shows a measurement that has high accuracy and high precision. The repeated measurements are both close to the true value and close to each other. For research endeavors, one requires both highly accurate and highly precise data. For rapid cycle quality improvement, data needs to be accurate, but not necessarily highly precise initially. As improvement cycles continue, the level of precision is refined. There are statistical methods that can be employed initially to ensure accuracy within defined margins of error when an improvement cycle begins.

Future Trends

The transformation of healthcare has and will continue to require a meaningful integration of data into bedside care, population health models, and sophisticated strategies to translate analytics into improvements in outcomes. At its core, quality improvement not only requires an attention to data collection and processing but also requires the people and organizational structures to assure effective workflows to translate data into information that can drive better healthcare outcomes. In order to be meaningful, analytics for quality improvement must be sensitive to and incorporate clinical, operational, and financial perspectives. The most proximal future of analytics will involve sophisticated technologies for predictive analytics and risk stratification, driving care through clinical decision support. Acceleration of those processes will harness technologies such as machine learning and artificial intelligence to create greater efficiencies than the otherwise manual strategies of analyzing population-based data to improve health.

References

1. Wills MJ (2014) Decisions through data: analytics in healthcare. J Healthc Manag 59:254–262
2. Department of Health and Human Services Centers for Medicare & Medicaid Services (2010) Medicare and Medicaid programs; electronic health record incentive program; final rule. Fed Regist 75(144):44313–44588
3. Abelson R, Creswell J (2013) In second look, few savings from digital health records. The New York Times. https://www.nytimes.com/2013/01/11/business/electronic-records-systems-have-not-reduced-health-costs-report-says.html. Accessed 28 July 2015
4. Procter R (2009) Health informatics topic scope. In: U.S. National Library of Medicine, Health Services Research Information Central. https://hsric.nlm.nih.gov/hsric_public/display_links/717
5. Macias CG, Bartley KA, Rodkey TL et al (2015) Creating a clinical systems integration strategy to drive improvement. Current Treat Options Peds 1:334–346. https://doi.org/10.1007/s40746-015-0031-7

6. Richardson JE, Ash JS, Sittig DF et al (2010) Multiple perspectives on the meaning of clinical decision support. AMIA Annu Symp Proc 2010:1427–1431
7. Strategy Institute (2013) Proceedings from the Second National Summit on Data Analytics for Healthcare, Toronto
8. Adams J, Garets D (2014) The healthcare analytics evolution: moving from descriptive to predictive to prescriptive. In: Gensinger R (ed) Analytics in healthcare: an introduction. HIMSS, Chicago, pp 13–20
9. Macias CG, Loveless JN, Jackson AJ et al (2017) Delivering value through evidence-based practice. Clin Ped Emerg Med 18(2):89–97
10. Raghupathi W, Raghupathi V (2014) Big data analytics in healthcare: promise and potential. Health Inf Sci Syst 2:3. https://doi.org/10.1186/2047-2501-2-3
11. Burghard C (2012) Big data and analytics key to accountable care success.. IDC Health Insights
12. Institute for Healthcare Improvement (2016) Improvement tip: taking the journey to "Jiseki"..http://www.ihi.org/resources/Pages/ImprovementStories/ImprovementTipTaketheJourneytoJiseki.aspx. Accessed 7 December 2016
13. MedeAnalytics (2012) Healthcare Analytics Maturity Framework. https://www.scribd.com/document/330016789/MedeAnalytics-Healthcare-Analytics-Maturity-Framework-MA-HAMF-0212?doc_id=330016789&download=truc&order=469192010
14. Sanders D (2013) 7 Essential practices for data governance in healthcare.. Health Catalyst. https://www.healthcatalyst.com/wp-content/uploads/2013/09/Insights-7EssentialPracticesforDataGovernanccinHealthcare.pdf
15. Schwarzwald H, Macias CG (2018) Population health management in pediatrics. In: Kline MW (ed) Rudolph's pediatrics, 23rd edn. McGraw-Hill Education, New York, pp 21–24
16. Paul R, Melendez E, Wathen B et al (2018) A quality improvement collaborative for pediatric sepsis: lessons learned. Pediatric Quality & Safety 3(1):e051. https://doi.org/10.1097/pq9.0000000000000051
17. Cruz AT, Perry AM, Williams EA et al (2011) Implementation of goal-directed therapy for children with suspected sepsis in the emergency department. Pediatrics 3:e758–e766. https://doi.org/10.1542/peds.2010-2895
18. Goldenberg JN (2016) The breadth and burden of data collection in clinical practice. Neurol Clin Pract 6(1):81–86. https://doi.org/10.1212/CPJ.0000000000000209
19. Disch J, Sinioris M (2012) The quality burden. Nurs Clin N Am 47(3):395–405. https://doi.org/10.1016/j.cnur.2012.05.010
20. Harder B, Comarow A (2015) Hospital quality reporting by US News and World Report. JAMA 313:19. https://doi.org/10.1001/jama.2015.4566
21. Ferris TG, Torchiana DF (2010) Public release of clinical outcomes data–online CABG report cards. NEJM 363(17):1593–1595. https://doi.org/10.1056/NEJMp1009423
22. Mack MJ, Herbert M, Prince S et al (2005) Does reporting of coronary artery bypass grafting from administrative databases accurately reflect actual clinical outcomes? J Thoracic Cardiovasc Surg 129(6):1309–1317. https://doi.org/10.1016/j.jtcvs.2004.10.036

Additional Resources-Further Reading

IOM (Institute of Medicine) (2015) Vital Signs: Core metrics for health and health care progress. The National Academies Press, Washington DC
Kaprielian VS, Silberberg M, McDonald MA et al (2013) Teaching population health: a competency map approach to education. Academic Med 88(5):626–637. https://doi.org/10.1097/ACM.0b013e31828acf27

Office of Disease Prevention and Health Promotion (2011) Social determinants of health. http://www.healthypeople.gov. Accessed 20 August 2016

Stiefel M, Nolan K, Institute for Healthcare Improvement (2012) A guide to measuring the triple aim: population health, experience of care and per capita cost. IHI Innovation Series white paper. http://www.ihi.org/resources/Pages/IHIWhitePapers/AGuidetoMeasuringTripleAim.aspx

Stoto MA (2013) Population health in the affordable health care act era. Academy Health, Washington D.C

Taveras EM, Gortmaker SL, Hohman KH et al (2011) Randomized controlled trial to improve primary care to prevent and manage childhood obesity: the High Five for Kids study. Arch Pediatr Adolesc Med 165(8):714–722. https://doi.org/10.1001/archpediatrics.2011.44

Yu YR, Abbas PI, Smith CM et al (2016) Time-driven activity-based costing to identify opportunities for cost reduction in pediatric appendectomy. J Pediatr Surg 51:1962–1966. https://doi.org/10.1016/j.jpedsurg.2016.09.019

Chapter 7
Utilization Management, Case Management, and Care Coordination

Angelo P. Giardino and Michelle A. Lyn

Executive Summary

Utilization management (UM) is the mix of clinical, administrative, and financial methods used to evaluate the appropriateness, processes, facilities, and providers of care applied to an individual and a total population of patients. Case management (CM) is a centralization of the planning, arranging, and follow-up of a member's specific health services in order to manage utilization, effectiveness, cost, and quality of health care. Care coordination (CC) includes case management and involves processes that organize and connect personnel and other resources needed to carry out all required patient care activities and is characterized by the effective exchange of information among participants responsible for different aspects of care. CM and CC are used to monitor and coordinate services and supports rendered to members including those special populations with medical complexity which require high cost or intensive services.

The underlying reason to integrate the frameworks of utilization management, case management, and care coordination is to make sure that health care is delivered to the patient and the population efficiently and effectively where such activities directly impact the quality of outcomes. This contrasts with the older concept of utilization review as a sole means to control resources and the cost of care. Intrinsic to UM, CM, and CC are structured programs and methodologies that incorporate indicators, monitors, and benchmarks that track and note trends in the processes and outcomes of care as planned and delivered. Previously, the responsibilities of UM

A. P. Giardino (✉)
University of Utah School of Medicine, Salt Lake City, UT, USA

M. A. Lyn
Baylor College of Medicine, Houston, TX, USA

Texas Children's Hospital, Houston, TX, USA

© American College of Medical Quality (ACMQ) 2021
A. P. Giardino et al. (eds.), *Medical Quality Management*,
https://doi.org/10.1007/978-3-030-48080-6_7

professionals were seen as distinct, but the value of connecting UM with quality and safety management is becoming clear and is now driven by a shift from fee for service reimbursement to the more outcome-oriented value-based models. The essential need for CM and CC aligned with UM processes is now seen as overlapping and essential to high-quality, cost-effective care delivery models. Two care models that utilize the data and approaches involved with UM, CM, and CC are the *chronic care model* and the *patient-* and *family-centered medical homes*. These two models figure prominently in the move from fee for service to value-based alternative payment models. Aligned UM and CC approaches are part of the operational infrastructure necessary to improve healthcare while being cost-effective in an era of limited resources.

Learning Objectives

Upon completion of this chapter, readers should be able to

- Review current definitions of utilization management (UM), case management (CM), and care coordination (CC)
- Discuss processes and methods of UM
- Discuss the processes and methods of CM and CC
- Evaluate outcomes and the return on investment for UM, CM, and CC
- Describe the regulatory, accreditation, and oversight programs for UM and CM
- Review two care delivery models: the chronic care model and the patient- and family-centered medical homes and their connection to UM, CM, and CC

Introduction

The Institute of Medicine describes utilization management as part of a complex balancing act between ensuring that people get needed medical care without spending so much that other important social objectives are compromised and discouraging unnecessary and inappropriate medical services without jeopardizing necessary high-quality care [1]. Insurers, hospitals, and healthcare professionals as well as public and private agencies have developed a variety of UM, CM, and CC programs in an evolving effort to comprehensively manage costs, decrease fragmentation of healthcare delivery, promote high-quality care, and enhance the patients' experience with the healthcare system. The purpose and scope of these programs vary with the type of organization but often focus on accomplishing higher levels of coordinated care that achieve improved outcomes. Historically, insurers used UM programs as a self-contained cost management tool. Case management performed for insurers and managed care organizations (MCOs) typically focused more on benefits management and resource utilization. Hospitals used case management to provide information to payers and assist with discharge planning. More recently, aligning UM with the quality of care delivered has led to a recognition of the potential value of an enhanced connection among UM and CM programs as well as the emerging value of a more comprehensive CC approach to care which ultimately seeks to deliver the right care to the right patient at the right time. This chapter first addresses UM processes and programs then moves to address the underlying principles of effective CM and CC. It concludes with a brief description of two important care models, namely, the chronic care model and the patient- and family-centered medical homes, both of which are facilitated by well-designed CC that is informed by UM data.

Components of Utilization Management Systems

The UM process includes interventions that take place before, during, and after a clinical event occurs. The process that occurs before the clinical event is called *prior authorization* or *precertification*. While the clinical event is happening, the process is called *concurrent review*; if the patient is in a facility, it will also include discharge planning. After the clinical event has occurred, the process is called *retrospective review* or *retro review*. The overall UM process should be as nonintrusive to the delivery of care as possible and be able to stop inappropriate care before it does harm. In order for UM programs to be successful, several critical factors must be in place [2]:

- Utilization of data and information that can be easily compared between providers, patients, payers, and other stakeholders (e.g., the Pennsylvania Healthcare Cost Containment Council information).
- Continued improvement in UM processes to keep pace with the complex care and new technology being used for credentialing.
- Utilization of up-to-date technology that does not duplicate the administrative burden of providers and patients.
- Safeguards in place to protect individual patient data and information as identified in the Health Insurance Portability and Accountability Act (HIPAA) and other regulations.
- Utilization of evidence-based medicine, patient and provider satisfaction measures, cost of operations, and clinical outcomes in determining the appropriateness and the success of UM efforts.
- Determinations are reliable, consistent, and follow the policy of the UM program.
- Responsiveness to patients and providers through a grievance and appeals program, quality monitoring system, and trending of the decisions of care (especially denials of care).

- Must occur without delaying care. There needs to be a process in place that reviews alternatives of care, placement of care, and providers of care in a timely fashion.
- Must follow the coverage and benefit that is provided to the patient.

Effective Utilization Management

According to the American College of Medical Quality's *Core Curriculum for Medical Quality Management*, there are nine key tasks that ensure UM is consistent and relevant, integrated into the organization and that the process is legitimatized among clinicians, patients, and other stakeholders [2].

1. Determine Priority Areas

Priority areas may be related to the use of healthcare resources, quality outcomes, regulatory compliance, and overall financial health of the organization. For many healthcare organizations, the majority of their revenue is spent on clinical care. The right questions will improve the clinical and financial health of the organization.

2. Identify Needed Information and Critical Stakeholders

Data are required to guide the UM process. The data must be accurate, timely, relevant, and easily collectable at a reasonable cost. The methodology of using the data must be transparent and appropriate. Stakeholder buy-in from senior management, providers, and patients is key to successful UM.

3. Establish Appropriate Benchmarks

Benchmarks must be chosen that will identify desired levels of performance. Benchmarks can represent the process or outcome of care. When evidence-based medicine does not have an appropriate benchmark for the study, an expert panel of clinicians may suggest a standard. Benchmarks may be internally or externally generated.

4. Design, Data Collection, and Data Management Procedures

There is presently no accepted methodology for UM studies. The National Committee for Quality Assurance (NCQA) has identified a generic improvement activity form that may be used by UM plans [2]. Appropriate determination of the sample size, procedure, and types of data to be used (administrative or clinical) is critical when evaluating performance for UM.

5. Implement Data Collection and Management Procedures

This includes the allocation of human and financial resources for UM. It is important to have policies and procedures in place to determine who will be allowed to collect the data, what will be the main source of the data, and where, when, and with what frequency the information is shared. Policies and procedures must also be consistent and uniform across patients, providers, organizations, and other stakeholders. The cost of data collection must be evaluated.

6. Evaluate the Data and Present Results

There should be a common methodology and statistical analysis used in interpreting the data. Results must be presented in a fashion that recognizes speculation and ensures that the methodology and statistical analysis of the study have been transparent and that the results can be attributed to the intervention.

7. Develop Guidelines, Policies, and Procedures

Once an area for improvement in structure, process, or outcome is identified, new guidelines must be developed by the organization. This change in process should be managed by the organization and include key stakeholders (e.g., clinicians) affected by the change.

8. Implement Guidelines, Policies, and Procedures

System change can occur only if UM guidelines, policies, and procedures are implemented, followed, and re-evaluated on a regular basis.

9. Continuously Review the Task List

Each of the nine tasks identified should be reviewed on a regular basis by the people or the body responsible for UM in the organization in order to build a culture of constant improvement.

The Institute of Medicine empaneled a blue ribbon committee to explore the value of UM within the healthcare system, and they challenged purchasers, review organizations, physicians, and patients to accept responsibility for the reasonable and fair conduct of utilization management and the appropriate use of medical care [1]. See Table 7.1.

Processes, Procedures, and Timing of Utilization Management

The UM plan usually contains operational procedures related to prior authorization, concurrent review, and retrospective review. While each of these can be applied differently by each entity performing the UM programs, standard procedures and reasoning behind each of the three processes exist. Fundamental to the UM process is the establishment of medical necessity. Medical necessity is a time-honored concept that is common to both publicly and privately managed health benefits. When a healthcare provider, namely, a physician, orders a service or procedure, it will be covered only if it is deemed both (1) medically necessary and (2) a covered benefit. The UM professional generally reviews the requested service for appropriateness (i.e., medical necessity) and benefit eligibility. According to Stanford University's

Table 7.1 Responsibilities of stakeholders for utilization management

Stakeholders	Responsibilities
Employers and purchasers	As financers of both utilization management and health services, employers are in the best position to exert influence on the conduct of utilization management
	Employers should also examine other aspects of their health benefit plans for impediments to the appropriate use of medical services or the rational payment for these services
Utilization management organizations	Although good business and legal judgment should dictate prudent behavior, those who provide utilization management services also have a moral obligation not to harm the patients whose medical care they review and influence
	With respect to practitioners and individual providers of care, good business sense should dictate that review organizations encourage provider acceptance and cooperation by:
	Using sound clinical criteria that are open to examination
	Involving the medical community in criteria development
	Minimizing the administrative burdens placed on hospitals and physicians
	Clarifying and simplifying processes for appealing negative judgments
Practitioners and institutions	Healthcare practitioners and institutions are responsible for:
	Cooperating with the reasonable efforts of payers, including utilization management, to ensure that payments are for appropriate care within the terms of a patient's benefit plan
	Constructively challenging unreasonable utilization management programs and specific decisions that threaten patient safety or damage patient privacy
	Informing patients about treatment options, risks, and benefits and then considering their preferences
	Seeking to ensure that patients get needed services, which may mean locating an alternative source of care if the patient cannot pay and the provider cannot give free treatment
	Staying current with scientific literature on the necessity and effectiveness of medical services in their areas of practice
Patients	Patients and potential patients are the weakest strand in the web of responsibilities for the appropriate use of medical services. When ill, individuals may not be able to act in an informed and prudent way. And whether well or ill, individuals may find both their benefit plans and their medical care difficult to understand and evaluate. Nonetheless, health plan members should try to understand their responsibilities under the plan

Adapted from "Controlling Costs and Changing Patient Care?: The Role of Utilization Management," by the Institute of Medicine Committee on Utilization Management by Third Parties, pp. 6–9, 1989, Washington, DC: The National Academies Press. Adapted with permission

Center for Health Policy, the determination of medical necessity has, over time, become an increasingly important aspect of healthcare coverage:

> Understanding *medical necessity* is important for everyone. It is important for consumers because, ultimately, the decisions about coverage and treatment affect their lives and they need the information to make prudent choices. It is important for providers because they must now share treatment decision authority with managed care medical directors with whom they may disagree. It is important for the courts because they are the referees of last

resort, although poorly equipped to play that role. It is important for states and the federal government because they must mediate the conflict between clinical professionals, managed care decision makers, and the public over the use and definition of this term, and they need to understand how best to do that. It is important for the regulators and accreditors, because they must apply the laws and standards for high-quality professional performance [3].

Medically necessary services must be reasonably expected to produce the intended results for the patient to whom they are delivered, and medically necessary services should have expected benefits that outweigh potential harmful effects. Often times, medically necessary services are considered a standard of care supported by some level of evidence in the professional literature or at least a consensus of expert opinion.

Prior Authorization or Precertification

The first process is prior authorization or precertification, which is performed before a clinical intervention takes place. The purpose of this process is to make sure the clinical intervention is appropriate and takes place in the right setting and time and that the clinician has the expertise to do the clinical intervention. All these criteria should be measured on the basis of evidence-based medicine for that particular condition. Milliman and Interqual are some of the vendors that have developed commercially available criteria for prior authorization [4, 5]. Prior authorization can also be used as a vital communication link within a healthcare organization by gathering information that will help the patient have a better outcome and distributing it to other parts of the organization. This improves care coordination for the patient and the organization.

An example of this is a patient who is going in for a hip replacement. Once prior authorization information is received, it is transferred to a nurse who can call the patient to determine the individual's needs for rehabilitation (e.g., can the patient go home with appropriate support or does the patient need a placement in a rehabilitation facility). The nurse can also set up a satisfaction survey that will follow the patient after the episode of care is completed. If the organization doing the prior authorization is also a payer of claims, the notification and approval will be sent to the finance area to make sure funds are available to pay the providers of the intervention. The prior authorization process will also notify other components of the UM program (including concurrent review and retrospective review) to ensure they are performed in a timely and appropriate manner.

Concurrent Review and Discharge Planning

Concurrent review is the management of resources by evaluating the necessity, appropriateness, and efficiency of the use of medical services, procedures, and levels of care while a patient is in a facility. This process usually takes place during urgent or elective acute hospital admissions. The purpose of concurrent review is to deliver efficient, effective healthcare, to reduce the occurrence of over-, under-, or misuse of inpatient services, and to promote patient safety and the best outcome during an inpatient stay. As with the prior authorization process, concurrent review is connected to other processes of care including quality monitoring of the patient's hospital stay, coordinating with discharge planning, and identifying appropriate next levels of care. Concurrent review also helps identify patients who may benefit from disease management or case management and transfers data to finance for appropriate reimbursement. Criteria for concurrent review can vary by the organization performing the service, as long as it follows the principles of evidence-based medicine. Two recognized sources of criteria for concurrent review are Milliman Care Guidelines and Qualis Health-McKesson's InterQual Criteria [4, 5]. A basic principle widely quoted among utilization of management professionals is that concurrent review should begin on admission.

Discharge planning is the process of arranging for the next level of care for patients as they are ready to leave the facility and may be considered part of the concurrent review process. Discharge planning is initiated when patients are first admitted to the hospital and takes into consideration the medical conditions, social and environmental concerns, financial status, and other variables to make certain that the patients receive the appropriate placement and services once they leave the facility. Discharge planning is usually a team effort involving nurses, social workers, primary and specialty physicians, and the patient or patient advocate.

Retrospective Review

Retrospective review is the process of reviewing healthcare interventions and charges after the care has been delivered and the bill is submitted. Retrospective review determines whether the care was appropriate and provided at the most efficient and effective level with the best outcomes. It also determines if the bill was coded correctly according to Current Procedural Terminology (CPT), Centers for Medicare and Medicaid (CMS), International Classification of Diseases-10 (ICD-10), or other guidelines. Retrospective review should be a secondary look at the healthcare interventions and charges. Ideally, only minimal discrepancies should be identified if all guidelines and institutional procedures were completed during the inpatient hospitalization. Retrospective review should be used to collect data on quality and utilization by healthcare organizations, physicians, and other providers of care.

Interrater Reliability Assessment

Whenever a UM process has the potential to be evaluated by different reviewers, an *interrater reliability assessment* is required. Interrater reliability assessment is defined as the process of monitoring and evaluating clinical reviewers' understanding of medical review criteria and the consistency with which different reviewers apply the same criteria in making decisions. This important step is needed to certify that the review process decisions are made in a consistent manner according to evidence-based medicine criteria. Interrater reliability is usually assessed on a quarterly or semiannual basis. Reviewers whose decisions are not consistent with the criteria are usually reeducated and retested.

Denials and Audits

Healthcare organizations risk significant financial losses if there are lapses in the UM plan. Denials and audits from payers, including the Centers for Medicare & Medicaid Services (CMS), can occur when there are perceived deficits in the operational procedures of the UM plan. Common deficits can include

- Lack of clinical documentation
- Errors in interpretation of level of care
- Late submission of clinical information
- Failure to obtain prior authorization
- Differences in interpretation of medical necessity for admission utilizing available frameworks (e.g., Milliman Care Guidelines [4] and Qualis Health-McKesson's InterQual Criteria [5])

CMS oversees several different Recovery Audit Programs, such as those for Medicare FFS, Part C, and Part D. States oversee their own Medicaid Recovery Audit Programs in accordance with federal guidelines set by CMS. The Medicare Fee for Service (FFS) Recovery Audit Program's mission is to identify and correct improper Medicare and Medicaid payments through the efficient detection and collection of overpayments made on claims of healthcare services provided to Medicare and Medicaid beneficiaries, to identify underpayments to providers, and to provide information that allows the Centers for Medicare & Medicaid Services (CMS) to implement actions that will prevent future improper payments in all 50 states [6]. The program is authorized under Section 1893(h) of the Social Security Act (the Act) [7]. It has been in effect since 2005 and was expanded nationwide in 2010.

CMS uses several types of contractors to verify that claims are paid based on Medicare guidelines. One type of contractor used is a Recovery Auditor, also known as a Recovery Audit Contractor (RAC) [6]. Section 1893(h)(8) of the Act requires the Secretary [of Health and Human Services] to "annually submit to Congress a report on the use of recovery audit contractors…" [7] In addition, "each such report shall include information on the performance of such contractors in identifying underpayments and overpayments and recouping overpayments, including an evaluation of the comparative performance of such contractors and savings to the program…" [7] As required by the Act, RACs are paid on a contingency fee basis [7]. The amount of the contingency fee is a percentage of the improper payment recovered from or reimbursed to providers. The RACs negotiate their contingency fees at the time of the contract award. The base contingency fees range from 9.0 to 12.5% for all claim types, except durable medical equipment (DME). The contingency fees for DME claims range from 14.0 to 17.5%. The RAC must return the contingency fee if an improper payment determination is overturned at any level of appeal. Providers who disagree with a RAC's improper payment determination may utilize the multilevel administrative appeals process under Section 1869 of the Act. See Figs. 7.1 and 7.2.

Provider appeals are the counterbalance to payer denials. A UM appeal for a denied service activity or level of care typically takes the form of a provider letter of appeal and incorporates the details necessitating the service or level of care for each patient, any supporting documentation for the quality and quantity of care rendered, and is strengthened if national guidelines or protocols exist and are included as well. Disagreements between providers and payers are inevitable, so planning for the receiving of denials and the need for appeals are necessary for all healthcare organizations. An organized operational structure and process for the management of appeals and audits should be developed for each healthcare organization, especially with the perceived increase in external auditing on the part of payers and government programs. A framework for the development of a denial and appeals management process that ensures more favorable outcomes could be the Five Ws which

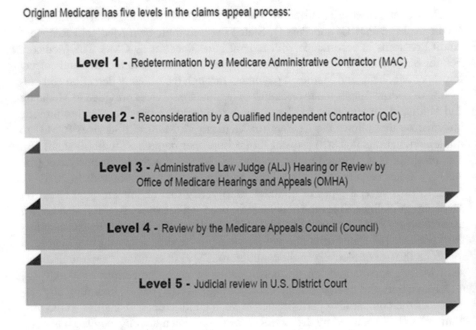

APPEALING MEDICARE DECISIONS

Original Medicare has five levels in the claims appeal process:

Level 1 - Redetermination by a Medicare Administrative Contractor (MAC)

Level 2 - Reconsideration by a Qualified Independent Contractor (QIC)

Level 3 - Administrative Law Judge (ALJ) Hearing or Review by Office of Medicare Hearings and Appeals (OMHA)

Level 4 - Review by the Medicare Appeals Council (Council)

Level 5 - Judicial review in U.S. District Court

Fig. 7.1 CMS/Medicare levels of appeal. https://www.cms.gov/Outreach-and-Education/Medicare-Learning-Network-MLN/MLNProducts/Downloads/MedicareAppealsProcess.pdf

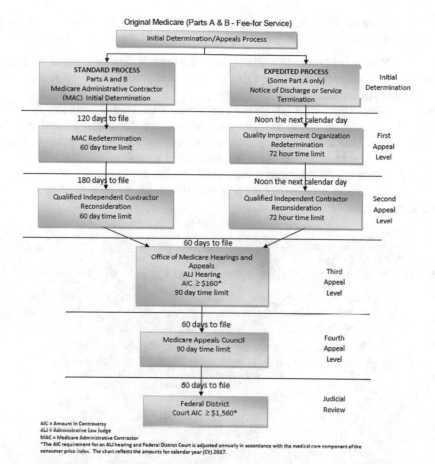

Redetermination: Performed by Medicare Administrative Contractors (MACs), the request for redetermination must be received by the MAC within 120 calendar days of the date a party receives the initial (or revised initial) determination, and written notice of the redetermination is expected to be mailed or otherwise transmitted by the MAC within 60 calendar days of receipt of the request for redetermination.

Reconsideration: Performed by Qualified Independent Contractors (QICs), the request for reconsideration must be filed with the QIC within 180 calendar days of the date the party receives the Medicare Redetermination Notice. The QICs are expected to mail or otherwise transmit notice of the reconsideration within 60 calendar days of receipt of the request for reconsideration.

Administrative Law Judge (ALJ): ALJ hearings require a minimum amount in controversy and a request for a hearing must be filed within 60 calendar days of the date the party receives the reconsideration notice. Generally, ALJs are expected to issue a decision, dismissal order, or remand to the QIC within 90 calendar days of the date the request for hearing is received. If an ALJ does not act in a timely manner, the appellant may choose to escalate that appeal to the next level of review if certain conditions are met.

Judicial Review (Federal District Court Review): Appeals to Federal district court must be filed within 60 calendar days of the date a party receives notice of the Appeals Council's decision, but the federal court does not have a deadline to issue its decisions. For CY 2015, the minimum amount in controversy was $1,460

Fig. 7.2 Original Medicare (Parts A and B – fee for service) appeals process. https://www.cms. gov/Medicare/Appeals-and-Grievances/OrgMedFFSAppeals/

refers to basic questions that address necessary information gathering and problem solving. Example of the Five Ws as applied to the UM program are as follows:

Who?   Who is the person or department in the organization designated to receive the letters of notification of appeals or audits and who will be responsible for addressing the appeals?

Why?   Why is there a denial? (lack of documentation, lack of notification, etc.)

What?   What action should be taken when there is a notification? Should there be an appeal? Should there be acceptance of the decision? If there is an appeal, how many levels should the organization be prepared to appeal?

When?   When are the deadlines for appeal?

Where?   Is there an error in the UM process? Where are these areas of opportunity for improvement?

Case Study • • •

The application of the UM five Ws in a pediatric patient with asthma

A pediatric patient with severe asthma develops respiratory distress and fever. The patient requires emergent admission to the hospital for respiratory support. The patient responds rapidly to interventions and is discharged within 48 h. The level of care assigned is denied by the payer due to lack of medical necessity and the short duration of care. Applying the Five Ws approach, we see:

- *Who* is the patient? Age, risk factors, previous hospitalizations, and underlying disease process?
- *What* were the presenting symptoms and signs? What type of interventions did the patient receive? What was the initial level of care? What questions need to be addressed in the UM plan?
- *Why* did this patient require inpatient care? Are clinical criteria present to justify medical necessity? Is there substantial documentation of medical necessity?
- *Where* was the patient admitted? ICU vs. acute care?
- *When* was the assessment of level of care made by the institution? When were the details communicated to the payer? When should there be an appeal?

The details of the answers to the questions listed above should guide the reviewer to assign the appropriate level of care. For this example, the level of care should be assigned the moment the decision is made for extended clinical care, evaluation, and management in the hospital setting. If a review of the UM process for this patient is appropriate and the level of care assigned is within the guidelines, there can be an appeal. The appeal should include substantive information for medical necessity.

Organizational Design of Utilization Management

Typically, the person responsible for the UM program is a healthcare professional with several years of experience in the field of healthcare utilization, quality, risk management, and safety (see Chap. 8).

It is imperative that the UM program have clinical input from practitioners who must comply with the UM program. This is usually done through a UM committee or a practitioner advisory committee. A senior clinician should lead the UM committee, and the committee should include several practicing physicians from different specialties and primary care. Some organizations have outside clinicians (who are not responsible to practice under the UM plan) help evaluate the validity and the appropriateness of the UM plan. The healthcare organization may also designate senior administrative leaders to serve on the committee. The functions of the committee are to:

- Design, develop, or plan program structure
- Develop UM program evaluation measures
- Identify opportunities to improve
- Identify performance indicators and metrics
- Identify organizational resources
- Align with organizational strategic plan
- Monitor the review activity
- Review progress of initiatives
- Develop senior leadership reports
- Track accreditation preparation
- Communicate with appropriate internal and external stakeholders
- Monitor resource utilization progress
- Evaluate program impact on workforce and senior leadership
- Hold meetings to present results
- Recognize and reward efforts
- Ensure accountability for program goals and objectives
- Present impact reports [2]

Committee meetings should be held on a regular schedule with support staff to help with the administrative aspects of the committee such as keeping meeting minutes. The committee should report to the decision makers in the healthcare organization.

Measuring the Effectiveness of UM Programs

Generally, the effectiveness of UM programs is measured in financial terms such as dollar savings or return on investment (ROI). While there may be no standardized methodologies across healthcare organizations on how to calculate ROI, the AHRQ does now have an ROI estimator calculator in the AHRQ Quality Indicators Toolkit [8]. Some programs merge quality and utilization programs and measure their effectiveness by using a balanced scorecard approach. The effectiveness of UM should, at minimum, be based on the following:

- Evidenced-based criteria
- Reliable, accurate, and defensible data that has been validated
- Appropriate clinical expert review
- Transparent methodology of effectiveness calculations

There are always challenges in the calculation of the effectiveness of UM. When looking at the results, one must consider the following potential problems: the sample size may be small or not appropriate for comparison, and the sample population may be different by demographics, severity, or culture.

As with most management processes in the healthcare setting, monitoring performance via data collection about the UM efforts allows for tracking and trending of what is working and what needs improvement to work better. Audits, both external, as the one described above, or internal, done by one's own organization, provide these data from which to construct charts and tables to display performance measures. At its most basic level, successful UM programs result in approvals and payments for appropriate levels of care, whereas failures result in denials and the need for appeals. Understanding the error trends for hospitals assists with building identifiable data sets for internal auditing of the hospital's UM program.

Case Study • • •
Texas Office of the Inspector General (OIG) Utilization Review Unit

In 2016, the Texas OIG provided an overview of its hospital utilization review process, procedures, and outcomes [9]. This document is useful in understanding the auditing of hospital information and the utility of establishing a quality UM department.

For Texas, the OIG developed the utilization review unit. The focus of the unit is stated as "Reviews of paid inpatient hospital claims for services provided to Medicaid recipients to assess the medical necessity for inpatient care, appropriateness of the Diagnosis Related Group (DRG) assignment, including whether diagnoses are supported by the information in the medical record and whether coding was consistent with federal coding guidelines, and quality of care provided during the inpatient stay." [9] The risk categories and methodology used to select claims for review are outlined in Table 7.2 below.

The process of review involves evaluation and validation of DRG for each patient selected. Identification of medical necessity utilizes MCG evidence-based care guidelines [10]. The utilization review unit must determine that the care provided met generally accepted standards of medical and hospital care practices. Once the review is completed, the hospital will receive a final notification letter with the results of the review and an explanation of each finding.

If the hospital disputes the findings, a Medical Appeals Section, established within the Texas Health and Human Services (HHSC) Medicaid Office of the Medical Director, manages the discrepancies.

Table 7.3 reveals the finding of the OIG office for fiscal years 2014 and 2015. The cumulative financial recovery for HHSC can be significant.

The utilization review unit listed the most common, recurring reasons contributing to denials and adjustment as follows [9]:

- Outpatient procedures billed as inpatient in an inpatient setting
- Diagnoses issues not supported by the medical record
- Coding issues (e.g., improper sequencing of obstetrical diagnoses)
- Treatment or care that was not provided on the initial admission resulting in readmission

Table 7.2 Categories and methodology for selection for review

Risk category	Methodology of selection	Percent of claims
Short stays	Random sample	50%
Newborns		
Complex and premature deliveries		
Admissions and readmissions	Random sample	25%
Psychiatric in-patient services	All identified claims	100%
Children's hospitals		
Freestanding psychiatric hospitals		
Rehabilitation hospitals		
Chemical dependency diagnoses		
Day outliers	Judgmental sample, based on length of stay and diagnoses submitted	A limited number (discretionary)
Cost outliers		

Reprinted from *Overview of Hospital Utilization Review*, by the Office of Inspector General, Texas Health and Human Services. Retrieved from https://oig.hhsc.texas.gov/sites/oig/files/documents/Overview-of-Hospital-Utilization-Review.pdf

Table 7.3 Findings of the OIG utilization review unit for fiscal years 2014 and 2015

Fiscal year	Total paid claims	Total dollars paid	Claims reviewed	Dollars recovered
2014	416,282	$1,550,101,372	28,378	$28,891,505
2015	383,914	$1,370,305,849	21,350	$15,536,822

Reprinted from *Overview of Hospital Utilization Review*, by the Office of Inspector General, Texas Health and Human Services. Retrieved from https://oig.hhsc.texas.gov/sites/oig/files/documents/Overview-of-Hospital-Utilization-Review.pdf

There has been some controversy over the value of UM. One concern identified is the cost of conducting UM may be greater than the savings obtained from the process. As discussed above, UM should be part of a group of interventions to decrease the overuse, underuse, and misuse of healthcare and improve individual and population outcomes. There should be a system in place that can identify patient safety issues that have been avoided by doing concurrent review in the hospital or identification of a quality problem that was reported before it became a major issue. The UM process also enhances the patient experience with the healthcare system in terms of discharge planning and follow-up when the patient is out of the hospital. Beneficial outcomes of UM are often represented in improved satisfaction survey results by the patient and providers.

Care Coordination and Case Management

> One challenge encountered throughout the care coordination field is the difficulty in distinguishing care coordination from other aspects or processes of care. Care coordination is a complex concept, intertwined with many other concepts relating to quality, delivery, and organization of care. In its broadest sense, almost all aspects of healthcare and its delivery can be understood as part of care coordination.
>
> Care Coordination Measures Atlas, Agency for Healthcare Research and Quality [11]

The Agency for Healthcare Research and Quality (AHRQ) defines care coordination (CC) as:

> …the deliberate organization of patient care activities between two or more participants (including the patient) involved in a patient's care to facilitate the appropriate delivery of healthcare services. Organizing care involves the marshalling of personnel and other resources needed to carry out all required patient care activities and is often managed by the exchange of information among participants responsible for different aspects of care [12].

AHRQ has developed a graphic to represent the many interrelated elements that may come together during effective care coordination. See Fig. 7.3. The central goal of care coordination is shown in the middle of the diagram. The 13 small circles represent possible participants, settings, and information important for care delivery and workflow in the clinical setting. The ring that connects the 13 circles is care coordination: anything that bridges gaps (i.e., white spaces between care delivery and workflow circles).

In addition, AHRQ takes a systems or human ecology approach to the many levels or varying perspectives necessary to understand care coordination including the patient/family, healthcare professional/organization, and healthcare system perspectives. See Table 7.4.

Case management is closely related to care coordination, and CM is often seen as a component of a broader CC approach. The ACMQ's *Core Curriculum for Medical Quality Management* defines case management (CM) as centralizing the planning, arranging, and follow-up of a patient or health plan member's specific health services in order to manage utilization, effectiveness, cost, and quality of

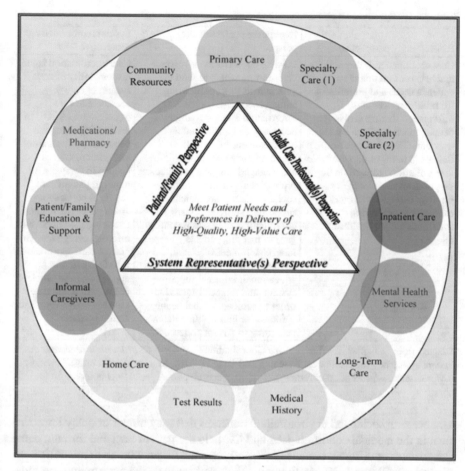

Fig. 7.3 AHRQ view of care coordination. Reprinted from "Chapter 2. What is Care Coordination?" in *Care Coordination Measures Atlas Update* by Agency for Healthcare Research and Quality, 2014, Retrieved from https://www.ahrq.gov/professionals/prevention-chronic-care/improve/coordination/atlas2014/chapter2.html

healthcare [2]. The Case Management Society of America (CMSA) defines CM as "...a collaborative process of assessment, planning, facilitation, care coordination, evaluation, and advocacy for options and services to meet an individual's and family's comprehensive needs through communication and available resources to promote quality, cost effective outcomes." [13] CM is used to monitor and coordinate medical and other services rendered to patients and health plan members including those who make up special populations, have specific diagnoses, or require high cost or intensive services.

The processes that underlie both CM and CC coordinate designated components of healthcare, such as appropriate referral to consultants, specialists, hospitals, and ancillary providers and services. These processes also help the patient or health plan

Table 7.4 Perspectives on care coordination

Patient/family perspective	Healthcare professional(s) perspective	System representative(s) perspective
Care coordination is any activity that helps ensure that the patient's needs and preferences for health services and information sharing across people, functions, sites are met over time. Patients perceive failures in terms of unreasonable levels of effort required on the part of themselves or their informal caregivers in order to meet care needs during transitions among healthcare entities	Clinical coordination involves determining where to send the patient next (e.g., sequencing among specialists), what information about the patient is necessary to transfer among healthcare entities, and how accountability and responsibility are managed among all healthcare professionals (doctors, nurses, social workers, care managers, supporting staff, etc.). Care coordination addresses potential gaps in meeting patients' interrelated medical, social, developmental, behavioral, educational, informal support system, and financial needs in order to achieve optimal health, wellness, or end-of-life outcomes, according to patient preferences	Care coordination is the responsibility of any system of care (e.g., accountable care organization [ACO]) to deliberately integrate personnel, information, and other resources needed to carry out all required patient care activities between and among care participants, including the patient and informal caregivers. The goal of care coordination is to facilitate the appropriate and efficient delivery of healthcare services both within and across systems

Adapted from "Chapter 2. What is Care Coordination?" in *Care Coordination Measures Atlas Update* by Agency for Healthcare Research and Quality, 2014, Retrieved from https://www.ahrq.gov/professionals/prevention-chronic-care/improve/coordination/atlas2014/chapter2.html

member with social and environmental concerns that may hinder or delay improvement in the medical condition. CM and CC help the patient navigate through complex systems or different organizations and avoid the fragmentation or misutilization of services. CM and CC are functions that work at both the system and the individual patient level. Frequent communication between and among the patient, the providers of care, and the case manager or care coordinator are essential.

Key components of a CM and CC program include the following:

- Screening and identification of conditions, populations, individual patients, and disease states for early detection of health problems
- Identifying and implementing effective interventions for individuals using evidence-based medicine and removing social environmental barriers to care
- Promoting and coordinating a collaborative team approach across various disciplines and levels of care
- Coordinating continuity of care through the course of the disease or condition to attain the best possible clinical outcome and improve quality of life
- Coordinating support and education for the patient, patient's family, and others involved in the patient's care to improve and sustain self-management behaviors and quality of life

- Ensuring that all providers of care and the patient know the care plan, have input into the care plan, and get regular reports on the progress of the patient according to the care plan

At times, CM has been seen as more of a payer or health plan function, as CC was seen as aligned with the functions and processes offered by a healthcare provider, but these lines have blurred as the healthcare system evolved with increasing integration of payer and provider roles as well as alternative payment models which promote the management of both care and utilization processes, e.g., DRGs, fixed payment models, and accountable care organizations. AHRQ notes that while all patients are likely to benefit from the basic elements of care coordination such as effective communication and the efficient exchange of information among care providers, from an efficiency standpoint, healthcare providers need to understand basic triage and stratification to determine which patients would likely benefit from higher levels of intensive CM and CC [14]. This requirement is particularly important for high-risk or high-cost populations.

It should be noted that paying for the staff who deliver the CM and CC services is viewed from the health plan side as part of the operational requirement. However, on the healthcare provider side in a fee-for-service environment, paying for additional staff and services essential to CM and CC remains problematic (hence the widespread enthusiasm for alternative payment models that may create a path forward to support healthcare provider CM and CC approaches).

Care Plans: A Key Document

> The formulation of a proactive plan of care is an essential element of case management and care coordination. CMS's definition of case management services (42 CFR §440.169(d)(2)) includes the…development and periodic revision of a specific care plan based on the information collected through an assessment or reassessment that specifies goals and actions to address the medical, social, educational needs, and other services needed by the eligible individual, including activities such as ensuring the active participation of the eligible individual and working with the individual (or the individual's authorized healthcare decision maker) and others to develop those goals and identify a course of action to respond to the assessed needs of the eligible individual [15].

The care plan for case management is usually individualized for the patient. The following process is an example of how an individual care plan is developed.

1. Identify the patient who needs a case management care plan. This may be done through the use of claims data, predictive modeling, or other sources of information.
2. Assign a case manager and or care coordinator to the patient.
3. Identify the diagnosis of the patient and how the case was referred.

4. Initiate patient assessment. This can be done using proprietary or off-the-shelf programs. The assessment should be for the patient's specific medical condition.
5. Coordinate with the providers of care after the assessment to determine their input to the assessment and a plan of care.
6. Develop a care plan, utilizing the inputs from the patient, the provider, and the other identified stakeholders of the patient. This care plan includes patient-identified areas for improvement and motivation to improve and provider-identified milestones of care that will get the member to the best outcome. Additionally, it is best to identify processes that will remove nonclinical obstacles that will be barriers to the success of the patient and the care plan.
7. Communicate the care plan to the patient, provider, and other stakeholders under HIPAA requirements and get their sign-off.
8. Continuously update the care plan and the progress made, changing it as needed with inputs from the patient, the provider, and the stakeholders.
9. Identify timeline and outcomes for the complete case management care plan.

Having an electronic or web-based system to produce, disseminate, and update the care plan makes it easier to be successful in meeting the case management goals and the objectives for the patient.

Accreditation and Regulatory Oversight of Utilization Management and Care Coordination

UM programs are subject to regulatory oversight that ensures that they are not limiting or inappropriately denying the use of healthcare by patients. The federal government has specific requirements for participation in Medicare that pertain to UM programs by vendors. Well-known accrediting organizations including, but not limited to, the Joint Commission, the American Association of Ambulatory Healthcare (AAAHC), the Utilization Review Accreditation Commission (URAC), and the National Committee for Quality Assurance (NCQA) each have standards related to UM, CM, and CC. Some of the accrediting organizations may certify the individual UM, CM, and CC programs as stand-alone entities and, depending on the organizational structure, may also include these elements as part of an integrated healthcare organization certification process (see Chap. 10). Table 7.5 lists the categories of assessment of a UM program for which URAC and NCQA have developed standards [16, 17]. Each of these categories has subcategories that further refine the standards for accreditation (see Appendices A and B).

URAC and the Case Management Society of America (CMSA) have developed standards or guiding principles for case management as well [18, 19].

URAC Case Management Accreditation Assessment Categories
- Case Management Program
- Case Management Staff
- Case Management Process
- Reporting Performance Measures to URAC
- Optional Designation: Transitions of Care

Adapted from Case Management Accreditation. In Utilization Review Accreditation Commission (URAC) Standards and Measures at a Glance, 2019, Retrieved from https://www.urac.org/standards-and-measures-glance. Copyright 2019 by URAC. Adapted with permission.

CMSA Guiding Principles for Case Management
- Use a patient-centric, collaborative partnership approach that is responsive to the individual patient's culture, preferences, needs, and values.
- Facilitate self-determination and self-management through the tenets of advocacy, shared and informed decision-making, counseling, and health education.
- Use a comprehensive, holistic, and compassionate approach to care delivery which integrates a patient's medical, behavioral, social, psychological, functional, and other needs.
- Practice cultural and linguistic sensitivity and maintain current knowledge of diverse populations within practice demographics.
- Implement evidence-based care guidelines as available and applicable to the practice setting and/or patient population served.
- Promote optimal patient safety at the individual, organizational, and community level.
- Promote the integration of behavioral change science and principles throughout the case management process.
- Facilitate awareness of and connections with community supports and resources.
- Foster safe and manageable navigation through the healthcare system to enhance the patient's timely access to services and the achievement of successful outcomes.
- Pursue professional knowledge and practice excellence and maintain competence in case management and health and human service delivery.
- Support systematic approaches to quality management and health outcomes improvement, implementation of practice innovations, and dissemination of knowledge and practice to the healthcare community.
- Maintain compliance with federal, state, and local rules and regulations and organizational, accreditation, and certification standards.

(continued)

> • Demonstrate knowledge, skills, and competency in the application of case management standards of practice and relevant codes of ethics and professional conduct.
>
> From Standards of Practice of Case Managers, pp. 12–13. Reprinted with permission, the Case Management Society of America, 6301 Ranch Drive, Little Rock, AR 72223, www.cmsa.org.

Table 7.5 Utilization management accreditation categories of assessment for organizations

NCQA utilization management accreditation measures	URAC utilization management accreditation measures
UM structure	Review criteria
Clinical criteria for UM decisions	Accessibility of review services
Communication services	On-site review services
Appropriate professionals	Initial screening
Timeliness of UM decisions	Initial clinical review
Clinical information	Peer clinical review
Denial notices	Peer-to-peer conversation
Policies for appeals	Time frames for initial UM decision
Appropriate handling of appeals	Notice of certification decisions
Evaluation of new technology	Notice of non-certification decisions
Satisfaction with the UM process	UM policy
Triage and referral for Behavioral Health care	Information upon which UM is conducted
Delegation of UM	UM appeals

Reproduced with permission from *A Summary of What NCQA Looks for When it Reviews an Organization* webpage by the National Committee for Quality Assurance (NCQA). Source: http://www.ncqa.org/tabid/413/Default.aspx. Last accessed: December 2017; and Adapted from *Health Utilization Management Accreditation, Version 7.3*, by Utilization Review Accreditation Commission (URAC), Retrieved from https://www.urac.org/standards-and-measures-glance, Copyright 2018 by URAC. Adapted with permission

Based on their guiding principles, the CMSA has established 13 standards of practice for case management and care coordination professionals to follow in their work [19]. See Table 7.6.

Frameworks for Understanding UM and CC

Evidence-Based Medicine and Evidence-Based Management Process

Stephen Shortell developed a process of care that links evidence-based medicine and evidence-based management [20]. According to the process, the two components necessary to improve the quality of medical care are advances in

Table 7.6 CMSA standards of practice for case management and care coordination professionals

Standard	Case manager action
Patient selection process for professional case management services	Identify those who are appropriate for and most likely to benefit from case management services available within a particular practice setting
Patient assessment	Complete a thorough individualized assessment that takes into account the unique cultural and linguistic needs of that patient
Care needs and opportunities identification	Identify care needs or opportunities that would benefit from case management interventions
Planning	Identify relevant care goals and interventions to manage patient's identified care needs and opportunities; document these in an individualized case management plan of care
Monitoring	Employ ongoing assessment with appropriate documentation to measure the patient's response to the plan of care
Outcomes	Maximize the patient's health, wellness, safety, physical functioning, adaptation, health knowledge, coping with chronic illness, engagement, and self-management abilities
Closure of professional case management services	Appropriately complete closure of case management services based upon established case closure guidelines
Facilitation, coordination, and collaboration	Facilitate coordination, communication, and collaboration with the patient, patient's family or family caregiver, involved members of the interprofessional healthcare team, and other stakeholders, in order to achieve target goals and maximize positive patient care outcomes
Qualifications for professional case managers	Maintain competence in her/his area(s) of practice by having one of the following:
	Current, active, and unrestricted licensure or certification in a health or human services discipline that allows the professional to conduct an assessment independently as permitted within the scope of practice of the discipline
	In a state that does not require licensure or certification, the individual must have a baccalaureate or graduate degree in social work or another health or human services field that promotes the physical, psychosocial, and/or vocational well-being of the persons being served
	The individual must have completed a supervised field experience in case management, health, or behavioral health as part of the degree requirements
Legal	Adhere to all applicable federal, state, and local laws and regulations, which have full force and effect of law, governing all aspects of case management practice including, but not limited to:
	Confidentiality and Patient Privacy: Adhere to federal, state, and local laws, as well as policies and procedures, governing patient privacy and confidentiality, and act in a manner consistent with the patient's best interest in all aspects of communication and recordkeeping
	Consent for Professional Case Management Services: Obtain appropriate consent before the implementation of case management services

(continued)

Table 7.6 (continued)

Standard	Case manager action
Ethics	Behave and practice ethically and adhere to the tenets of the code of ethics that underlie her/his professional credentials
Advocacy	Advocate for the patient, patient's family or family caregiver, at the service delivery, benefits administration, and policy-making levels
Cultural competency	Maintain awareness of and be responsive to cultural and linguistic diversity of the demographics of her/his work setting and to the specific patient and/or caregiver needs
Resource management and stewardship	Integrate factors related to quality, safety, access, and cost-effectiveness in assessing, planning, implementing, monitoring, and evaluation health resources for patient care
Professional responsibilities and scholarship	Engage in scholarly activities and maintain familiarity with current knowledge, competencies, case management-related research, and evidence-supported care innovations, etc. Identify best practices in case management and healthcare service delivery and apply such in transforming practice, as appropriate.

From Standards of Practice of Case Managers, pp. 20–30. Reprinted with permission, the Case Management Society of America, 6301 Ranch Drive, Little Rock, AR 72223, www.cmsa.org

evidence-based medicine that identify clinical practices leading to better care, including the content of providing care, and the knowledge of how to put evidence-based medicine into routine practice. These include disease registries, clinical guidelines, reminder systems, patient self-management education, physician feedback reports, and healthcare teams. The development of these techniques is enhanced by evidence-based management. Evidence-based management uses knowledge from human factors, high-reliability organizations, changes in organizational culture, development of high-performing teams, identification and correction of mistakes, and the continuous asking of and learning from how an organization improves.

T3 Translational Science

Complementary to this evidence-based medicine and management approach is the notion of *translational science*, where the findings from basic and controlled clinical trials are applied in the real-world setting [21]. In this translational framework, basic science answers the question, "What to do?" and is called T1; clinical effectiveness research answers the question, "Who benefits?" and is called T2. The applied translational work rooted in quality management and operations is called T3 work and addresses the question, "How best to deliver high-quality care to patients and families?" According to Dougherty and Conway, T3 work relies on having a shared leadership model among professionals, a focus on teamwork, an information system that provides essential data to plan and manage the initiatives, and the financial resources to implement all of the tasks and functions necessary to deliver the right care, to the right patient, at the right time [21].

Best Clinical and Administrative Practices Quality Framework

Closely aligned with evidenced-based management principles, T3 translational work is the approach popularized by the Center for Healthcare Strategies for Medicaid managed care organizations called the *Best Clinical and Administrative Practices (BCAP) Quality Framework* [22]. The BCAP framework is fundamentally based on a systematic assessment process that identifies the relevant population; stratifies the population based on risk, severity, or priority; conducts outreach to the targeted population; and finally, delivers interventions that are likely to achieve the desired change in outcome. The BCAP framework, now in its second decade of use, has been widely adopted by Medicaid managed care organizations and is credited with:

- Creating a culture of change and improvement
- Leveraging and building organizational infrastructure and care management programs (i.e., case management and care coordination)
- Facilitating the sharing of best practices among organizations
- Promoting standardization and efficiency
- Improving quality, customer satisfaction, financial, and clinical outcomes [22]

Evidence-based medicine, evidence-based management, T3, and BCAP are all part of the organizational processes that promote change and care transformation. Understanding the underlying models of care delivery is also essential to change and care transformation in care delivery practices. Care delivery impacts providers, patients, payers, and other stakeholders of healthcare, and two relevant models that make full use of UM and CC processes are discussed below, namely, the chronic care model and the patient-centered medical home.

Chronic Care Model

The chronic care model [23] has become a touchstone of care for people with any condition that requires ongoing self-management and interaction with the healthcare system. The model can be applied to systems and patients across various chronic illnesses. The systems that use this form of care delivery range in size from large multihospital healthcare organizations to single practitioner practices. Figure 7.4 illustrates the key elements of the chronic care model that lead to improved outcomes for chronically ill patients.

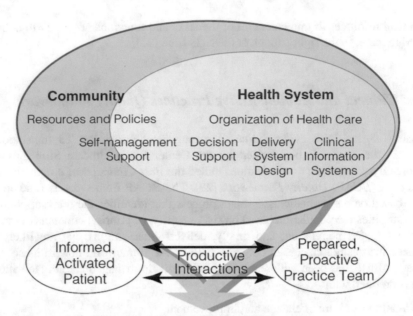

Functional and Clinical Outcomes

Fig. 7.4 Chronic care model components

Community = The model aims to mobilize community resources to meet the needs of patients, encourage patients to participate in effective community programs, partner with community organizations to support and to develop interventions that fill gaps in needed care and services, and advocate for policies and implementations that improve patient care.

Self-Management Support = This model empowers and prepares patients to manage their health and health care and emphasizes patients' central role in managing their health using effective self-management support strategies that include assessment, goal setting, action planning, problem solving, and follow-up.

Health System = This element aims to create the culture, organization, and mechanisms that promote safe, high-quality care through open encouragement and systematic handling of errors and quality concerns to improve care.

Decision Support = The model promotes clinical care that is consistent with scientific evidence and patient preferences. Patients should receive information about evidence-based guidelines to encourage their participation.

Delivery System Design = The model aims to assure the delivery of effective, efficient clinical care and self-management support through defining roles for each healthcare team member and through distributing tasks among team members who follow patients on a regular basis. The care delivered should be culturally sensitive and easily understood by the patient.

Clinical Information Systems = The model aims to organize patient and population data to facilitate efficient and effective care, make sure that the clinicians use timely reminders for patients and themselves, identify relevant subpopulations for proactive care, facilitate individual patient care planning and monitoring, share information with patients and providers to coordinate care, and continuously monitor the performance of the practice team and the care system.

Informed, Activated Patient = Patient who is aware and informed about their clinical circumstances and who is engaged with their healthcare provider to consider options and determine an appropriate course of action and is motivated to adhere to an agreed upon care plan.

Prepared, Proactive Practice Team = Healthcare provider who receives and reviews actionable data and reports that relate to specific patients and the patient population they serve. The provider

Patient-Centered Medical Home Model

The medical home is another model that has been around for some time and has been modified over the years by several organizations. Initially proposed by the American Academy of Pediatrics, the medical home is defined as an ideal manner of delivering primary care, characterized by care that is organized and "...accessible, continuous, comprehensive, family centered, coordinated, and compassionate...in an atmosphere of mutual responsibility and trust among clinicians, every child and adolescent, and caregiver(s)." [24, 25] The patient-centered medical home is defined as an approach to providing comprehensive primary care for children, youth, and adults. In this model, primary care is provided in a way that facilitates partnerships between individual patients and their personal physicians, broader care team, and when appropriate, the patient's family. The following is a slightly abridged version of the shared principles, as described by the Primary Care Collaborative, for primary care within advanced primary care models, including the medical home model. Approximately 350 organizations have signed on to this vision for primary care [26]:

1. *Person and Family Centered.* Primary care is focused on the whole person—their physical, emotional, psychological, and spiritual well-being, as well as cultural, linguistic, and social needs—and is grounded in mutually beneficial partnerships among clinicians, staff, individuals, and their families as equal members of the care team. Care delivery is customized based on individual and family strengths, preferences, values, goals, and experiences using strategies such as care planning and shared decision-making.
2. *Continuous.* Dynamic, trusted, respectful, and enduring relationships between individuals, families, and their clinical team members are hallmarks of primary care. There is continuity in relationships and in knowledge of the individual and their family or care partners that provides perspective and context throughout all stages of life including end-of-life care.
3. *Comprehensive and Equitable.* Primary care addresses the whole person with appropriate clinical and supportive services that include acute, chronic, and preventive care, behavioral and mental health, oral health, health promotion, and more, either in the practice's clinics or in collaboration with other clinicians outside the clinic. Providers seek out the impact of social determinants of health and societal inequities, and care delivery is tailored accordingly.

Fig. 7.4 (continued) has access and uses standardized care plans, evidence-based guidelines, and available resource referrals for additional support.
Productive Interactions = Information is shared between the patient and healthcare provider in a way that promotes attitudes, actions, and behavior changes that move toward relevant, effective care plans that are achievable.
Outcomes = The end result of care processes, e.g., blood sugar control in a diabetic patient. Reprinted from "Chronic Disease Management: What Will It Take to Improve Care for Chronic Illness?," by EH Wagner, 1998, *Effective Clinical Practice*, *1*(1), p. 3. Copyright 1998 by American College of Physicians–American Society of Internal Medicine. Reprinted with permission.

4. *Team Based and Collaborative.* Interdisciplinary teams, including individuals and families, work collaboratively and dynamically toward a common goal. The services they provide and the coordinated manner in which they work together are synergistic to better health.

5. *Coordinated and Integrated.* Primary care integrates the activities of those involved in an individual's care, across settings and services, and proactively communicates across the spectrum of care and collaborators, including individuals and their families or care partners. Primary care is actively engaged in transitions of care to achieve better health and seamless care delivery across the life span.

6. *Accessible.* Primary care is readily accessible, both in person and virtually, for all individuals regardless of linguistic, literacy, socioeconomic, cognitive, or physical barriers. As the first source of care, clinicians and staff are available and responsive when, where, and how individuals and families need them. Individuals are provided with easy, routine access to their health information.

7. *High Value.* Primary care achieves excellent, equitable outcomes for individuals and families, including using healthcare resources wisely and considering costs to patients, payers, and the system. Practices employ a systematic approach to measuring, reporting, and improving population health, quality, safety, and health equity.

A number of standards and external recognitions are available to practices that adopt the principles and operational strategies that underlie a patient-centered medical home. First, the Medical Home Index (MHI) is available free of charge from the Center for Medical Home Improvement and is a validated self-assessment and classification tool that measures broad indicators of observable, tangible behaviors and the process of care that represents *medical homeness* in the primary care setting [26]. The MHI assesses six domains: organizational capacity, chronic condition management, care coordination, community outreach, data management, and quality improvement and change, providing numeric scores for each domain and ranking the level of performance on a 4-point scale [27].

Secondly, NCQA provides a recognition program for PCMHs that has been widely adopted by more than 12,000 practices in the USA, representing 60,000 clinicians, and is supported by over 100 payers who provide incentive payments and coaching for practices recognized as medical homes by the NCQA [28]. The 2017 NCQA recognition program evaluates performance measures in six broad areas [28]:

- Team-based care and practice organization
- Knowing and managing patients
- Patient-centered access and continuity
- Care management and support
- Care coordination and care transitions
- Performance measurement and quality improvement

URAC also provides a certification process for PCMHs that evaluates practices within six focus areas: practice culture and patient centeredness, electronic capabilities, access to healthcare services, coordinated quality care, performance monitoring and improvement, and reporting performance measures [29]. URAC has identified essential standard elements needed for sustainable transformation from a physician practice or healthcare clinic into a patient-centered medical home; a URAC-certified PCMH:

- Provides enhanced access to primary care
- Improves delivery of preventive services
- Helps patients make healthy lifestyle choices
- Uses the latest health information technology and evidence-based medical approaches
- Reduces emergency room visits and hospitalizations
- Improves care coordination
- Provides high-quality disease management [29]

The value of recognition or certification as a medical home has been assessed as well. Participation in a medical home certification or recognition program clearly provides technical assistance and focus to the structure and delivery of a UM and CC program and helps champions within a practice setting or organization set priorities [30]. Additionally, depending on the payer market place, having a recognized or certified medical home may provide financial benefits to the provider which helps offset the investment of resources, at times considerable in terms of time and effort, to achieve that designation. Finally, once the recognition or certification is achieved, maintaining that status drives attention to quality measures and compliance with standards pertaining to "care coordination, access to care, patient-centeredness, comprehensiveness of care, and systems based on quality and safety." [30]

The Primary Care Collaborative (formerly Patient-Centered Primary Care Collaborative) released its analysis of 45 reports from peer-reviewed literature published in 2016 which showed that there is a growing body of literature that reports a positive effect on care delivery in cost, quality, and utilization [31] (see Fig. 7.5). The results are not unanimous; however, the analysis showed that the longer a practice has been operating as a patient-centered medical home, and the higher the medical complexity of the patient population being cared for, the more significant were the positive effects measured, especially in the cost savings realm.

Future Trends

Currently, UM is understood as not being a stand-alone process and, instead, is best combined with related quality, patient safety, and patient activation strategies to be successful. Information technology will likely streamline the processes of UM and enable CC. Having web-based capability with instant approval or denial logic embedded in the software will allow the processes to be more user-friendly and efficient and will help patients receive their clinical interventions in a timely fashion. Information flow will also decrease waste such as duplicate testing and consults

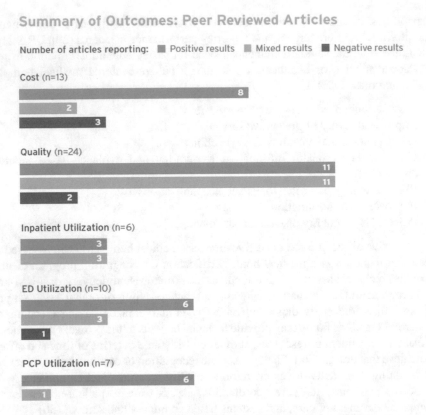

Fig. 7.5 Forty-five peer-reviewed articles published in 2016 report that patient-centered care delivery results in positive effects on cost, quality, and utilization. Reprinted from *The Impact of Primary Care Practice Transformation on Cost, Quality, and Utilization: A Systematic Review of Research Published in 2016 Executive Summary*, by Y Jabbarpour, et al., 2017, Primary Care Collaborative (formerly Patient-Centered Primary Care Collaborative) and Robert Graham Center. Retrieved from https://www.pcpcc.org/resource/impact-primary-care-practice-transformation-cost-quality-and-utilization. Reprinted with permission

as well as facilitate coordination and information sharing among providers and between providers and patients. Rapid data analysis can then be used to inform care guidelines, provider productivity, and patient safety initiatives.

The priorities that emerge from the transition from FFS to more value-based initiatives will likely impact the future of UM and CC. Programs will identify monitors and indicators of utilization such as referrals per thousand, high-cost diagnostic procedures per thousand, admissions to inpatient facilities per thousand, and the overall use of healthcare dollars per patient. These measures, when shared with providers, along with the relevant cost data, will likely have an impact on how providers practice and influence their use of evidenced-based medicine. Table 7.7 describes strategies and recommendations for care management that are also applicable to the combined case management (CM) and care coordination (CC) efforts discussed in this chapter.

Table 7.7 Key care management strategies and recommendations

Strategy	Recommendations for medical practice	Recommendations for health policy	Recommendations for health services research
Identify populations with modifiable risks	Use multiple metrics to identify patients with modifiable risks	Consider return on investment of providing CM services to patients with a broad set of eligibility requirements	Determine the benefits to different patient segments from CM services
	Develop risk-based approaches to identity patients most in need of care management (CM) services	Establish metrics to identify and track CM outcomes to determine success	Investigate the understanding of and parameters affecting modifiable risks.
		Implement value-based payment methodologies through State and Federal tax incentives to practices for achieving the triple aim	Develop/refine tools for risk stratification
			Develop predictive models to support risk stratification
Align CM services to the needs of the population	Tailor CM services, with input from patients, to meet specific needs of populations with different modifiable risks	Incentivize CM services through CMS transitional CM and chronic care coordination billing codes	Evaluate initiatives seeking to foster care alignment across providers
	Use EMR to facilitate care coordination and effective communication with patients and outreach to them	Provide variety of financial and non-financial supports to develop, implement and sustain CM	Create a framework for aligning CM services across the medical neighborhood to reduce potentially harmful duplication of these services
		Reward CM programs that achieve the triple aim	Determine how best to implement CM services across the spectrum of long-term services and supports
Identify and train personnel appropriate to the needed CM services	Determine who should provide CM services given population needs and practice context	Incentivize care manager training through loans or tuition subsidies	Determine what team-building activities best support delivery of CM services
	Identify needed skills, appropriate training, and licensure requirements	Develop CM certification programs that recognize functional expertise	Design protocols for workflow that accommodate CM services in different contexts
	Implement interprofessional team-based approaches to care[23]		Develop models for interprofessional education that bridge trainees at all levels and practicing health care professionals

Note: The term "care management" as used in this table is similar to how this chapter uses the combination of case management and care coordination. Reprinted from *Care Management: Implications for Medical Practice, Health Policy, and Health Services Research*, by T Farrell, et al., 2015, Retrieved from https://www.ahrq.gov/sites/default/files/publications/files/caremgmt-brief.pdf.

Appendices

Appendix A

HEALTH UTILIZATION MANAGEMENT V7.3

ORGANIZATIONAL STRUCTURE
CORE 1: Organizational Structure
CORE 2: Organization Documents

POLICIES AND PROCEDURES
CORE 3: Policy and Procedure Maintenance, Review and Approval

REGULATORY COMPLIANCE
CORE 4: Regulatory Compliance

INTER-DEPARTMENTAL COORDINATION
CORE 5: Inter-Departmental Coordination

OVERSIGHT OF DELEGATED FUNCTIONS
CORE 6: Delegation Review Criteria
CORE 7: Delegation Review
CORE 8: Delegation Contracts
CORE 9: Delegation Oversight

MARKETING AND SALES COMMUNICATIONS
CORE 10: Review of Marketing and Sales Materials

BUSINESS RELATIONSHIPS
CORE 11: Written Business Agreements
CORE 12: Client Satisfaction

INFORMATION MANAGEMENT
CORE 13: Information Management
CORE 14: Business Continuity
CORE 15: Information Confidentiality and Security
CORE 16: Confidentiality of Individually-Identifiable Health Information

QUALITY MANAGEMENT
CORE 17: Quality Management Program
CORE 18: Quality Management Program Resources
CORE 19: Quality Management Program Requirements
CORE 20: Quality Management Committee
CORE 21: Quality Management Documentation
CORE 22: Quality Improvement Projects
CORE 23: Quality Improvement Project Requirements
CORE 24: Quality Improvement Projects: Consumer Organizations

STAFF QUALIFICATIONS
CORE 25: Job Descriptions
CORE 26: Staff Qualifications

STAFF MANAGEMENT
CORE 27: Staff Training Program
CORE 28: Staff Operational Tools and Support
CORE 29: Staff Assessment Program

Reprinted from Health Utilization Management Accreditation. In Utilization Review Accreditation Commission (URAC) Standards and Measures at a Glance, 2019, Retrieved from https://www.urac.org/standards-and-measures-glance. Copyright 2019 by URAC. Reprinted with permission.

Appendix B

A Summary of What NCQA Looks for When It Reviews an Organization

Utilization Management (UM)

1. UM Structure (UM 1)

   - Does the organization have a written description of its program for managing care?
   - Is the program evaluated and approved annually?
   - Is a senior physician involved in the program's operation?
   - Are behavioral health aspects described in the program description, and if so, is a behavioral health practitioner involved in them?

2. Clinical Criteria for UM Decisions (UM 2)

   - Are criteria and procedures for approving and denying care clearly documented?
   - Are practitioners involved in procedures development?
   - Does the organization review and revise criteria regularly?
   - Can practitioners obtain the criteria upon request?
   - Does the organization evaluate the consistency with which the criteria are applied?

3. Communication Services (UM 3)

   - Are UM staff accessible to practitioners and members to discuss UM issues?

4. Appropriate Professionals (UM 4)

   - Do qualified health professionals oversee all review decisions?
   - Does an appropriate practitioner review any denial of care based on medical necessity?
   - Does the organization have written job description with qualification for practitioners that review denials of care based on medical necessity?

5. Timeliness of UM Decisions (UM 5)

   - Does the organization make decisions regarding coverage within the time frames specified in NCQA's standards and guidelines?
   - Does the organization notify members and practitioners of coverage decisions within the required time frames?

6. Clinical Information (UM 6)

   - When determining whether to approve or deny coverage based on medical necessity, does the organization gather relevant information and consult with the treating physician?
   - Does the organization assist with a member's transition to other care when benefits end?

7. Denial Notices (UM 7)

- Does the organization clearly communicate the reason for denial of service in writing to both the members and treating practitioners?
- Does the organization provide the treating practitioner with the opportunity to discuss the reason for the denial with the organization's appropriate practitioner reviewer?
- Is the appeal process outlined clearly in all denial notifications?

8. Policies for Appeals (UM 8)

- Does the organization have written policies and procedures for the appropriate handling of preservice, post-service, and expedited members' appeals?
- Does the organization have procedures for providing member access to all documents relevant to an appeal and provide members with the opportunity to submit comments, documents, or other information relating to an appeal?
- Are appeal reviewers disinterested parties (i.e., not involved in the initial denial decision)?
- Are same-or-similar-specialty reviewers (i.e., practitioners in the same or a similar specialty who treat the condition under appeal) involved in appeals?
- Does the organization have procedures for allowing an authorized representative to act on behalf of a member?
- Are members notified of further appeal rights?

9. Appropriate Handling of Appeals (UM 9)

- Does the organization have a full and fair process for resolving member appeals?
- Does the organization follow the policies outlined in UM 8?

10. Evaluation of New Technology (UM 10)

- Does the plan have a written description of the process it uses to determine whether or not it will cover new medical technologies or new applications of existing technologies, and has it implemented the process?

11. Satisfaction with the UM Process (UM 11)

- Does the organization evaluate member and practitioner satisfaction with its process for determining coverage, and does it address areas of dissatisfaction?

12. Triage and Referral for Behavioral Healthcare (UM 14)

- Does the organization prioritize or make referrals for behavioral healthcare based on accepted definitions for the level of urgency and setting?
- Depending on the case, are these decisions made by qualified staff or a behavioral health professional?

13. Delegation of UM (UM 15)

- If the organization delegates decisions on approval or denial of coverage to a third party, is the decision-making process—including the responsibilities of the organization and the delegated party—clearly documented?
- Does the organization evaluate and approve the delegated party's plan on a regular basis?

Reproduced with permission from *A Summary of What NCQA Looks for When It Reviews an Organization* by the National Committee for Quality Assurance (NCQA). Source: http://www.ncqa.org/tabid/413/Default.aspx. Last accessed: December 2017.

References

1. Institute of Medicine (1989) Controlling costs and changing patient care?: the role of utilization management. The National Academies Press, Washington, DC
2. American College of Medical Quality (2005) Core curriculum for medical quality management. Jones and Bartlett, Sudbury
3. Singer S, Bergthold L, Vorhaus C, Olson S, Mutchnick I, Goh YY, Zimmerman S, Enthoven A (1999) Decreasing variation in medical necessity decision. In: Final report to the California healthcare foundation, grant number 98–5021, Center for Health Policy, Stanford University. https://www.chcf.org/wp-content/uploads/2017/12/PDF-medicalnec.pdf
4. Milliman, Inc (2019) Milliman care guidelines register. https://www.mcg.com/care-guidelines/care-guidelines/
5. Qualis Health (2008) McKesson releases InterQual Criteria Version 3.0 register. https://www.changehealthcare.com/solutions/interqual
6. Centers for Medicaid and Medicare Services (2019) Medicare fee for service recovery audit program. https://www.cms.gov/Research-Statistics-Data-and-Systems/Monitoring-Programs/Medicare-FFS-Compliance-Programs/Recovery-Audit-Program/
7. Social Security Board (1983) Social Security Act. Section 1893, Medicare integrity program. https://www.ssa.gov/OP_Home/ssact/title18/1893.htm
8. Agency for Healthcare Research and Quality (2016) The toolkit for using the AHRQ quality indicators: how to improve hospital quality and safety. https://www.ahrq.gov/professionals/systems/hospital/qitoolkit/index.html
9. Texas Office of Inspector General (OIG) (2016) Overview of hospital utilization review. https://oig.hhsc.texas.gov/sites/oig/files/documents/Overview-of-Hospital-Utilization-Review.pdf
10. MCG Health (2019) Industry-leading informed healthcare strategies. https://www.mcg.com/care-guidelines/care-guidelines/
11. Agency for Healthcare Research and Quality (2014) Chapter 1: Background. In: Care coordination measures atlas update. https://www.ahrq.gov/professionals/prevention-chronic-care/improve/coordination/atlas2014/chapter1.html
12. Agency for Healthcare Research and Quality (2014) Chapter 2: What is care coordination? In: Care coordination measures atlas update. https://www.ahrq.gov/professionals/prevention-chronic-care/improve/coordination/atlas2014/chapter2.html
13. Case Management Society of America (2010) What is a case manager? http://www.cmsa.org/who-we-are/what-is-a-case-manager/
14. Farrell T, Tomoaia-Cotisel A, Scammon D, Day J, Day R, Magill M. Care Management: Implications for Medical Practice, health Policy, and Health Services Research (2015)

Prepared by Econometrica, Inc. under Contract No. HHSA2902007 TO No. 5 (eds) AHRQ Publication No. 15-0018-EF. Rockville: Agency for Healthcare Research and Quality. https://www.ahrq.gov/sites/default/files/publications/files/caremgmt-brief.pdf

15. Agency for Healthcare Research and Quality (2014) Table 3: Relation between the care coordination measurement framework and other key sources. In: Care coordination measures atlas update. https://www.ahrq.gov/professionals/prevention-chronic-care/improve/coordination/atlas2014/chapter3tab3.html

16. Utilization Review Accreditation Commission (URAC) (2018) Health utilization management accreditation, Version 7.3. https://www.urac.org/sites/default/files/standards_measures/pdf/Health%20Utilization%20Management%20v7.3%20Standards%20at%20a%20Glance.pdf

17. National Committee for Quality Assurance (NCQA). A summary of what NCQA looks for when it reviews an organization. http://www.ncqa.org/tabid/413/Default.aspx

18. Utilization Review Accreditation Commission (URAC) (2018) Case management accreditation, Version 6.0. https://www.urac.org/sites/default/files/standards_measures/pdf/Case%20Management%20v6.0%20Standards%20Only.pdf

19. Case Management of America (CMSA) (2016) Standards of practice of case managers. https://www.miccsi.org/wp-content/uploads/2017/03/CMSA-Standards-2016.pdf

20. Shortell SM, Rundall TG, Hsu J (2007) Improving patient care by linking evidence-based medicine and evidence-based management. JAMA 298(6):673–676. https://doi.org/10.1001/jama.298.6.673

21. Dougherty D, Conway PH (2008) The "3Ts" road map to transform US health care: the "how" of high-quality care. JAMA 299(19):2319–2321

22. Center for Health Care Strategies, Inc (2006) A guide to the BCAP quality framework. https://www.chcs.org/resource/bcap-quality-framework/

23. Wagner EH (1998) Chronic disease management: what will it take to improve care for chronic illness? Eff Clin Pract 1(1):2–4

24. American Academy of Pediatrics (1992) Ad hoc task force on definition of the medical home. Pediatrics 90:774. http://pediatrics.aappublications.org/content/pediatrics/90/5/774.full.pdf

25. American Academy of Pediatrics (2002) Policy statement: the medical home. Pediatrics 110:1. http://pediatrics.aappublications.org/content/pediatrics/110/1/184.full.pdf

26. Primary Care Collaborative (2017) Shared principles of primary care. https://www.pcpcc.org/about/shared-principles

27. Center for Medical Home Improvement (2006) The medical home index: pediatric. Measuring the organization and delivery of pediatric primary care for all children, youth and families. https://medicalhomeinfo.aap.org/tools-resources/Documents/CMHI-MHI-Pediatric_Full-Version.pdf

28. National Committee for Quality Assurance (NCQA) (2008) Standards and guidelines for accreditation. http://www.ncqa.org/tabid/691/Default.aspx. Accessed 16 Oct 2008

29. URAC Releases Standards for Patient Centered Medical Home Certification (2017) URAC organization. https://www.urac.org/press-room/urac-releases-standards-patient-centered-medical-home-certification. Accessed 22 Feb 2017

30. Kreimer S (2015) PCMH accreditation: is it worth it? Medical economics. https://www.medicaleconomics.com/health-law-policy/pcmh-accreditation-it-worth-it. Accessed 2 July 2015

31. Jabbarpour Y, De Marchis E, Bazemore A, Grundy P (2016) The impact of primary care practice transformation on cost, quality, and utilization: a systematic review of research published in 2016. Executive summary. Primary care collaborative (formerly patient-centered primary care collaborative). Robert Graham Center. https://www.pcpcc.org/sites/default/files/resources/pcmh_evidence_es_071417%20FINAL.pdf

Additional Resources and Further Reading

Centers for Medicare and Medicaid Services, Medicare Learning Network (2017) Medicare parts A & B appeals process. https://www.cms.gov/Outreach-and-Education/Medicare-Learning-Network-MLN/MLNProducts/downloads/MedicareAppealsprocess.pdf. Accessed June 2017

Centers for Medicare and Medicaid Services (2017) Original medicare (Fee-for-service) appeals. https://www.cms.gov/Medicare/Appeals-and-Grievances/OrgMedFFSAppeals/index.html. Accessed Nov 2017

Institute of Medicine (US) Committee on the Health Professions Education Summit (2003) In: Greiner AC, Knebel E (eds) Health professions education: a bridge to quality. National Academies Press, Washington, DC

The SCAN Foundation (2013) Achieving person-centered care through care coordination. https://www.thescanfoundation.org/achieving-person-centered-care-through-care-coordination

Varkey P (ed) (2009) Medical quality management: theory and practice, 2nd edn. Boston, Jones and Bartlett Publishers

Chapter 8
Organization Design and Management

Robert McLean, Jennifer Hooks, and Carrie Guttman

Executive Summary

The inherent financial and service-driven complexities of the healthcare industry and its systems require a mosaic approach to organizational structures and processes. Healthcare institutions must develop organizational structures in response to the requirements of dynamic external and internal stakeholders whose interests and motives do not categorically coincide. Organizations must be structured to embody the specific needs of their identity and mission. Therefore, multiple structural approaches have evolved to accommodate the explicit concerns of organizations whether a large academic medical center, large group practice, smaller community hospital, or an integrated healthcare system.

As healthcare organizations examine how to design and adapt their management structures to ensure quality is being measured and improved, considerations around the functioning of systems and the management of change become crucial.

R. McLean (✉)
Yale New Haven Health System, New Haven, CT, USA

J. Hooks
Medical University of South Carolina, Charleston, SC, USA

C. Guttman
Northeast Medical Group of Yale New Haven Health, New Haven, CT, USA

© American College of Medical Quality (ACMQ) 2021
A. P. Giardino et al. (eds.), *Medical Quality Management*,
https://doi.org/10.1007/978-3-030-48080-6_8

Learning Objectives

Upon completion of this chapter, readers will be able to:

- Describe the basics of organizational systems
- Discuss the key concepts of a learning organization
- Understand the role of clinical microsystems
- Describe the elements of successful quality improvement teams
- Understand the critical responsibilities of leadership and boards in quality improvement

Sociological Background

Two landmark reports from the Institute of Medicine (IOM), *To Err is Human* [1] and *Crossing the Quality Chasm* [2], were critical in raising the importance of quality as a major issue and priority concern for the entire field – framing the problem in ways resonant with physicians and providing endorsement by an authoritative voice for industrial and systems-based approaches to be used to solve the "quality chasm."

In order to conceive an efficient, cohesive matrix for structure, there must be a clear vision and an understanding of how quality is defined within the organization using the IOM's domains of healthcare quality to establish a starting point [3]. The challenge organizations face is how to structure care delivery systems that deliver each of the domains both at scale and at the point of care level. A commitment to high-quality care means this applies to every patient, every time, regardless of age, gender, payer, culture, or race.

So what systems need to be put in place and how can this be ensured?

How Systems Are Organized

Donald Berwick explained how a deeper understanding of systems is needed if the goal is to improve the functioning of a system [3]. A system of work is defined as any set of activities with a common aim – whether in an office visit, a hospital stay, or a visit to a lab to get blood tests drawn. Each of those groups of activities involves many steps performed by different individuals behaving in ways for different reasons.

Once a healthcare system recognizes it needs improvement, it must have mechanisms in place to learn how it must change.

Learning Organizations

The concept of a learning organization as described by Peter Senge in *The Fifth Discipline: The Art and Practice of the Learning Organization* is "an organization that is continually expanding its capacity to create its future" [4]. Organizations learn when the individuals who comprise them learn. Shared learning then serves to build a collective by which organizational learning evolves and proves efficacious. Senge's theory incorporates five key disciplines for all learning organizations:

1. *Systems Thinking*: The ability to see the big picture.
2. *Personal Mastery*: Organizations learn only through individuals who learn, and individual commitment to learning must be continuous and lifelong.
3. *Mental Models*: There are deeply ingrained assumptions, generalizations, and images that influence how individuals understand the world around them. Learning organizations continually identify, evaluate, and improve its members' mental models.
4. *Shared Vision*: Organizations are formed by large numbers of individuals who must develop a shared sense of identity and vision for the entire organization.
5. *Team Learning*: Individuals must align and develop as teams to create the desired results for the larger organization [4].

The World Health Organization (WHO) describes systems thinking as

> an approach to problem solving that views 'problems' as part of a wider, dynamic system. Systems thinking involves much more than a reaction to present outcomes or events. It demands a deeper understanding of the linkages, relationships, interactions, and behaviors among the elements to characterize the entire system. [5]

Considerations for effective implementation of these concepts into healthcare systems have been described. The conceptual foundation of the rapid-learning health system has both human and technological aspects. Human factors include the development of stakeholders motivated by a desire to continuously improve the system for patients. They understand the organization's leadership and decision-making culture and are willing to be vulnerable and transparent, learning both from mistakes and successes.

There is usually trust among all stakeholders in the health system (leaders, clinicians, and researchers) which facilitates change, collaboration, and the explicit identification of problems and innovative solutions. Technology is in place to support the use of current, robust data to guide evidence-based clinical and administrative decision-making and the development of reporting systems that are accessible system-wide, allowing learning to permeate organizations with actionable data. Making clinically relevant knowledge accessible at the point of care and thereby actionable by leveraging technology is a distinctive characteristic of rapid-learning health systems.

Six Conceptual Phases of a Practical Model for a Learning Health System

Based on experience at the Group Health Cooperative in Washington [6], six conceptual phases of a practical model for a learning health system were described:

1. *Scanning and Surveillance*: The rapid-learning process begins with problem identification and characterization. Learning health systems are inherently observant, and employees are frequently seeking new information and data from different sources.
2. *Design*: Participatory design involves key stakeholders to ensure that their ideas are considered and that end products meet their specific needs. By blending research evidence with daily experiences of a frontline workforce, a learning organization leverages evidence about what works in the context of its own setting, population, available resources, and organizational culture. The importance of context is reviewed later in this chapter.
3. *Implementation*: It is risky and often counterproductive to introduce wholesale innovations in complex systems without pilot testing on a small scale – the experiences of early adopters should guide this implementation and spread process.
4. *Evaluation*: Predefined evaluation with timely feedback ensures that implementation of a change can guide subsequent actions. Ideally, the evaluation includes feedback from everyone affected.
5. *Adjustment*: Learning health systems actively seek and apply objective evidence about improving care.
6. *Dissemination*: Open discussion of evaluation findings with internal stakeholders reinforces a learning culture. Learning healthcare systems require effective communication channels directed toward internal and external stakeholders.

Changing the way healthcare professionals view organizational learning and improvement strategies will continue to strengthen overall quality in healthcare. *Just culture* and *high reliability* are two organizational learning objectives warranting focus.

Just Culture

A *just culture* is a culture of shared responsibility, shared accountability, and professionalism. It describes an approach to understanding behavioral choices and investigating processes which creates a fair and safe environment where individuals can report errors in a nonpunitive environment. A just culture promotes understanding of risk in organizations as individuals take ownership for increased reporting of harm and near misses while learning from mistakes [7]. There is an appropriate balance between the benefits of a learning culture and the need to retain personal accountability [8]. It also enhances trust building, promotes retention of high performers, and leads to more effective safety and operational management.

High Reliability Organizations

High reliability organizations are those that deliver consistent, safe, and reliable processes and outcomes despite being faced with high-risk situations. Error management in the aviation industry has served as a model that healthcare has begun to follow [9]. Key components of a highly reliable organization include:

- Full leadership engagement in driving system safety and *just culture* accountability principles [7, 10].
- An organization-wide culture of team training and effective communication [11].
- Fostering collective mindfulness of workers: constant concern about possibility of failure, deference to expertise regardless of rank or status, ability to adapt when the unexpected occurs, ability to both concentrate on a specific task and have a sense of the bigger picture, and ability to alter and flatten hierarchy as best fits the situation [12].
- System-wide standardization and simplification of care processes [7, 10].
- Measurement of safety remains a challenge and must rely on valid rate-based measures [13].

Progress in achieving these high reliability organizational goals remains quite slow in the healthcare delivery area [14]. Each one of the components listed above faces great implementation challenges. Hospitals and healthcare systems need to utilize Robust Process Improvement (RPI) tools (Lean, Six Sigma, and change management) to achieve improvements in faulty processes and to sustain improvement.

While this large system view is an important perspective, organizations must be able to narrow their focus to much smaller units of functioning where implementation of change and improvement actually occurs, otherwise called clinical microsystems.

Clinical Microsystems: Where the Action Is

Challenges seen with quality improvement efforts are frequently technical in nature (inadequate data and analytics, lack of valid measures, lack of staff skilled in quality improvement work) but also include *adaptive* factors related to culture change and motivations which accompany a culture. So even with such an infrastructure in place, there is a clear need for leaders to successfully face both technical and adaptive challenges.

The size of the organization also appears to have an effect. A study of the Veterans Affairs system suggested that enacting quality improvement culture in larger, higher-complexity facilities appeared more difficult than in lower-complexity facilities [15]. Challenges to larger facilities include addressing need and assuring viability of the solution; providing adequate data collection and effective monitoring systems; attending to organizational cultures, capacities, and level of staff engagement; leadership efficiency; incentivizing participation; and securing long-term sustainability [16].

Focusing on smaller units, clinical microsystems, as local pilots for innovation and initiation of performance improvement projects will help leaders to "build the will for change" among individual clinicians [16]. Those clinicians need to see the differences between their practices and other high-quality centers and clinicians through analysis of reliable data presented transparently.

Nelson et al. define clinical microsystems as "the basic building blocks of all health systems" [17]. This might be a hospital unit ward or a small ambulatory practice site of just a few clinicians. These small systems typically have inputs, processes, outputs, and feedback loops, and the members of the system have a shared aim to protect, restore, or promote the patient's health. The functioning of microsystems depends on the intelligent use of data, quality of its connections to other related microsystems, and engaging everyone in the microsystem to consistently complete and improve their work.

Collections of interrelated microsystems providing care to shared populations of patients (e.g., cancer, women's health, cardiovascular, orthopedic) can be considered "mesosystems." These mesosystems exist within an overarching macrosystem: a hospital, a large group, or an integrated health system. In several organizations, these mesosystems are called service lines [18]. The service line approach organizes the management of inpatient and outpatient clinical services with a focus on patient diagnostic clusters. Services specific to each diagnostic cluster are then offered through multidisciplinary teams including clinicians, nurses, pharmacists, care coordinators, and other members of expanded teams. This approach may increase the efficiency and effectiveness of an organization's programs for patient care [19]. By focusing on defined diagnostic clusters, this approach may facilitate use of metrics, protocols, and care pathways that reduce unwanted variations in care and improve patient experiences and outcomes. Studies have not yet demonstrated that this approach is more effective than other management organizations in healthcare systems.

What do we know about theories of learning within either smaller microsystem units or mesosystems? Within the field of organizational learning, Rangachari explored how learning and improvement in healthcare settings depend on context [20]. There are two categories of knowledge that need to be learned or demonstrated:

- *Explicit knowledge* can be easily explicated and codified and is fact-based.
- *Tacit knowledge* may be hidden or embedded in routines or behaviors, is experience-based, and cannot be easily codified.

As entities within an organization or system, individuals or larger groups interact in different, dynamic ways that have significant impact on how they might share knowledge or learn from each other; network theory tries to understand these dynamics and how they impact learning and effectiveness. Some networks are *dense* with strong ties (like among peers working together or in similar positions), some are considered a *brokerage* with weak ties (separate non-redundant positions or groups), and some are *hierarchic* (a minority of actors stand apart as a central connection within the network).

A network approach suggests that different types of quality improvement activities may be more effectively learned and shared through varied network relationships. Rangachari indicates that the literature is not clear whether the structure of effective learning networks differs for each type of improvement activity or type of knowledge, but awareness of this construct is fundamental to understanding how learning occurs in healthcare systems [20]. Only then can management design and support effective structures for knowledge sharing and collective learning in their organizations.

One approach recently described by Pronovost and Marsteller involves an infrastructure establishing interdependence while allowing independence [21]. Termed a *fractal-based quality management infrastructure*, it creates a repeating structure for building and supporting quality improvement expertise, goal alignment, and communication at all levels of an organization. There is an explicit creation of connections both vertically among organizational levels to support accountability and horizontally, across units at the same level, to support peer learning. This model would seem to incorporate the strengths of larger organizations with accountability and more resources but also offers the balance of smaller, self-organizing teams (i.e., clinical microsystems) where more innovation and motivation tend to reside. In healthcare organizations, there is greater potential within these smaller teams for effective physician engagement in the process and in the performance improvement goal or vision. These small teams remain as independent clinical microsystems but with both vertical and horizontal connections within the larger organization and become a macrosystem. They are not grouped into larger mesosystem sub-units within the larger organization.

Case Study • • •
How the Fractal Model Accelerates Quality and Safety Improvement in the Ambulatory Setting

As healthcare organizations of all sizes and composition transition from fee for service to pay for performance, incentives now exist for robust investment in establishing innovative governance models more nimble at producing improved outcomes at scale. Many private payer and CMS (Medicare and Medicaid) value programs link revenue to quality delivery of clinical care, improved patient experience, and lower cost (utilization). Johns Hopkins Medicine (JHM) through clarity of governance and deliberate strategic planning has created the fractal-based quality management infrastructure to foster accelerated clinical quality and safety performance improvement and organi-

(continued)

zational learning across the health system. The term "fractal" denotes a mathematical set or a pattern in nature that repeats at every scale as the model expands, such as found in fern growth. Key components of the fractal management model include but are not limited to a core of experts providing local structures with leadership and support, alignment of goals across the organization, appropriate allocation of resources, built-in accountability, effective horizontal and vertical communication, staff training in quality improvement and safety science, consideration of the patient's perspective, and a repeating pattern of governance and leadership at all levels of the organization [21].

JHM functions as the umbrella organization for the Johns Hopkins University School of Medicine, 6 academic and community hospitals, 4 healthcare and surgery centers, and 40 primary care and specialty outpatient sites. Johns Hopkins Community Physicians manage more than 900,250 patient visits a year. In entirety, JHM physicians and affiliated clinicians conduct nearly two million non-ancillary ambulatory visits annually [22]. In order to accelerate performance improvement, JHM took a number of steps including establishing the Armstrong Institute for Patient Safety and Quality as the core entity that coordinates quality improvement across the system [23]. In 2014, JHM recognized the need to address ambulatory quality improvement needs and implemented the fractal model governance structure across all ambulatory sites. Although decentralized, accountability for safety and quality permeates throughout every level of the organization and ultimately rolls up to the JHM Board of Trustees. See Fig. 8.1.

JHM launched the Office of Johns Hopkins Physicians (OJHP) in order to establish direct and indirect oversight of clinicians caring for patients in the ambulatory setting. Accountability is established at the Board of Trustees level and cascades to the Ambulatory Quality Council and workgroups and then to the local performance improvement committees at the ambulatory practice level. If an ambulatory practice continues to report substandard performance metrics, its leaders as well as the ambulatory practice chief quality officer are required to create an action plan and present it to the Board of Trustees. The Armstrong Institute in turn leads and facilitates the quality and safety process throughout the JHM health system. JHM built into the governance structure mechanisms for drill down and improvement when local practices underperform [24]. Outcomes have been very positive. JHM has seen improvement on over a dozen value-based purchasing metrics that are components of the Maryland Medicaid Managed Care Organization in 2014, including well child care (ages 3–6) and adolescent well care (ages 12–21) [25].

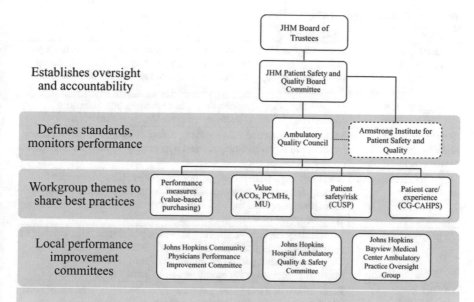

Fig. 8.1 Organization, scope, and accountability pathways of the Johns Hopkins Medicine (JHM) ambulatory medicine quality and safety oversight structure. Abbreviations: *OJHP* indicates Office of Johns Hopkins Physicians, *ACO* accountable care organization, *PCMH* patient-centered medical home, *MU* meaningful use of electronic health records, *CUSP* Comprehensive Unit-based Safety Program, *CG-CAHPS* Clinician and Group Consumer Assessment of Healthcare Providers and Systems. Reprinted from "Establishing an ambulatory medicine quality and safety oversight structure: leveraging the fractal model" by S.J. Kravet, et al., 2016, *Academic Medicine, 91*(7), p. 963. Copyright 2016 by Association of American Medical Colleges. Reprinted with permission. https://journals.lww.com/aca-demicmedicine/Fulltext/2016/07000/Establishing_an_Ambulatory_Medicine_Quality_and.25.aspx

Quality Improvement Teams

Given the complexity of the steps involved in healthcare delivery, whether for the inpatient or the outpatient setting, quality improvement (QI) initiatives require a team approach. Developing a QI team with a core set of principles is essential to the achievement of success in improvement initiatives. A research project funded by the National Institute for Health Research, Health Services, and Delivery Research (NIHR, HS, & DR) programs in the UK developed a substantial list of characteristics of good QI teams shown in Table 8.1 [26].

Engaging team members that have the right blend of these principles can be challenging, particularly in small practices. Depending on practice size, team members may function in one or more team roles, which means additional responsibilities. QI teams' primary function is to manage the overall planning and implementation of quality improvement project initiatives with focused objectives. Teams of up to seven members in size are most effective. Typical roles in successful QI teams are noted in Table 8.2 [27].

Table 8.1 Characteristics of a high-performing interdisciplinary team

Themes	Descriptions
Leadership and management	Having a clear leader of the team, with clear direction and management capacity to enhance efficiency and effectiveness; democratic; shared power; support/supervision; personal development aligned with line management; leader who acts and listens
Communication	Individuals with communication skills; ensuring that there are appropriate systems to promote communication within the team
Personal rewards, training, and development	Learning; training and development; career development opportunities; incorporates individual rewards and opportunity; morale and motivation
Appropriate resources and procedures	Structures (e.g., team meetings, organizational factors, team members working from the same location); ensuring that appropriate procedures are in place to uphold the vision of the service (e.g., communication systems, appropriate referral criteria, etc.)
Appropriate skill mix	Sufficient/appropriate skills, competencies, practitioner mix, balance of personalities; ability to make the most of other team members' backgrounds; having a full complement of staff, with timely replacement/coverage for empty or absent posts
Climate	Team culture of trust; valuing contributions; nurturing consensus; need to create an inter-professional atmosphere
Individual characteristics	Knowledge; experience; initiative; knowing strengths and weaknesses; listening skills; reflexive practice; desire to work on the same goals
Clarity of vision	Having a clear set of values that drive the direction of the service and the care provided; portraying a uniform and consistent external image
Quality and outcomes of care	Patient-centered focus; outcomes and satisfaction; encouraging feedback; capturing and recording evidence of the effectiveness of care and using that as part of a feedback cycle to improve care
Respecting and understanding roles	Sharing power; joint effort; autonomy

Reprinted from "Ten principles of good interdisciplinary team work" by S.A. Nancarrow et al., 2013, *Human Resources for Health, 11*(9), p. 9. Licensed under a Creative Commons Attribution 2.0 Generic License: https://creativecommons.org/licenses/by/2.0/#

Team Strategies and Tools to Enhance Performance and Patient Safety (TeamSTEPPS™) is a systematic approach developed by the Department of Defense and the Agency for Healthcare Research and Quality (AHRQ) to integrate team-work into practice [28]. It is an evidence-based framework to optimize team performance and designed to improve quality, safety, and efficiency across the healthcare delivery system. It focuses on four teachable-learnable skills: leadership, situation monitoring, mutual support, and communication [28].

An array of skills, knowledge, and expertise is needed for the members; however, the leader role, regardless of profession, is a key role in achieving overall project success. Reports suggest that clinician leadership is a key factor influencing clinical

Table 8.2 Typical roles in quality improvement teams

Role	Responsibilities
Clinical leader	Has enough authority in the organization to test and implement a change and to deal with issues that arise
	Understands both the clinical implications of proposed changes and the consequences such a change might trigger in other parts of the system
Day-to-day leadership	Is the driver of the project, assuring tests are implemented and overseeing data collection
	Understands not only the details of the system but also the various effects of making change(s) in the system
	Needs to be able to work effectively with the physician champion(s)
Technical expertise	Knows the subject intimately and understands the processes of care
	An expert on improvement methods can provide additional technical support by helping the team determine what to measure, assisting in design of simple, effective measurement tools, and providing guidance on collection, interpretation, and display of data
Project sponsor	Has executive authority and can provide liaison with other areas of the organization
	Serves as link to senior management and the strategic aims of the organization
	Provides resources and overcomes barriers on behalf of the team
	Is not a day-to-day participant in team meetings and testing but reviews team's progress on a regular basis

Adapted from www.IHI.org with permission of the Institute for Healthcare Improvement, ©2019

acceptance and involvement in QI [29]. Through involvement in governance, leaders can shape the quality vision and directly influence system decisions about implementation and cost-quality trade-offs [30].

Leadership Responsibilities

There is a critical role for management of healthcare organizations to inspire and lead culture change in a manner that recognizes that the Triple Aim [31] of healthcare improvement, improving the patient experience of care, including quality and satisfaction; improving the health of populations; and reducing the per capita cost of healthcare, has evolved into the Quadruple Aim [32] which includes the work-life balance of healthcare providers. Without attention from organization leaders, clinicians will not be adequately engaged, and quality improvement efforts will not succeed.

Leadership holds the responsibility to direct its organization to create or support necessary structures to inspire, motivate, and create a culture that holds quality and continuous performance improvement as core values. What leadership requirements are necessary for quality leaders? Five responsibilities are essential: advocacy and spokesmanship; policy, planning, and vision; delivery system decision support; analysis and control of quality; and external liaison and representation [33].

Advocacy and Spokesmanship

Medical quality leadership takes the lead in articulating and stimulating discussion of quality values with clinical and administrative staff, raises philosophy and purpose of quality in the institution, and advocates for it in many forums, from administrative meetings to departmental specialty conferences.

Policy, Planning, and Vision

How well is the quality perspective represented in strategic discussions? Does it rate the prominence given to cost reduction, profit margins, and market share? Here, the leader is expected to identify and present the competitive advantages of quality and, most importantly, lead the development of the organization's formal policies on quality management. Policy design includes consideration of objectives, quality management methods, resources, staffing, and impact. And, as an extension of this effort, the leader is responsible for creating a vision of future quality improvement needs for the institution.

Delivery System Decision Support

Most health and medical care organizations are constantly considering a redesign of their delivery systems. Many are developing greater internal integration of departments and more sophisticated information systems to track patients, services, and financial transactions. Others are involved in discussions about mergers and acquisitions. Pushing integration, leaders in QI must be able to relate to many levels of authority and bridge gaps in culture and perception [34]. The medical quality leader should play a key role in redesign and reengineering efforts and keep them oriented to achieve overall clinical and business quality and safety.

Analysis and Control of Quality

Within the existing system, there is an ongoing need to identify and collect quality data, conduct the required analyses, and act on the results to stimulate continuous improvement in the delivery system. The quality leader is expected to coordinate team processes in deciding which information is relevant and manage subsequent data feedback.

External Liaison and Representation

Purchasers, regulators, and consumers now seek information on institutional quality of care. The chief executive is the quality leader in a symbolic sense, establishing a culture with quality values and a continuous improvement philosophy. The expectation is for the medical quality leader to fully represent those values in practice, helping the organization to meet and exceed professional and accreditation standards. When industry purchasers and oversight groups request data, examples of continuous improvement gains, and detailed descriptions of quality management practices, someone must respond. The medical quality leader typically assumes the leadership and coordinating responsibility for the same.

Thus, to fulfill the responsibilities presented above, quality management leaders act in several key roles within the quality system. First, quality leaders must be *content experts*, guiding the institution to a clear and effective system based on state-of-the-art quality philosophies and methods. Second, they must act as *educators*, continuously teaching and updating clinical and administrative staff on primary and advanced knowledge, skills, and innovations that have developed in the quality field. The quality leader must spend time explaining why and how quality management contributes to the institution's objectives. Third, they must act as *process experts*, using interpersonal communication and group skills to lead management and clinical personnel through the development and the usage of a system of quality management. Finally, quality leaders must be able and willing to act as *evaluators*, constantly assessing the state of their quality management system and searching for ways to improve its design and operations.

Leadership Roles and Strategies

Once we recognize that strategic decisions affect quality, it becomes clear that quality management leaders must have a voice in the *direction* of the organization (strategy) and in the *execution* of the strategies (operations).

There are numerous reports of reengineering and quality improvement protocols that have been used to guide efforts, some demonstrating breakthrough success [35].

Some in healthcare organization leadership have adopted a construct called *Hoshin planning* from other production industries as a way to link strategic planning and execution. The components of the Japanese words *Hoshin Kanri* define four components that are continually revisited: *Ho*, direction; *Shin*, focus; *Kan*, alignment; and *Ri*, reason [36]. The main focus of *Hoshin Kanri* is to deploy and track only a few priorities at each level of the organization. *Hoshin planning* is intended to link strategic planning (high-level, long-term) with operational planning and implementation (frontline, short-term), ensuring that the best visions and intentions are realized [36].

The elements of *Hoshin* are directed at making this two-pronged effort (strategic and operational) meld into one organization-wide, smoothly integrated endeavor. The methods of *Hoshin* can be captured by noting the essential elements [36]:

- The QI effort is intended to be inclusive of staff at all levels. Thus, it is consistent with participative total quality management that crosses levels and functions, from top executives and managers toward all levels of personnel.
- The leadership of the organization must buy into and visibly support the planning process, particularly the interest in listening to lower-level staff and the encouragement of cross-functional teams. The kickoff effort is the first of these high-visibility opportunities for leaders. A second opportunity is ongoing leader attention to team efforts and outcomes.

- Resources are substantial and, as in other quality management efforts, are used to support significant training at the start, with coaching and advisory services as ongoing provision.

Hoshin planning relies on a participative base in establishing goals and strategies that are followed by a publicizing of the progress with appropriate metrics. Implementation is tracked with regular performance reviews that are charted and posted for all to see, in open ways that characterize a *just culture*.

Quality Leadership Structure

Leadership of quality within a healthcare organization is dependent upon many structural considerations including whether the organization is an inpatient or out-patient facility or a combination thereof; whether the organization is geographically compact or widely spread; and whether it is affiliated with an academic health center or medical school, which may have parallel but intertwined, personnel and structures. Quality improvement historically began in controlled inpatient settings under the auspices of programs named quality assurance or utilization review. Therefore, leadership has focused on the inpatient setting where data was accumulated and quality improvement then implemented. Leaders now need to have the background or resources in place to expand to the outpatient realm. A parallel leadership structure might be necessary. In some situations, leadership might need to organize quality oversight with a position like a chief quality officer (CQO) into inpatient and outpatient positions.

Governance and Quality Oversight

The role of the governing board in quality management has historically been passive oversight. Boards typically consisted of community leaders and non-medical individuals who did not have expertise or adequate knowledge in medical affairs or quality issues. However, the Institute of Medicine reports *To Err is* Human [1] and *Crossing the Quality* Chasm [2] raised great awareness of deficiencies in quality and safety in our healthcare delivery systems. As well, the Sarbanes–Oxley Act was passed in 2002 after high-profile corporate malfeasance and the ensuing media attention and government investigation. This law mandated a much greater oversight responsibility for boards across all corporate entities.

How much should an organization's board be involved in quality oversight or should a CQO have a specific office or hierarchy for adequate implementation and monitoring? Answers might need to be different based on size and historical/cultural considerations for different organizations.

Healthcare organizations in this environment need to clearly establish distinctions between governance and management with regard to quality and safety and where lines of accountability reside [37]. There has, historically, been wide variation and ambiguity in hospitals and healthcare systems around the authority and responsibility of governing boards [38]. Boards need to be structured with the right composition of individuals who understand issues around quality and safety and who can help establish policies and oversight to appropriately execute commitments made to ongoing performance improvement in these areas [39]. A study comparing hospital boards found that higher-performing hospitals tended to have more physicians involved in governance [40]. The evolution of the important roles that boards play in healthcare organizations' approaches to these areas is demonstrated by the increasing frequency of assigning oversight responsibility for the organizations' patient care quality and safety functions to a standing board committee and by the increasing amounts of board meeting time spent on these topics [41].

Yet, there are wide variations. Jha and Epstein surveyed hospital board chairs and found that programmatic emphasis on quality was not uniformly high and that formal education of board members on quality was widely variable across institutions [42]. There was an association of higher-performing institutions with higher levels of quality engagement by its board.

While board composition and attention to quality are necessary, they are not sufficient to develop an organizational culture. The framing to clinicians and other healthcare providers of what and who is being measured and how that relates to accountability is a critical communication component of organizational culture [43]. Early in the journey of an organization toward improved patient quality and safety, measurement tends to focus on process measures. However, to enhance accountability to patients and other external entities, outcome measures gradually take on more focus and prioritization. Outcome transparency requires significant physician engagement [44].

While measurement is critical to drive performance improvement of any type, issues arise around validity of quality measures in healthcare. Unlike more controlled variables in many production industries, healthcare delivered to individuals across populations is highly complex with myriad variables that cannot always be anticipated. Clinicians are particularly concerned about whether measures truly represent the quality of care provided or are significantly influenced by systematic and random error [45]. Leadership and boards must recognize such concerns can lead to loss of credibility in the quality and measurement arena with clinicians, who are critically needed to influence local organizational culture.

Leadership and governing boards can influence organizational culture in several ways, including establishing a framework for consistent accountability; promoting transparency; reinforcing training of teamwork; maintaining open, safe, and effective communication; and publicly visible, consistent involvement of senior leadership in gathering frontline provider insights to directly influence operational decisions [7].

Beyond these governance issues, setting the appropriate support structures in place is critical. The organization's health information technology must be structured to work with, and be adequately responsive to, the needs of quality leadership. Data is necessary to measure outcomes and drive decision-making. Adequate analytics are also needed to interpret and relay data in ways that make it understandable and actionable to constituents. Leaders must adequately source the necessary data and analytics resources, as well as qualified personnel, to effectively support the health information technology framework within an organization.

The Challenge of Burnout

Accurate and credible data must underlie the rationale for performance improvement within healthcare organizations. Physicians and other clinicians are trained to make decisions based on scientifically proven, data-driven evidence. Therefore, engaging them requires framing of the necessity for performance improvement as the logical conclusion based on data.

The Institute for Healthcare Improvement (IHI) Framework for engaging physicians in a shared quality agenda summarizes well a leadership to-do list to assist with change management [46]:

• Discover common purpose.
• Reframe values and beliefs.
• Segment the engagement plan.
• Use "engaging" improvement methods.
• Show courage.
• Adopt an engaging style.

In recent years, there has been increasing attention on the concept of burnout and how various aspects of the professional life of clinicians, in the changing environment of healthcare delivery, contribute to dissatisfaction and frustration. It is not surprising that burnout appears to be affected by the local culture in which the clinician practices. In addition to the adverse effect of physician burnout on quality of care, there are recognized effects on patient safety, patient satisfaction, and financial implications for organizations, including costs associated with physician turnover and decreased productivity. Healthcare organizations have a responsibility to develop strategies to reduce physician burnout and promote engagement [47].

A 2013 survey of nearly 4000 physicians and scientists noted that the leadership qualities of supervisors appeared to impact the well-being and satisfaction survey scores of individual physicians at the Mayo Clinic [29]. Recognizing the increasing role that the problem of physician burnout plays in our healthcare systems, Shanafelt and Noseworthy propose nine organizational strategies to promote physician engagement and reduce burnout [48]:

- Acknowledge and assess the problem.
- Harness the power of leadership.
- Develop and implement targeted work unit interventions.
- Cultivate community at work.
- Use rewards and incentives wisely.
- Align values and strengthen culture.
- Promote flexibility and work-life integration.
- Provide resources to promote resilience and self-care.
- Facilitate and fund organizational science.

Notably, clinicians and staff engaged in quality improvement activities have shown increased engagement and a lower incidence of burnout [48].

Future Trends

When considering the future of the organization and managerial aspects of quality management, several areas will evolve:

- The growing complexity of the quality management effort, coupled with the size of the investment, will give rise to management challenges (e.g., who leads, how much investment in QI, pressures to adopt new technologies).
- The need to consider how leadership and management are linked to risk management, patient advocacy, safety, and other quality metrics will be increasingly raised.
- Maintaining the investment in quality management will be challenged in light of continuing cost pressures and the requirement to demonstrate a return on investment.
- Increasing emphasis on *Value* in healthcare delivery, defined as (Quality + Outcomes)/Cost, means that healthcare quality management of the future can no longer stand alone to continue to be successful.
- How improvements in quality will fit in with more general corporate organizational strategy and can be integrated into strategy formulation processes.

References

1. Kohn LT, Corrigan JM, Donaldson MS (eds) (2000) To err is human: building a safer health system. National Academies Press, Washington, DC
2. Institute of Medicine (2001) Crossing the quality chasm: a new health system for the 21st century. The National Academies Press, Washington, DC
3. Berwick DM (1996) A primer on leading the improvement of systems. BMJ 312:619. https://doi.org/10.1136/bmj.312.7031.619
4. Senge PM (1990) The fifth discipline: the art and practice of the learning organization. Random House, London

5. De Savigny D, Adam T (eds) (2009) Systems thinking for health systems strengthening. Alliance for Health Policy and Systems Research, World Health Organization, Geneva
6. Greene SM, Reid RJ, Larson EB (2012) Implementing the learning health system: from concept to action. Ann Intern Med 157:207–210. https://doi.org/10.7326/0003-4819-157-3-201208070-00012
7. Frankel AS, Leonard MW, Denham CR (2006) Fair and just culture, team behavior, and leadership engagement: the tools to achieve high reliability. Health Serv Res 41:1690–1709
8. Marx D (2001) Patient safety and the "just culture": a primer for health care executives. Trustees of Columbia University in the City of New York. https://www.chpso.org/sites/main/files/file-attachments/marx_primer.pdf
9. Helmreich RL (2000) On error management: lessons from aviation. BMJ 320:781–785. https://doi.org/10.1136/bmj.320.7237.781
10. Cochrane BS, Hagins M, Picciano G et al (2017) High reliability in healthcare: creating the culture and mindset for patient safety. Health Manage Forum 30:61–68. https://doi.org/10.1177/0840470416689314
11. Baker DP, Day R, Salas E (2006) Teamwork as an essential component of high-reliability organizations. Health Serv Res 41:1576–1598
12. Weick KE, Sutcliffe KM (2001) Managing the unexpected: assuring high performance in an age of complexity, 1st edn. Jossey-Bass, San Francisco
13. Pronovost PJ, Berenholz SM, Goeschel CA et al (2006) Creating high reliability in health care organizations. Health Serv Res 41:1599–1617. https://doi.org/10.1111/j.1475-6773.2006.00567.x
14. Chassin MR, Loeb JM (2013) High-reliability health care: getting there from here. Milbank Q 91:459–490
15. Koron-Djakovic D, Canamucia A, Lempa M et al (2016) Organization complexity and primary care providers' perceptions of quality improvement culture within the Veterans Health Administration. Am J Med Qual 31(2):139–146. https://doi.org/10.1177/1062860614559743
16. Gupta R, Moriates C (2017) Swimming upstream: creating a culture of high-value care. Acad Med 92(5):597–601. https://doi.org/10.1097/ACM.0000000000001485
17. Nelson EC, Godfrey MM, Batalden PB et al (2008) Clinical microsystems, part 1: the building blocks of health systems. Jt Comm J Qual Patient Saf 34(7):367–378
18. Monitor, Independent Regulator for NHS Foundation Trusts (2009) Service-line management: an overview. Monitor, London. https://www.gov.uk/government/publications/service-line-management-an-introduction-for-nhs-foundation-trusts
19. Nasrabad RR (2016) Service line management: a new paradigm in health care system. Int J Med Res Health Sci 5(12):208–211
20. Rangachari P (2010) Knowledge sharing and organizational learning in the context of hospital infection prevention. Q Manage Health Care 19(1):34–46. https://doi.org/10.1097/QMH.0b013e3181ccbd1d
21. Pronovost PJ, Marsteller JA (2014) Creating a fractal-based quality management infrastructure. J Health Organ Manage 28(4):576–586
22. Johns Hopkins Medicine (2017) Excellence and discovery: an overview. http://www.hopkinsmedicine.org/about/downloads/jhm-overview.pdf. Accessed 19 Mar 2017
23. Austin JM, Demski R, Callender T et al (2017) From board to bedside: how the application of financial structures to safety and quality can drive accountability in a large health system. Jt Comm J Qual Patient Saf 43(4):166–175. https://doi.org/10.1016/j.jcjq.2017.01.001
24. Kravet SJ, Bailey J, Demski R, Pronovost P (2016) Establishing an ambulatory medicine quality and safety oversight structure: leveraging the fractal model. Acad Med 91(7):962–966. https://doi.org/10.1097/ACM.0000000000001102
25. Interview with Johns Hopkins leaders, April 5–7, 2017
26. Nancarrow SA, Booth A, Ariss S et al (2013) Ten principles of good interdisciplinary team work. Hum Resour Health 11:19. https://doi.org/10.1186/1478-4491-11-19

27. Institute for Healthcare Improvement (2019) Science of improvement: forming the team. http://www.ihi.org/resources/Pages/HowtoImprove/ScienceofImprovementFormingtheTeam.aspx. Accessed 14 May 2019
28. Agency for Healthcare Research and Quality (2019) About Team STEPPS. Rockville, MD. http://www.ahrq.gov/teamstepps/about-teamstepps/index.html
29. Shanafelt TD, Gorringe G, Menaker R et al (2015) Impact of organizational leadership on physician burnout and satisfaction. Mayo Clin Proc 90(4):432–440. https://doi.org/10.1016/j.mayocp.2015.01.012
30. Weiner BJ, Shortell SM, Alexander JA (1997) Promoting clinical involvement in the hospital quality improvement efforts: the effects of top management, board, and physician leadership. Health Serv Res 32:491–510
31. Berwick DM, Nolan TW, Whittington J (2008) The triple aim: care, health, and cost. Health Aff 27(3):759–769. https://doi.org/10.1377/hlthaff.27.3.759
32. Bodenheimer T, Sinsky C (2014) From triple to quadruple aim: care of the patient requires care of the provider. Ann Fam Med 12:573–576
33. Ziegenfuss JT (1997) Five responsibilities of medical quality leaders. Am J Med Qual 12(4):175–176. https://doi.org/10.1177/0885713X9701200401
34. Ashkenas RN, Francis SC (2000) Integration managers: special leaders for special times. Harv Bus Rev 78(6):108–116
35. Nackel JG (1995) Breakthrough delivery systems: applying business process innovation. J Soc Health Syst 5(1):11–21
36. Hutchins D (2008) Hoshin kanri: the strategic approach to continuous improvement. Gower Publishing Co, Burlington. https://www.henryford.com/hcp/academic/pathology/production-system/wednesdays-words/2011-articles/march-9-2011
37. Goeschel CA, Wachter RM, Pronovost PJ (2010) Responsibility for quality improvement and patient safety: hospital board and medical staff leadership challenges. Chest 138(1):171–178. https://doi.org/10.1378/chest.09-2051
38. Alexander JA, Lee SY (2006) Does governance matter? Board configuration and performance in not-for-profit hospitals. Milbank Q 84(4):733–758. https://doi.org/10.1111/j.1468-0009.2006.00466.x
39. Orlikoff JE, Totten MK (2003) Trustee workbook 2: best practices in governance: what makes great boards great. Trustee 56(4):15–18
40. Prybil LD (2006) Size, composition, and culture of high-performing hospital boards. Am J Med Qual 21(4):224–229. https://doi.org/10.1177/1062860606289628
41. Prybil LD, Peterson R, Brezinski P et al (2010) Board oversight of patient care quality in community health systems. Am J Med Qual 25:34–41. https://doi.org/10.1177/1062860609352804
42. Jha AK, Epstein AM (2010) Hospital governance and the quality of care. Health Aff 29:182–187. https://doi.org/10.1377/hlthaff.2009.0297
43. Pronovost PJ, Sexton B (2005) Assessing safety culture: guidelines and recommendations. Qual Saf Health Care 14(4):231–233. https://doi.org/10.1136/qshc.2005.015180
44. Pross C, Geissler A, Busse R (2017) Measuring, reporting, and rewarding quality of care in 5 nations: 5 policy levers to enhance hospital quality accountability. Milbank Q 95(1):136–183. https://doi.org/10.1111/1468-0009.12248
45. Pronovost PJ, Miller M, Wachter RM (2007) The GAAP in quality measurement and reporting. JAMA 298(15):1800–1802. https://doi.org/10.1001/jama.298.15.1800-2
46. Reinertsen JL, Gosfield AG, Rupp W et al (2007) Engaging physicians in a shared quality agenda. IHI Innovation Series white paper. Institute for Healthcare Improvement, Cambridge
47. Shanafelt T, Goh J, Sinsky C (2017) The business case for investing in physician well-being. JAMA Intern Med 177(12):1826–1832. https://doi.org/10.1001/jamainternmed.2017.4340
48. Shanafelt TD, Noseworthy JH (2017) Executive leadership and physician well-being: nine organizational strategies to promote engagement and reduce burnout. Mayo Clin Proc 92(1):129–146

Additional Reading

Agency for Healthcare Research and Quality (2013) Practice facilitation handbook: module 14. creating quality improvement teams and QI plans. http://www.ahrq.gov/professionals/prevention-chronic-care/improve/system/pfhandbook/mod14.html. Accessed May 2013

Ziegenfuss JT (1991) Organizational barriers to quality improvement in medical and health care organizations. Qual Assur Util Rev 6(4):115–122

Ziegenfuss JT (1994) Toward a general procedure for quality improvement: the double track process. Am J Med Qual 9(2):90–97

Chapter 9
Economics and Finance in Medical Quality Management

Donald Fetterolf and Rahul K. Shah

Executive Summary

Recent, costly expansions within the healthcare delivery system, in addition to heightened corporate involvement, have led to an increasing focus on the cost of care versus the value received. Improvements in medical care and its delivery come at a price, but not all costs yield value at the patient level. The greatest current challenge in the economics of health care is to balance a business-oriented focus centered on the financial orientation of medical organizations with a patient-oriented focus on short- and long-term gains created by QI methods. This challenge is doubly difficult since both an analysis of the real costs of healthcare for a particular activity may be hard to calculate and the perceived value of outcomes is often difficult to express in a way that allows strict economic analysis.

As the next generation of quality management continues to evolve, medical quality managers, along with other institutional leaders, must balance the trade-off between elements of quality and the costs that society can tolerate as it continuously seeks to improve the health of its population [1–4]. Indeed, newer approaches for reviewing the value of quality initiatives are multidisciplinary and must consider financial, clinical, operational, and intangible variables.

Significant pressure is applied by the payer community to document the return on investment (ROI) of quality improvement activities. Large company benefit managers typically demand to know what the ROI is for clinical quality improvement activities and whether or not these activities are worth purchasing [5]. It is not uncommon for a health plan executive to be asked, "If you just don't do all of those quality initiatives, could you give me a lower premium cost?" The usual quick

D. Fetterolf (✉)
Fetterolf Healthcare Consulting, Imperial, PA, USA

R. K. Shah
Children's National Hospital, Washington, DC, USA

© American College of Medical Quality (ACMQ) 2021
A. P. Giardino et al. (eds.), *Medical Quality Management*,
https://doi.org/10.1007/978-3-030-48080-6_9

response is that there is value to quality initiatives that have a definite return on investment, but that answer falls short. The real response is a complex one that must be assembled from the facts, provided in a short time, and is often not easy to articulate. Similarly, basic operational questions to quality managers—Why do you think you need another nurse in the quality area? Could you do with less? Can you justify the increase in the budget that you are requesting?—can be very difficult to answer in a cost-sensitive environment. The value of quality must be condensed into understandable and relatable economic terms that the organization and society as a whole will understand and accept. Simply put, you need to monetize the quality efforts you oversee.

The lesson for physicians responsible for quality programs who understand the economics and politics of healthcare is that any major change, planned or unexpected, will have numerous consequences. Predicting the result of the dynamics of change becomes infinitely more complicated when the outcome is not definitive— or even tangible—but rather is a consequence of shifting resources that affect the cost of healthcare, alter the quality of healthcare, or impinge on access to services [6].

In the end, quality professionals are tasked with assessing the value of the programs they implement and, for their superiors, whether that value is worth the cost of completing the program. They need to present the results in a convincing, clear way, period.

This chapter reviews the fundamentals of economics, finance, and politics of medical quality and illustrates how these three fields interact and can be used by the reader to prepare and defend the business case for quality. The information within this chapter is intended to introduce basic concepts that can be useful regardless of which direction the system will move in the next 5 years.

Learning Objectives

Upon completion of this chapter, readers should be able to:

1. Understand the historical evolution of how quality programs have developed an economic emphasis.
2. Discuss the economic and policy events that caused the government to become involved with medical quality.
3. Discuss the general business principles and key concepts in economic theory that the medical quality practitioner must understand.
4. Understand key financial and accounting concepts and detail how these tools are used in new models of care delivery analysis and operations.
5. Develop a structure for organizing the economic value of quality in financial and nonfinancial terms for senior management and public presentations.
6. Organize how to present "the business case for quality" in a business environment.

7. Develop an approach to the construction and delivery of a quality presentation that defines the value of a quality department or quality initiative.
8. Outline the roles of American values and health policy in which medical quality practitioners should approach their tasks.

Historical Perspective

The evolution of medical quality efforts in the United States has in many ways paralleled or followed similar developments in the business world. Quality-oriented activities have progressed from an inspection-based approach to data-driven, analytic methods using principles of statistical quality control. At the same time, the approach of medical quality professionals has become increasingly entwined in a variety of business activities. The progression of this process can be divided into the stages of quality assurance, statistical quality control in continuous quality improvement, and outcomes-focused analysis, all of which are addressed in detail in Chaps. 2, 3, and 8. The move from many quality improvement teams from the basements of hospitals to the C-suite and boardrooms demonstrates the crucial need for healthcare quality improvement executives to understand the role of financial literacy in their work.

The early stages of quality analysis in medicine focused on a largely inspection-based mode of quality assurance. Focus was on sentinel event monitoring, clinical pathology conferences, outlier reporting such as transfusion reactions, etc. The focused attention to these matters was often considered a professional responsibility rather than a business one, and while it was understood that costs were associated with poor quality, regular reporting was largely in the form of descriptive statistics and patient care. Performing these types of activities required a considerable effort and cost, which was borne by the hospitals and health plans as a grudging part of "overhead" without the need for exhaustive justification. Examples of inspection type statistics include the following:

- Physician credentialing and certification
- Institutional credentialing and certification
- Procedure-specific credentialing
- Utilization management process adequacy reviews such as length of stay monitoring
- Technology assessment /medical policy of new and emerging technology
- Adverse occurrence and "sentinel event" reviews
- External accreditation such as the Joint Commission (formerly known as JACHO)

The next iteration in quality review came with the widespread adoption of management tools, now well familiar to students of Deming [7] and Juran [8], as businesses began to demand that these tools be employed in healthcare as they were in other industries. Statistical quality control measures used included run charts, control charts, and various similar methods to detect trends and statistical measures for improving quality. Again, the focus was largely at a professional level, with the intent to improve the quality of medicine. Quality programs spent considerable amounts of time to explain why lengths of stay at their hospital were longer for such and such a diagnosis, etc. functioning not only to identify outlier practices but also to serve as defensive units when criticism of public reporting came to bear. Both seemed valuable, but exact methods for calculating the value of quality improvement activities remained elusive. Quality was felt to be created by reducing unnecessary variation. Examples of the analysis in these types of activities include the following:

- Diagnosis-specific admissions variation
- Targeted surgical variation including rates of procedures, complications, etc.
- Targeted ambulatory surgery variation
- Physician statistical cost/mortality profiling
- Pharmaceutical profiling

A third movement in the development of quality improvement occurred as the attention on outcomes moved from a statistically driven focus to a quantitative design to include even less tangible measures of impact such as patient satisfaction and the patient's perception of care. There was a recognized value in other areas aside from monetary expense, but the intangible nature of many of the related outcomes made proper financial analysis problematic. This next generation of quality assessment was much more sophisticated and nuanced and required much more complex analytics. As a result, quality assessments were seen as costly quantitative measures, increasingly questioned by nonclinical management concerned with overall costs.

Each of the following trends in quality improvement carried its own challenges in estimating the impact or value of an initiative, and determining a return on an investment in these programs became increasingly problematic:

- Selected claims-based outcomes
- Member satisfaction/perception of health
- Clinical outcomes measures
- Disease specific patient perceptions
- Linkage of programs to disability/absenteeism
- Life event risk intervention analysis
- Social-small area analysis, e.g., the Dartmouth Atlas study
- Functional status and well-being
- Health risk appraisals

The sophistication of data collection and analytics led to increasingly sophisticated methods of internal reporting that were handled by larger institutions capable of aggregating and reporting this data. Ultimately, it spilled into the realm of public reporting.

Physician-level public reporting of clinical outcomes has been discussed for a number of years, but with increasing shifts to consumer-driven healthcare programs and the expanded availability of data, the public is questioning why more information is not made accessible. Subtle, important nuances in interpreting healthcare data that are well known to statisticians and physicians are viewed skeptically by eager but less sophisticated advocates of public reporting as roadblocks in the public's quest to find good physicians and eliminate ineffective or dangerous practitioners. Early attempts to profile hospitals in order of unadjusted mortality rates provide a ready example for how complicated a simple question can become. That public pressure will accelerate public disclosure is certain, with uncertain results.

Simultaneously, consolidating large data sets in enterprise data warehouses in government and insurer organizations has led to the possibility that informatics-driven evaluation of processes may build on the previous activities. Predictive modeling, data mining, and the application of a variety of sophisticated techniques for locating and abstracting information related to medical quality initiatives are being utilized at unprecedented rates. This field is in its infancy, and time will tell if the hype can lead to significant, beneficial advances in the field of quality and finance.

Throughout the 1980s, 1990s, and to the present, the amount of available information has increased greatly, as has the analytic capability to evaluate it. Multiple organizations have sprung up to create meaningful measures to define quality, resulting in a plethora of potential outcome measures. The National Committee for Quality Assurance (NCQA), the National Quality Forum (NQF), and numerous governmental agencies, business coalitions, and healthcare professional associations are involved. The Centers for Medicare & Medicaid Services (CMS) has, for example, released a listing of almost 300 indicators it believes are important [9].

Once one develops a list of appropriate measures one feels best identifies what *quality medicine* may be, the concept of *pay for performance* is never far behind. An overriding question remains as to how to use it to calculate the value of different medical interventions and the potential for return on investment of quality initiatives designed to improve the care of individuals at large and within organizations. To best understand how to do this, we need to start at the beginning.

Basic Concepts in Business and Economics

Imparting in-depth knowledge of business economics and finance is beyond the purview of a single chapter in a textbook directed at fundamental concepts of medical quality. Yet, the business of economics and finance within the healthcare industry has become increasingly important for all healthcare professionals. The main categories of economics, accounting, and finance will be reviewed briefly, particularly as they relate to quality professionals.

Economics

A common misunderstanding among clinically trained healthcare professionals is that economics is all about money. In fact, *economics* focuses on the creation, evolution, and delivery of *value* which may include nonmonetary elements such as labor forces, factors that alter the business cycle, the influence of history, and the general thoughts and motives of the gross population. Business schools divide the study of economics into *macroeconomics* and *microeconomics*.

Macroeconomics

Macroeconomics typically deals with the big picture in the structure and performance of the industrial market as well as the behavior of society at large. The money supply and how it affects wages, prices, employment, inflation, long-term growth, and productivity make up a major part of this topic. Macroeconomics focuses primarily on the behavior of the economy as a whole, its total output, and activity at the national or international level. It also deals with these activities over time and studies how they affect the wealth of nations and overall business cycles.

Macroeconomics usually focuses on overall markets rather than on a specific small region or product but can be applied locally. Students of the subject recognize that it is an inexact science that has developed a variety of approaches. Keynesian economics was developed in the earlier part of the twentieth century, and its tenets were frequently quoted as guiding principles until the late twentieth century. Keynesian economics focuses on the importance of consumer aggregate demand within the economy as an economic force and is often referenced in models of healthcare consumption. The Keynesian approach has since been supplemented by a variety of theoretical constructs that continue to evolve [10]. These theoretical constructs or models for economics develop other theories around drivers of the healthcare economy, particularly as demand can be altered by other economic forces such as the presence of health insurance, government mandates, disease management programs, etc.

Regulation of the monetary supply by the Federal Reserve Board presents a *monetarist* approach to economics that is relatively recent and fueled by complex econometric computer models. Considerable disagreement arises among various schools of economics as to what the best approach may be, how the market responds to various drivers, and what a government's best course of action may be. A second or *fiscal* approach looks at other factors that affect the economy such as taxation, government spending on various activities, or legislative interventions. These theories are also influenced, in part, by the political views of individual analysts who, for example, might emphasize the role of business and organizations over the perceived need to improve the quality of life for the general public or the need to redistribute wealth to optimize the economy.

The healthcare system as a whole is clearly an issue in macroeconomics now that the overall cost of healthcare is over 17% of the gross domestic product of the United States [11]. As the healthcare delivery system has expanded, it has assumed an increasingly large role in the overall economy including manufacturing, labor, and the economies of governments. Economists have noted a close relationship between consumption spending and disposable income [12]. Clearly, current trends in the use of disposable income in healthcare spending are unsustainable from a mathematical perspective. Historical changes in the US economy during economic recessions have resulted in considerable pressure on large businesses to reduce healthcare expenditures as they become an increasing portion of a company's expenses and, in a way, make the company less competitive in world markets. One of the most salient examples of such problems driving down the financial competitiveness of a multinational corporation is the problem faced by General Motors, one of the "big three" automakers in the United States, whose financial responsibility for health benefits for current and retired workers is over $50 billion. An understanding of the structure of macroeconomics is useful for quality professionals as the economic environment in healthcare becomes increasingly complicated.

Microeconomics

The second portion of typical course work in economics focuses on microeconomics or *the economics of the firm*. In contrast to macroeconomics, which centers on industrial market structure and performance, microeconomics focuses on the effects of these various forces on individual firms and regions or market segments. In healthcare, microeconomic studies focus on individual physician practices, the workings of hospital markets and service areas, and the nuances of physician payment systems. Market demand and demand curves are of interest to various kinds of individual companies seeking to set the price and volume of services they offer. This area of economics is clearly relevant to a medical care system that has grown substantially during the past five decades, particularly with the support of government subsidies.

Microeconomics is also concerned with the behavior of individuals as they relate to an organization. How individuals view the price of a company's service is related to the utility that they attribute to these services. In organizations that appear to offer commodities—and healthcare is increasingly being positioned as a commodity—payers, at the individual or business level, may be indifferent to which provider is used and will pay higher prices or move to different providers only when more complex relationships alter their demand, such as changes in co-pay structure or high-deductible health plan designs.

Microeconomic analysis has the ability to evaluate consumer behavior in the purchase of healthcare services. Large insurance carriers conduct market research and an ensuing mathematical review to anticipate ways in which consumer behavior can be altered, such as through various types of charges and perceived quality. For example, insurers and payers are interested in the types of incentives that may change the likelihood that consumers will seek health services, particularly as this likelihood relates to pricing—the so-called price elasticity of demand.

Price Elasticity of Demand Among Purchasers of Health Insurance Services

Insurers—indeed sellers of many products—note that certain price points will move customers in the direction of their product. For example, insurers and managed care organizations report that as little as a $10 per member per month (PMPM), out-of-pocket cost can cause a consumer to shift from one type of health provider to another. Physicians often are firmly convinced that their patients will come to them forever because they believe that the definitive bond is the relationship between the doctor and the patient. Actual practice, however, suggests that a consumer will shift to a different physician to obtain a savings of $8 to $10 PMPM. The easier it is for the patient to shift plans and networks, the more "elastic" the relationship is between individuals and the choice of purchasing services by a given physician. Many factors affect the elasticity of demand. Examples include:

- The presence of equivalent substitutes (the perception among some patients that all doctors are equal or offer commodity services)
- The penetration of the product into the community (patients will pick HMOs if many are available in the marketplace but may be less inclined to do so when managed care develops in an indemnity market)
- The income profile of the consumer purchasing the product

Microeconomic principles come to play in a number of economic analyses in healthcare, from the development of hospital services to the management of medical practices. Understanding basic tenets of macroeconomics and microeconomics should be on the basic checklist for clinicians working in the quality management field. One ignores these concepts at one's own peril.

Monopoly and Monopsony Markets

The response of individuals in *monopoly* or *monopsony* markets is also of interest to large insurance carriers, in both *highly concentrated* and *unconcentrated* labor markets. In a monopoly, a seller of services represents a dominant or unique vendor position and can set higher prices for their services than others in more competitive markets. In highly concentrated markets, which have only a few insurers for a region, individuals and businesses may find that this effect drives increased premiums. They may state that, "High barriers to entry" in the market prevent the competition from lowering prices. Similar complaints arise in a monopsony market situation when a sole community provider of healthcare services, such as a regional rural hospital or a university hospital system, negotiates higher fees for its services with a health plan.

In a monopsony, the purchaser of services represents an exclusive position in the market. The federal government, with respect to Medicare services, can be thought of as monopsonistic, when it is the dominant payer of clinicians in a region. The effects in this case concern the public and government officials as the costs of healthcare rise. This issue is also of concern to physicians, who represent a segment of the labor force that must contract with various organizations. For example, the behavior of primary care and specialist physicians likely varies in different types of markets depending on the level of the physician's market control. In markets with a dominant insurer and an oversupply or undersupply of a particular type of physician specialty, these factors greatly affect the physicians' interpretations of how aggressive they can be with the payer. Physicians who are in short supply and in high demand can negotiate higher-than-normal fees for their services. Physicians who are in more plentiful supply may feel more downward pressure on their fees; they become *price takers*. In markets that are highly fragmented across many payers, the behavior of physicians and insurers would vary according to whether physician specialties are over or under represented.

Clearly, the leverage that a payer or a health plan has over physicians is also related to economic forces. How closely physicians are tied to a health plan directly influences their need or desire to participate in mandated quality initiatives. The economics of the behaviors of patients and providers has been studied with much interest. Textbooks that combine micro- and macroeconomics and a solid knowledge of the healthcare system [3, 4, 13–16] are worth reviewing by all medical care professionals—and by quality professionals in particular.

The importance of economics to healthcare professionals in general, and to quality managers in particular, is becoming increasingly evident as the overall effect of the healthcare system on the general economy becomes more prominent and more acute. It will be the responsibility of the next generation of quality leaders to have a thorough understanding of general economic principles so that the *economic value* of their work can be presented. Understanding economic forces and their relationship to the business community is an important capability, if not a compulsory skill, needed at all levels of management in healthcare organizations. Training in economics can be obtained through graduate-level courses, although several less difficult avenues are possible. Intensive short courses offered by graduate business schools, brief introductory training sessions offered through professional societies, and instructional audiotapes are available [17]. Health economics has developed into a specialty in its own right, and entire texts are available on the subject [13, 18, 19].

Case Study • • •
Macroeconomic Issues

Health plan actuaries predict a flattening in the healthcare cost trend because costs "can't keep getting higher." They also note that economic analyses in a CMS report by the federal government suggest considerable debate about the

(continued)

leveling of costs in the near future. They admit that "provider reform" efforts by the federal government to control costs are doomed to failure and that costs could keep going up.

The Chief Medical Officer is asked to comment. He notes that costs are up in every category. He also notes that various classes of emerging technologies continue to arrive in increasing numbers and that the demographics of the plan suggest that the aging population will continue to have a great effect on cost. The Vice President of Provider Relations observes that vertical and horizontal market consolidation in the area, as well as declining hospital margins, will make it unlikely that simple price controls will be effective, because reimbursements to hospitals may need to go up this year. He admits that providers also have not had a fee increase for some time, are being hit with rising malpractice premiums, and are unlikely to settle for any reduction in fees. He concedes that physicians may be leaving the state because of low reimbursement and high malpractice premiums and that Medicare recently had to retreat from a planned reduction in physician payment. In his view, multiple economic factors seem to point to continuously increasing costs. The group concludes that the percentage of the gross national product attributed to healthcare, now edging to 18%, will rise even higher. These national trends are likely to be reflected in local health plans as well cost drivers.

The Chief Medical Officer is asked to participate in a workgroup in the plan to brainstorm methods of cost control. Several managers believe that cutting payments to physicians is the only way to reduce consumption of medical services. Others argue that better management of individuals will be the most cost-effective method. Still others maintain that the days of managed care are over and that real cost savings will come through reducing unnecessary variation by applying quality tools. The COO takes a naïve, simplistic approach and tells the Chief Medical Officer, "Tell me how you will take 5% out of the healthcare system. That seems like a simple enough assignment if there really is a lot of waste. Let us know by our staff meeting next week."

What should the Chief Medical Officer's advice to the group be?

Accounting

Why do quality management professionals need to develop a working knowledge of accounting, let alone take a course in this subject? The reason is that basic accounting principles are used in a variety of analyses and are the language of business. Accounting is the main method used to record business transactions and to present them to other business professionals to communicate cost and movement of money. Although health professionals need not perform accounting procedures, they still must understand and appreciate basic accounting principles in much the same way that those pursuing internal medicine rather than surgery must have a thorough knowledge of anatomy.

Types of Financial Accounting Reporting Tools

Medical quality managers are called on to review and understand the significance of a wide variety of financial information. Financial information can take many forms in a health plan or hospital [20].

Financial Statements

Financial statements include the balance sheet, the income statement, the statement of cash flows, and the similar documents. These are used to communicate with external entities, such as the Internal Revenue Service, auditors, investors, banks, and state governments.

Important features of financial statements are often expressed as ratios. These ratios include the *current ratio* (current assets divided by current liabilities), the *quick ratio* (current assets minus inventories divided by current liabilities), and various forms of debt and profit ratios. These statistics provide an estimate of how "solid" the company is or whether its assets are sufficient to cover the debt it carries. Similar ratios reflect the return on activity of the company. For example, ROI, *return on assets* (ROA), *return on equity* (ROE), and *earnings per share* (EPS) of stock are typically used. In these statistics, the amount of net earnings or revenue is divided by the numbers used for summarizing the asset base, by outstanding equity, or by outstanding shares of stock, respectively. For medical managers, the most frequently requested statistic is the ROI—the amount of money returning to the organization for the financial investment in an initiative. This statistic is particularly difficult to obtain accurately in medical management activities in which clinical returns often are not easily converted to financial equivalents.

Balance Sheets

A *balance sheet* presents a financial picture of a company or organization at a fixed point in time (see Table 9.1). As such, it is a snapshot that records the organization's assets, liabilities, and, in the case of a publicly owned company, the owner's equity.

In its simplest form, the balance sheet provides a picture of a company's financial position in terms of its current assets and liabilities. It typically presents several derivative statistics, often depicted as ratios (e.g., current ratio, quick ratio) that show how much and to what degree a company's assets and liabilities are committed to hard assets, outstanding loans, liabilities of other types, taxes, and other areas. The liquidity of the organization's assets, or the ability of the company to move cash, is an important part of this statement. A quality leader or executive must be able to cogently speak to and address their organization's balance sheet. Of course, your healthcare entity's balance sheet may be quite sophisticated and several pages long, but once the fundamental parts are broken down, it looks very similar to the example above.

Table 9.1 Sample balance sheet

Balance sheet: ABC Medical Corporation	As of December 31
Assets	
Current assets	
Cash	$50,000
Accounts receivable	$35,000
Total current assets	$85,000
Noncurrent assets	
Land	$200,000
Medical office building	$1,579,000
Equipment (net of accumulated depreciation)	$250,000
Total noncurrent assets	$2,029,000
Total assets	**$2,114,000**
Liabilities	
Current liabilities	
Accounts payable to suppliers	$25,000
Salaries payable to employees	$32,000
Taxes owed	$52,000
Total current liabilities	$109,000
Noncurrent liabilities	
Notes payable to lenders	$150,000
Total liabilities	**$259,000**
Shareholders' equity	
Common stock	$1,500,000
Retained earnings	$355,000
Total shareholders' equity	**$1,855,000**
Total liabilities and shareholders' equity	**$2,114,000**

Income Statements

Probably more important to practicing managers than the financial statement or the balance sheet is the *income statement*, which is useful in the ongoing evaluation of a business or modeled initiative. In the standard income statement, sources of revenue are listed at the top of the sheet, expenses are listed below in numerated line item form, and a final net income is given at the bottom. This format is typically used to communicate the sales efforts of the organization or the company and the costs that must be subtracted from profits.

Quality professionals should also recognize that while recording information in accounting ledgers, they must consider the *accounting basis*. Many physicians or nurses initially entering hospital or managed care environments are accustomed to the cash accounting, or *cash-basis accounting*, used in their practices. Here, revenue and costs are recognized in the month or period in which they occur. For a variety of reasons, large operating concerns, for which revenue and expenses may not match neatly in each month, follow *accrual-based accounting*. In this approach, companies record revenue and expenses in the period in which they were incurred, regardless of the time in which money may have actually changed hands or a check was received. Accrual-based accounting requires regular upkeep of accounting ledgers but is more appropriate than cash-based accounting for organizations that have cash flows that are not closely temporally linked.

In healthcare, real profitability and future growth are assessed with *earnings before interest and taxes (EBIT)*. This element is important in the income statements of both for-profit and not-for-profit healthcare companies because it identifies the real earnings of a company. The expanded concept of *earnings before interest, taxes, depreciation, and amortization (EBITDA)* is often used in income statements when estimates of cash profitability are desired. Interest, taxes, depreciation, and amortization are used in financial and tax accounting to reduce taxable profits. Thus, EBIT and EBITDA represent earnings that are available for reinvestment in the company and are important in estimating profitability, the capital structure of the company, and other important concepts in both taxed and tax-exempt organizations.

Statement of Cash Flows

Another important accounting reporting tool is the *statement of cash flows*. This type of statement typically shows the sources of cash received by the organization or company and provides an overview of whether the organization can shift its liquid assets around in its operations. A statement of cash flows is typically of more interest to financial managers than to medical quality professionals, but its existence and general structure are worth reviewing.

The statement of cash flows accounts for the cash moving through the organization from *operating, investing,* and *financing activities*. A sample is shown in Table 9.2. Selling goods or services is the predominant method for realizing operating cash flows. The acquisition of noncurrent assets, particularly property and equipment, makes up the investing section of the statement and is needed for the company to function. Finally, the company's efforts to obtain cash for short- and long-term use are described in the financing section of the statement.

Statements of cash flow assess the effect of ongoing operations on the liquidity of the corporation and describe the relationships among the various components. The statement may reveal that the company is out of balance with respect to cash inflows and outflows, a situation that can precipitate a *cash crisis* in which insufficient cash is available to meet the needs of the corporation. Alternatively, the statement may show the availability of too much cash, which suggests that the company is not making the best use of this resource.

Table 9.2 Sample statement
of cash flows

Cash flows: ABC medical corporation	For current year
Operations	
Cash flow from operations	$1,662,000
Investing	
Sale of noncurrent assets	$0
Acquisition of noncurrent assets	–$30,000
Total cash flow from investing	–$30,000
Financing	
Issue of partner stock	$50,000
Dividends	–$2000
Total cash flow from financing	$48,000
Net change in cash flow	**$1,680,000**

Annual Reports

A company's *annual report* is designed to provide an overview of the company and its financial position. The president and persons involved in running the company direct the report to stockholders and stakeholders. The report typically contains annual and quarterly financial statements, a balance sheet, an income statement, and a statement of cash flow along with other information such as a letter from the company president and a statement from an independent auditor. People who review these documents are often most interested in the supplementary information at the end of the report, particularly the management letter provided by the independent auditor. Areas of concern documented in the management letter may raise red flags among those concerned about the organization's assets and its prospects for growth and performance. As a quality leader or executive, an understanding of one's organizational annual report, as well as that of those organizations that your healthcare entity does business with (e.g., hospital association, prime vendors, etc.), is crucial. There is an abundance of information in a well-constructed annual report that can help the quality professional understand the potential for collaboration and building of synergies with business partners.

Types of Accounting Systems

Generally Accepted Accounting Principles

Many of the accepted accounting principles in the United States have been developed through a centralized method called *generally accepted accounting principles* (GAAP). Annual reports, balance sheets, and similar types of accounting documents are prepared using GAAP. These principles are set by general approval from three main formal organizations: the American Institute of Certified Public Accountants (AICPA), the Securities and Exchange Commission (SEC), and the Financial Accounting Standards Board (FASB). These organizations gained influence in the development of accounting principles during the mid- to late twentieth century. These accounting principles, however, have not been adopted universally, and in many countries, other, sometimes completely different, accounting systems may be operating. Recently, several international organizations have sought to standardize financial accounting methods for use in international commerce.

Statutory Accounting Standards

Accounting and financial reporting can also include a variety of *statutory accounting standards* that are developed by government agencies. Statutory accounting principles are standardized, often on a national or state-by-state basis, and are used by departments of health and departments of insurance to regulate health plans. Like income tax forms, statutory reporting forms contain a variety of financial and sometimes clinical or utilization information that is useful to the state or federal government. Statutory information may be calculated using certain algorithms that better allow state regulators to determine effectiveness, solvency, and similar aspects of a health plan or hospital management.

The efforts of the National Association of Insurance Commissioners (NAIC) to develop *model laws* [21] that outline standardized recommendations for writing legislative and statutory requirements have contributed significantly to generating order in the healthcare industry. Widespread adoption of these principles has helped foster a relatively consistent approach across the country in the insurance industry.

Managerial Accounting

In addition to offering financial accounting, business schools typically offer a course in *managerial accounting* that focuses more on the day-to-day operations of the corporation. The approaches used in managerial accounting are often not part of GAAP but are adopted regularly by organizations for internal use. The purpose of these approaches is to provide senior management with a clear view of financial events in the company.

An important concept in managerial accounting is *contribution income*, which is reflected in the *contribution income statement*. In this variation of the income statement, revenues and expenses are listed on a per-unit-of-production basis. Thus, the revenues from an individual item (such as a surgical procedure or service) are linked with its expenses to show the *contribution margin*, or profit, from the sale of each item. Fixed expenses or fixed overhead must also be taken into consideration, and these items are presented later in the contribution income statement. See Table 9.3 for a comparison of a contribution income statement to a regular income statement.

The value of this approach is that the overall profit can be calculated easily once the *break-even point* is known (i.e., the point at which the contribution margin from the sale of a certain number of widgets equals the amount of the fixed expenses or overhead). The application of this approach to medical management initiatives is

Table 9.3 Differences between a regular income statement and a contribution income statement

Form of a regular income statement		
Standard income statements generally reflect sources of revenue and expenses and then define the difference as net profit		
Revenues		
Revenue	$100	
Expenses		
Variable expense	$60	
Fixed expense	$20	
Profit/loss	**$20**	

Form of a contributions income statement		
A contribution income statement presents variable revenues and expenses separately from fixed expenses and notes the relationship between the volume of business activity and the ultimate profitability of the organization		
	Per member per year	Total
Members affected		$50,000
Revenues		
Variable revenues/savings	$7	$350,000
Expenses		
Variable expenses/unit	($5)	($250,000)
Contribution margin	$2	$100,000
Fixed expenses		$46,000
Profit/loss		**$54,000**

In this example, the break-even point would occur when 23,000 members were treated; at this point, the revenues would equal the remaining expenses (i.e., 23,000 members times the contribution margin of $2 per member would generate $46,000, the amount needed to meet the fixed expenses.) above this point, the marginal profit of the effort would accrue at a rate of $2 per member per year

clear. If a certain medical cost savings per member per month (PMPM) is anticipated from an intervention that costs a known amount, the number of individuals who need to be treated per month to cover the monthly cost—or the overall cost and overall fixed expenses of the initiative (the break-even point)—can be calculated. From these figures, the amount of profit from each additional member treated per month (the *marginal profit*) can be calculated. *Marginal cost* is calculated in a like manner.

Other organizations outside of the government statutory accounting efforts also set out to develop standard accounting processes. Many of these represent managerial accounting approaches to evaluate specific problems in the industry in which they are found. An example of such an effort includes the Population Health Alliance to standardize the reporting for estimating the economic impact of medical management programs [22, 23]. These are particularly relevant to quality managers because disease management evaluation is often included within the realm of accreditation programs. Another example of standardized reporting of what are essentially finan-

Table 9.4 Example of activity-based cost accounting

Product	A	B	C	Total
Revenue				
Variable revenue	$50	$50	$20	$120
Expenses				
Variable expense	$30	$5	$5	$40
Fixed expense	$15	$30	$5	$50
Profit/loss	**$5**	**$15**	**$10**	**$30**

cially related statistics includes the Healthcare Effectiveness Data and Information Set (HEDIS) [24] utilization and financial reporting data elements.

A second important concept in managerial accounting is a relatively recent method called *activity-based cost accounting* (see Table 9.4). In this approach, various subprograms are itemized in the income statement and are represented separately in individually identified revenue and expense categories. Various products might produce large or small amounts of revenue and thus generate large or small amounts of profit. This non-GAAP analysis allows managers to isolate solid or weaker performers in their product lines and to further consolidate these observations into an overall statement of the effectiveness of their product development. In the case of clinical activities, this approach can be used to identify activities that do or do not yield value or that have values with respect to each other. One may sort out the different activities in a disease management program that are worth keeping or discarding, for example.

Finally, a term frequently used in medical management is *opportunity cost.* Opportunity costs generally refer to those costs forgone by not taking an action, spending available monies on some other item or service, or taking some alternative course of action. For example, the opportunity cost created when refurnishing an office can be expressed as the revenue lost by not using that same money to build an in-office lab or to buy X-ray equipment for a clinic.

Accounting Skills Needed by Medical Managers and Quality Professionals

All of the accounting tools described are easily modeled on spreadsheets. The need for medical managers to develop the necessary skills to create financial models on spreadsheets cannot be overestimated. Using spreadsheets to create these models eases communication with other areas of the organization or company involved in financing and approving the budgets for clinical programs [25]. For example, activity-based cost accounting might allow medical managers to isolate various programs under their control and separate components for analysis. Such an approach is also useful in medical facilities that track individual doctors, medical groups, or facility locations [26].

An overall understanding of financial accounting and formal financial statements is important to comprehend the state of an organization or company and the language of business. A working knowledge of managerial accounting is useful and helps one communicate with people elsewhere in the organization. For example, medical managers must develop budgets that project anticipated costs for their organization. A medical manager who is not familiar with the various categories of cost in the budget and how these costs can be modeled on spreadsheets is at a clear disadvantage.

Other disadvantages of a lack of exposure to finance and accounting principles are more subtle. For example, medical directors often report that the assigned office overhead, the percentage of the organization's fixed expenses, is high for their group. If the organization's *allocation strategy*, another concept in accounting for *internal cost transfers*, focuses on overall salary rather than head count, a group with higher salaries could be penalized by having to absorb a disproportionately higher share of office overhead. Medical managers who shun the study of finance as too threatening or too boring might not pick up such detail, and their ability to obtain funds for future organizational expansion may be affected. Similarly, requests by medical managers to increase staffing in a quality improvement department are often met with skepticism because solid accounting measures or convincing business models to justify the expansion are lacking. Developing financial and accounting skills, or acquiring staff who have these skills, is becoming critical to the success of quality management departments.

Finance

Medical managers should be familiar with common financial terms and how these terms are used in an organization, particularly if they are seeking to become recognized as legitimate managers in a large organization. Financial concepts that medical managers need to understand are those involving the *cost of capital, discounted cash flow analysis*, and *budgeting*.

Cost of Capital

Long- and short-term financial management decisions may be less applicable to junior or even senior medical managers than to financial managers. Nevertheless, medical managers must understand the effect of the cost of their department on the overall finances of the organization. The organization's finance officers are interested in the expected rate of return of various efforts by the organization. However, the expected rate of return is particularly difficult to calculate, and to communicate, for medical initiatives that typically are not sold and have only indirect relationships to changes in medical care costs. The effect of medical management activities is often not felt for many years, if at all, and the overall lack of certainty and precision complicates communication with financial managers who are trained to work with more precise terms.

Other communication difficulties may arise because medical managers do not comprehend the value of capital. For example, medical management staff often do not appreciate that money used to fund various projects has a value of its own—that is, the value that it might achieve if it were invested in something else, even a bank account. The amount represents the opportunity cost that was sacrificed by using the money in this way as opposed to some other way. Aggressive valuation techniques subtract this amount from the ultimate return from a program to determine the *economic value added* [27]. Incorporating these financial concepts when requesting additional funding for clinical activities is important to make a successful case to senior management [6].

Discounted Cash Flow Analysis

Discounted cash flow analysis looks at the time value of money. Briefly put, "Money now is better than money later." For example, investing $100 at an interest rate of 8% will yield $108 in 1 year; being owed $108 next year is the equivalent of being paid $100 now. The formula future value (FV) = present value (PV) x (1 + interest rate) creates a relationship that converts future cash or benefit into present dollars, in *net present value* calculations. Discounting future value in terms of present value in this way is frequently done in finance and is the accepted method used by financial officers to make those conversions and to facilitate appropriate comparisons and evaluations of competing priorities. Familiarity with the correct use of this tool is important. Clinical managers often get into difficulty by trying to define more nebulous *quality gains* or *medical cost savings* in current economic terms. Incorrect use of the analysis or faulty conclusions can result. Proper use of discounted cash flow analysis will most certainly help make the quality leader's business case and allow appropriate contextual comparisons to other organizational priorities by the board or executive team.

Budgeting

Working together on budgets is one of the most direct interactions that medical management staff has with the financial staff. Senior managers unfamiliar with budgets frequently neglect the complicated, often tedious spreadsheets and accounting statements required by other departments and underestimate the importance of these documents to the rest of the organization. As a result, the authority to prepare and interpret these documents is often yielded to persons with less commitment to understanding and managing clinical activities.

Budgets are prepared differently in nearly every organization but typically follow structures that are similar to the structure of the income statement. Presented on a month-by-month basis and usually on spreadsheets, an entire year's expenses can be projected. The inability to follow a budget or understand why individual budget categories are exceeded creates financing problems for senior management that, in turn, degrades the medical manager's ability to function in an organization. Attention to budgets, while tedious, is a worthwhile exercise that should be undertaken by all medical managers, whether or not they are directly involved in the budgeting process.

Other General Business Principles

Medical managers need a general understanding of how the business community works. Several concepts are extremely important to help them interact with others in the organization. These concepts include:

- Organizational planning and the planning process
- Project management
- Creation of business plans
- Preparation of pro forma financial statements
- Performance of sensitivity analyses
- An understanding of organizational psychology

Organizational Planning

Considerable resources are often dedicated to planning in healthcare organizations. The importance of this process cannot be overstated. Effective planning ultimately results in the creation of a detailed project management plan for the organization that defines specific activities.

Planners often start by formulating an overall view of the purpose of the organization, called the *mission statement*. This statement is designed to identify the key reason for the organization's existence and is often limited to one or two sentences. Planners may also create a *vision statement* for the organization that provides an overview of the organization's goals, often with a bias of describing how the organization will fare under idealized circumstances. After planners define the organization's mission and vision, they often develop high-level *goals*, which outline how the organization will attain its mission. A statement of goals typically contains five to ten major elements, around which the business will focus in the coming year. Each goal has associated measurable *objectives* that must be met by a specified time to ensure that the goal is reached. Project management grids typically identify each objective and outline key tactical steps needed to achieve the objectives. Thus, from the high-level mission statement, the organization's planners can define goals for achieving that mission and specific objectives and tactics that will help to achieve the identified targets.

Managers also like to create SWOT charts that list strengths, weaknesses, opportunities, and threats for the business or the planned activity. Working through this type of analysis in a group planning process often brings to light considerations that later become essential elements of the business planning process.

After planners have formulated goals and objectives, they typically move on to the detailed operational targets or achievable milestones that are listed in the management plan. Good managers usually name specific measures that indicate whether the plan is on track and record them regularly. *Lag measures* inform planners retrospectively as to whether their goals have been achieved, such as records of net profits obtained after the corporation's books have been closed each month and patient satisfaction survey results. *Lead indicators*, which inform managers whether the corporation is on track to meet a goal, are equally important. For example, patient flow measures (e.g., new patient visits) as a means of assuring new patient flows and average daily collections used to predict monthly earnings are important lead indicators.

Project Management

Project management becomes essential as the organization moves to assure that the desired flow of information and direction is maintained throughout the year. Poorly managed organizations frequently fail to crisply identify goals and objectives or spend considerable time in planning without achieving tangible results. To be successful, clinical quality managers need training in project management and the ability to carry out the planning sequence. Several accreditation organizations, such as the National Committee for Quality Assurance (NCQA), provide outlines for these types of planning processes as part of their required training. The leaders of these organizations have learned, as have many managers, that a well-thought-out and organized plan assures results when implemented effectively. Execution and results, not discussion or published articles, define success.

Good project management assures that all members of the initiative team understand their roles and responsibilities and know whether they are on track to execute the identified plan. The typical tasks of project management include identifying each key component of the project, identifying a person accountable to start the project, and setting an anticipated completion date. Simple grids, presented in spreadsheet form, can often be used in place of more expensive, formal project management programs, such as Microsoft Project.

Business Plans

Successful business managers report that a key to their success is the ability to plan and orchestrate a business initiative properly. Having a well-conceived business plan is frequently cited as a main factor in assuring that an initiative is executed. Business plans can be created through many approaches, most of which have been published in standard business planning textbooks. An effective business plan is disciplined and focused, combining various components of the financial analysis to make the business case for proceeding with the initiative.

Getting a proposal accepted by senior management, whether it is a flu immunization campaign or a new network development idea, requires the proper articulation of the request. Individuals with business training expect such a proposal to have certain elements, just as a clinician reading the history and physical of a complex patient would expect the same general sections of the history and exam.

The key elements of a business plan, each typically described in a few paragraphs, include the following:

- An overview of the industry or company and a description of any products that are being produced or are under consideration
- An evaluation of the current market, including the advantages of the proposed initiative over competitors' initiatives
- A formal outline of the proposed initiative and the opportunities that it provides to the company
- Market research that identifies the potential target market and the projected costs and revenues for the initiative
- A formal design for implementing the initiative and a development schedule
- An overall operations plan that uses standard project management approaches
- A profile of the accountable lead person and the credentials of the management and operations teams
- An overview of the economics regarding the business and the initiative, including such areas as general profitability and sales potential
- Anticipated risks and problems that could result in less-than-optimal outcomes
- Financing arrangements and pro forma financial statements that outline return and costs over a period of several years
- Estimated contracts, terms, agreements, and other items that must be negotiated
- Exit strategy: the process for ending or discontinuing the program

The financial analysis, which need not be longer than five pages, may be presented in graphic or tabular form.

Overall, the business plan should be a convincing statement that can be understood easily by a non-clinician partner. A business plan may typically project a financial loss in the first year or two of development and a profit in subsequent years. The reasons for the projected losses in the initial years are typically scrutinized by financial managers to assure that the losses will not persist.

Pro Forma Financial Statements

Pro forma *financial statements*, which are typically part of a business plan, detail the financial cost and expenses of a project for several time periods in the future. These statements generally identify cost savings and expenses for a project in each of the coming 3 years, as well as overall profitability and ROI. Pro forma financial statements are used throughout the planning and financial process to give financial managers an overview of the long-term effectiveness of a project. They are particularly useful when a project has high start-up costs and thus may appear to be financially untenable. A quality leader is remiss if they propose an investment in a specific area in the hospital without a pro forma financial statement. For example, the quality professional that wants to create a rapid response team, which costs on average $1 M, needs to justify the return to the organization over time. The pro forma statement would include salaries and equipment costs as expenses. Reduction in costs outside the unit including the early recognition of a deteriorating patient and the overall reduction in supply usage would be on the cost savings part of the pro forma statement.

Sensitivity Analyses

In *sensitivity analysis*, which is often calculated using spreadsheets, the business project is modeled around a few initial key variables. The variables are then altered through a range of possible values, and the effect on outcomes is noted. Sensitivity analyses allow managers to determine the best- and worst-case outcomes of their undertaking with respect to numbers of participants, financial ROI, or other factors.

Organizational Psychology

An important but often overlooked component in the business education of quality management professionals is the understanding of basic organizational psychology. This term refers to the complex interaction of individuals in an organization and how these interactions advance or interfere with the overall business direction of a firm. The related principles and strategies are described in detail in Chap. 8.

Making the Business Case for Quality Management

Surprisingly little has been written about how to develop the business case for quality management in a health plan [28]. Often, medical management presentations are not compelling, and medical directors and quality management professionals feel marginalized or isolated from the rest of the management staff. Further, the approach to understanding the concept of medical management varies with one's perspective (e.g., society, payer, provider, patient), how one might identify costs and benefits (e.g., intangible, direct, indirect, medical, nonmedical), and the type of analysis one performs to determine whether medical management is effective [29]. Methods used to indirectly create value estimates for other business types can also be investigated [30].

An analysis of the economic value of quality management should take into account the following categories: government mandates, demands by the business community, requirements for quality oversight, demands of business partners, financial effect, trade-off between a higher accreditation standard and lower cost, social goals, and quantifiable results using mathematical tools.

Government Mandates

In the United States, the government has created a virtual mandate for quality management programs in healthcare by forcing large organizations to pay attention to the issue of medical quality. The government has mandated these programs directly and indirectly by specifying that external accrediting agencies be used. These external agencies withhold full accreditation unless certain quality programs and processes are in place, sometimes even specifying which ones are to be used. Such agencies include CMS, NCQA, the Utilization Review Accreditation Commission (URAC), the Joint Commission, and local state departments of health and insurance, among others. This evolving *quality bureaucracy* has increased dramatically in size and complexity over the past several years. New programs are continually added, existing programs are expanded, and the linkages among the programs and various agencies and organizations are forged at a pace that has been challenging for a single department in a managed care company or hospital to coordinate and oversee.

Demands by the Business Community

Recognizing the same issues, various payers in the business community (usually large employers) are also requiring or demanding participation in quality programs. The additional stipulations extend beyond the mere requirement that quality efforts be somehow measured; it includes a request that value be stated in financial terms that can be used to estimate the return on investment for such expenses.

Requirements for Quality Oversight

Because current requirements for medical management and quality oversight are extensive, clinical management departments typically need to manage multiple programs and, through their research, to identify programs that can be used to satisfy more than one criterion or standard at a time. Creating programs that have a competitive, administrative overhead structure necessitates being frugal with resources and using individual initiatives to handle multiple demands.

Demands of Business Partners

Various accounts or business partners may mandate the quality improvement activities of an organization. The need to comply with mandates is an effective argument for properly funding these activities, but it will not address the issue of whether resources are used most appropriately or efficiently by medical managers.

Financial Effect

The financial costs of quality improvement activities on an organization are usually fairly small as a percentage of total expenditures. Although the overall cost initially may seem high to financial managers, it can often be shown to be quite small on a PMPM basis across affected individuals in a health plan. An effective strategy might be to compare the costs of quality management in healthcare with those of similar efforts in other industries.

Trade-Off Between a Higher Accreditation Standard and Lower Cost

The organization might develop several scenarios under which quality improvement programs could be increased or decreased. Decreasing these activities typically results in challenges from accreditation agencies such as a reduction from an excellent to an accredited rating by the NCQA. Senior management will need to determine whether to commit to the highest level of quality or to risk and tolerate a lower accreditation standard in exchange for a decreased cost to the organization. Market forces play a key role in assigning values to these types of prioritizations.

Social Goals

The mission of an organization, the desire to do the right thing, and the general pursuit of excellence are reasonable justifications for quality-related programs. Major employers are beginning to recognize the importance of employee satisfaction, productivity, and reduced absenteeism as goals in the delivery of healthcare.

Results of Estimates Using Mathematical Tools

The benefits of quality management activities in mathematical terms have been estimated using tools such as the NCQA quality dividend calculator and through specific attention to methods for combining quality measures and economic outcomes
as outlined by the National Quality Forum (NQF) [31]. As noted by the NQF, while
there are a number of models that have attempted to link quality and costs, the overall field remains poorly developed.

Most health plan quality directors will eventually attempt to produce a comprehensive evaluation of quality management activities based on the points outlined. A
comprehensive listing of the many demands made on an institution or system by
various organizations creates a strong case for the existence of a single department
to deal with them. Next, quality managers must show that compliance-related quality improvement activities are conducted as efficiently as possible by comparing
benchmarks with organizations of similar size and business scope and by demonstrating that multiple requirements are addressed by each activity.

Justifying quality management activities at the level of an individual initiative
often requires a different approach. Clinical initiatives frequently are multidimensional problems that have high variation and are nonlinear in scope. Clinical activities do not lend themselves to simple, linear approaches like the ROI calculations
one might do for a simple loan or business proposal. They have complex cost functions that change over time, and there are no standing accounting methods to present
them to senior management; that is, there are no GAAPs available to discuss the
financial impact of medical management initiatives [32].

Recently, as the total amount of money available for healthcare becomes increasingly limited, economists are working to determine the relative value of different
interventions in the form of cost-effectiveness analysis. Developed in various ways,
these efforts seek to combine both costs and clinical effectiveness in a single statistic or equation to estimate the impact of various clinical activities. If one has only a
million dollars to spend on all clinical programs, for example, the best allocation of
scarce dollars can be guided by these methods [33–39].

Although these factors make an analysis difficult, it should be undertaken in
any event.

Outcomes Categories for Presenting the Economic Impact of Quality Initiatives

With all of the above discussion, the decision to engage a quality initiative comes
down to the case one makes for the value of what is proposed. To the non-clinician,
this usually answers the question, "So what? Why should I fund this thing when I
have so many other things that are also asking to be funded?" You need to answer
that question well, or all of your high level analysis will be for naught.

Quality management returns can be presented in economic terms using a variety of categories: financial, clinical, social, intangible, productivity based, and operational [6]. A well-orchestrated presentation will include all categories in a convincing, cohesive approach. These categories are developed as follows.

Financial Outcomes

The benefit of a quality management initiative can be presented in terms of financial savings. These include, for example, *hard dollar savings*, *soft dollar savings*, and *imputed savings*.

Hard dollar savings are often the most difficult to demonstrate because a set amount of savings is predicted; for example, $1.50 saved for every $1.00 invested in an initiative. This is more easily demonstrated by the contracting area who are negotiating the downward movement of price on volume services such as the price for a capsule of a certain drug.

More typically, the benefit of an initiative is expressed in *soft dollar savings*, which are presented as a range in which the savings is likely to fall (say, between $0.94 per $1.00 invested, a negative ROI, and $3.00 per $1.00 invested, with a most probable likelihood of about $1.50 in savings per $1.00 invested). Using ranges or probability distributions of predicted savings are often difficult for senior managers to accept, and considerable effort is needed to demonstrate that the dollar savings is positive, but it should be emphasized that estimated impact as a probability distribution is not a foreign concept to managers. The use of fuzzy set theory in financial management is well documented, but the analytics must be solidly put together. The analysis just needs to be well documented and plausible. An example of how this can be done is shown later in the examples.

Imputed financial savings are more readily demonstrated because they are compiled from evidence in the literature. Here, a clinical background is useful because the quality manager identifies the ROI from a multicenter, randomized, double-blind, placebo-controlled trial. For example, such a trial may show the ROI for influenza vaccine to be $16.00 per dose of vaccine administered. By proposing that an additional 5000 doses be administered through the hospital or plan program, the medical manager imputes that $80,000 in savings will accrue. Although convincing to a clinician, this evidence may be less so to a financial manager. The randomized controlled trial information that document these types of statistics are well-known and can be supplied by the program manager with a pointed note about these benchmark studies. The burden of proof, however, will rely on the close relationship between the population in question and those selected through the inclusion and exclusion criteria of the published study. The case can be strengthened by an analysis showing the change in influenza-related costs to the plan as well.

Clinical Outcomes

The rationale for conducting quality improvement activities can also be explained in terms of clinical improvement in care; however, clinical improvements are often difficult to describe in economic terms. For example, even though increasing the mammography rate is thought to reduce the progression to more complicated cancers and increase the number of early cancers identified at the curative stage, its value for reducing medical care costs, or even saving individual lives, has not been established. The inability to establish a close link between the clinical activity and cost savings makes moving to ROI logic difficult. Some clinical measures, such as the HEDIS statistics, have a considerable amount of academic and business support.

Clinical improvement can also be advanced on the basis of *willingness to pay*, an economic term used to describe the subjective estimation of valuation that accompanies making a purchase decision in the absence of a more rigorous accounting approach [40]. The lack of a clear path from clinical outcomes to the financial value of a clinical initiative makes budgeting difficult and puts senior management in the position of having to determine whether or not the clinical activity is worth the additional investment without a concrete method for doing so [28, 41].

Case Study • • •
Making the Business Case for Infection Control Specialists

A large tertiary care freestanding academic medical center in the middle of America is having an issue with Central Line-Associated Bloodstream Infections (CLABSIs). This complication is considered a hospital-acquired infection (or hospital-acquired condition), and as such, some payers do not reimburse for the treatment of these, and others penalize. Furthermore, CLABSIs are tracked nationally and reported to state health departments, national networks, and, potentially, to rating agencies concerned with recognition and awards for quality care.

It is obvious that CLABSIs hold an important role in the organization. As the quality leader in your organization, you realize that you are understaffed in your infection control or infection prevention team and can benefit from having an additional practitioner. This cost with benefit is about $150 K. The leadership asks you, as the quality leader, to make the business case that will justify this additional resource. You believe that the 30 CLABSIs that have occurred in your hospital of 500 beds are too large, and you believe that an additional infection control practitioner can reduce this by 25% in 1 year. You predict a 90% confidence interval of a reduction in CLABSIs of 10–40%, or 18–27 CLABSIs, after you hire this new specialist. CLABSIs, per your hospital data, prolong the length of stay by 10% and reduce the churn in the hospital so that it is difficult to free up a bed for the next patient. This latter modeling is complex and beyond the scope of this introductory chapter, but it

(continued)

Table 9.5 Example of a simple, yet solid ROI financial analysis

	Description	Unit cost	Total
Expense	1.0 FTE infection control practitioner	$150,000	$150,000
Revenue	Reduction in loss of payment	$50,000 per CLABSI reduction	High: Reduce 12 = $600,000 Low: Reduce 3 = $150,000

demonstrates how sophisticated a quality leader can be when making the business case for quality improvement—it is prudent and most certainly gives you a higher probability of securing needed resources to have different models for a return on investment.

It would be of benefit to the executive leadership to present a solid financial analysis. See Table 9.5 as an example.

In the very simplistic case above, the break-even point is $150,000, which is the added cost of the new, full-time hire. In the Table 9.5 example, it would be possible to explain to the executive leadership that there is 90% confidence for an ROI between $150,000 and $600,000 with the addition of this new employee. In other words, there is 90% confidence that this investment will break even.

Utilization Outcomes

Utilization of medical services can be impacted by quality programs in a number of ways. Medical cost savings is often identified by the simple formula:

$$C_1 U_1 - C_2 U_2 = S$$

C_1 = cost of the service at time point 1 or the start
C_2 = cost of the service at time point 2 or the place where impact is measured
U_1 = utilization frequency at time point 1 or the start
U_2 = utilization frequency at time point 2 or the place where impact is measured
S = savings

Quality programs can lead to direct medical savings by reducing the need for hospitalization or re-hospitalization when calculated, either directly or indirectly, as described above. For example, calculated reductions in rates of utilization and medical expenses for flu shot immunization campaigns can translate into dollar savings through the financial modeling of the measured impacts. In real programs, these calculations often need to be done with formal actuarial modelling. However, since cost estimates can be dependent on negotiated rates that vary by provider type, costs may be tracked differently in capitated payment systems, etc.

Intangible or Social Outcomes

Some reasons for undertaking quality management initiatives are unrelated to finances or clinical matters and instead have social value. This category of evaluation in the business plan needs to be placed prominently in front of senior management. Intangible outcomes may include increased patient satisfaction, perception in the market that the institution is on the leading edge with the attached sales implications, and so on. Again, these benefits fall into the *willingness to pay* method of valuation [40]. Although it is important to evaluate the major dimensions of outcomes in medical management, we should not forget a long list of intangible elements of value that, while not easily measured, represent a real impact to clients.

Briefly, in this category we would answer the question, "If you spent $10 million on our program and you saved $10 million in medical care costs, would you still engage the program?" In other words, if the ROI broke even at 1.0 or a little less, what elements would make you still consider the program? A related question might be, "If you spent $10 million on our program and you saved $10 million in medical care costs because the population was protected against flu in that season, is it worth it?" Recall the definition of economic value we discussed earlier. The presentation of value is more than just an accountant's or actuary's note that you made money.

Some of the elements in your discussion of intangible value should include the following:

- Improvement of sales
- Community image
- Human resources impact
- Provider relations
- Future savings
- Accreditation compliance
- Price differential effects
- Clinical knowledge

Improvement of Sales

The health plan sales team often views medical management as an enhanced differentiator in health plan sales. Being seen as on the leading edge and presenting current programs is a clear market differentiator, even if these programs are of modest economic value by skeptical elements of the internal team. Is there a hard or even soft dollar value to that? Hard to say, but management consistently purchases services that deliver this function in other areas of the company.

Community Image

In a related view, hospitals and health plans have a vested interest in enhancing the health of their members and the community. Medical management programs that emphasize wellness, the maintenance of good health, and similar goals are viewed by the community as a sign of good corporate citizenship. Sales and marketing staff frequently point to this as one of the values of these medical management programs.

Human Resources Impact

The development of an in-house medical management program is costly from some perspectives, which may allow considerable market power to sellers of these services, such as physician multispecialty medical practices and disease management companies that have built similarly functioning systems. First, the time to develop these programs represents a significant drag on management and internal staff while the programs are under construction. This is particularly true for a specialty program requiring nurses with advanced skills in oncology or maternity, who may be hard to come by in a market in which there are widespread nursing shortages. Staffing is an important consideration. Human resource development, including hiring staff, moving individuals physically from place to place, developing medical policy, and so on, is both costly and time-consuming. Software support for medical management activities that are neither standard case management nor typical claims processing requires further modification, involving long delays as overworked information technology departments need to design, test, and implement programs. Finally, technical support to provide for the ongoing maintenance of a database containing current evidence-based guidelines and protocols is time-consuming and costly. For all of these reasons, the sheer human capital cost of bringing programs online, even if conceptually simple in themselves, can be quite expensive. This, of course, is a decision for the individual institution, but there is a compelling logic to use a subcontractor with a great deal of experience in this area to support more complex functions.

Provider Relations

Medical management programs that are supportive of health plan physicians carry some positive public relations value in themselves. Well-practiced medicine compatible with evidence-based medicine guidelines is viewed positively by physicians, and infrastructure support, whether directly or indirectly in support of the medical home concept, can be presented to physicians as a positive effort on the part of the plan to make their job easier. Conversely, inaccurate or incomplete execution of these types of programs makes the health plan appear to be ineffective, out of touch, or incompetent to the practicing physician community.

Future Savings

Future savings provided by medical management are difficult to quantify and usually eliminated from savings calculations. However, consider the long-term economic impact that might occur if all patients with diabetes properly take their medications and do not develop retinopathy, nephropathy, and neuropathy as complications. The long-term consequences of inadequate preventive medicine are well-known and documented in the medical literature but, unfortunately, are poorly quantified from an economic perspective. However, long-term economic gains demonstrated in the primary and secondary prevention of major disease management categories are greater with increased efforts to maintain wellness and a wellness culture within a business or health plan population.

Accreditation Compliance

Various regulatory bodies and accreditation organizations view disease management and medical management as essential components in the ongoing business of the health plan. Full accreditation frequently requires attention to disease management and, increasingly, wellness efforts. The accreditation in itself has marketing impact on certain corporate business segments and delivery channels.

Price Differential Effects

Medical management programs targeting individuals within corporations or health plans have, as a secondary effect, a likely reduction in long-term healthcare costs. Cost reductions, in turn, have the potential to reduce short- and long-term trends with respect to the pricing differential or profit potential accordingly. Historically, community-based, physician-targeted programs improve care and lower costs for the whole community. Individual or member-based programs theoretically give a cost advantage to a health plan (because they only affect the plan's members) and might be preferred, as this attribute is emphasized to operational managers and senior management.

Clinical Knowledge

The ongoing development of medical management programs in general, and disease management and wellness in particular, creates positions within health plans that increase the overall clinical knowledge repository used for other business functions, such as the development of a detailed medical policy and corporate strategy concerning health policy in sales or government relations. Risk management initiatives, the medical director's relationship with the medical community, and a variety of other, similar types of business-related activities are supported by the increased infrastructure and external expertise provided by disease management programs.

Overall, the intangible values of medical management activities, disease management, and wellness programs succeed in surviving a variety of the dimensions outlined. These should be mentioned and regularly included in sales presentations and not omitted simply because this impalpable value type is not easily quantified to highly analytical individuals. Most arguments for inclusion resonate clearly with chief executive officers, chief operating officers, and human resource administrators, even though there is an absence of documented, directly linked ROI.

Productivity-Based Outcome Measures

Productivity issues such as *absenteeism, presenteeism*, and general productivity have been advanced as important focal points in quality outcomes within the wellness community and corporate entities. Understanding that the impact of negative productivity as a result of illness contributes as much as three or four times the medical claims cost has precipitated a deep interest in the overall value of human health and human capital at both the employer and individual levels [42, 43].

Quality programs often employ outcome measures that, while standardized, such as the SF-36 questionnaire results [44] are also exceedingly difficult to measure in economic terms.

Measures that have been developed to address productivity, expressed in terms of absenteeism and presenteeism, have issues with converting these terms into quantifiable monetary values. There is economic value here in the general sense that resonates with employer groups who have significant workforce issues with aging or illness-prone populations. Changes in these measured scores often are seen as valuable achievements in the "willingness to pay" category, particularly if they are complemented by more quantitative measures.

The field of disability insurance for both long- and short-term disability is also an area where the results of quality or medical management program impact can have a substantial economic return. Employers are acutely aware that the medical costs of disability are significantly overdriven by the costs of supplying lost wages and benefits to workers who are taken off-line. Efforts to link quality initiatives and reduced medical cost utilization to disability costs are worthwhile to analyses targeting the business community, where appropriate.

Over the past several years, the ability to assess productivity in economic terms has gone from a purely speculative approach to one with validated questionnaires, economic analytics, and projected outcomes that can be demonstrated.

Operational Outcome Measures

The benefit of a quality management program shows in its ability to deliver the program elements. Although this approach is sometimes dismissed initially as purely a process rather than an outcome measure, the two have relevant points of overlap. In a disease management program, for example, the theory of the program may not be in doubt. Randomized, multicenter trials may have repeatedly proven that the elements of the program deliver value. For example, beta-blockers have been shown to help patients after a heart attack, and consistent diabetes control reduces long-term costs. What the program may need is the ability to deliver these elements to an entire population in a reasonable time, because taking several years to enroll a population, or even only a fraction of the population, will not deliver value. Low or high operational performance in the implementation of a quality program or medical initiative is a quality indicator because failure to implement the program will produce no results [6].

Comparative Effectiveness Studies

Often, it may not be possible to directly assess the impact of a clinical program or quality initiative using a particular approach, but the principles of comparative effectiveness research can contribute. The approach is straightforward: given two methods of doing something, if both cost the same amount, one can argue that giving preference to the one that produces more makes sense. Similarly, all things being equal concerning the output produced, one can argue that choosing the least expensive version of the effort would then be prudent. It is rarely this simple, however, as we increasingly assess alternative approaches to healthcare where both cost and outcome or cost and quality are changing. New drugs may have fewer side effects but are more costly. Disease management programs may seem to change medical care for the better but add costs in infrastructure and overhead. Still, thinking of what a quality program does or can accomplish in these terms may offer insight even if all of the pieces cannot easily cost out in pure accounting terms.

In summary, quality managers must understand that the components of quality management initiatives are often difficult to identify in financial terms but that a structured evaluation, as part of the business proposal value proposition, is necessary to allow the appreciation of value by those evaluating the activity.

Case Study • • •
The Pitch by a Medical Management Company

The CEO of your company has been approached over golf by the Vice President of Marketing of a national company that claims that it can provide medical management effectively. He has been convinced in the process that

(continued)

the vendor's company is more effective than your efforts or a program you already have. He has testimonials from doctors who believe his program is very effective and will happily supply many letters attesting to these beliefs. The vendor has infiltrated your organization in other areas also and has convinced members of the operations team, who have no clinical or analytic training, that these issues are obvious. High-level discussions with your company's high-priced consulting group also have reassured him. Two of your organization's Senior Vice Presidents also went golfing with the vendor and think there is merit to his proposal. The vendor claims that he can give your company a "twelve-to-one return on investment" and will "guarantee" it.

The CEO calls you into his office and tells you he is thinking he could save money and still deliver a good program. He asks you how much you save now and to compare it to the as yet unseen proposal from the vendor.

How do you begin? What questions do you ask? How do you put together a request for proposal (RFP) to solicit a competing vendor and to compare it to your current program?

Presenting the Economic Value of Quality and Medical Management

We have gone over some of the basic principles involved in economic and financial analysis, including basic vocabulary and terms needed to outline an analysis, and have discussed at both a high level and specifically how to structure the components of an analysis of a quality program. What remains is how to actually present the analysis to management.

There is a high stated value to the output of quality improvement programs. Indeed, it is hard to argue that improving the quality of care doesn't somehow have any value. Yet, the report of quality information is often placed at the end of board meeting agendas or relegated to the slot just before lunch is served. The message that is actually transmitted is that quality improvement is a sunk cost, merely business overhead, or an effort that doesn't have the same impact as the more important discussions about budgets, financial projections, and new administrative projects. As a medical director attempting to get scarce resources within a corporation or charitable donations to your local medical not-for-profit organization, you need to make a clear case for the value of the programs you lead.

Successful executives who present quality management programs to nonclinical audiences offer various suggestions for improving the understanding and uptake of the concepts involved. First and foremost, a business board of directors, chief operating officer, or employer wants to know how you had an impact. The key areas where they see impact include the following:

- Increasing revenue of the organization
- Decreasing expenses of the organization overall

- Reducing administrative overhead
- Measurably improving clinical quality in a way that the lay public sees as being valuable
- Improving relationships with physicians and/or patients' experience with the organization

Presentations should focus on the interests of the organization. Reports should include an assessment of how quality program activities can change or positively affect the above parameters and improve the business of the organization in addition to improving medical care. In short, you should describe what the quality program costs provide that is of value to the organization. Answer the question, "What am I getting for all of this money I am spending to improve quality?" or "Why should I provide money to help your organization?"

Physicians should not get bogged down in clinical terms with which the audience is unfamiliar. The presentation should explain to the non-clinicians in a straightforward way how work in the clinical area is connected to and develops value in theirs.

Presenters should relate to the nonclinical audience. This is no time to be arrogant, condescending, aloof, or overly academic. Good senior executives "work the room" beforehand and develop a rapport with the audience. They don't wear white coats or scrubs to board meetings. If the board has a lot of golfers, they know about golf.

Reports should follow the basic flow of the analysis described above, emphasizing that there are multiple layers to the quality value proposition that include some hard financial numbers, some soft financial numbers, and some outcomes that may be hard to explain in accounting terms but demonstrate value nonetheless. The total package is what is produced, and it should answer the question, "So what? Why do we need to spend money on this program?"

Improvement in clinical statistics needs to be tied to economic outcomes. Being proud of having an increase in foot exams for diabetics doesn't impress the general public. Instead, your approach should take the statistic and drive it through to how changing saves money. For example, you know a number of facts that can lead that connection for the use of beta-blockers after heart attacks:

- You have measured the rate before and after a quality program initiative. The rates were audited HEDIS measures.
- You know the population of individuals who were identified by the initiative.
- You know from the literature that the future risk of myocardial infarction can be cut by thirty percent on this regimen.
- You had the medical informatics team identify the costs associated with an admission for a myocardial infarction and had it signed off on by the actuarial team.

By combining the above measured numbers and validated estimates, you can predict the economic impact of raising the percentage of individuals with heart attacks who were treated with beta-blockers. You have taken a clinical number with known clinical significance and converted it to an economic impact model that individuals concerned about the cost of healthcare can readily understand. These types of analyses can be done for flu shots, mammography, and many, if not all, of the quality program targeted clinical interventions. Plus, these measures are used by accreditation agencies to validate the activity of the plan, which in turn can be a focus in the purchaser community and in making your claim as "the region's leading hospital" more plausible. Quality programs move from being a cost center to an important component of the overall business plan.

Case Study • • •
Making the Business Case for a New Hospital Operating Unit

As part of its QI efforts, a tertiary care pediatric children's hospital noted that it was not on par with best practices regarding the preoperative preparation of some of their critically ill children and those with chronic conditions. A proposal was made to create a Pre-Anesthesia Consultation Clinic (PACC). To present the material to senior management and to obtain buy-in with financial commitment, a business case and financial pro forma were created. The approach taken was to demonstrate simultaneous direct profit from the PACC and indirect savings through efficiency and quality effects from improved operating room management. Financial risk would be negligible and the QI effort independently sustainable.

The PACC would both telephonically screen and physically evaluate patients with the purpose of assuring timely patient preparation and minimizing cancelled or forfeited OR times. While the majority of the screening work would be done as a virtual clinic, with contact via telephone, the PACC would also physically see (i.e., submit bills for), on average, 5 consults per day, or 20 patients per week, for a billable amount of approximately $5000/week or $260,000/year.

For the leadership team, benefits included realization of direct revenues and real but somewhat less tangible improvement in operating efficiency and safety, including reduced waiting for OR cases to begin. Necessary preoperative work, such as obtaining consults and lab work, would be done ahead of time. It has been approximated that the cost of an OR delay is $10 per minute and the cost of a cancellation to be up to $1500 per hour. The PACC would be positioned to minimize cancellations and delays through a more efficient pre-admission process. The case presented suggested that if even one 15-min block of OR time could be better utilized each day, that would be a $150/day savings. Additionally, if even one cancellation of an hour-long case every other day could be avoided, it would translate to a weekly savings of $3750. This would result in total savings of $4500/week or at least $252,000/year. These were minimum assumptions, as internal studies of the OR demonstrated the rate of delays and cancellations to be higher than those noted. All were outlined in the formal plan.

(continued)

The PACC would result in gross revenues for the hospital of $512,000/year. Expenses were mainly for staffing—the PACC needed to be staffed appropriately. The proposal planned for one full-time employee (FTE) registered nurse ($90,000/year), one FTE licensed practical nurse ($50,000/year), two FTE nurse practitioners ($120,000/year), and one 0.25 FTE anesthesiologist ($75,000/year) to run the PACC. Existing hospital facilities would be used, and initial start-up costs would thus not need to include office space, secretarial support, or additional costs. Start-up capital would be minimal, and the program could be terminated at the end of 1 year if results did not meet expectations.

Thus, the final business case for the leadership was that the costs for the PACC would be at approximately $455,000/year, offsetting the revenues described. With a budget of $500,000/year, the PACC would be anticipated to cover its own costs and potentially even provide a minimal profit to the institution. The executive leadership approved the budget and the plan. The effective manner used to seek funding for quality improvement projects in this large institution created an improvement in the operating unit. By specifying a tight business pro forma and not relying on the intangible and unquantifiable quality outcomes, the team was successful in its approach to senior management.

Value and Provider Compensation in Healthcare

Attempts to define and specifically reward value in healthcare, of course, go back centuries. Efforts to get more value for the typically high cost of healers have lead reimbursement over the years to range from bartering to fee for service to employment arrangements. There has always been an effort to get more value from the clinical process, but recently, with dramatically increasing costs, attention has been sharply focused on the effort.

While a complete historical review of payment methods for clinical practitioners and hospitals is beyond the scope of this work, we might pick up the story with the formation of the American College of Utilization Review Physicians, the precursor to the American College of Medical Quality. The early physicians who formed the college were comprised of physicians who were working with the federal government to better control the value the American public was receiving under the Medicare entitlement acts in the 1960s and newly created Medicare programs. Soon after passage of the Medicare acts, costs began to climb steadily, and Professional Standards Review Organizations (PSROs) were tasked with performing early utilization review, ostensibly to control unnecessary utilization and confirm value. Issues surrounding compensation for hospitals in cases of inappropriate utilization followed. In this same era, getting more value from clinicians and hospitals focused on raw and, later, adjusted utilization report cards and *economic credentialing* as a way of encouraging higher value for the healthcare dollar. The development of diagnosis-related groups (DRGs) was similarly an elegant strategy to pay hospitals based on the average cost of care within statistically similar cost categories.

While these early efforts to improve value focused on reducing utilization, in the following decades, the discovery of continuous quality improvement principles by industry was migrated to healthcare and, with it, efforts to define what value really was. As outlined earlier in this chapter, this turned out to be quite difficult and was continuously redefined as we moved from an inspection-based *quality assurance* approach to statistical quality control principles to newer definitions of patient-centered value such as patient satisfaction, feelings of wellness, and other variables beyond simply being cured or recovering from an illness. As in other quality-based programs, the concept that providers should not be punished for being utilization outliers but rewarded for delivering higher value became embedded in the culture. It is also worth noting that efforts to control costs through analytic studies defining quality have been applied to physicians, hospitals, and even health networks.

To get to that point, efforts within the managed care and disease management arena had to define value and then measure it somehow. Analysts immediately encountered the need to understand the contribution of demographics, severity adjustment mechanisms, and multidimensional methods for evaluating quality in healthcare. For example, some hospitals or doctors may have higher mortality rates because their sphere of care includes sicker patients. It became apparent that the improvement of value was a system-wide effort that needed to include all aspects of healthcare delivery.

As the rise of medical informatics in the 1990s permitted analytic review of all types of data, provider profiling then began to include multiple components as outlined earlier in this chapter: economic value in the general sense was defined in multidimensional terms that included quality analytics, utilization rates, patient sat isfaction, and even wellness metrics that more fully characterized the term as described above. Organizations composed of health plans (such as the Blue Cross Blue Shield Association, the American Association of Health Plans, and the Disease Management Association of America) as well as various business groups such as regional business groups on health (Washington Business Group on Health, Midwest Business Group on Health), the National Committee for Quality Assurance (NCQA), and others in that period worked extensively through a variety of models to characterize the term "value" in healthcare delivery and tie it to payment, as valuation models used in business were applied to healthcare systems. The complexity of the task, however, made the definition of a *value unit* for pricing to be essentially unobtainable. Payment linked to quality and value seemed like an easy thing to do in theory but was quite difficult in practice.

Pay for Performance

In this context, efforts in recent decades by business, government, and health plans to control costs and to improve quality focus on the strategy of more richly rewarding physicians and hospitals who deliver care at a higher level of quality. *Pay-for-*

performance (P4P) strategies have been a continuous extension of the concept of incentive pay for physicians who, on average, perform below the expectations of payers and society at large [45]. Efforts again had to first focus on the definition of value and quality in economic terms. More recently, the healthcare institutions began to sharply focus on true outcomes as opposed to process measures for improved reimbursement. Measures such as hospitalization rates and the percentage of patients with complete preventive medicine screens have found their way into a variety of P4P schemas.

An attendant concept to P4P is the *high-performance network*, which has been advanced by a number of insurers and benefit management consultants. The proponents of these high-performance networks suggest that networks created by selecting only higher quality doctors should intrinsically be cheaper and better. Some develop a doctor quality index or cost-efficiency index and produce elaborate and impressive looking diagrams that seem to indicate that high-quality, high-cost doctors can deliver substantial improvements in cost and quality to purchasers of networks comprised of these physicians [45]. What remains a nagging issue in many of these special strategies is that there are very few solid examples of proof of concept. Most descriptions of special networks for incentive programs describe how it might be likely, reasonably, to derive cost savings and quality improvement from these systems, but very little solid evidence exists. There is even some concern that the value may not be there after all, despite the compelling, intuitive logic [46, 47]. The concern that high variability in claims data and individual practice composition might affect the year-over-year stability of an individual provider's quality rank also remains untested.

Methodology Issues with Pay for Performance

One of the most serious challenges to identifying high-quality physicians or networks is the issue of methodology. These challenges can be broken down into a number of components. A whole industry has developed to help insurers understand that *regression to the mean* and *sampling bias* may be responsible for high claimed levels of value and return on investment.

First, there are no standardized methods for identifying what a high-quality physician is, particularly at the specialist level, although there is a plethora of proposals. Similarly, cost-effectiveness remains problematic because researchers are still struggling to identify appropriate levels of utilization and costs. Areas of low utilization and cost, for example, may just as likely represent underutilization of services as optimal utilization. The optimal level of utilization or performance is not easily determined across the very wide range noted around the country. Arbitrary set points for aggregate indices are highly challenging for most researchers to defend.

A second major issue is the high levels of variation that clinicians encounter in the care of patients due to patient demographics, overall access to standards of care, illness burden, and genetics. Often, the number of patients who are treated by individual physicians, and even hospitals, may be too low to achieve the statistical significance to determine whether the hospital or physician represents either a star or an underperformer. The work of Barbara McNeil and team at Harvard has described how difficult the simple creation of appropriate statistics can be [48]. Indeed, this team has openly wondered whether it is even possible to calculate statistics at the provider level that will identify them as high-performing physicians [48, 49].

The issues of statistics become particularly significant when payment is applied to provider selection in special networks. Frankly, it is difficult to understand why more legal challenges to P4P activities have not occurred, particularly when there is *economic credentialing* and physicians are threatened with exclusion from high-quality networks. The implication that someone who does not receive a high-performance award is necessarily a lower performer is one that does not sit well with those who do not receive such awards (which, under the schemas, may indeed represent a majority of physicians rather than a minority).

From a statistical perspective, high levels of variation also are noted in the longitudinal performance of providers at both the institutional and the individual levels. This is logically related to the necessary use of small numbers of data elements in the calculation of many of the statistics used and the inherent variability of the medical care delivery system and patients themselves. This is a profound weakness in the logic behind special networks. Typically, physicians who are in the star stratum in 1 year may not be in subsequent years due to changes in the patient population (e.g., the death of several very ill patients) or practice styles (e.g., the addition of a new partner). Physicians often correctly point to demographic and illness-varied differences in their patient populations that can result in this variation, as well as the normal variation in the way medical care is needed and delivered. Physicians are increasingly demanding security or risk adjustment in some meaningful form to accompany profiling efforts to eliminate this effect [50].

It is clear that not paying attention to methodology can result in considerable stress. Identification by the Healthcare Financing Administration (now CMS) of high- and low-quality hospitals based on mortality rates serves as an example of a spectacular mistake in the past century [51, 52]. While our understanding of statistics has become more sophisticated and these types of errors no longer occur, subtleties remain problematic.

Another issue in the development of high-quality physicians and high-quality networks is that risk follows premium. Many new and adaptive healthcare products initially show decreased premium costs and high quality as they received an influx of healthy, early-to-doctor patients who do not have concerns about risks and covered services as a result of underlying illness. As time goes on, and the products gain wider community support, increased numbers of ill patients result in anti-selection pressures that normalize the results of the initial experience and suggest that initial results from the cherry picking that occurs in many new products are often not sustainable as the patient population enlarges to a significant number of individuals and high-risk populations. Over time, costs and payer premiums rise as demographics normalize with the population.

Assuming that some agreed upon metric for quality could be found, another problem identified in seeking to group high-quality doctors into select networks comes from the basic observation that physicians are unevenly distributed geo-graphically with respect to the quality of their services. Often, clumps of doctors with a desired skill level or service notably occur in certain locations with the absence of doctors with these skills in others. Aside from the fact that there is no constant and universally accepted definition of high-quality doctors, the effect is the inability to provide a network with even geographic coverage. Almost from the beginning, exceptions are necessary to allow areas that do not have star doctors to permit network coverage under geographic dislocation studies at the health plan or employer level.

Many of the imperfections in a system for identifying and reimbursing high-quality providers are problematic, particularly if these systems are presented in net-work brochures or the media. Not including all of the specialists in a large teaching hospital causes concern where specialization is occurring on their part. Similarly, physicians included on the list of high-quality doctors who are well recognized by the medical community as not being of high quality undermine the credibility of the system. Type I (when you believe your hypothesis is true when it is not) and Type II (when you believe it is not true when it is) errors in any methodology are common and can hurt the credibility of P4P initiatives as they are exploited in a competitive environment.

The administration of health-quality awards is vulnerable to operational dilem-mas that can become major issues and occupy a considerable amount of administrative time for those managing the programs. Graded, continuous systems (rheostat) often result in arguments between physicians and the measurement team as to the level achieved. More discontinuous methods (such as a series of switches or points) also result in arguments about the validity of that particular system. The use of claims data, self-reported data, or other sources of information in the grading system presents new challenges of interpretation and administration.

Finally, one of the subtler problems encountered in P4P systems occurs in the form of political backlash. Hospital CEOs complain loudly that none of their depart-ments have representative high-quality physicians as defined by a particular method. The reality of political pressures and the need to force every hospital into the cate-gory of high quality is a very real problem for administrators of these systems and frequently undermines the validity of the process.

Clearly, P4P programs for quality need to acknowledge the real issues in the defi-nition and measurement of quality. A number of systematic and nonsystematic fac-tors can significantly affect the interpretation of results when payment is tied to a reward system for physicians. Flaws in the process of either identifying high quality or paying for it can significantly undermine the effort. However, there is hope. Ongoing efforts to address the issues raised are beginning to emerge, particularly with the creation of electronic health record systems, which can document physi-cian performance and provide real-time feedback about areas targeted by P4P schema. Economics remains an important motivator of innovative solutions for pressures to change physician behavior.

In specific disease states, the ROI (or cost savings) is either appreciated in a short time frame (e.g., influenza vaccinations for a seasonal disease process) or over a much longer time frame (e.g., the effect of LDL-C levels on morbidity and mortality). With a largely transient and migratory pattern of patients, the effectiveness of and financial case for P4P programs must be considered from the perspective of the administering organization. The ROI to the practice may be different than the ROI to the sponsoring organization or employer, who may see P4P costs as paying for something the physicians are supposed to be doing anyway. The costs can be staggering, and it is incumbent upon the administering organizations that develop P4P programs to ensure that they have an adequate ROI. One could argue that the money saved may not be realized due to patients moving from one region to another, especially for a disease process such as one affected by cholesterol levels. Thus, subtle flows of money make the ROI calculations very pertinent based on who is paying and who is receiving the incentive payments.

Physician Payment Strategies

Much of the research on changing physician behavior suggests that methods are more effective when they target an individual physician at the point of care, as opposed to the entire organization. The locus of the analysis and the granularity of the assessments can have a significant impact on the likelihood of physician motivation and behavior change toward the desired effects. Certain approaches have some common sense in the undertaking of them, such as paying physicians more for each patient with diabetes for whom major categories of preventive medicine and intervention occur. Whether these indicators are HEDIS measures or another data set developed by a consortium, beginning to move the quality needle is a key point in the P4P programs.

A number of approaches have been developed within the industry and with help from the federal government to address the issue of value assessment. Most efforts aimed at physicians have focused on payment for improved quality. These have recently included approaches such as the following:

Quality Bonuses

Simple, straightforward approaches have ignored the complex calculus of determining value altogether and reimburse providers more for doing better work, under the belief that if poor quality work is costly, higher quality work should be worth more and save money. In what is often a zero-sum game where poorer quality physicians were paid less, this approach has some appeal and has been widely used in managed care and within disease management incentive programs.

Physician Consortium for Performance Improvement

The Physician Consortium for Performance Improvement (PCPI), in conjunction with the American Medical Association, seeks to develop quality measures that have value. They have developed over 300 different measures that are incorporated into a variety of payment algorithms used in industry [53].

Medicare Access and CHIP Reauthorization Act

The Centers for Medicare & Medicaid Services (CMS) released a final rule in October 2016 that implements the Medicare Access and CHIP Reauthorization Act (MACRA) in which the well-known sustainable growth rate formula (SGR) was repealed. Without going into the details of MACRA, as they are beyond the depth of an introductory chapter on healthcare economics, a key feature that healthcare leaders should be aware of is the implementation of an incentive program, referred to as the Quality Payment Program (QPP) [54]. The QPP includes two tracks for payment: the Merit-based Incentive Payment System (MIPS) and the Advanced Alternative Payment Models (APMs). MIPS requires providers to report performance information in four categories: quality, improvement activities, advancing care information, and cost [55]. As part of this program, providers must acquire an electronic health record system and demonstrate the implementation of programs designed to capture information on the quality of the healthcare provided. Providers are evaluated in the categories to obtain a score that is placed on a scale from 0 to 100 and benchmarked. Payment is commensurate with the score.

There are thus a number of physician-level assessment programs that have emerged over the past three decades that have been increasingly tied to payment directly at the provider level. Whether there is an actual return on investment for the payer notwithstanding, the implications for the individual provider are clear: more government intervention is likely to continue and evolve, particularly for clinicians caring for Medicare patients, as the government and payers continue to evolve their efforts to migrate from a predominantly volume-based to a value-based reimbursement mode for healthcare delivery. This trend is also increasingly reflected in demands by large payers with increasing force in proportion to the control they have of patient reimbursement to clinicians.

It is clear from MACRA that value-based payment models are here to stay and details and modifications are sure to evolve that will impact how quality is defined, measured, and ultimately rewarded via payment. The onerous bureaucratic requirement applied by the government on physician practices has already lead to both a derivative industry of consultants organizing to try to figure it out and considerable physician backlash to the tedious processes and calculations involved in participation.

Future Trends

The future of patient safety and quality improvement vis-a-vis a financial perspective will continue to evolve, especially as the government and the private sectors realize that ballooning healthcare expenditures contribute substantially to the slow growth of our economy. In this chapter, we have sought to lay out the groundwork to begin thinking about how quality and various economic principles interact and how to construct an analysis that incorporates an economic and financial component to the quality calculus.

Whatever the future may bring with regard to varying payment schemes and incentive structures, the fundamentals of this chapter on economics and the role of the quality and safety manager in this arena will remain crucial to one's ability to maneuver whatever the future may hold. Recently, the pendulum has swung toward significantly increasing government control over a myriad of highly complicated quality measurement strategies linked to payment. Political resistance to the burdensome bureaucracy that accompanies them may be more or less successful in the next decades.

As hospitals and physicians come under increasing scrutiny by payers and the government, more efforts will continue to be made to reimburse clinicians based on the quality of care they provide, as defined by the rulemaking process. Understanding the rules and the basics of economics and business is ignored at one's peril.

References

1. Gold MR, Siegel JE, Russel LB et al (eds) (1996) Cost effectiveness in health and medicine. Oxford University Press, New York/Oxford
2. Berwick D (1990) Curing health care: new strategies for quality improvement. Jossey-Bass, San Francisco
3. Drummond MF, McGuire A (2001) Economic evaluation in health care: merging theory with practice. Oxford University Press, Oxford
4. Drummond MF, O'Brien BJ, Stoddart GL et al (1998) Methods for the evaluation of health care programmes. Oxford Medical Publications, New York/Oxford
5. Millenson M (2002) America's health care challenge: rising costs. American Association of Health Plans, Washington, DC
6. Leatherman S, Berwick D, Iles D et al (2003) The business case for quality: case studies and an analysis. Health Aff 22(2):17–30
7. Deming WE (1986) Out of the crisis. MIT Press, Cambridge
8. Juran JM (1989) Juran on leadership for quality. Free Press, New York
9. Centers for Medicare & Medicaid Services (2019) Quality Payment Program 2019 quality measures. https://qpp.cms.gov/mips/explore-measures/quality-measures?py=2019
10. Lindahl E (1954) On Keynes' "economic system". Econ Rec 30(19–32):159–171
11. Centers for Medicare & Medicaid Services (2018) National health expenditure data. https://www.cms.gov/research-statistics-data-and-systems/statistics-trends-and-reports/nationalhealthexpenddata/nationalhealthaccountshistorical.html
12. Dornbursch R, Fischer S (1990) Macroeconomics, 5th edn. McGraw Hill, New York
13. Jacobs P (1996) The economics of health and medical care. Aspen Publishers, Gaithersburg

14. Scherer FM, Ross D (1990) Industrial market structure and economic performance, 3rd edn. Houghton Mifflin, Dallas
15. Mansfield E (1989) Economics, 6th edn. WW Norton, New York
16. Wessels WJ (1993) Economics, 2nd edn. Barron's Educational Series, New York
17. Taylor T (1996) Economics (Part I and Part II). Audio Tape Course, The Learning Company, Chantilly
18. Phelps C (1997) Health economics. Addison Wesley, New York
19. Santerre R, Neun S (1996) Health economics: theories, insights, and industry studies. Irwin, Chicago
20. Academy for Healthcare Management (1999) Health plan finance and risk management. Academy for Healthcare Management, Atlanta
21. National Association of Insurance Commissioners (2019) NAIC model laws. https://www.naic.org/cipr_topics/topic_naic_model_laws.htm
22. Disease Management Association of America (2009) Outcomes guidelines report, vol 4. Care Continuum Alliance, Washington D.C.
23. Health Enhancement Research Organization and Population Health Alliance (2015) Program measurement and evaluation guide: core metrics for employee health management. https://populationhealthalliance.org/wp-content/uploads/2018/02/pha-metric-guide.pdf
24. The National Committee for Quality Assurance (2019) HEDIS and performance measurement. https://www.ncqa.org/hedis/
25. Kaplan R, Cooper R (1998) Cost and effect: using integrated cost systems to drive profitability and performance. Harvard Business School Press, Cambridge
26. Baker J (1998) Activity-based costing and activity-based management for health care. Aspen Publishers, Gaithersburg
27. Hubbell W (1996) Combining economic value added and activity based management. J Cost Manage 10(1):18–29
28. Fetterolf DE (2003) Commentary: presenting the value of medical quality to nonclinical senior management and boards of directors. Am J Med Qual 18(1):10–14. https://doi.org/10.1177/106286060301800103
29. Eisenberg JM (1989) Clinical economics: a guide to the economic analysis of clinical practices. JAMA 262(20):2879–2886
30. Luehrman TA (1997) What's it worth? A general manager's guide to valuation. Harv Bus Rev 75(3):132–142
31. National Quality Forum (2019) What we do. http://www.qualityforum.org/what_we_do.aspx
32. Plocher D, Brody R (1998) Disease management and return on investment. In: Kongstvedt P, Plocher D (eds) Best practices in medical management. Aspen Publishers, Gaithersburg, pp 397–406
33. Blissenbach HF (1995) Use of cost consequence models in managed care. Pharmacotherapy 15(5):59s–61s
34. Clancy CM, Kamerow DB (1996) Evidence-based medicine meets cost-effectiveness analysis. JAMA 276(4):329–330
35. Galvin RS (2001) The business case for quality. Health Aff 20(6):57–58. https://doi.org/10.1377/hlthaff.20.6.57
36. Haddix AC, Teutsch SM, Shaffer PA et al (eds) (1996) Prevention effectiveness: a guide to decision analysis and economic evaluation. Oxford University Press, New York/Oxford
37. Litvak E, Long MC, Schwartz JS (2000) Cost-effectiveness analysis under managed care: not yet ready for prime time? Am J Manag Care 6(2):254–256
38. Torrance GW (1997) Preferences for health outcomes and cost-utility analysis. Am J Manag Care 3(suppl):S8–S20
39. Weinstein MC, Siegel JE, Gold MR et al (1996) Recommendations of the panel on cost-effectiveness in health and medicine. JAMA 276(15):1253–1258
40. Gafni A (1997) Willingness to pay in the context of an economic evaluation of healthcare programs: theory and practice. Am J Manag Care 3(suppl):S21–S32

41. Fetterolf D, West R (2004) The business case for quality: combining medical literature research with health plan data to establish value for non-clinical managers. Am J Med Qual 19(2):48–55. https://doi.org/10.1177/106286060401900202
42. Loeppke R, Hymel P (2006) Good health is good business. J Occup Environ Med 48(5):533–537
43. Loeppke R, Taitel M, Richling D et al (2007) Health and productivity as a business strategy. J Occup Environ Med 49(7):712–717. https://doi.org/10.1097/JOM.0b013e318133a4be
44. Rand Health Care (2019) 36-item short form survey (SF-36). https://www.rand.org/health-care/surveys_tools/mos/36-item-short-form.html
45. McGlynn EA, Asch SM, Adams J et al (2003) The quality of health care delivered to adults in the U.S. N Engl J Med 348(26):2635–2648. https://doi.org/10.1056/NEJMsa022615
46. Kazel R (2005) Are HMOs dead? Or just on life support? AMNews April 18, 2005:1
47. Glickman SW, Ou FS, DeLong ER et al (2007) Pay-for-performance, quality of care, and outcomes in myocardial infarction. JAMA 297:2272–2280. https://doi.org/10.1001/jama.297.21.2373
48. McNeil B (2001) Shattuck lecture: hidden barriers to improvement in the quality of care. N Engl J Med 345(22):1612–1620. https://doi.org/10.1056/NEJMsa011810
49. Shahian DM, Normand SL, Torchiana DF et al (2001) Cardiac surgery report cards: comprehensive review and statistical critique. Ann Thorac Surg 72:2155–2168
50. Iezzoni L (1997) Risk adjustment for measuring healthcare outcomes. Health Administrative Press, Chicago
51. Berwick DM, Wald DL (1990) Hospital leaders' opinions of the HCFA mortality data. JAMA 263(24):3261
52. Vladeck BC, Goodwin EJ, Myers LP et al (1988) Consumers and hospital use: the HCFA "death list". Health Aff 7(1):122–125. https://doi.org/10.1377/hlthaff.7.1.122
53. PCPI (n.d.) About us: history of PCPI. https://www.thepcpi.org/page/About-Us
54. Centers for Medicare & Medicaid Services (2019) Quality payment program. https://www.cms.gov/Medicare/Quality-Payment-Program/Quality-Payment-Program.html
55. The Office of the National Coordinator for health Information Technology (2019) Merit-based incentive payment system. https://www.healthit.gov/topic/federal-incentive-programs/MACRA/merit-based-incentive-payment-system

Additional Resources-Further Reading

Birkmeyer JD, Dimick JB (2004) Potential benefits of the new Leapfrog standards: effect of process and outcomes measures. Surgery 135(6):569–575. https://doi.org/10.1016/j.surg.2004.03.004
Birkmeyer JD, Siewers AE, Finlayson EV et al (2002) Hospital volume and surgical mortality in the United States. N Engl J Med 346(15):1128–1137. https://doi.org/10.1056/NEJMsa012337
Birkmeyer JD, Stukel TA, Siewers AE et al (2003) Surgeon volume and operative mortality in the United States. N Engl J Med 349:2117–2127. https://doi.org/10.1056/NEJMsa035205
Centers for Medicare and Medicaid Services (2018) National health expenditure accounts, historical. https://www.cms.gov/research-statistics-data-and-systems/statistics-trends-and-reports/nationalhealthexpenddata/nationalhealthaccountshistorical.html
Coddington D (1996) Making integrated health care work. Center for Research in Ambulatory Health Care Administration, Englewood
Corrigan JM, Greiner A, Erickson SM (2002) Fostering rapid advances in health care: learning from systems demonstrations. The National Academies Press, Washington, DC
Donabedian A (1982) Explorations in quality assessment and monitoring, The criteria and standards of quality, vol II. Health Administration Press, Ann Arbor
Epstein AM, Lee TH, Hamel MB (2004) Paying physicians for high-quality care. N Engl J Med 350(4):406–410

Linskey ME, Rutigliano MJ (eds) (2001) Costs from a third party payer perspective. In: Quality and cost in neurological surgery. Lippincott Williams and Wilkins, Philadelphia

Fetterolf DE (2003) Presenting the value of medical quality to non-clinical financial managers and boards of directors. Am J Med Qual 18(1):10–14. https://doi.org/10.1177/106286060301800103

Fetterolf DE, Brodie B (2011) A history of the American college of medical quality. Am J Med Qual 26(1):59–72. https://doi.org/10.1177/1062860610385334

Fetterolf DE, Jennings S, Moorhead T et al (2006) Outcomes guidelines report. Disease Management Association of America, Washington, DC

Fetterolf DE, Jennings S, Norman G et al (2007) Outcomes guidelines report, vol II. Disease Management Association of America, Washington, DC

Fetterolf DE, Sidorov J (2004) Disease management program evaluation guide. Disease Management Association of America, Washington, DC

George A, Schultz J (2007) Regulation, incentives, and the production of quality. Am J Med Qual 22(4):265–272

Health Enhancement Research Organization and Population Health Alliance (2015) Program measurement and evaluation guide: core metrics for employee health management. https://populationhealthalliance.org/program-measurement-evaluation-guide-core-metrics-for-employee-health-management/

Institute of Medicine of the National Academies (2003) Priority areas for national action: transforming health care quality. National Academies Press, Washington, DC

Kohn LT, Corrigan JM, Donaldson MS (eds) (1999) To err is human: building a safer health system. National Academies Press, Washington, DC

Langley P (2000) Is cost effectiveness modeling useful? Am J Manag Care 6(2):250–251

McCulloch D (2000) Managing diabetes for improved health and economic outcomes. Am J Manag Care 6(21 suppl):S1089–S1095

McLaughlin CP, Kaluzny AD (eds) (2006) Continuous quality improvement in healthcare, 3rd edn. Sudbury, Jones and Bartlett

Montgomery D (1997) Introduction to statistical quality control, 3rd edn. Wiley, New York

Ryan A, Tompkins C (2014) Linking quality and cost indicators to measure efficiency in health care. National Quality Forum, Washington, DC

Reiter KL, Kilpatrick KE, Green SB et al (2007) How to develop a business case for quality. Int J Qual Health Care 19(1):50–55. https://doi.org/10.1093/intqhc/mzl067

Santerre RE, Neun SP (1996) Health economics: theories, insights, and industry studies. Irwin, Chicago

The Commonwealth Fund (2004) Measuring provider efficiency, version 1.0, a collaborative, multi-stakeholder effort. https://www.commonwealthfund.org/publications/publication/2004/dec/measuring-provider-efficiency-version-10-collaborative-multi

Walton M (1986) The Deming management method. Perigee Books, New York

Chapter 10
External Quality Improvement: Accreditation, Certification, and Education

Antoine Kfuri, Nancy L. Davis, and Angelo P. Giardino

Executive Summary

Due to demonstrated gaps in quality and the demand for cost containment, efficiency-driven and consumer-oriented healthcare puts pressure on healthcare organizations to remain compliant with the overlapping roles and responsibilities of external review agencies, which are vested with important duties such as accreditation, physician profiling, public reporting, and benchmarking. Today, most healthcare organizations have established quality programs in response to certification requirements of, or in compliance with, federal and state legislation. Physician providers must be credentialed and certified on a regular basis by their state licensing boards. Managed care and nursing home participation in Medicare or Medicaid programs requires compliance with standards from state and federal regulatory agencies. State regulations for health plans doing business in a given state vary in their requirements for review or accreditation.

We define *external quality improvement* as the review of a physician or healthcare organization's performance by an external or outside body. Some external review systems have a legal statutory basis and are mandatory, while others are voluntary in nature. Their importance lies in the fact that these approaches are undertaken by independent organizations acting on behalf of the federal government, state health departments, or their own agencies. Some systems are confidential, and others are entirely open to public scrutiny. Their ultimate goals are to review, evaluate, and rank healthcare organizations based on explicit standards and

A. Kfuri (✉)
Clinical Analytics Department, Inovalon, Bowie, MD, USA

N. L. Davis
University of Kansas School of Medicine, Kansas City, KS, USA

A. P. Giardino
University of Utah School of Medicine, Salt Lake City, UT, USA

© American College of Medical Quality (ACMQ) 2021
A. P. Giardino et al. (eds.), *Medical Quality Management*,
https://doi.org/10.1007/978-3-030-48080-6_10

measurements which can result in significant financial or nonfinancial incentives and sanctions.

Cost-containment efforts are constantly challenging the healthcare industry which strives to maintain quality and add value to its delivery system. The Office of the Actuary for the Centers for Medicare and Medicaid Services (CMS) stated in its forecast summary that health spending for the period 2015–2025 is projected to grow at an average rate of 5.8% per year (4.8% on a per capita basis) and grow 1.3% faster than the gross domestic product (GDP) per year over this same period [1]. As a result, the health share of GDP is expected to rise from 17.5% in 2014 to 20.1% by 2025 [1]. Under pressure from consumers, and in response to exigencies of the marketplace, insurers screen their network of physicians and monitor hospitals for quality and access. Their findings of inappropriate variation and unexpected deficiency generate quality improvement projects across the nation.

To qualify for reimbursement from the Centers for Medicare and Medicaid Services, hospitals must be reviewed by CMS or through accreditation by the Joint Commission. Legislative and regulatory mandates, market demands for accreditation by consumer groups and payers, and quality improvement efforts by healthcare providers are the backbone for external quality improvement and define the critical role played by these accrediting organizations in the certification of quality in healthcare.

This chapter presents information on external quality improvement programs and organizations, including their most recent reports and updated changes. These recent changes have a direct influence on the accreditation and education processes, taking into consideration a more transparent and objectively assessed credentialing mechanism that reflects an evidence-based and patient-centered quality of care.

Learning Objectives

After completion of this chapter, readers should be able to:

- Identify the foremost accrediting agencies and outline their roles and responsibilities
- Discuss the concepts of physician profiling, public performance reporting, and benchmarking
- Describe the Healthcare Effectiveness Data and Information Set (HEDIS)®, the Physician Quality Reporting System (PQRS), the CMS Five-Star Quality Rating System, the Accountable Care Organization (ACO), and the Baldrige Performance Excellence Program
- Discuss the certification and credentialing processes and their role in quality improvement
- Understand the role of continuing education in quality improvement

History

Beginning in the mid-1990s, American industries and manufacturers started regaining their competitive edge among industrial nations by adopting Total Quality Management (TQM) [2] and *Lean Manufacturing* [3] to eliminate waste, thus reducing variation and improving efficiency. However, the escalating costs of workforce health benefits kept US manufacturers and businesses at a competitive disadvantage in global markets. While it is true that our healthcare system is becoming technologically advanced, the cost of care far outstrips any perceived societal gains.

The Henry J. Kaiser Family Foundation released the 2019 Employer Health Benefits Survey based on extensive data collected for the 2018 benefit period. For employer-sponsored health insurance, the average annual premium was $7188 for single coverage and $20,576 for family coverage, which represents a 4% and 5% increase, respectively, from the prior year. Notably, family coverage premiums have increased 22% since 2013 and 54% since 2008. The Kaiser report places these increases in context, pointing out that during the comparable period, worker's wages increased 3.4% and inflation increased only 2%. On average, workers contributed 18% of the premium for single coverage and 30% for family coverage in 2018, which amounts to $1242 and $6015, respectively. The average contribution amount has increased 25% over the last 5 years and 71% over the last 10 years. Additionally, 82% of workers have a general annual deductible that must be met prior to services being paid for by the health plan. The average deductible for single coverage is $1655, which represents a 36% increase over the last 5 years and a 100% increase over the last 10 years. Even after meeting the deductible, most workers are also required to pay a copayment or coinsurance when they receive care. The average copayment is $25 to see a primary care physician, $40 for a specialist, and $326 per hospital admission. Average coinsurance rates are 18% for primary care, 19% for specialty care, and 20% for hospital stays [4].

The market demand for cost control is compounded by the baby boomer effect. A Health Affair 2015 *Datawatch* report showed that the Medicare per capita spending for beneficiaries with traditional Medicare over age 65 peaks among beneficiaries in the mid-1990s and then declines, varying by type of service with advancing age [5]. Between the years 2000 and 2011, the peak age for Medicare per capita spending increased from 92 to 96. The amount of Medicare per capita spending at peak age has also increased, from $9557 in 2000 (adjusted for inflation) to $15,015 in 2011 if Part D is excluded and to $16,145 including Part D [5]. It is estimated that population aging will impact medical costs over the next five decades in the United States. Specifically, that aging will have a greater impact on per capita costs with regard to diseases for which the ratio of costs for older versus younger patients is greater, such as congestive heart failure (CHF), coronary artery disease (CAD), and diabetes [6]. The projected cost change per capita for aging was 48% for CAD and 75% for CHF compared to a mere 4% change for asthma [6]. Alemayehu et al. also found that nearly one-third of lifetime expenditures are incurred during middle age and nearly half during the senior years [7].

Healthcare reform is a precept intended to effect change in healthcare policy, to expand care options and patient access, and to improve the overall quality of healthcare. Through governmental legislation, healthcare reform seeks to decrease healthcare costs, expand available coverage and the populations served, and ensure the appropriate and timely delivery of healthcare services.

Historical Summary of Healthcare Reforms

1965 President Lyndon Johnson enacted legislation that introduced Medicare, covering both hospital (Part A) and supplemental medical (Part B) insurance for senior citizens. The legislation also introduced Medicaid, which permitted the federal government to partially fund a program for the poor, with the program managed and co-financed by the individual states [8].

1985 The Consolidated Omnibus Budget Reconciliation Act of 1985 (COBRA) amended the Employee Retirement Income Security Act of 1974 (ERISA) to give some employees the ability to continue health insurance coverage after leaving employment [9].

1996 The Health Insurance Portability and Accountability Act (HIPAA) not only protects health insurance coverage for workers and their families when they change or lose their jobs, it also made health insurance companies cover pre-existing conditions [10]. If such condition had been diagnosed before purchasing insurance, insurance companies are required to cover it after the patient has 1 year of continuous coverage. If such condition was already covered on their current policy, new insurance policies due to changing jobs, etc. have to cover the condition immediately.

1997 The Balanced Budget Act of 1997 introduced two new major federal healthcare insurance programs, Part C of Medicare and the State Children's Health Insurance Program or SCHIP [11]. Part C formalized long-standing "Managed Medicare" (HMO, etc.) demonstration projects and SCHIP were established to provide health insurance to children in families at or below 200% of the federal poverty line. Many other "entitlement" changes and additions were made to Parts A and B of fee-for-service (FFS) Medicare and to Medicaid within an omnibus law that also made changes to the Food Stamp and other federal programs.

2000 The Medicare, Medicaid, and SCHIP Benefits Improvement and Protection Act (BIPA) effectively reversed some of the cuts to the three named programs in the Balanced Budget Act of 1997 because of congressional concern that providers would stop providing services.

2003 The Medicare Prescription Drug, Improvement, and Modernization Act (also known as the Medicare Modernization Act or MMA) introduced supplementary optional coverage within Medicare for self-administered prescription drugs and, as the name suggests, also changed the other three existing parts of Medicare law.

(continued)

2010 The Patient Protection and Affordable Care Act, called PPACA or ACA but also known as Obamacare, was enacted, providing for the phased introduction over multiple years of a comprehensive system of mandated health insurance reforms designed to eliminate "some of the worst practices of the insurance companies"—pre-existing condition screening and premium loadings, policy cancellations on technicalities when illness seems imminent, and annual and lifetime coverage caps. It also sets a minimum ratio of direct healthcare spending to premium income and creates price competition bolstered by the creation of three standard insurance coverage levels to enable like-for-like comparisons by consumers and a web-based health insurance exchange where consumers can compare prices and purchase plans. The system preserves private insurance and private healthcare providers and provides subsidies in the form of income tax reductions to enable lower-income Americans to buy insurance. PPACA also made many changes to the 1997, 2000, and 2003 laws that had previously changed Medicare and further expanded eligibility for Medicaid (that expansion was later ruled by the Supreme Court to be at the discretion of the states).

2015 The Medicare Access and CHIP Reauthorization Act (MACRA) made significant changes to the process by which many Medicare Part B services are reimbursed and also extended SCHIP.

CMS' Center for Clinical Standards and Quality (CCSQ) has a steadfast focus on improving outcomes, beneficiaries' experience of care, and population health, while also aiming to reduce healthcare costs through improvement. CMS has various quality initiatives that touch every aspect of the healthcare system. Some initiatives focus on publicly reporting quality measures for nursing homes, home health agencies, hospitals, and kidney dialysis facilities. Consumers can use the quality measures information that is available on www.medicare.gov for these healthcare settings to assist them in making healthcare choices or decisions.

Quality Initiatives

Since 1965, several changes have been made to these programs. In 1982, the Tax Equity and Fiscal Responsibility Act made it easier and more attractive for health maintenance organizations to contract with Medicare and expanded CMS' quality oversight efforts through Peer Review Organizations (PROs). PROs scrutinize medical case records and disallow payment to hospitals whenever a physician's care is judged to be unnecessary or inadequate.

Quality Improvement Organizations

The term Peer Review Organization or PRO was officially changed to Quality Improvement Organization (QIO) as per the Federal Register on May 24, 2002, in large part, to reflect this new emphasis on population-based quality improvement [12]. CMS contracts with QIOs in 3-year cycles, referred to as *Scope of Work*. Due to escalating expenditures, and in response to the Balanced Budget Act of 1997, CMS continues to develop quality improvement programs in hospitals, physicians' offices, home health agencies, and nursing homes. The QIO Program is a key component of CMS' broad agenda to improve care for Medicare beneficiaries [13]. CMS' quality agenda includes public reporting of quality measures, known as National Quality Initiatives, to help Medicare beneficiaries make informed choices about local healthcare services. CMS' quality improvement program includes pay-for-performance demonstrations, payment and coverage policies, collaboration with state agencies to administer survey and certification programs for healthcare providers, and strategic alliances at the national level to create momentum for transformational change at the local level [13].

Accountable Care Organizations

Accountable Care Organizations (ACOs) are groups of doctors, hospitals, and other healthcare providers who come together voluntarily to give coordinated high-quality care to the patients they serve. Coordinated care helps ensure that patients, especially the chronically ill, get the right care at the right time, with the goal of avoiding unnecessary duplication of services and preventing medical errors [14]. When an ACO succeeds in both delivering high-quality care and spending healthcare dollars more wisely, it will share in the savings it achieves for the Medicare program.

Medicare offers several ACO programs, including:

- Medicare Shared Savings Program, for fee-for-service beneficiaries
- ACO Investment Model, for Medicare Shared Savings Program ACOs to test prepaid savings in rural and underserved areas
- Advance Payment ACO Model, for certain eligible providers already in or interested in the Medicare Shared Savings Program
- Comprehensive End-Stage Renal Disease (ESRD) Care Initiative, for beneficiaries receiving dialysis services
- Next Generation ACO Model, for ACOs experienced in managing care for populations of patients
- Pioneer ACO Model, for healthcare organizations and providers already experienced in coordinating care for patients across care settings [14]

Medicare Access and CHIP Reauthorization Act (MACRA) Quality Payment Program

Beginning January 1, 2017, CMS was required by law to implement a quality payment incentive program, referred to as the Quality Payment Program, which was designed to reward value and outcomes in one of two ways: the Merit-based Incentive Payment System (MIPS) or Advanced Alternative Payment Models (APMs). Clinicians and practices choose which of these two tracks to follow based on practice size, specialty, location, and patient population [15].

Merit-Based Incentive Payment System

MIPS updates and consolidates previous programs that include the Medicare Electronic Health Records (EHR) Incentive Program for Eligible Clinicians, Physician Quality Reporting System (PQRS), and the Value-Based Payment Modifier (VBM). Within MIPS, performance is measured through the data that eligible clinicians report in four areas:

- *Quality*: Category covers the quality of the care delivered, based on performance measures created by CMS and medical professional and stakeholder groups. Six measures of performance are selected that best fit the eligible clinician's practice.
- *Improvement activities*: Category includes an inventory of activities that are meant to improve care processes, enhance patient engagement in care, and increase access to care. The inventory allows the clinician to choose the activities appropriate to his or her practice.
- *Promoting interoperability*: Category focuses on patient engagement and the electronic exchange of health information using certified EHR technology. High performers proactively share information with other clinicians or the patient in a comprehensive manner.
- *Cost*: The cost of the care provided is calculated by CMS based on the clinician's Medicare claims. MIPS uses cost measures to gauge the total cost of care during the year or during a hospital stay [16].

Advanced Alternative Payment Models

An Alternative Payment Model (APM) is a payment approach that provides eligible clinicians added incentive payments to provide high-quality and cost-efficient care. APMs can apply to a specific clinical condition, a care episode, or a population [17]. Advanced APMs, which are a track of the CMS Quality Payment Program, meet these three criteria: (1) participants are required to use certified EHR technology, (2) payment is based on quality measures comparable to those used in MIPS, and (3) either the APM is a Medical Home Model expanded under CMS Innovation Center authority or participants are required to bear significant financial risk [18]. Table 10.1 lists the range of conditions, episodes, and populations addressed in the Advanced APMs approach.

Table 10.1 CMS listing of 2019 advanced APMs

Advanced APM	Overview
Bundled Payments for Care Improvement (BPCI) Advanced	The Bundled Payments for Care Improvement (BPCI) initiative is a model of care which links payments for the multiple services beneficiaries receive during a clinical episode of care
Comprehensive ESRD Care (CEC) – Two-Sided Risk	The Comprehensive ESRD Care (CEC) Model is designed to identify, test, and evaluate new ways to improve care for Medicare beneficiaries with end-stage renal disease (ESRD). Through the CEC Model, CMS partners with healthcare providers and suppliers to test the effectiveness of a new payment and service delivery model in providing beneficiaries with person-centered, high-quality care
Comprehensive Primary Care Plus (CPC+)	Comprehensive Primary Care Plus (CPC+) is a national advanced primary care medical home model that aims to strengthen primary care through regionally based multi-payer payment reform and care delivery transformation
Medicare Shared Savings Program – Track 2, Track 3, Level E of the BASIC track, the ENHANCED track	The Shared Savings Program is a voluntary program that encourages groups of doctors, hospitals, and other healthcare providers to come together as an ACO to provide coordinated, high-quality care to their Medicare patients. ACOs participating in Track 2, Track 3, Level E of the BASIC track, and the ENHANCED track may share in savings or repay Medicare losses depending on performance. These ACOs may share in a greater portion of savings than ACOs participating in Track 1 or Levels A, B, C, or D of the BASIC track. ACOs in the ENHANCED track take on the greatest amount of risk but may share in the greatest portion of savings if successful
Medicare Accountable Care Organization (ACO) Track 1+ Model	The Medicare ACO Track 1+ is a time-limited model for Track 1 Medicare Shared Savings Program ACOs. Track 1+ Model ACOs assume limited downside risk (less than Track 2 or Track 3)
Next Generation ACO Model	Building upon experience from the Pioneer ACO Model and the Shared Savings Program, the Next Generation ACO Model offers a new opportunity in accountable care – one that sets predictable financial targets, enables providers and beneficiaries greater opportunities to coordinate care, and aims to attain the highest quality standards of care
Oncology Care Model (OCM) – Two-Sided Risk	Under the Oncology Care Model (OCM), physician practices have entered into payment arrangements that include financial and performance accountability for episodes of care surrounding chemotherapy administration to cancer patients
Comprehensive Care for Joint Replacement (CJR) Payment Model (Track 1-CEHRT)	The Comprehensive Care for Joint Replacement (CJR) model aims to support better and more efficient care for beneficiaries undergoing the most common inpatient surgeries for Medicare beneficiaries: hip and knee replacements
Vermont Medicare ACO Initiative (as part of the Vermont All-Payer ACO Model)	The Vermont All-Payer Accountable Care Organization (ACO) Model is the Centers for Medicare & Medicaid Services' (CMS) new test of an alternative payment model in which the most significant payers throughout the entire state – Medicare, Medicaid, and commercial healthcare payers – incentivize healthcare value and quality, with a focus on health outcomes, under the same payment structure for the majority of providers throughout the state's care delivery system and transform healthcare for the entire state and its population

(continued)

Table 10.1   (continued)

Advanced APM	Overview
Maryland All-Payer Model (Care Redesign Program)	The Care Redesign Program (CRP) is a voluntary program within the Maryland All-Payer Model that advances efforts to redesign and better coordinate care in Maryland. The CRP provides hospitals participating in the Maryland All-Payer Model the opportunity to partner with and provide incentives and resources to certain providers. In exchange, suppliers offer activities and processes that aim to improve quality of care and reduce the growth in total cost of care for Maryland Medicare beneficiaries
Maryland Total Cost of Care Model (Maryland Primary Care Program)	The Maryland Total Cost of Care Model builds on the success of the Maryland All-Payer Model by creating greater incentives for healthcare providers to coordinate with each other and provide patient-centered care and by committing the state to a sustainable growth rate in per capita total cost of care spending for Medicare beneficiaries
Maryland Total Cost of Care Model (Care Redesign Program)	The Care Redesign Program (CRP) allows hospitals to make incentive payments to non-hospital healthcare providers who partner and collaborate with the hospital and perform care redesign activities aimed at improving quality of care. A participating hospital may only make incentive payments if it has attained certain savings under its fixed global budget and the total amount of incentive payment made cannot exceed such savings

Adapted from "Advanced Alternative Payment Models (APMs)" by the Centers for Medicare & Medicaid Services, 2019. Retrieved from https://qpp.cms.gov/apms/advanced-apms

CMS Quality Rating Systems

CMS has created a number of quality rating systems to help consumers, their families, and caregivers compare services. The ratings support the efforts of CMS to improve the level of accountability for the care provided by physicians, hospitals, and other providers, as well as drive improvements in Medicare quality [19]. Table 10.2 below describes the CMS quality rating systems.

Healthcare Effectiveness Data and Information Set (HEDIS)

The Healthcare Effectiveness Data and Information Set (HEDIS) is a widely-used set of performance measures in the managed care industry, developed and maintained by the National Committee for Quality Assurance (NCQA) [20]. HEDIS is a tool used by more than 90% of America's health plans to measure performance on important dimensions of care and service. HEDIS consists of 94 measures addressing a broad range of important health issues across six domains of care: the effectiveness, access/availability, and experience of care; utilization/risk-adjusted utilization; health plan descriptive information; and measures collected using electronic clinical data systems [20].

Table 10.2 CMS publicly reported quality ratings

Programs/reporting website	Data sources	Measures
Plan Compare website • Medicare Advantage Quality Improvement Program • Medicare Part C & D Star Ratings Program	• AHRQ Consumer Assessment of Healthcare Providers and Systems (CAHPS) Patient Surveys • CMS Health Outcomes Survey • NCQA' Healthcare Effectiveness Data and Information Set (HEDIS) • Medicare claims data	• Staying healthy: screenings, tests, and vaccines • Managing chronic (long-term) conditions • Plan responsiveness and care • Health plan customer service • Drug plan customer service • Member experience with the drug plan • Drug pricing and patient safety • Member complaints, problems getting services, and choosing to leave the plan
Physician Compare website (Includes performance scores for individual physicians, physician groups, and Accountable Care Organizations) • Physician Compare Initiative • Quality Payment Program • Accountable Care Organization Shared Savings Program	• AHRQ Clinician & Group Consumer Assessment of Healthcare Providers & Systems (CG-CAHPS) Patient Survey for the Merit-based Incentive Payment System (MIPS) • Medicare claims data	• Innovative payment model participation • Electronic health record technology participation • Quality of patient care performance measures • Timely care, appointments, and information • Communication • Health promotion and education • Clinician rating • Office staff rating • Attention to patient medicine cost
Hospital Compare website • Hospital Inpatient Quality Reporting Program • Inpatient Psychiatric Facility Quality Reporting Program • Hospital Outpatient Quality Reporting Program	• AHRQ Hospital Consumer Assessment of Healthcare Providers and Systems (HCAHPS) Patient Survey • Medicare claims data	• Nurse communication • Doctor communication • Responsiveness of hospital staff • Communication about medicines • Discharge information • Care transition • Cleanliness of hospital environment • Quietness of hospital environment • Hospital rating • Willingness to recommend

Program/Website	Data Sources	Performance Measures
Nursing Home Compare website • Nursing Home Quality Initiative • Skilled Nursing Facility Quality Reporting Program	• CMS health inspection database • CMS Minimum Data Set (MDS) • Medicare claims data	• Facility cleanliness and safety • Staffing ratios • Quality of resident care performance measures
Long-Term Care Hospital (LTCH) Compare website • Long-Term Care Hospital Quality Reporting Program	• CMS Long-term Care Hospital (LTCH) Continuity Assessment Record and Evaluation (CARE) Data Set • CDC National Healthcare Safety Network (NHSN) • Medicare claims data	• Complications • Effective care • Infections • Flu prevention • Readmissions • Successful return to home and community • Payment and value of care
Inpatient Rehabilitation Facility (IRF) Compare website • Inpatient Rehabilitation Facility Quality Reporting Program	• CMS Inpatient Rehabilitation Facility – Patient Assessment Instrument (IRF-PAI) • CDC National Healthcare Safety Network (NHSN) • Medicare claims data	• Conditions treated • Complications • Effective care • Infections • Flu prevention • Readmissions • Successful return to home and community • Payment and value of care
Home Health Compare website • Home Health Quality Reporting Program	• CMS Outcome and Assessment Information Set (OASIS) • AHRQ Home Health Consumer Assessment of Healthcare Providers & Systems (HHCAHPS) Patient Survey	• Managing daily activities • Managing pain and treating symptoms • Preventing harm • Preventing unplanned hospital care • Payment and value of care • Home health team communication • Willingness to recommend

(continued)

Table 10.2 (continued)

Programs/reporting website	Data sources	Measures
Hospice Compare website • Hospice Quality Reporting Program	• CMS Hospice Item Set (HIS) • AHRQ Consumer Assessment of Healthcare Providers and Systems (CAHPS) Hospice Family Experience Survey	• Quality of patient care performance measures • Communication with family • Getting timely help • Treating patient with respect • Emotional and spiritual support • Help for pain and symptoms • Training family to care for patient • Hospice rating • Willingness to recommend
Dialysis Facility Compare website • End-Stage Renal Disease Quality Incentive Program	• CMS Consolidated Renal Operations in a Web-enabled Network (CROWN) • CDC National Healthcare Safety Network (NHSN) • AHRQ In-Center Hemodialysis Consumer Assessment of Healthcare Providers and Systems (ICH CAHPS) Patient Survey • Medicare claims data	• Quality of patient care performance measures • Doctor communication and caring • Dialysis center staff and operations • Providing information to patients • Doctor rating • Dialysis Center Staff rating • Dialysis Center rating

Adapted from "Quality Initiatives/Patient Assessment Instruments" and "Prescription Drug Coverage" by the Centers for Medicare & Medicaid Services, n.d. Retrieved from https://www.cms.gov/Medicare/Medicare.html

Individual measures revolve around screening, prevention and wellness, chronic condition management, measures targeted toward children and adolescents, measures targeted toward older adults, measures of value and utilization, as well as consumer and patient engagement and experience.

Because so many plans use HEDIS, and because the measures are so specifically defined, HEDIS can be used to make comparisons among plans. To ensure that HEDIS stays current, the NCQA has established a process to evolve the measurement set each year through its Committee on Performance Measurement.

Baldrige National Quality Program

The Malcolm Baldrige National Quality Improvement Act of 1987 was signed by President Ronald Reagan, establishing the program and making quality a national priority. Today, the Baldrige National Quality Program is being modeled in more than 40 states, Europe, and the Far East.

The Baldrige Excellence Framework [21] is widely used as an assessment and improvement tool. In 1999, the categories of education and healthcare were added to the original three categories of manufacturing, service, and small business. In 2007, a nonprofit category was added. To date, more than 1600 US organizations have applied for the Baldrige Award within the more than 30 independent Baldrige-based state and regional award programs, covering nearly all 50 states. The leadership and performance management framework for the healthcare sector empowers health organizations to accomplish their mission, improve results, and become more competitive. The seven critical areas of focus of the Baldrige Excellence Framework in Health Care [22] are displayed in Fig. 10.1.

The Baldrige Health Care Criteria are designed to help organizations use an integrated approach to organizational performance management, resulting in the following goals:

- Improved healthcare quality
- Improved organizational sustainability
- Improved organizational effectiveness
- Improved organizational capabilities
- Improved organizational learning
- Delivery of value to patients
- Delivery of value to customers
- More effective healthcare provider
- More capable healthcare provider
- Improved provider learning

The criteria are embedded in core values and concepts. They are applicable to high-performing healthcare organizations that integrate key performance and operational requirements within a results-oriented framework which create a basis for action and feedback. Every healthcare application is examined and scored through consensus on a point value system. The items that are evaluated under the criteria framework are displayed in Table 10.3 [22].

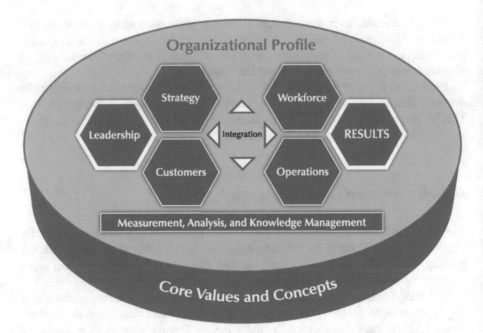

Fig. 10.1 Baldrige Excellence Framework's seven critical areas of focus. Reprinted from "2017–2018 Baldridge Excellence Framework: A Systems Approach to Improving Your Organization's Performance (Health Care)" by US Department of Commerce, National Institute of Standards and Technology, 2017. Retrieved from https://www.nist.gov/baldrige

Table 10.3 2017 Baldrige Health Care criteria for performance excellence item listing

Criteria	Item listing
1. Leadership	1.1 Senior Leadership 1.2 Governance & Societal Contributions
2. Strategy	2.1 Strategy Development 2.2 Strategy Implementation
3. Customers	3.1 Customer Listening 3.2 Customer Engagement
4. Measurement, Analysis, and Knowledge Management	4.1 Measurement, Analysis, and Improvement of Organizational Performance 4.2 Information and Knowledge Management
5. Workforce	5.1 Workforce Environment 5.2 Workforce Engagement
6. Operations	6.1 Work Processes 6.2 Operational Effectiveness
7. Results	7.1 Health Care and Process Results 7.2 Customer-Focused Results 7.3 Workforce-Focused Results 7.4 Leadership and Governance Results 7.5 Financial, Market, and Strategy Results

Adapted from "Baldrige Health Care Criteria for Performance Excellence Categories and Items" by US Department of Commerce, National Institute of Standards and Technology, 2019. Retrieved from https://www.nist.gov/baldrige/baldrige-criteria-commentary-health-care

Evaluators use the *Steps Toward Mature Processes* to help identify and assess appropriate scores relative to the organization's level of performance in each of the areas of focus [21] (see Fig. 10.2). Every applicant receives a detailed feedback report based on an independent external assessment conducted by a panel of specially trained, recognized experts [23].

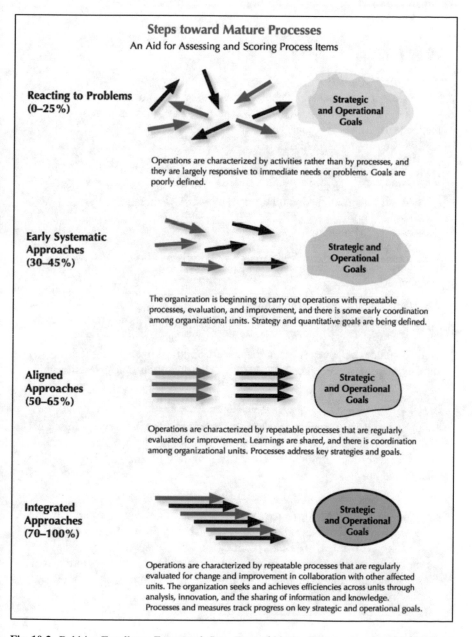

Fig. 10.2 Baldrige Excellence Framework *Steps Toward Mature Processes* scoring aid. Reprinted from "2017–2018 Baldridge Excellence Framework: A Systems Approach to Improving Your Organization's Performance (Health Care)" by US Department of Commerce, National Institute of Standards and Technology, 2017. Retrieved from https://www.nist.gov/baldrige

The criteria for performance excellence emphasize continuous performance improvement, innovation, and the integration of processes and results. The Baldrige Criteria, Lean, and Six Sigma are complementary; many organizations use Baldrige to develop an overall performance map to identify areas that need improvement and then use Six Sigma, Lean, or both to design operations or improve processes within the organization.

Case Study • • •

The Baldrige Application

This is a hypothetical applicant, Arroyo Fresco Community Health Center, used for Baldrige training exercises. The full case study is available at the National Institute of Standards and Technology's Baldrige Performance Excellence Program website [24].

A) Application responses of the hypothetical applicant, Arroyo Fresco Community Health Center (AF), addressing criteria item 4.1: Measurement, Analysis, and Improvement of Organizational Performance.

Item Worksheet: Item 4.1

Measurement, Analysis, and Improvement of Organizational Performance

Relevant Key Factors

4.1a Performance Measurement
A key element of AF's measurement, analysis, and improvement of organizational performance is its automated FOCUS scorecard, which uses a commercially available balanced scorecard software application customized to reflect the key measures needed by AF to track daily operations and overall organizational performance.

4.1b Performance Analysis and Review
Using the FOCUS scorecard posted on the intranet for progress against plan and performance against relevant comparisons, senior leaders review organizational performance monthly. They use a variety of analytical methods to ensure that conclusions are valid.

4.1c Performance Improvement
Senior leaders use performance review findings and key comparative and competitive data to project future performance based on an extrapolation of historic trends—unless they can identify an anticipated action or change in circumstances that will result in a discontinuous change. Any differences in these projections and those originally projected are identified, discussed, and reconciled.

(continued)

Adapted from "2017 Baldrige Case Study: Arroyo Fresco Community Health Center" by US Department of Commerce, National Institute of Standards and Technology, 2017. Retrieved from https://www.nist.gov/baldrige/2017-arroyo-fresco-community-health-center-case-study

B) Baldrige feedback report addressing Arroyo Fresco Community Health Center's performance on criteria item 4.1: Measurement, Analysis, and Improvement of Organizational Performance.

4.1 Measurement, Analysis, and Improvement of Organizational Performance
Your score in this Criteria item for the Consensus Review is in the 30–45 percentage range.

Strengths
4.1(a) Real-time integration of data into the FOCUS scorecard enables measurement agility, with the ability to update any FOCUS area quickly as needs are identified or circumstances change. This agility may help AF provide efficient and effective care.

4.1(b) The customizable FOCUS scorecard aligns data and information pulled from the electronic health record (EHR) and other systems. Metrics are aligned with the SPP to track progress on achieving strategic objectives and action plans.

Opportunities for Improvement
4.1(b,c) It is not clear how AF systematically tracks progress on achieving action plans and strategic objectives and closes gaps between actual and projected performance or how some measures align with objectives or the vision. For example, some FOCUS data and action plans do not include measures or milestones…In addition, some measures are annual and do not clearly align with objectives….Alignment and measurement of progress against stated objectives may help AF better allocate resources to close gaps and improve patients' health.

Adapted from "2017 Baldrige Case Study: Arroyo Fresco Community Health Center" by U.S. Department of Commerce, National Institute of Standards and Technology, 2017. Retrieved from https://www.nist.gov/baldrige/2017-arroyo-fresco-community-health-center-case-study.

Accreditation and Certification

Accreditation and certification are quality improvement and assurance processes that entail review by an external body to ensure an organization, facility, or provider meets recognized standards of care, competencies, and regulations. The accreditation process in particular helps streamline operations, identify gaps in compliance, improve quality of care, and decrease variation in care practices across departments. There are several external agencies, including regulatory ones, that assist with medical quality management, accreditation, and certification efforts. We present a synopsis of these agencies that, along with QI efforts, assist in leading to safer and more effective healthcare systems.

National Committee for Quality Assurance

The National Committee for Quality Assurance (NCQA) is a private, 501(c)(3) nonprofit organization dedicated to improving healthcare quality. Since its founding in 1990, NCQA has been a central figure in driving improvement throughout the healthcare system and helping to elevate the issue of healthcare quality to the top of the national agenda. The range of evaluative programs offered by NCQA is broad and includes accreditation, certification, and physician recognition programs [25]. These programs apply to organizations and individuals ranging from health plans (including health maintenance organizations [HMOs] and preferred provider organizations [PPOs]) to physician networks, medical groups, and even individual physicians. NCQA has helped to build consensus around important healthcare quality issues by working with large employers, policymakers, doctors, patients, and health plans to decide what is important, how to measure it, and how to promote improvement.

Survey teams of physicians and managed care experts, rather than staff, conduct NCQA's accreditation survey process. In addition to an on-site review, NCQA requires submission of (and includes in the accreditation scoring process) data on key clinical and service measures such as mammography screening rates, smoking cessation efforts, and consumer satisfaction (HEDIS). The State of Health Care Quality Report is produced annually by NCQA to monitor and report on performance trends over time, track variations in patterns of care, and provide recommendations for future quality improvement [26].

Among the most remarkable achievements influenced by systematic measurement, reporting, and improvement of quality is the increase in the percentage of heart attack patients who are discharged from the hospital on beta-blocker drugs to prevent second, often fatal, heart attacks. When NCQA began measuring this lifesaving treatment in 1996, fewer than two in three patients were receiving the right care. But in 2016, nearly 86% of heart attack patients received beta-blockers, and every plan that reported on its performance had beta-blocker treatment rates of 80% or higher [27]. This single improvement has saved the lives of thousands of people. This is a prime example of a successful external quality improvement program that resulted in beta-blocker treatment rates so high and variation from plan to plan so low that it is almost uniformly adopted by healthcare providers. Notably, this measure has been retired from the HEDIS data set and replaced by a measure of persistence of treatment. Health plans in every state, the District of Columbia, and Puerto Rico are NCQA accredited. These plans cover 109 million Americans or 70.5% of all Americans enrolled in health plans.

Utilization Review Accreditation Commission

Founded in 1990, the Utilization Review Accreditation Commission (URAC) is the independent leader in promoting healthcare quality through accreditation, certification, and measurement. URAC is a nonprofit organization developing evidence-based measures and standards through inclusive engagement with a range of stakeholders committed to improving the quality of healthcare [28]. Their portfolio of accreditation and certification programs span the healthcare industry, addressing healthcare management, healthcare operations, health plans, pharmacies, telehealth providers, physician practices, and more. URAC accreditation is a symbol of excellence for organizations to showcase their validated commitment to quality and accountability [28].

URAC's accreditation programs vary widely and include, but are not limited to, health plans; healthcare management programs, including case and disease management programs; pharmacy and accountable care organizations; and provider integration and coordination programs [29]. Any organization that has to meet specific standards, including hospitals, HMOs, PPOs, ACOs, healthcare centers, health plans, health networks, and provider groups can seek accreditation in case and health utilization management, including workers' compensation, disease management, consumer education and support programs, and HIPAA privacy and security accreditation programs [29]. URAC's Pharmacy Quality Management Accreditation programs include the Specialty Pharmacy Accreditation, Community Pharmacy Accreditation, Pharmacy Benefit Management Accreditation, and the Drug Therapy Management Accreditation [29].

URAC offers two accreditations for health plans: a Health Plan Accreditation and a Health Plan with Health Insurance Marketplace Accreditation, which allows health plans to participate in health insurance exchanges in all 50 states and the District of Columbia. Measuring health plan quality and performance is important to help consumers make an informed choice. Measuring performance, and the public reporting of results, is central to monitoring quality and quality improvement, as well as holding health plans and their providers accountable for the care they provide.

The Joint Commission

Founded in 1951, the Joint Commission evaluates and accredits nearly 21,000 healthcare organizations and programs in the United States, including hospitals and healthcare organizations that provide ambulatory and office-based surgery, behavioral health services, home healthcare, nursing care center services, and laboratory services. An independent, not-for-profit organization, the Joint Commission is the nation's oldest and largest standards setting and accrediting body in healthcare. It also has two nonprofit affiliate organizations: the Joint Commission Center for Transforming Healthcare aims to solve healthcare's most critical safety and quality problems, and Joint Commission Resources (JCR) provides consulting services, educational services, and publications; Joint Commission International, a division of JCR, accredits and certifies international healthcare organizations.

The Joint Commission's state-of-the-art standards focus on patient safety and quality of care. Standards are updated regularly to reflect the rapid advances in healthcare and medicine. The hospital accreditation standards number more than 250 and address everything from patient rights and education, infection control, medication management, and preventing medical errors to how the hospital verifies that its doctors, nurses, and other staff are qualified and competent; how it prepares for emergencies; and how it collects data on its performance and uses that data to improve itself [30]. To earn and maintain the Joint Commission's Gold Seal of Approval®, an organization undergoes an on-site survey by a Joint Commission survey team at least once every 3 years. (Laboratories are surveyed every 2 years.) [31]

In 2004, the Joint Commission began using a new accreditation process called *Shared Visions-New Pathways*, which shifts the focus from survey preparation to the continuous improvement of operational systems that directly affect the quality and safety of patient care [32]. With the active engagement of physicians and other care-givers, the new accreditation process emphasizes periodic performance reviews, on-site surveys directed by the priority focus process, and on-site evaluations of compliance with standards relating to patients' care experience [33]. In 2006, the Joint Commission began conducting on-site accreditation surveys and certification reviews on an unannounced basis [33].

In 2002, the Joint Commission established its National Patient Safety Goals (NPSGs) program, and the first set of NPSGs was effective January 1, 2003 [34]. The NPSGs were established to help accredited organizations address specific areas of concern in regard to patient safety. In 2017, National Patient Safety Goal 07.06.01 (implement evidence-based practices to prevent indwelling catheter-associated urinary tract infections) expanded for inclusion in the Nursing Care Center Accreditation program and has also been revised for the Hospital and Critical Access Hospital Accreditation programs. Previously, a note for the NPSG excluded pediatric populations. That note has been removed based on new evidence-based practices. A new note provides references and links to supporting literature [34].

Also, in 2017, there are new and revised elements of performance for the Hospital and Critical Access Hospital Accreditation. The Joint Commission requires a quality improvement program in all hospitals with residency training programs. Hospitals devise QI programs based on the Commission's guidelines for "practitioner-specific" data collection in the areas of patient care, medical and clinical knowledge, and practice-based learning and improvement. Those QI programs are then incorporated into residency training manuals as core competencies in quality management.

International Organization for Standardization

International Organization for Standardization (ISO) is an independent, non-governmental international organization with a membership of 163 national standards bodies. It is the world's largest developer and publisher of international standards and comprises a network of the national standards institutes of multiple countries [35]. ISO has published more than 21,000 International Standards and related documents, covering almost every industry, from technology, food safety, and agriculture, to healthcare. The vast majority of ISO standards are specific to a particular process or industry. However, ISO 9001 is limited to quality [36] and yet is a *generic management system* of standards, meaning that the same standard can be applied to any organization, large or small, in any sector and to any business, government agency, or healthcare entity.

There are over one million companies and organizations in over 170 countries certified within the scope of ISO 9001. This standard is based on a number of quality management principles including a strong customer focus, the motivation and implication of top management, the process approach, and continual improvement. ISO 9001 puts greater emphasis on leadership engagement, helps address organizational risks and opportunities in a structured manner, uses multiple management systems, and addresses supply chain management [36]. It provides a framework for healthcare organizations to tackle the demands placed upon them. The standard is highly generic and versatile and is applicable to all healthcare organizations, regardless of their size or subsector. ISO 9001:2015 sets the criteria for a quality management system and is the only standard that can be certified to [36] (although this is not a requirement). It is a useful framework with which to evaluate and improve quality and operations within a healthcare organization.

If a healthcare provider is certified in ISO 9001, any other survey process for healthcare quality certifications will be much simpler and less costly regarding both preparation and compliance demonstration. ISO certification helps improve documentation and patient records, while focusing on patient care, satisfaction, and safety. While ISO is not intended to replace the Joint Commission, URAC, NCQA, or CMS, it does make the compliance demonstration process much easier to manage, less time-consuming, and less costly. Some of the International Standards that are available for the healthcare industry are displayed in Table 10.4.

Table 10.4 Some of International Organization for Standardization's available standards for healthcare

Tech committee #	Title
TC 76	Transfusion, infusion and injection, and blood processing equipment for medical and pharmaceutical use
TC 84	Devices for administration of medicinal products and catheters
TC 121	Anesthetic and respiratory equipment
TC 150	Implants for surgery
TC 168	Prosthetics and orthotics
TC 170	Surgical instruments
TC 173	Assistive products
TC 194	Biological and clinical evaluation of medical devices
TC 198	Sterilization of healthcare products
TC 209	Cleanrooms and associated controlled environments
TC 210	Quality management and corresponding general aspects for medical devices
TC 215	Health informatics
TC 304	Healthcare organization management

Adapted from "Technical Committees" by International Organization of Standardization, n.d. Retrieved from https://www.iso.org/technical-committees.html?s=HEALTH_AND_MEDICINE. Reprinted with permission

Physician Profiling

Physician profiling is a process whereby doctors are rated on measures and standards of quality of care and cost-efficiency. Physician profiling creates a way to compare physicians with their peers. It allows payers to compare networks, groups, and individual physicians with metrics that track quality, utilization, cost, and prescribing practices against group, network, and national benchmarks. Showing physicians how their performance compares to other physicians helps to improve clinical, quality, and cost-related outcomes. Physician profiling can also be used in the allocation of funds generated by shared savings and other pay-for-performance payment models.

Physicians must find the data and analytic methodologies credible for profiling to have the desired effect on physician behavior. For example, physicians must be convinced that the payer has addressed the challenge of comparing physicians with disparate patient populations. This can be accomplished with risk-adjusted efficiency profiles that take into account the potential that a particular physician's patients may present with an illness or disease that requires a greater degree of care, may be chronic rather than acute, and may differ in the duration of care than another physician's patients.

The American Academy of Family Physicians (AAFP) has issued guidelines for a fair and effective physician performance reporting program [37]:

1. Support the physician/patient relationship.
2. Have as its purpose to assess and improve the quality of patient care and clinical outcomes.
3. Clearly define what is being measured, how performance scores are calculated, and how those scores are compared to peers.
4. Utilize criteria for comparison purposes that are based on valid peer groups, evidence-based statistical norms, and/or evidence-based clinical policies.
5. Select measurement goals which are actionable so physicians can easily act as needed to achieve improved quality of care.
6. Involve physicians in the selection of performance measures and the development of a feedback process and appeals process.
7. Explicitly describe the data sources on which measurement is based, e.g., administrative/claims, medical records, surveys, registry, etc.
8. Clearly report on the validity, accuracy, reliability, and limitations of data utilized when reporting results and when providing physician feedback.
9. Allow physicians to identify their individual patients who are not receiving indicated clinical interventions to support improvement relative to stated measurement.
10. Provide physicians performance profiles and allow review and reconciliation period prior to publication.

(continued)

11. Provide consumers adequate guidance about how to interpret the physician performance information and explicitly describe any limitations in the data in lay terms.

Reprinted with permission from Public Reporting of Physician Performance, Guiding Principles, 1999, Communications Copyright ©1999 American Academy of Family Physicians. All Rights Reserved

Physician profiling is more common in managed care. Profiling is based on certain data that is used to benchmark providers against other comparable providers, select and recruit providers into a managed care organization (MCO) network, and pay incentives to providers based on performance. Some examples of the metrics used in provider profiling include wait time to schedule an appointment, hospital admissions, emergency department visits, out-of-network referrals, member satisfaction, and compliance with MCO clinical guidelines. MCOs can also use these data for utilization management and quality improvement initiatives targeting individual providers and groups of providers.

Public Reporting

Public reporting of healthcare quality data allows consumers, payers, and healthcare providers to access information about how clinicians, clinics, hospitals, long-term care facilities, and insurance plans perform on healthcare quality measures [38]. *Report cards*, also called *citizen report cards*, consumer reports, provider profiles, performance reports, quality assessment reports, score cards, league tables, and other reporting websites fall under the umbrella of *public reports* which serve to enable patients to compare provider performance on measures of healthcare quality and outcomes. These tools can also help providers assess their own practices and consider the performance of other providers.

Hospitals and other healthcare institutions are subject to public reporting. Healthcare quality data is often provided by regional collaboratives but can also be shared by health insurance plans as well as state, local, and federal government agencies. Public reporting of healthcare institutions began with rankings of the best hospitals in the nation based on mortality rates, medical errors, and possible infection rates. Such efforts have been successful. An important strategy is the public dissemination of timely, relevant, and reliable information on healthcare quality that can be used effectively by the consumer, healthcare payers, and hospitals. Advocates for public reporting argue that it will inject competition into the health system. In addition, it could help providers to improve by benchmarking their performance against others, encourage private insurers and public programs to reward quality and efficiency, and help patients make informed choices [39].

Case Study • • •

Publishing Patient Reviews Online

The University of Utah Health Care (UUHC) system is made up of four hospitals and ten community clinics, with 1.4 million patient visits annually [40], and in 2012, it became the first health system in the United States to publish patient reviews online [41]. In order to understand and address increasingly frequent patient complaints—from scheduling delays and insufficient way finding to poor communication, inadequate care coordination, and lack of professionalism—UUHC began collecting patient feedback via the Press Ganey Medical Practice Survey and putting the results on its public website. It posts roughly 100,000 reviews a year, complete with 5-star ratings based on the survey data and unedited free-response comments, both positive and negative, unless they could be considered libelous or compromise patient privacy [41].

UUHC quickly discovered that the patient reviews were effective motivators. Physicians wanted to know how they measured up against their colleagues within the system and their peers across the country. System executives noted, "The natural tendency toward competition began to drive improvements in patient satisfaction....High performers were recognized, and low performers were offered coaching" [40]. At the outset, only 4% of UUHC physicians ranked in the top 10th percentile for patient satisfaction compared to their peers nationally; by 2014, half of all physicians who had received at least 30 reviews scored in the top 10th percentile, and one-quarter were in the top percentile [42]. Transparency with patient reviews also served as a catalyst for continuous innovation toward optimizing the patient experience. Improvements resulting from physician-driven initiatives intended to address patient criticism include extended clinic hours to reduce wait times for an appointment, refined processes for handing off patients from one provider to another, and, for one community clinic, on-site childcare during appointments and home well-baby visits for newborns [40–42].

Not only did UUHC see a significant increase in patient satisfaction, but the new culture of physician engagement and innovation also led to better quality of care and better margins. Prior to the initiative, quality metrics were average compared to those of other teaching hospitals, but since instituting the Press Ganey Patient Survey, UUHC has been consistently ranked among the top ten academic medical centers in the country by the University HealthSystem Consortium, a comparison of the nation's teaching hospitals based on quality and safety [40]. Safer care and improved patient satisfaction translate to a lower rate of malpractice litigation. On a per-dollar-of-revenue-collected basis, UUHC malpractice premiums have fallen [42]. In the first 4 years of the initiative, premiums declined at a rate that exceeded national trends, even despite a significant increase in the number of physicians practicing [40].

(continued)

UUHC also experienced increased revenue due to a rise in patient volumes. Publicly sharing patient feedback fosters a sense of trust with patients and the community and can help patients make more informed decisions about where they go for care. In the first 13 months after going live with patient reviews, website traffic more than doubled [42]. According to an online poll, 48% of UUHC patients said physician ratings and other patients' comments influenced their choice of physician, while another 29% said they were somewhat influenced by the reviews [42]. When patients were asked what is most important to know about their physician, other patient reviews ranked second, just behind the physician's specialty [42]. This bold patient satisfaction initiative has evolved into a model for cultural transformation focused on improved quality and safety, lower costs, reduced variability in performance, and enhanced professionalism and communication.

The Leapfrog Group

The Leapfrog Group is a national nonprofit organization founded in 2000 that is driving a movement for improved quality in healthcare. Its mission is "to trigger giant leaps forward in the safety, quality and affordability of U.S. healthcare by using transparency to support informed healthcare decisions and promote high-value care" [43]. The Leapfrog Hospital Survey collects and reports hospital performance, empowering consumers to find the highest-value care and giving them the lifesaving information they need to make informed decisions. Another Leapfrog Group initiative, the Hospital Safety Grade, assigns letter grades to hospitals based on their record of patient safety, helping consumers protect themselves and their families from errors, injuries, accidents, and infections. It developed this approach with many of the nation's largest corporations and in partnership with public agencies such as CMS, the US Office of Personnel Management, and the Department of Defense.

Four hospital quality and safety practices are the focus of Leapfrog's hospital rating program [44]:

1. *Computer Physician Order Entry (CPOE)*: Hospital staff enter medication orders via computers linked to software designed to prevent prescribing errors.
2. *Evidence-Based Hospital Referral (EBHR)*: Hospital refers patients needing certain complex medical procedures to hospitals offering the best survival odds based on scientifically valid criteria, such as the number of times a hospital performs a procedure each year.
3. *ICU Physician Staffing (IPS)*: Hospital staffs ICUs with doctors who have special training in critical care medicine.
4. *Leapfrog Safe Practices Score*: Assesses hospital's progress on a range of National Quality Forum (NQF)-endorsed Safe Practices.

The Leapfrog Group has grown exponentially—now reporting data on more than 2000 hospitals with regional partnerships in 36 states [45]. They started a national campaign to reduce early elective deliveries, launched a pay-for-performance program, and designed the Leapfrog Hospital Safety Grade to empower consumers to make better choices. The Leapfrog Hospital Survey is the nation's gold standard in evaluating hospital performance on quality, safety, and resource use, using national performance measures to evaluate individual facilities. Leapfrog issues a series of reports annually detailing their aggregate findings on the prior year's hospital performance nationwide. Highlights from the 2018 series note that although most reporting hospitals use the recommended bar code medication administration (BCMA) system, only one-third fully meet Leapfrog's standard for safe and effective implementation of the system, most often failing by not scanning both the patient and medication at least 95% of the time; only one in five hospitals that electively deliver very low birth weight babies meet Leapfrog's standard which includes treating large numbers of these babies, having outstanding outcomes, and giving mothers steroids prior to a baby's birth; and more than six in ten hospitals are achieving infection ratios of between 0.000 and 1.000 on each of the five healthcare-associated infections measured, which is better than predicted [46].

There is some evidence that public reporting of healthcare quality data improves the quality of care. Effects appear strongest in competitive markets, especially for nursing home facilities and health insurance plans [47]. Table 10.5 provides a summary of public reporting entities. More state agencies are increasingly reporting state data over the Internet.

Table 10.5 Public reporting entities

Public reporting entity	Format	Beneficiary	Performance measures
CMS: QualityNet [48]	QIO Data APU	Non-public providers	AMI, heart failure, pneumonia, surgical care
Hospital Quality Alliance/ CMS: Hospital Compare [49]	Hospital Compare	Public hospitals	22 clinical processes 30-day mortality
The Joint Commission: Quality Check [50]	ORYX	Hospitals	Outcome measures
Cal Hospital Care [51]	Report Card Hospital Rating	Consumer Health plans	Patient satisfaction measures Patient experience Specific medical conditions
National Quality Forum [52]	Hospitals	Consumer hospitals	Healthcare-associated infections (HAI) project
Institute for Healthcare Improvement[53]	Medical Groups Hospital Rating	Consumer public	Safety, effectiveness, patient-centeredness, timeliness, efficiency, equity
The Leapfrog Group[45]	Survey results Hospital rating	Public Payers	Patient safety Hospital quality
Healthgrades [54]	Compare Data	Physicians Hospitals	Credentials of physicians Hospital rates

QIO Quality Improvement Organization
AMI Acute myocardial infarction
APU Annual Payment Update
ORYX Performance Tool for Joint Commission

Teaching Quality Improvement

Undergraduate Medical Education

In response to the Institute of Medicine (IOM) Committee on Healthcare in America reports *To Err Is Human*, released in 1999, and *Crossing the Quality Chasm*, published in 2001, the Association of American Medical Colleges (AAMC) developed the ongoing Medical School Objectives Project (MSOP) [55]. The project sought to address two fundamental questions: (1) What should medical students learn about quality of care issues (learning objectives)? (2) What kinds of educational experiences would allow students to achieve those learning objectives (educational strategies)? The MSOP groups learning objectives into three main areas:

- The ability to critically evaluate the knowledge base supporting good patient care
- An understanding of the gap between prevailing practices and best practices and the steps necessary to close that gap
- Participating in closing the gap between prevailing and best practices [55]

Experience has shown that there is no lack of opportunity to integrate quality into medical education, but what is lacking is the integration of quality improvement tools (measurement and intervention) and the modeling of best practices by faculty and staff.

In 2014, the AAMC published its Core Entrustable Professional Activities (EPAs) for Entering Residency and later developed comprehensive toolkits for each of the EPAs that describe competencies for graduating medical students, including systems-based activities essential to healthcare quality improvement and patient safety [56]. When this content is included in medical school, graduates enter residency training with the knowledge and skills needed to practice quality improvement in their specialty training.

The Institute for Healthcare Improvement (IHI), a nonprofit organization, has become the foundation for improvement science and education. Its Open School provides online and in-person curricula including modules, faculty guides, networking, and projects for teaching healthcare quality improvement and patient safety [57]. An important part of IHI's work is to incorporate the teaching of quality improvement into health professional education curricula. Eight knowledge domains were identified as essential core content that all health profession students should learn as an integral part of their training [58].

Quality Improvement Knowledge Domains for Health Professional Education

1. *Healthcare as a process, system.* The interdependent people (e.g., patients, families, eligible populations, caregivers), procedures, activities, and technologies of health care giving that come together to meet the need(s) of individuals and communities.

(continued)

2. *Variation and measurement.* The use of measurement to understand the variation across and within systems to improve the design and redesign of healthcare.
3. *Customer/beneficiary knowledge.* Identification of the person, persons, or groups of persons for whom healthcare is provided or may be provided in the future; an understanding of their needs and preferences and of the relationship of healthcare to those needs and preferences.
4. *Leading, following, and making changes in healthcare.* The methods and skills for designing and testing change in complex organizational caregiving arrangements, including the general and strategic management of people and the healthcare work they do in organizations.
5. *Collaboration.* The knowledge, methods, and skills needed to work effectively in groups, to understand and value the perspectives and responsibilities of others, and the capacity to foster the same in others, including an understanding of the implications of such work.
6. *Social context and accountability.* An understanding of the social contexts (i.e., local, regional, national, global) of health caregiving and the way that expectations arising from them are made explicit. This specifically includes an understanding of the financial impact and costs of healthcare.
7. *Developing new locally useful knowledge.* The recognition of the need for new knowledge in personal daily health professional practice and the skill to develop new knowledge through empiric testing.
8. *Professional subject matter.* The health professional knowledge appropriate for a specific discipline and the ability to apply and connect it to all of the above.

Reprinted from www.IHI.org with permission of the Institute for Healthcare Improvement, ©2019

Assessment of competency in medical education is crucial for quality improvement. Effective assessment tools and faculty development are necessary to ensure that only those students and trainees who are competent advance to the next level of training and, ultimately, to practice. Use of case studies, simulators, and observations in practice will ensure that learners can apply the new knowledge they acquire.

A study conducted by Gould et al. used second-year medical students in community-based primary care practices to collect baseline data for diabetes care, implement a results-specific intervention, and reassess quality indicators 6 months later [59]. They found that documentation of specific indicators increased, along with actual improvement of clinical measures. Thus, medical students can be a resource to improve patient care by participating in QI projects in clinical practice.

Graduate Medical Education

The Accreditation Council for Graduate Medical Education (ACGME) adopted general competencies in 1999 that incorporate the knowledge and recognition of quality of care issues. Implementation of the ACGME's core competencies is being promulgated through the ACGME's Outcome Project [60]. The core competencies were later adopted by the American Board of Medical Specialties (ABMS) as content for lifelong clinical practice [61]. The six general competency areas are as follows [60]:

1. *Patient care.* Provide patient care that is compassionate, appropriate, and effective for the treatment of health problems and the promotion of health.
2. *Medical knowledge.* Demonstrate knowledge about established and evolving bio-medical, clinical, and cognate (e.g., epidemiological, social-behavioral) sciences and the application of this knowledge to patient care.
3. *Practice-based learning and improvement.* Demonstrate the ability to investigate and evaluate patient care practices, to appraise and assimilate scientific evidence, and to improve patient care practices.
4. *Professionalism.* Demonstrate a commitment to carrying out professional responsibilities, to adhering to ethical principles, and to showing sensitivity to a diverse patient population.
5. *Interpersonal and communication skills.* Demonstrate interpersonal and communication skills that result in effective information exchange and teaming with patients, patients' families, and professional associates.
6. *Systems-based practice.* Demonstrate an awareness of and a responsiveness to the larger context and system of healthcare and the ability to effectively call on system resources to provide care that is of optimal value.

While ACGME has linked accreditation of graduate medical education programs to demonstrations that residents in training are proficient in the core competencies, there is variability between programs and questions regarding the effectiveness of various teaching methods. This is particularly true of practice-based learning and improvements and systems-based practice competencies where quality improvement concepts are most important. A systematic review of the effectiveness of teaching quality improvement to clinicians, conducted in 2007, produced evidence of this variability [62]. Teaching methods included didactic and experiential learning, and, while most evaluated learning, few used validated assessment instruments. Assessments of attitudes showed mixed results, and only 8 out of 28 studies of clinical outcomes reported beneficial effects. Clearly, more study is needed to ascertain how best to teach the concepts of quality improvement and to actually improve clinical outcomes.

Ogrinc et al. developed a framework for teaching medical students and residents systems-based practice and practice-based learning and improvement based on a review of the literature [63]. Training, educational objectives, and methodology recommendations were made depending on the learners' skill levels. For example, students at the novice level might develop an understanding of systems-based practice, measure a process, and try a test of change (e.g., Plan, Do, Study, Act [PDSA] cycle) on a system that is familiar to them. An early resident, with mentoring by faculty, might conduct an assessment of his or her own patients' needs and engage other members of the healthcare team to implement an intervention for improvement. An advanced resident might build on his or her changes to practice, remeasuring and modifying as needed.

For novice learners, intensive, experiential, interdisciplinary training can facilitate improvements in patient care. Varkey et al. found their interdisciplinary QI curriculum created an opportunity for learners in varying disciplines to learn from each other's successes and failures, share resources, develop an understanding of the health system, and stimulate future professional interactions [64]. The learner team successfully completed a QI project in outpatient medication reconciliation as a part of the curriculum.

In 2014, the ACGME introduced its Clinical Learning Environment Review (CLER) initiative. It is designed to provide US clinical settings affiliated with ACGME-accredited institutions with periodic feedback that addresses six focus areas including patient safety, healthcare quality, care transitions, supervision, well-being, and professionalism [65]. ACGME makes CLER visits to teaching institutions every 24–36 months and provides feedback on their proficiency in each of the focus areas. While not a part of the formal accreditation process, it is expected that teaching centers engage trainees in patient quality and safety in meaningful ways. This new approach to graduate medical education led to the realization that many faculty members were themselves not proficient in healthcare quality improvement principles, and faculty development efforts escalated. The 2018 ACGME CLER report found that while improvements had been made in many areas, there are still systematic concerns regarding transitions of care, aligning trainee QI projects with organizational priorities, and trainee reporting of errors and near misses [66].

Teaching quality improvement and patient safety to both learners and faculty has centered on three major areas which include the use of formal curricula to teach concepts or methods, education for specific skills related to safety and quality as a core part of doctoring, and real-life QI initiatives that involve trainees as active participants [67]. While ideal, it is often difficult to involve trainees in ongoing organizational QI due to their training schedules, lack of expertise, and lack of faculty mentors.

Continuing Medical Education

The melding of quality improvement and continuing medical education (CME) has been discussed for decades but did not become a reality until the introduction of maintenance of certification (MOC) in 2000. It was then that the American Board of Medical Specialties determined that board certification of physicians should do more to ensure the continuous competence of physicians. At that time, most certifying boards required a written exam every 6–10 years, depending on specialty, to maintain certified status. Some boards required no recertification. Based on the core competencies developed by ACGME and adopted by ABMS, the new requirements for ongoing MOC have four components:

- *Part I: Professionalism and Professional Standing* – Requires a valid, unrestricted medical license
- *Part II: Lifelong Learning and Self-Assessment* – Requires educational and self-assessment activities determined by each specialty board
- *Part III: Assessment of Knowledge, Judgment, and Skills* – Requires demonstration of specialty-specific knowledge and skills through a written exam and other evaluations
- *Part IV: Improvement in Medical Practice* – Requires demonstration of the use of evidence and best practices compared to peers and national benchmarks [68]

It is this fourth component that truly calls for the integration of quality improvement and CME. Certifying boards and corresponding medical specialty societies have developed modules to fulfill MOC Part IV. Generally, these have been modeled after the PDSA cycle for improvement. In these modules, physicians are asked to perform an assessment of their current practice, which might include a survey or chart abstraction. The results of the assessment are compared with peers and national benchmarks. Next, physicians are directed to plan interventions for improvement, which may include education or systems-based process interventions. Sometime after implementation of the intervention(s), usually 6 months, the physician is asked to reassess their practice and then compare results to peers and national benchmarks. Once the module is complete, the board-certified physician is credited with completion of MOC Part IV.

In 2010, the American Board of Medical Specialties introduced the Multispecialty MOC Portfolio Program to better align MOC requirements with practice-based quality improvement efforts. Through this program, board-certified physicians can receive credit for ongoing, practice-based quality improvement rather than completing online modules or other activities that may not be relevant to their practice [69]. While intended to recognize ongoing, practice-based QI, the Portfolio Program has garnered limited success. Originally, 22 of the ABMS's 24 member boards recognized the Portfolio Program as a means to earn Part IV credit. Over time, several boards have opted out, and less than 2% of board-certified physicians utilize portfolio to meet their requirements.

In addition to meeting requirements for MOC, physicians may also receive CME credit for participating in performance improvement activities. In 2005, the American Medical Association (AMA), the American Academy of Family Physicians, and the American Osteopathic Association agreed to criteria for awarding CME credit for such activities. Physicians cannot self-report performance improvement CME activities but must work with an approved CME provider that awards the credit. In order to give added value to performance improvement CME activities, the credit scheme allows participants to receive five credits for each stage of the project: Stage A, practice assessment; Stage B, intervention(s); and Stage C, remeasurement and reflection on new knowledge and practice. When all 3 stages are complete, the physician is rewarded with 5 additional credits for a total of 20. This was the first movement away from time as the metric for CME credit. Credit for performance improvement CME is not based on the time the physician spent but the relative value of the activity. Twenty credits are almost half of the annual CME credit necessary for most physicians for licensure, board certification, and other CME credit requirements.

In 2007, the Accreditation Council for Continuing Medical Education (ACCME) set forth new criteria for accreditation to incentivize CME providers to integrate quality and performance improvement, collaboration, and higher levels of outcome measures into their programs [70]. These new criteria came in response to criticism that traditional CME is not effective in improving physician performance and, ultimately, patient care. ACCME's updated criteria for accreditation with commendation in 2016 put even more emphasis on continuous quality improvement through team-based learning and population health interventions [71].

In 2017, the ACCME and the ABMS partnered to further attempt to streamline the requirements for MOC and CME. A collaborative pilot allowed ACCME-accredited providers to design their CME activities to meet MOC requirements and report physician participation directly to their certifying board. This allowed for the documentation of both CME and MOC requirements through one activity [72].

CME is a $2 billion-plus industry in the United States, over half of which is funded by the pharmaceutical industry [73]. Critics maintain that CME is influenced by that funding and that more emphasis must be placed on evidence-based needs assessment and filling performance gaps in clinical practice. Integrating quality improvement methods and data with educational activities better serves the needs of physicians, the healthcare system, and the patients they serve.

There are several barriers to integration of CME and quality improvement. First, QI and CME departments are usually in different areas of the organization. This is true in hospitals, medical schools, and other healthcare organizations. Quality improvement is often viewed as a nursing-oriented function, while CME is considered physician oriented. While much rhetoric is devoted to the team approach, it is often difficult to implement. The CME office often is not aware that data is being collected or of the results. Quality management areas see CME as an externally driven and funded activity that is not continuous in nature and that has no overarching, long-term goal that fits into the organization's goals for patient care. Second, education often is not the solution for improving performance. Lapses may not be an issue of knowing better but of doing better. Other systems-based processes or barriers frequently affect practice. Third, many areas of medicine have no evidence-based performance measures. There are no quality data available in many areas where education is needed. CME developers cannot depend on the quality agenda alone to direct their programs. Finally, external funding has traditionally been crucial to CME units. They have often been expected to be at least self-sustaining and preferably profit centers for the organization, which has led to a dependence on external funding, largely from the pharmaceutical industry, to sustain

CME. Organizations fund quality management with the assumption that increased quality will decrease overhead.

How, then, can quality improvement and CME best be integrated? Communication is the key. Staff in the two areas should communicate regularly on a strategic as well as an operational level. Quality improvement priorities of the organization should be a part of the CME program, and individual quality projects should always consider CME as part of the improvement intervention. CME planners should always consider quality data as well as quality improvement processes and tools as part of the educational activity.

Performance data can serve as a needs assessment to identify gaps in knowledge and skills. It can also be used as outcomes data to show if education has an impact on improving physician performance and healthcare outcomes. Staff who are cross-trained in education and quality can serve both purposes well. Increasing awareness in both disciplines will ensure better utilization and improve effectiveness in both areas.

Future Trends

As healthcare evolves in its commitment to incorporate elements of the science of healthcare delivery (as described in Chap. 2), consumers and payers have become increasingly interested in performance data; patient-centered, high-quality care; cost containment; and the delivery of adequate and appropriate health services. External quality improvement is at the forefront of healthcare concerns which allows accrediting agencies to tighten their processes for heightened compliance and allows the federal government and other payers to demand more accountability for quality and efficient pay for performance.

Teaching quality improvement across the continuum of medical education is increasingly important, and formal instruction in quality improvement concepts means that students are exposed to quality patient safety techniques prior to the clinical setting. Participation in quality programs, pay-for-performance, and continuing professional development will become a routine part of the medical professional's functional pursuits.

Funding shifts for CME caused by decreasing external funding from pharmaceutical companies and other commercial sources, along with an increased emphasis on practice outcomes, will provide further incentives for integrating institutional quality priorities with educational interventions for improvement.

As healthcare professionals' time constraints increase and revenues decrease, there will be more emphasis on streamlining regulatory and educational requirements so that continuous professional development is more practice-based and relevant to the individual's practice improvement needs with documented improvements counting for more than one regulatory requirement.

References

1. Centers for Medicare & Medicaid Services (2019) National Health Expenditure Projections 2015–2025. https://www.cms.gov/Research-Statistics-Data-and-Systems/Statistics-Trends-and-Reports/NationalHealthExpendData/Downloads/Proj2015.pdf
2. Free Management Library (n.d.) Total quality management. http://www.managementhelp.org/quality/tqm/tqm.htm
3. American Society for Quality (2019) What is lean? https://asq.org/quality-resources/lean
4. Kaiser Family Foundation (2019) Employer Health Benefits 2019 Summary of Findings. https://www.kff.org/report-section/ehbs-2019-summary-of-findings/
5. Neuman P, Cubanski J, Damico A (2015) Medicare per capita spending by age and service: new data highlights oldest beneficiaries. Health Aff Datawatch 34(2):335–339. https://doi.org/10.1377/hlthaff.2014.1371
6. Garrett N, Martini EM (2007) The boomers are coming: a total cost of care model of the impact of population aging on the cost of chronic conditions in the United States. Dis Manag 10(2):51–60. https://doi.org/10.1089/dis.2006.630
7. Alemayehu B, Warner KE (2004) The lifetime distribution of health care costs. Health Serv Res 39(3):627–642. https://doi.org/10.1111/j.1475-6773.2004.00248.x
8. U.S. Centers for Medicare and Medicaid Services (2018) CMS' program history. https://www.cms.gov/About-CMS/Agency-information/History/
9. U.S. Centers for Medicare and Medicaid Services (n.d.) COBRA continuation coverage questions and answers. https://www.cms.gov/CCIIO/Programs-and-Initiatives/Other-Insurance-Protections/cobra_qna.html
10. U.S. Department of Health & Human Services (2017) HIPAA for professionals. https://www.hhs.gov/hipaa/for-professionals/index.html
11. Agency for Healthcare Research and Quality (2017) Federal Balance Budget Act of 1997: excerpts. http://www.ahrq.gov/professionals/quality-patient-safety/quality-resources/tools/chtoolbx/fbba97.html
12. Register F (2002) Office of inspector general-health care: Medicare and Medicaid programs; peer review organizations: name and other changes-technical amendments. Fed Regist 67(101):36539–36540
13. U.S. Centers for Medicare and Medicaid Services (2018) Quality improvement organizations. https://www.cms.gov/Medicare/Quality-Initiatives-Patient-Assessment-Instruments/QualityImprovementOrgs/index.html?redirect=/qualityimprovementorgs
14. Centers for Medicare & Medicaid Services (2019) Accountable Care Organizations (ACOs): general information. https://innovation.cms.gov/initiatives/ACO/
15. Centers for Medicare & Medicaid Services (n.d.) Quality payment program overview. https://qpp.cms.gov/about/qpp-overview
16. Centers for Medicare & Medicaid Services (n.d.) MIPS overview. https://qpp.cms.gov/mips/overview
17. Centers for Medicare & Medicaid Services (n.d.) APMs overview. https://qpp.cms.gov/apms/overview
18. Centers for Medicare & Medicaid Services (n.d.) Advanced Alternative Payment Models (APMs). https://qpp.cms.gov/apms/advanced-apms
19. Centers for Medicare & Medicaid Services (2016) 2017 star ratings. https://www.cms.gov/newsroom/fact-sheets/2017-star-ratings
20. National Committee for Quality Assurance (2019) HEDIS and performance measurement. https://www.ncqa.org/hedis/
21. U.S. Department of Commerce, National Institute of Standards and Technology (2017) Baldrige Performance Excellence Program: how Baldrige works. https://www.nist.gov/baldrige/how-baldrige-works
22. U.S. Department of Commerce, National Institute of Standards and Technology (2019) Baldrige Health Care criteria for performance excellence categories and items. https://www.nist.gov/baldrige/baldrige-criteria-commentary-health-care

23. U.S. Department of Commerce, National Institute of Standards and Technology (2018) The Baldrige feedback report. https://www.nist.gov/baldrige/baldrige-award/feedback-report
24. U.S. Department of Commerce, National Institute of Standards and Technology (2017) Baldridge Performance Excellence Program 2017 Arroyo Fresco Community Health Center Case Study. https://www.nist.gov/baldrige/2017-arroyo-fresco-community-health-center-case-study
25. National Committee for Quality Assurance (2019). About NCQA. http://www.ncqa.org/about-ncqa
26. National Committee for Quality Assurance (2019) State of health care quality. https://www.ncqa.org/report-cards/health-plans/state-of-health-care-quality-report/
27. National Committee for Quality Assurance (2019) Persistence of Beta-Blocker Treatment after a heart attack (PBH). https://www.ncqa.org/hedis/measures/persistence-of-beta-blocker-treatment-after-a-heart-attack/
28. URAC (2019) About URAC. https://www.urac.org/about-urac
29. URAC (2019) URAC: standards and measures at a glance. https://www.urac.org/standards-and-measures-glance
30. The Joint Commission (2018) Facts about Joint Commission standards. https://www.jointcommission.org/facts_about_joint_commission_accreditation_standards/
31. The Joint Commission (2019) Achieve the Gold Seal of Approval®. https://www.jointcommission.org/achievethegoldseal.aspx
32. Healthcare News (2002) Joint Commission debuts new accreditation process "Shared Visions-New Pathways" will redirect the focus of the accreditation process. Healthcare News Nov 2002
33. The Joint Commission (2018) Facts about the on-site survey process. https://www.jointcommission.org/facts_about_the_on-site_survey_process/
34. The Joint Commission (2018) Facts about the National Patient Safety Goals. https://www.jointcommission.org/facts_about_the_national_patient_safety_goals/
35. International Organization for Standardization (ISO) (n.d.) All about ISO. https://www.iso.org/about-us.html
36. International Organization for Standardization (n.d.) ISO 9000 family – quality management. https://www.iso.org/iso-9001-quality-management.html
37. American Academy of Family Physicians (2019) Public reporting of physician performance, guiding principles. http://www.aafp.org/about/policies/all/physician-profiling.html
38. James J (2012) Health policy brief: public reporting on quality and costs. Health Aff 2012:1–5. https://www.healthaffairs.org/do/10.1377/hpb20120308.53696/full/
39. Colmers J (2007) Public reporting and transparency. The Commonwealth Fund. https://www.commonwealthfund.org/publications/fund-reports/2007/feb/public-reporting-and-transparency
40. Lee VS, Miller T, Daniels C et al (2016) Creating the exceptional patient experience in one academic health system. Acad Med 91:338–334. https://doi.org/10.1097/ACM.0000000000001007
41. Lee VS (2017) Why my health system collects and publishes patient reviews. In STAT. https://www.statnews.com/2017/02/21/patient-reviews-help-improve-health-care/. Accessed 21 Oct 2019
42. Lee VS (2016) Why doctors shouldn't be afraid of online reviews. In HBR.org. https://hbr.org/2016/03/why-doctors-shouldnt-be-afraid-of-online-reviews. Accessed 21 Oct 2019
43. The Leapfrog Group (n.d.) Mission and vision. http://www.leapfroggroup.org/about/mission-and-vision
44. The Leapfrog Group (2009) Fact sheet. https://www.bcbsil.com/provider/pdf/7_leapfrog_fact_sheet.pdf
45. The Leapfrog Group (n.d.) About us. http://www.leapfroggroup.org/about
46. The Leapfrog Group (2018) Leapfrog Hospital Survey Report Series Issued in 2018. http://www.leapfroggroup.org/ratings-reports/leapfrog-hospital-survey-report-series-issued-2018
47. Totten AM, Wagner J, Tiwari A, et al (2012) Public reporting as a quality improvement strategy. In closing the quality gap: revisiting the state of the science, Evidence report no. 208. Agency for Healthcare Research and Quality, Rockville

48. QualityNet (n.d.) Public reporting overview. https://www.qualitynet.org/dcs/ContentServer?c=Page&pagename=QnetPublic%2FPage%2FQnetTier2&cid=1121785350618
49. Centers for Medicare and Medicaid Services re.gov (2016) Hospital compare. https://www.cms.gov/medicare/quality-initiatives-patient-assessment-instruments/hospitalqualityinits/hospitalcompare.html
50. The Joint Commission (2018) Quality check. https://www.qualitycheck.org/
51. Cal Hospital Compare (2019) About. http://calhospitalcompare.org/about/
52. National Quality Forum (2019) About us. http://www.qualityforum.org/About_NQF/
53. Institute for Healthcare Improvement (2019) About us. http://www.ihi.org/about/Pages/default.aspx
54. Healthgrades Operating Company (2019) Quality and transparency. https://www.healthgrades.com/quality/
55. Association of American Medical Colleges (2001) Report V contemporary issues in medicine: quality of care, medical school objectives project. Washington, DC
56. Obeso V, Brown D, Aiyer M, et al (eds) (2017) Core EPAs for entering residency. Toolkits for the 13 Core EPAs. Association of American Medical Colleges, Washington, DC. https://www.aamc.org/initiatives/coreepas/publicationsandpresentations/
57. Institute for Healthcare Improvement (2019) Open school. http://www.ihi.org/education/ihiopenschool/
58. Institute for Health Care Improvement (1998) Knowledge domains for health professional students seeking competency in the continual improvement and innovation of health care. Boston. http://www.ihi.org/education/IHIOpenSchool/resources/Pages/Publications/EightKnowledgeDomainsForHealthProfessionStudents.aspx
59. Gould BE, Grey MR, Huntington CG et al (2002) Improving patient care outcomes by teaching quality improvement to medical students in community-based practices. Acad Med 77(10):1011–1018
60. Swing SR (2007) The ACGME outcome project: retrospective and prospective. Med Teach 29(7):648–654. https://doi.org/10.1080/01421590701392903
61. American Board of Medical Specialties (2017) Steps toward initial certification and MOC. http://www.abms.org/board-certification/steps-toward-initial-certification-and-moc/. Accessed 7 Apr 2017
62. Boonyasai RT, Windish DM, Chakraborti C et al (2007) Effectiveness of teaching quality improvement to clinicians. JAMA 298(9):1023–1037. https://doi.org/10.1001/jama.298.9.1023
63. Ogrinc G, Headrick LA, Mutha S et al (2003) A framework for teaching medical students and residents about practice-based learning and improvement, synthesized from a literature review. Acad Med 78(7):748–756
64. Varkey P, Reller MK, Smith A et al (2006) An experiential interdisciplinary quality improvement education initiative. Am J Med Qual 21(5):317–322. https://doi.org/10.1177/1062860606291136
65. Accreditation Council for Graduate Medical Education (2019) Clinical Learning Environment Review (CLER). https://acgme.org/What-We-Do/Initiatives/Clinical-Learning-Environment-Review-CLER
66. Co JPT, Weiss KB, Koh NJ, Wagner R (2018) CLER National Report Findings 2018: Executive Summary. Accreditation Council for Graduate Medical Education, Chicago
67. Wong BM, Levinson W, Shojania KG (2012) Quality improvement in medical education: current state and future directions. Med Educ 46:107–119. https://doi.org/10.1111/j.1365-2923.2011.04154.x
68. American Board of Medical Specialties (2019) Board certification, assessed through a four-part framework. https://www.abms.org/board-certification/a-trusted-credential/assessed-through-a-four-part-framework/
69. American Board of Medical Specialties (2019) About portfolio program. https://mocportfolioprogram.org/about-us/

70. Accreditation Council for Continuing Medical Education (2007) ACCME policy updates. http://www.accme.org/sites/default/files/null/409_ACCME%20Policy%20Updates%20 2007_20070824.pdf
71. Accreditation Council for Continuing Medical Education (2019) Accreditation criteria. http:// www.accme.org/accreditation-rules/accreditation-criteria
72. Accreditation Council for Continuing Medical Education (2019) CME in support of MOC. http://www.accme.org/cme-support-moc
73. Accreditation Council for Continuing Medical Education (2015) ACCME 2015 Data Report. http://www.accme.org/publications/accme-2015-data-report. Accessed 7 April 2017

Additional Reading-Further Resources

Accreditation Council for Continuing Medical Education (ACCME). Updated Criteria for Accreditation: http://www.accme.org/accreditation-rules/accreditation-criteria
American Academy of Family Physicians. Activities Eligible for Prescribed Credit: https://www. aafp.org/cme/creditsys/about/activity-types.html
American Board of Medical Specialties. Maintenance of Certification Competencies and Criteria: http://www.abms.org/board-certification/steps-toward-initial-certification-and-moc/
American Medical Association Physicians Recognition Award: https://www.ama-assn.org/ education/apply-ama-physician-recognition-award

Chapter 11
The Interface Between Quality Improvement and Law

Angelo P. Giardino and Marc T. Edwards

Executive Summary

A solid legal footing provides the framework and benchmarks for credible, persuasive, accountable quality management activities. Medical quality management (MQM) should reflect prevailing societal preferences, establishing a balance between the interests of patients, practitioners, institutional providers, health plans, regulatory agencies, and the general public. Legal standards help to ensure that these preferences are honored and bring clarity and accountability to the process. The quality of care delivered in a facility or health plan is directly influenced by the organization's quality improvement (QI) activities, including regulatory and accreditation compliance, provider credentialing, risk management, and clinical peer review.

As medical care has become increasingly complex, government actions via laws and regulations have also become more complicated to address the many aspects of the evolving healthcare system. Particularly in the face of limits on resources, or where healthcare benefits are restricted or limited, MQM decision-making must be done in a transparent and ethical manner that is fully compliant with relevant laws and regulations. The purpose of this chapter is to provide a working knowledge of legal issues related to clinical quality, provide a context to better understand some of the current challenges, and provide benchmarks in MQM.

A. P. Giardino (✉)
University of Utah School of Medicine, Salt Lake City, UT, USA

M. T. Edwards
University of North Carolina School of Medicine, Chapel Hill, NC, USA

© American College of Medical Quality (ACMQ) 2021
A. P. Giardino et al. (eds.), *Medical Quality Management*,
https://doi.org/10.1007/978-3-030-48080-6_11

Learning Objectives

Upon completion of this chapter, readers should be able to

- Identify the basic concepts related to legal issues in healthcare
- Discuss the impact of government and court decisions on the practice of medical quality management
- Explain the impact of federal and state laws on healthcare provision
- Discuss peer review protections and the creation of the National Practitioner Data Bank (NPDB)
- Understand best practices for clinical peer review in pursuit of quality and safety
- Identify pertinent issues related to the Health Insurance Portability and Accountability Act (HIPAA) of 1996
- Discuss the role of the Healthcare Quality Improvement Act (HCQIA) of 1986 in peer reviews
- Understand the Patient Safety and Quality Improvement Act of 2005
- Discuss legal issues related to medical errors and transparency
- Explain the effects of malpractice, antitrust legislation, and risk management on healthcare practice
- Present the basic framework for alternatives to litigation in resolving disputes

History

One of the first documented legal codes was based on Sumerian and Akkadian laws [1]. It was compiled by Hammurabi, who ruled Babylonia between 1795 and 1750 BC [2]. The Code of Hammurabi contains a number of regulations related to what physician actions are permissible, physician payment rates, and reimbursement of the patient for damages as the result of an operation. Under this code, physicians were judged based on quality and outcomes—an ancient pay-for-performance initiative. As societies became more regulated, the legal profession and government increased their oversight, proscribing and prescribing certain actions and activities.

Ethical and legal codes and principles can be found in writings from ancient civilizations in Greece and India. For example, Hippocrates' writings (fifth century BC) contain physicians' principles and patients' rights [3]. Sushruta, a renowned Ayurvedic surgeon from India (sixth century BC), documented that he required his students to use fruits, vegetables, and artificial models of the human body for surgery training [4]. The basic concepts found in ethical and legal documents evolved in parallel with the development of modern healthcare. They are embodied in the administrative and financial activities that support the delivery of care, and they are published and disseminated by medical associations.

Clinical peer review, now a pivotal element of healthcare evaluation and oversight, has been evolving for over a century. After Medicare was signed into law, peer review programs were widely adopted as a result of conditions of participation that required quality assurance and utilization review activities [5]. The current legal framework for MQM reflects societal preferences on how to balance the interests of patients, practitioners, institutional providers, health plans, regulatory agencies, and the general public. Legal standards help to ensure that these preferences are honored.

Role of Government

The government uses laws and regulations to codify actions it believes to be appropriate in specific circumstances for the protection of the population. These laws and regulations aim to decrease unnecessary variation and complexity.

Federal law preempts state laws in most cases [5]. For example, the Employee Retirement Income Security Act of 1974 (ERISA) establishes minimum standards for pension and other health insurance plans provided by private employers. The Act supports private industry by regulating and protecting the interests of employee benefit plan participants and their beneficiaries, establishing rules of conduct for plan fiduciaries, and by simplifying the creation of multistate or national benefit plans. Because it preempts state law, ERISA permits private companies to offer health plans and benefits nationwide without running afoul of state insurance regulations. In civil lawsuits, ERISA forbids financial awards to beneficiaries for pain and suffering and punitive damages for gross negligence in the mismanagement of the healthcare plans. This legislation and its impact on certain litigation is at the core of an ongoing debate between state and federal regulations pertaining to the degree of protection and accountability of the fiduciary and the right of the beneficiary to be compensated as a result of harm.

The government supports medical quality professionals through regulations and by providing governmental and government-sponsored organizations. These include the Agency for Healthcare Research and Quality (AHRQ), which fosters and facilitates evidenced-based medicine and guideline development, and the National Academy of Medicine, which was known as the Institute of Medicine (IOM) prior to July 2015. The IOM was instrumental in promoting a quality and safety agenda in healthcare via its landmark reports on medical errors, patient safety, and quality improvement [6, 7]. Specifically, in its 2001 report, *Crossing the Quality Chasm*, the IOM challenged healthcare organizations to take an active role in improving care by focusing on six major domains: safety, timeliness, effectiveness, efficacy, equity, and a patient-centered approach [7]. US healthcare organizations responded by implementing QI activities to make medical care safer for patients. Most recently, the Patient Protection and Affordable Care Act of 2010 established the National Quality Strategy (NQS), which incorporates the six quality domains and speaks to a set of aims, priorities, and levers directed at improving the quality and safety of healthcare in the United States.

The National Quality Strategy (NQS) was first published in March 2011 as the National Strategy for Quality Improvement in Healthcare and is led by the Agency for Healthcare Research and Quality (AHRQ) on behalf of the U.S. Department of Health and Human

Services (HHS). The NQS was developed through a transparent and collaborative process with input from…[m]ore than 300 groups, organizations, and individuals, representing all sectors of the healthcare industry and the general public… Based on this input, the National Quality Strategy established a set of three overarching aims building on the Institute for Healthcare Improvement's Triple Aim®, supported by six priorities that address the most common health concerns that Americans face, and nine levers stakeholders can use to align their core business or organizational functions to drive improvement on the aims and priorities [8].

Table 11.1 outlines these components of NQS.

Table 11.1 National Quality Strategy

Component	Details
Aims	1. Better care: Improve the overall quality by making healthcare more patient-centered, reliable, accessible, and safe. 2. Healthy people/healthy communities: Improve the health of the US population by supporting proven interventions to address behavioral, social, and environmental determinants of health in addition to delivering higher-quality care. 3. Affordable care: Reduce the cost of quality healthcare for individuals, families, employers, and government.
Priorities	1. Making care safer by reducing harm caused in the delivery of care 2. Ensuring that each person and family are engaged as partners in their care 3. Promoting effective communication and coordination of care 4. Promoting the most effective prevention and treatment practices for the leading causes of mortality, starting with cardiovascular disease 5. Working with communities to promote the wide use of best practices to enable healthy living 6. Making quality care more affordable for individuals, families, employers, and governments by developing and spreading new healthcare delivery models
Levers	1. Measurement and feedback: Provide performance feedback to plans and providers to improve care. 2. Public reporting: Compare treatment results, costs, and patient experience for consumers. 3. Learning and technical assistance: Foster learning environments that offer training, resources, tools, and guidance to help organizations achieve quality improvement goals. 4. Certification, accreditation, and regulation: Adopt or adhere to approaches to meet safety and quality standards. 5. Consumer incentives and benefit designs: Help consumers adopt healthy behaviors and make informed decisions. 6. Payment: Reward and incentivize providers to deliver high-quality, patient-centered care. 7. Health information technology: Improve communication, transparency, and efficiency for better coordinated health and healthcare. 8. Innovation and diffusion: Foster innovation in healthcare quality improvement and facilitate rapid adoption within and across organizations and communities. 9. Workforce development: Investing in people to prepare the next generation of healthcare professionals and support lifelong learning for providers.

Adapted from *About the National Quality Strategy,* by the Agency for Healthcare Research and Quality, 2016, Retrieved from https://www.ahrq.gov/workingforquality/about/nqs-fact-sheets/fact-sheet.html.

Of note, in the 2015 annual update to Congress on the NQS, AHRQ reported that key indicators on healthcare quality were improving, stating:

Across the National Quality Strategy's six priorities, the 2014 report finds that half of the patient safety measures improved, led by a 17 percent reduction in rates of hospital-acquired conditions; person-centered care improved steadily, especially for children; care coordination improved as providers enhanced discharge processes and adopted health information technologies; effective treatment in hospitals improved, as indicated by measures publicly reported by the Centers for Medicare & Medicaid Services on the Hospital Compare website; healthy living improved in about half of the measures followed, led by increased administration of selected adolescent vaccines from 2008 to 2012; and care affordability worsened from 2002 to 2010 and then leveled off. After years without improvement, the rate of un-insurance among adults ages 18-64 decreased substantially during the first half of 2014. In order to obtain high-quality care, Americans must first gain entry into the healthcare system, and millions have done so by enrolling in the healthcare marketplaces that have expanded coverage to 17.6 million people through provisions of the Affordable Care Act, including both Medicaid expansion and Health Insurance Marketplaces. As of June 30, 2015, about 9.9 million consumers had effectuated Health Insurance Marketplace coverage, and about 84 percent, or more than 8.3 million consumers, were receiving an advanced premium tax credit to make their premiums more affordable throughout the year [9].

Public Laws and Regulation to Ensure Quality

Some laws require quality assurance (QA) activities in addition to QI activities. QA activities focus on compliance with accepted standards or guidelines. In contrast, QI activities focus on measures, processes, and outcomes in an ongoing, iterative course of action to actively improve results.

State-mandated facility inspections and professional licensure constitute the ground floor level of quality (i.e., minimum requirements to practice medicine or to provide care in a facility). While licensure is important, it does not assure high-quality healthcare.

Some public interest groups have attempted to use licensure and public sanctions as a measure of the effectiveness of a State Board of Medicine's ability to protect the population. One such method would calculate the proportion of disciplinary actions taken against physicians versus the number of licensed physicians in the state. Such a ratio is potentially misleading, however, as it may include licensed physicians who are not in active practice, are solely involved in research, or do not reside or practice in multiple states where they may be licensed.

States are responsible for a substantial amount of oversight including the licensure of inpatient facilities and healthcare professionals. They also regulate managed care and other insurance products when outside the domain of ERISA. The federal government has a significant impact on Medicare (federally sponsored) and Medicaid (jointly funded, federal and state-sponsored) programs, which affects a high percentage of the population in most states.

Health and safety standards provide a foundation for improving quality and protecting patients. States have looked to nationally recognized accreditors, such as the

Joint Commission, National Committee on Quality Assurance (NCQA), and Utilization Review Accreditation Commission (URAC), as sources for standards. For example, many state agencies that oversee Medicaid managed care require the collection and reporting of NCQA's HEDIS data.

Most hospitals demonstrate compliance with Medicare conditions of participation in conjunction with oversight by an accrediting agency. The Joint Commission is a private, not-for-profit organization that accredits the majority of hospitals that participate in Medicare. Hospitals accredited by the Joint Commission are considered to be in compliance with the requirements for Medicare participation. Under the Medicare statute, Joint Commission–accredited hospitals are considered to have met requirements for Medicare certification (42 USC §1395x [e] and §1395bb). In recent years, other organizations such as DNV GL Healthcare and the Center for Improvement in Healthcare Quality (CIHQ) have competed for this business.

The activity of these accrediting organizations has not gone without government scrutiny. As early as 2004, in its Report to Congressional Requesters, *Centers for Medicare and Medicaid Services Needs Additional Authority to Adequately Oversee Patient Safety in Hospitals*, the Government Accountability Office reported that the Joint Commission's pre-2004 hospital accreditation process did not identify a number of the hospitals' deficiencies in Medicare requirements noted by state surveys [10]. Suggestions were made to the U.S. Centers for Medicare and Medicaid Services (CMS) to modify the oversight process.

Despite calls for improvement, a recent *Wall Street Journal* investigation again called attention to a quality accreditation disconnect [11]. According to the investigation, the Joint Commission accredits about 80% of U.S. hospitals, and after reviewing hundreds of inspection reports, "Nearly 350 hospitals maintained accreditation in 2014 despite Medicare deviations, and more than a third of those had further violations in 2015 and 2016." [11]

As a volume purchaser of healthcare, CMS affects how care is delivered to seniors and the disabled. It also has a significant impact on commercial insurance carriers and Medicaid. CMS's reimbursement and coverage rules affect a large percentage of hospitalized and ambulatory patients. Changes in Medicare coverage make it necessary for hospitals to modify policies and procedures, educate staff, and maintain ongoing oversight.

The Deficit Reduction Act of 2005 directed Health and Human Services (HHS) to identify a number of preventable inpatient complications, the occurrence of which would no longer be reimbursed by Medicare. This new rule, mandated under Section 5001(c) of Public Law 109–171, was published as a final rule on July 31, 2008 in the Inpatient Prospective Payment System (IPPS). At that time, CMS slated ten categories of conditions for the Hospital Acquired Conditions (HACs) "no payment list." [12] Monetary implications began October 1, 2008. Essentially, the initiative penalizes hospitals performing in the bottom 25% on the HAC measures as compared to their peers. New HACs were added in the final rule for 2013. The categories for HACs are listed below:

- Foreign object retained after surgery
- Air embolism

- Blood incompatibility
- Stage III and IV pressure ulcers
- Falls and trauma

  - Fractures
  - Dislocations
  - Intracranial injuries
  - Crushing injuries
  - Burn
  - Other injuries

- Manifestations of poor glycemic control

  - Diabetic ketoacidosis
  - Nonketotic hyperosmolar coma
  - Hypoglycemic coma
  - Secondary diabetes with ketoacidosis
  - Secondary diabetes with hyperosmolarity

- Catheter-associated urinary tract infection (UTI)
- Vascular catheter-associated infection
- Surgical site infection, mediastinitis, following coronary artery bypass graft (CABG)
- Surgical site infection following bariatric surgery for obesity

  - Laparoscopic gastric bypass
  - Gastroenterostomy
  - Laparoscopic gastric restrictive surgery

- Surgical site infection following certain orthopedic procedures

  - Spine
  - Neck
  - Shoulder
  - Elbow

- Surgical site infection following cardiac implantable electronic device (CIED)
- Deep vein thrombosis (DVT)/pulmonary embolism (PE) following certain orthopedic procedures

  - Total knee replacement
  - Hip replacement

- Iatrogenic pneumothorax with venous catheterization [12]

Programs designed to prevent these complications (e.g., policies, procedures) will likely result in a decreased incidence of these events at hospitals across the country. For fiscal year 2018, Medicare penalized 751 of 3306 hospitals evaluated for their measured performance on the HAC indicators with a 1% payment reduction [13].

Patient Safety and Quality Improvement Act

The Patient Safety and Quality Improvement Act of 2005 (the Act) created a general framework to support and protect voluntary initiatives to improve quality and patient safety in all healthcare settings through reporting to patient safety organizations (PSOs). It includes protections against reprisals for good-faith reporters of patient safety concerns, which include any circumstance involving patient safety, and encompasses patient safety events (both incidents and near misses) and unsafe conditions:

- *Incident*: A patient safety event that reached the patient, whether or not the patient was harmed
- *Near miss (or close call)*: A patient safety event that did not reach the patient
- *Unsafe condition*: Any circumstance that increases the probability of a patient safety event [14]

The Act opened the door to standardized, large-scale data aggregation and information sharing. It has potential to stimulate development of a culture of safety in healthcare, but faces challenges from ongoing litigation over patient safety work product (PSWP) protections. PSWP is the regulatory term primarily used to describe the data and activities protected under the Act. Broadly speaking, it includes any information which could result in improved patient safety, quality, or outcomes. It involves two dimensions of activity:

- Data collected within the provider's patient safety evaluation system (PSES) for purposes of reporting to a PSO, such as interviews with staff, event reports, data reports, and copies of records
- Analyses conducted within the provider's PSES, such as clinical peer review and root cause analysis (RCA)

For provider organizations, the distinction between data collected and analyses is important because collected data is subject to the dropout provision of the final rule, which allows time to assess whether the data is subject to statutory reporting requirements or other restrictions that would prohibit a primary designation as PSWP. Analyses conducted within the PSES are always protected and cannot be removed. The regulations do not restrict the use of analytic methods such as RCA or peer review outside the PSES. Analyses may always be recreated or repeated from original source material.

The original medical record and hospital financial systems transactions are never considered PSWP. Nor is material that exists or is developed outside a PSES or material required to meet statutory reporting obligations. Nevertheless, copies of such data can be entered into the PSES and reported to a PSO for further data aggregation and other objectives. Those copies are eligible for protection even if the source material is not.

Eligible work product enjoys both confidentiality and privilege protections. In general, it may not be disclosed, used in disciplinary proceedings, or subjected to subpoena or legal discovery. There are several narrowly defined exceptions to this principle. The specific details are given in §3.204 and §3.206 of the PSO Final Rule. The privilege protections are subject to enforcement by the courts. The confidentiality provisions are subject to enforcement via civil monetary penalties imposed by the Office of Civil Rights on behalf of the Secretary of the Department of Health and Human Services.

Patient Safety Organization Activity

Patient safety organizations are designated by statute to receive *patient safety work product* from contracted providers. The Patient Safety Act includes specific criteria for certification as a "listed" PSO. The final rule defines the requirements and process for initial certification and continued listing. The process of reporting PSWP to a PSO confers the privileges and protections of the Act. The role of the PSO is to work with multiple healthcare organizations and their associated clinicians to identify, analyze, and reduce the risks and hazards associated with patient care. The PSO brings special expertise to complement the work that providers are already doing. This may include

- Receipt and analysis of patient safety work product
- Feedback to promote a culture of safety and reduce patient risk
- Large-scale data aggregation and analysis
- Best practice recommendations
- Consultative support for quality and safety improvement [14]

Patient safety evaluation system (PSES) is the regulatory term used to describe the provider's process and protected space for collecting, managing, and analyzing information about patient safety events for the purpose of reporting to a PSO. Most providers already manage this sensitive information in relation to their risk management or quality management program. An element of the PSES is the identification of the types of information that the organization wants to collect, manage, and analyze for the purpose of reporting to a PSO. Once that is done, the details of documentation and PSO reporting can be worked out. While the regulations do not specifically require documentation of the PSES, most organizations should consider developing a policy and procedure. Such documentation will prove helpful in the event that the organization's assertions of federal protections to PSWP are challenged.

The Patient Safety Act also authorized the development of *Common Formats for Event Reporting* for reporting patient safety events to PSOs [15]. PSOs are responsible to support Common Formats whenever possible in their data collection work. These Common Formats are sets of standards for patient safety–related data which are intended to enable interoperability and data sharing on a national level. The Common Formats include form specifications for various types of event reports, a meta-data registry with data element attributes and technical specifications, a complete data dictionary defining XML data file requirements for reporting to the national database, and a common set of definitions of patient safety concerns [15]. Data elements within the Common Formats can be either *structured data*, which can be aggregated within and across provider organizations, or *narrative information*, which cannot be aggregated, but provide the necessary details about an individual event or condition needed to understand patient safety concerns at the provider and/ or PSO levels [15].

AHRQ established a process for developing Common Formats that is evidence-based, harmonizes across governmental health agencies, incorporates feedback from the private sector, and permits timely updating of clinically sensitive formats [16]. AHRQ has released initial and revised sets of Common Formats for hospitals, an initial set for community pharmacies, and beta versions for hospital readmissions, hospital surveillance (through medical record review), and nursing homes [16].

While the original intent of PSOs focused on encouraging contracted providers to establish PSESs and to collect and report PSWP, in recent years, they have expanded their activities to promote protected sharing and learning from events by creating forums such as *Safe Table* discussions [17]. Safe Tables are a method to foster discussion that promotes a culture of trust. They can be conducted either in person or via virtual meetings, and can focus on a single setting or include a variety of settings. PSOs can host Safe Tables regionally with broad participation or in a more focused fashion with targeted audiences such as specific units or types of care providers, e.g., obstetrics units [14]. The California Hospital PSO defines the objectives of a Safe Table as: 1) to generate candid discussion and share organizations' experiences on patient safety and quality issues; 2) to exchange information about best practices relative to patient safety and, 3) to encourage coordinated/collaborative efforts and new partnerships [18]. Examples provided by AHRQ of topics discussed at Safe Tables include failure to inform patients of abnormal test results, factors related to falls, prevention of health care–associated infections, and responses to patient violence and aggression [14].

Healthcare Quality Improvement Act and Peer Review Protection

Clinical peer review is an activity whereby healthcare professionals evaluate each other's clinical performance with the goal of improving quality, safety, and the cost of care. This includes routine clinical peer review programs found in all US hospitals, which invariably include retrospective medical record review of the quality of care [19]. Clinical peer review appears to be the dominant mode of adverse event analysis in the hospital setting. The scope of hospital peer review programs varies widely and may include other activity ranging from ongoing professional practice evaluation to physician health programs. Peer review methods are also used to assess clinical competence in licensing, credentialing, and privileging decisions. At that level, it affords providers a fair hearing process that protects their rights. All these forms of peer review activity help to protect patients.

Most commonly, the routine clinical peer review process is administered separately from credentialing activity, even if its results inform credentialing decisions. It is best performed by healthcare professionals who are not in direct economic competition with the individual under review and who are attuned to identifying opportunities for improvement in the system of care. The peer review process generally compares the provider's performance with evidence-based standards and the practice of peers within the same specialty with similar patients. It may also examine whether the provider's care falls within the scope of the patient's insurance benefits. Peer review regulatory requirements may vary from state to state (e.g., whether the physician conducting review must be in active practice).

Prevailing peer review practices, which focus narrowly on questions of standard of care, have long been criticized for being out of touch with modern QI methods. Nevertheless, a best practice model has been described which conforms to them. The QI model for clinical peer review includes the standardization of the review process, a focus on identifying opportunities for improved performance (as opposed to casting blame for error); promotion of self-reporting of adverse events, near misses, and hazardous conditions; the quality of case review; timely performance feedback; recognition of clinical excellence; a solid connection between the peer review program and the organization's quality improvement process; and attentive program governance [20].

The Healthcare Quality Improvement Act of 1986 (HCQIA) (42 USC § 11,101–11,152) addressed the need to simultaneously protect peer review and prevent its abuse by providing immunity protection only for good faith activity, irrespective of available state-specific protections [21]. It was enacted at a time when the number of malpractice cases was rising, with increasingly large settlements. Malpractice and the perceived risks of healthcare were in the public eye; the time was ripe for actions to ensure patient safety. Physicians reportedly considered early retirement or the elimination of certain procedures from their practices to reduce the risks and costs of malpractice. Oversight of physicians and other professionals (e.g., licensure, credentialing) was being strengthened. It was, therefore, important to make it safe for physicians to participate in peer review activities.

The HCQIA provides immunity to bodies that conduct peer review through a formally defined process that extends notice and fair hearing rights to any provider whose clinical privileges are threatened. Covered entities include hospitals, managed care organizations, professional societies, or committees of physicians at a national, state, or local level. The expressed objective of these organizations should be to improve the quality of healthcare. The protection afforded by the act is *qualified immunity* from damages under state and federal law if the provisions of the act (§ 11,112) are followed. The Act relates to deliberations of professional review bodies and actions that affect clinical privileges. Individuals who take part in these activities are also protected (see *Imperial v Suburban Hosp. Assn., Inc.*, 37 F3d 1026 [4th Cir 199]; *Decker v IHC Hospitals, Inc.*, 982 F2d 433 [10th Cir 1995]). It establishes immunity from liability only, not immunity from suit. The Act specifically denies immunity for claims alleging civil rights violations (42 USC §11,111[b] professional review) [21].

Requirements for Peer Review Activities to Be Granted Immunity from Liability Damages

1. The review and the resultant action must adversely affect the physician's clinical privileges and be based on clinical competence or conduct issues.
2. The action taken must be imposed with the reasonable belief that it will improve the quality of care.
3. The physician must be provided with due process rights within a specific time frame. The procedure for providing appeal rights and time frames are clearly stated in the act. The physician must be made aware of the following:

   - The potential adverse action.
   - The basis for the action.
   - The right to request a hearing (within not less than 30 days).
   - The hearing process and the witnesses to be called.
   - He or she can be represented by counsel and may cross-examine the witnesses and present evidence.
   - The hearing is to be recorded with the production of a written report, a copy of which is presented to the physician.

4. Actions taken must be reported within a specified time frame to the data bank.

Adapted from *Title IV of Public Law 99–660*, by U.S. Department of Health & Human Services, Retrieved from https://www.npdb.hrsa.gov/resources/titleIv.jsp.

In the context of an accusation of a violation of civil rights, peer review protection can be pierced. In one civil rights case, *Russell Adkins v Christie* 488 F.3d 1324 (11th Cir 2007), a three-judge panel of the 11th U.S. Circuit Court of Appeals requested review of peer review records to investigate a potential civil rights violation. The physician alleged that an action had been taken based on his race. The court decided that rooting out "insidious discrimination" had priority over the need to keep private peer review deliberations secret. The judges ruled the information contained in the peer review was integral to the charge of racial discrimination, and found that the physician had been subjected to a higher level of review which resulted in the termination of his privileges.

Peer review protection is provided only if the peer review is conducted in good faith with the prime objective of the activity being to improve the quality of healthcare. The review and resultant action must be based in clinical competence or professional conduct issues. The process for appeals is specifically documented in the act. Challenges may be made to the immunity of the deliberations by allegation of peer review being conducted in bad faith if:

- The case is related to a civil rights claim
- The physician is not made aware of the potential adverse action and his due process rights within the specified time frame
- Procedural requirements were not met (i.e., the physician is not provided his due process rights and/or a fair hearing was not offered)
- The action was taken to decrease competition (e.g., collusion between members of the peer review panel who were direct competitors of the physician under review)
- The action was not taken with the main objective to improve care, but rather to remove a troublesome staff member or to silence a "malcontent" or whistle blower [21].

As a result, most hospital medical staff bylaws are structured to conform to the requirements of HCQIA. In practice, covered entities may forfeit protections under the Act by failing to follow and document these procedures. If the peer review process is misused for economic or anti-competitive purposes to achieve an advantage of one provider or provider organization over another, the legal protections are forfeited. The case described below, which progressed through the court system over several years, provides valuable insights into how the peer review process must adhere to the principles of good faith and must only be used for quality improvement purposes. When used to damage someone's reputation and achieve a competitive advantage, the peer review privilege is forfeited, and civil damages may be awarded.

Case Study • • •
Misuse of the Peer Review Process for Economic Purposes: A Cautionary Tale.

According to the Supreme Court of Texas' May 22, 2015 decision, a cardiac surgeon practiced at Hospital A from 1998 until 2012, where he developed a robotic cardiac surgery program and built a reputation for "quality patient care, technical excellence, and outstanding professionalism in heart and general surgery." [22, 23] When it became known to Hospital A leaders that the cardiac surgeon was willing to associate himself with Hospital B, a competitor in the marketplace, Hospital A's leaders began a "whisper campaign" against the surgeon. Specifically, at a November 2011 meeting, a medical leader from Hospital A displayed data to referring physicians implying that the cardiac surgeon had a higher than expected mortality rate. This Hospital A medical leader manipulated the presented data and failed to use generally accepted scientific methodologies for peer comparison. Despite

(continued)

Hospital A's peer review committee repudiation of the medical leader's comparative data display, the manipulated data continued to be disseminated within the referring medical community. In addition, a Hospital A administrator in January 2012 publicly ridiculed the cardiac surgeon's skills and alerted physicians, nurses, and other administrators that he had targeted the cardiac surgeon because of the surgeon's association with the competitor Hospital B. He specifically stated that targeting the cardiac surgeon was meant as a preemptive warning to other physicians who sought to leave Hospital A for Hospital B and that the administrator would not tolerate physicians taking business from Hospital A.

From news coverage of the case, we know that the cardiac surgeon brought a suit against Hospital A in 2012 alleging it misused the peer review process and falsified data to damage his reputation and to harm his practice after he associated with Hospital B in addition to his work at Hospital A [24]. During a two-week trial in March 2017, a jury found that Hospital A had defamed the cardiac surgeon and awarded him 6.4 million dollars in damages. Specifically, the jury found that Hospital A made false statements about the cardiac surgeon's competence and surgical mortality rates and that Hospital A had shared manipulated peer review data with referring cardiologists. The rarity of such cases making it to trial was noted in one news article reporting on the case: "The verdict is extremely unusual. Typically, defamation cases are solved outside of courts, especially because it is difficult for physicians to prove the peer review process was used in a detrimental way, as is necessary in Texas for physicians to access the otherwise confidential data." [24]

In May 2017, a state district judge upheld the jury verdict and award to the cardiac surgeon against Hospital A which was found to have defamed the cardiac surgeon who brought the lawsuit "in an effort to protect its business from other hospitals and competitors." [25] Again, the news coverage comments on the central role of the peer review process and its potential misuse:

> [The cardiac surgeon's] case turned on peer review, a confidential process conducted by committees of physicians to weed out bad doctors. [The cardiac surgeon], however, alleged that [Hospital A] misused the process, manipulating data on the outcome of his surgeries to suggest that his patients were more likely to die. The jury… determined that a comment from a [Hospital A] employee about [the cardiac surgeon's] "bad quality, high mortality rates, unnecessary surgeries," was false and damaged [the cardiac surgeon's] reputation… The jury also found another employee's comment about the hospital's decision to share [the cardiac surgeon's] peer review data with referring cardiologists in the name of safety and transparency to be false and defamatory [25].

On August 15, 2019, a state appeals court upheld the $6.4 million jury award. In a 67-page ruling, the appeals court stated, "We conclude that there was evidence that [Hospital A]…published the individual surgeon mortality data by presenting it to other doctors, who were capable of understanding its defamatory import." [26]

The National Practitioner Data Bank

Although the HCQIA established federal peer review protection for institutions and individuals engaged in peer review, another major provision, the creation of the National Practitioner Data Bank (NPDB), was not realized until after the publication of the final regulations in 1989. The NPDB was intended to restrict the ability of incompetent physicians to move from state to state unscrutinized. Hospitals, state medical boards, and other healthcare entities who engage in formal peer review activities are required to report disciplinary actions they have taken to the NPDB. An entity that fails to report as required may lose HCQIA protections for 3 years. Data Bank content was further amended by the 1990 Omnibus Budget Reconciliation Act (OBRA), which added a requirement that adverse determinations (findings and actions) by peer review of private accreditation entities should be reported to the NPDB [27]. The NPDB collects the following types of data:

- Professional review actions taken by hospitals, HMOs, and other entities that result in reduction, suspension, revoking of clinical privileges, restriction, or termination of privileges or membership in a healthcare entity. Any action that adversely affects the clinical privileges of a physician for a period longer than 30 days must be reported.
- Acceptance of the surrender of clinical privileges or restriction of privileges while the physician is under investigation by the healthcare entity concerning issues of incompetence or improper professional conduct, or as an alternative to conducting an investigation.
- Professional board actions that result in a change in licensure status.
- Exclusion from Medicare-Medicaid programs and sanctions.
- Malpractice payments and settlements made on behalf of physicians [28].

The HCQIA (§ 11,135) requires hospitals to query the NPDB in their initial credentialing and bi-annual provider recredentialing processes.

Credentialing

Credentialing is the process of obtaining, verifying, and assessing information to determine the qualifications of a healthcare professional to provide services to a patient. The credentialing process examines the training, education, and actual experience of the healthcare professional. This may include data such as the number of times a surgeon has performed a certain procedure and the clinical outcomes for the patients.

Specific criteria for credentialing are well outlined by many organizations. These include the NCQA, Utilization Review Accreditation Commission (URAC), the Joint Commission, and others. Some states may also have specific criteria for healthcare professionals that must be followed. The following are the general processes involved in credentialing:

- Primary source verification

  - Medical school graduation
  - Residency
  - Specialty boards
  - State license
  - Drug enforcement certificate
  - History of professional liability
  - Clinical privileges
  - Malpractice insurance
  - Work history

- Application and attestation

  - Reason for any inability to perform essential clinical functions
  - Lack of present illegal drug use or chemical dependency
  - History of loss of license-felony convictions
  - History of change in privileges or disciplinary action
  - Correctness and completeness of application

- Verification

  - National Practitioner Data Bank
  - Healthcare Integrity and Protection Data Bank
  - Licensure limitations
  - Medicare and Medicaid sanctions

- Initial site visit

  - May be required for primary care physicians and some specialists
  - Criteria for credentialing

When conducted according to these criteria, credentialing is an up-front process that protects patients, healthcare systems, and physicians from potential quality and utilization issues. Some healthcare organizations break the credentialing process into two components. The first is the contracting component, which determines whether the physician meets the criteria to have a contract with the healthcare organization. The second is the actual clinical appropriateness of the physician in terms of privileges to care for specific types of patients or disease processes. For example, all general surgeons may have a contract to provide surgery to a population, but only some general surgeons will have privileges to provide thyroid surgery within their contract.

As noted in the HCQIA § 11,135, "a hospital which does not request the information respecting a physician or practitioner [during the credentialing process] as required under subsection (a) of this section is presumed to have knowledge of any information reported under this subchapter to the Secretary with respect to the physician or practitioner." [21]

The HCQIA specifically states who may have access to the Data Bank:

- A hospital that requests information concerning a physician, dentist, or other healthcare practitioner who is on its medical staff (courtesy or otherwise) or has clinical privileges at the hospital
- A physician, dentist, or other healthcare practitioner who requests information concerning himself or herself
- Boards of Medical Examiners or other state licensing boards
- Healthcare entities which have entered, or may be entering, employment or affiliation relationships with a physician, dentist, or other healthcare practitioner; or to which the physician, dentist, or other healthcare practitioner has applied for clinical privileges or appointment to the medical staff
- An attorney, or individual representing himself or herself, who has filed a medical malpractice action or claim in a state or federal court or other adjudicative body against a hospital, and who requests information regarding a specific physician, dentist, or other healthcare practitioner who is also named in the action or claim, provided that this information will be disclosed only upon the submission of evidence that the hospital failed to request information from the Data Bank as required by Sec. 60.10(a), and may be used solely with respect to litigation resulting from the action or claim against the hospital
- A healthcare entity with respect to professional review activity [21]

The HCQIA allows the U.S. Department of Health and Human Services (HHS) to promulgate regulations that allow a healthcare practitioner to challenge information reported to HHS (42 USC §11,136 [2]). According to the NPDB Guidebook, a practitioner may contact the reporting entity directly to request a correction [28]. At any time, the practitioner may add a Subject Statement to the report. Once a Subject Statement is processed, the NPDB copies anyone who received the report within the prior 3 years. The Subject Statement becomes a permanent part of the record and is included whenever the report is disclosed [28].

The subject of a report also has the right to enter the report into Dispute Status by challenging either the facts of the report or whether it was submitted in accordance with NPDB reporting requirements, including the eligibility of the entity to report to the NPDB [28]. If the subject is unable to resolve issues with the entity, he or she may request dispute resolution by the NBDP. Dispute resolution cannot address the validity of the underlying reasons for the report or whether due process was followed. The Agency's determination is final.

HIPAA Regulations

HIPAA is the well-known acronym for the Health Insurance Portability and Accountability Act of 1996 (Public Law 104–191) [29]. HIPAA amended the Internal Revenue Code of 1986 to improve portability and continuity of health insurance coverage in the group and individual markets to combat waste, fraud, and abuse in health insurance and healthcare delivery, to promote the use of medical savings accounts, to improve access to long-term care services and coverage, and to simplify the administration of health insurance, among other purposes.

HIPAA had profound effects on healthcare administration. Of the many rules promulgated as a result of this Act, those related to the privacy and security of healthcare information are most relevant to healthcare quality improvement.

The Privacy Rule

The Privacy Rule is comprised of regulations that govern the use and disclosure of protected health information (PHI), either in electronic or paper form. PHI is any health-related information, health status, or information relating to healthcare provisions, payment, and any other identifiable or specific material contained in the medical record. Specific exceptions to this rule include reporting to law enforcement officials' evidence of child abuse and reporting infectious disease. The key to disclosure of PHI between health professionals is that the minimum amount of information necessary should be released. Covered entities (defined in the rule as those who are "covered by the regulations") must also track the release of this PHI and must designate an individual to be responsible for educating all staff on the Privacy Rule and overseeing the confidentiality provisions of HIPAA. Covered entities are required to have designated privacy officers and policies and procedures used to educate the facility or office staff and to ensure compliance with the act.

The Privacy Rule gives the patient the right to review their medical record and to correct any errors. The covered entity can disclose information as part of ongoing treatment, payment during normal operations of the facility or office, and through written authorization by the patient. The privacy officer is responsible for ensuring that these privacy activities occur consistently, in addition to ensuring compliance with other HIPAA requirements. Upon initially accessing care, patients are provided with a privacy notice (i.e., an explanation of the organization's use of information and the patient's rights regarding its use and release of the information contained in the medical records). The patient's acknowledgment of receipt of this information must be retained.

The Security Rule

The Security Rule consists of security safeguards for PHI stored electronically and promotes the goal of maintaining the integrity and availability of electronic PHI.

The Enforcement Rule

The Enforcement Rule, issued in 2006, sets penalties for violations of HIPAA rules and creates a structure for investigations and hearings related to violations.

Administrative Simplification Rule

The Administrative Simplification Rule is comprised of the following standards:

Transactions and Code Sets Standards   The HIPAA transactions and code sets standards mandated the simplification of data collection and aggregation through the creation of universal data sets and the fostering of interoperability of programs, including electronic data interchange (EDI) functions, which was meant to standardize the electronic exchange of patient information. Common codes have the following advantages [29]:

- Facilitating electronic filing of health claims
- Decreasing costs of electronic interactions in the long term
- Decreasing the errors that result in rejected claims
- Providing a more universal system for data collection and interoperability between various systems and programs, including claim adjudication of health data collection
- Improving transparency related to the delivery of healthcare

Identifier Standards for Employers and Providers   As part of HIPAA, a unique identifier was created for all covered entities using electronic data interchange (EDI). The Employer Identification Number (EIN) was established for organizations who hire healthcare providers, and a National Provider Identifier (NPI) was instituted for individual providers. Covered healthcare providers and all health plans and healthcare clearinghouses must use the unique identifiers in the administrative and financial transactions adopted under HIPAA [30].

Healthcare Integrity and Protection Data Bank

HIPAA also established the Healthcare Integrity and Protection Data Bank (HIPDB), which collects reports on final adverse actions including the following [31]:

- Civil judgments from federal and state courts related to the provisions of goods and services, findings against healthcare providers and suppliers, and actions taken by federal or state agencies against healthcare providers and suppliers related to licensing and certification
- Exclusion from participation in federal or state healthcare programs
- Federal or state criminal convictions against health suppliers and providers

These data sets could be data mined to identify circumstances that lead to increased risk of fraud and abuse. The HIPDB was merged into the NPDB under the Affordable Care Act of 2010 [32].

The HITECH Act

In 2009, HIPAA was further modified by the Health Information Technology for Economic and Clinical Health Act (HITECH Act). The HITECH Act provided a major financial stimulus for investment in electronic health records alongside the development of federal health information technology standards. It also extended HIPAA privacy and security protections to business associates of covered entities. This includes the associated criminal and civil penalties applicable to violations.

Basics of Malpractice

Medical malpractice and the problems associated with it remain an important issue in the US medical community. The general concept of professional malpractice can be traced to English legal theory as early as the fourteenth century; however, it was not until the mid-nineteenth century that it began to be applied in real-world situations [5, 33, 34]. Today, an American doctor has a greater chance of being sued than any other doctor in the world. While some feel that it serves to weed out bad doctors, malpractice also can adversely affect physicians who practice within the standards of reasonable care.

Medical malpractice is an act or omission by a healthcare provider that deviates from accepted standards of practice in the medical community and causes harm or injury to the patient. Fear of malpractice results in the practice of defensive medicine, which may put patients at risk for unnecessary treatments and testing, and may further deplete limited resources. Concerns about malpractice may hinder open clinical quality management activities (e.g., access to quality management documents may be limited due to the fear of releasing potentially damaging information) [34].

Negligence is the most common cause for malpractice cases wherein the defendant physician is accused of failing to exercise due care. In the majority of these cases, four specific elements are required to prove negligence:

- **Duty to treat**: Based on the existence of a patient–physician contractual relationship to provide care. A duty does not exist where no relationship is established between the doctor and patient; but when a relationship is established, such as covering patients for a colleague, a duty of reasonable care follows.
- **Breach of duty to provide a reasonable standard of care:** Physicians are required to provide the same reasonable and ordinary care, skill, and diligence as other physicians in the same area of practice. To establish a breach of a standard of professional care, expert witnesses are often called to testify in court as to what appropriate care would be. Expert witnesses are usually physicians of the same specialty or have education and experience similar to the physician accused of malpractice.

- **Causation:** The patient must show a direct relationship between the alleged breach of duty and a subsequent injury, i.e., the outcome would not have occurred but for the physician's action or failure to act. The proximate cause is not required to be the sole cause of the action, but only a significant factor.
- **Evidence of injury/damages:** The patient must have suffered emotional or physical harm.

Bishop and colleagues conducted a retrospective analysis of malpractice claims, from both inpatient and outpatient settings, paid on behalf of physicians using data from the NPDB [35]. In 2009, there were 10,739 malpractice claims identified to have been paid on behalf of physicians, approximately 47% of which were from inpatient settings (4910 claims), 43% from the outpatient setting (4448 claims), and 9% involved both inpatient and outpatient settings (966 claims). Major injury and death were the most common outcomes for both inpatient- and outpatient-related claims accounting for 74% of inpatient claims, 67% of outpatient claims, and 72% of those related to both settings. Event types varied by setting with the most common inpatient type being surgical (34%), the most common in outpatient care being diagnostic error (46%), and for those involving both inpatient and outpatient settings being surgical (32%). Looking at the second and third most common event types, diagnostic errors and treatment/medical errors were identified for inpatient claims at 21% and 20%, respectively; for outpatient treatment, medical errors and surgical at 30% and 14%, respectively; and claims associated with both settings again mirrored the inpatient setting at 27% and 24%, respectively. Finally, for the 10,739 claims from 2009 identified in the NPDB, the average payment amount was $363,000 for those from the inpatient setting, $290,000 for those from the outpatient setting, and $300,000 from those claims associated with both settings [35].

An analysis by Hickson and Pichert with the National Patient Safety Foundation states that when a healthcare injury occurs, the patient and the family are entitled to a prompt explanation of how the injury occurred and its short- and long-term effects [36]. Furthermore, when an error contributed to the injury, the patient and the family should receive a truthful and compassionate explanation about the error and the remedies available to the patient. Finally, they should be informed that the factors involved in the injury will be investigated so that steps can be taken to reduce the likelihood of a similar injury to other patients. Hickson and colleagues conducted one of the earliest systematic studies examining reasons for bringing medical malpractice suits. They reported on 368 closed cases involving families in Florida who experienced permanent injuries or deaths involving perinatal care from 1986 to 1989 [37]. Surveys were completed by 127 (35%) of the families. In this study, the reasons that families brought suits in these cases were the following:

- 33% were advised by acquaintances.
- 24% recognized a cover-up.
- 24% needed money.
- 23% perceived their child as having no future.
- 20% received inadequate information.
- 19% sought revenge or protection from future harm [37].

The parents studied expressed significant dissatisfaction with physician–patient communication as evidenced by the following views expressed by respondents to the closed case perinatal malpractice study:

- 13% believed physicians would not listen.
- 32% believed physicians would not talk openly.
- 48% believed the physicians attempted to mislead them.
- 70% expressed that physicians did not warn them about long-term neurodevelopmental problems to be expected in their child [37].

Greenberg and colleagues conducted a study for the RAND Corporation on data from 2001 to 2005 in order to determine if a relationship existed between patient safety activities and malpractice claims [38]. Using a sophisticated health service research design, counties in California were assessed for malpractice activity and patient safety initiatives. The authors recognized that the decision to bring a malpractice suit is complicated and depends on many factors. However, the intuitive relationship between improved patient safety performance and decreased malpractice activity, and the opposite tenet that less patient safety work would be associated with more malpractice suits being filed, was confirmed in this study. In support of this transparent communication approach, Wu cites a plaintiff's attorney's observations about why patients bring law suits:

> In over 25 years of representing both physicians and patients, it became apparent that a large percentage of patient dissatisfaction was generated by physician attitude and denial, rather than the negligence itself. In fact, my experience has been that close to half of the malpractice cases could have been avoided through disclosure or apology but instead were relegated to litigation. What the majority of patients really wanted was simply an honest explanation of what happened, and if appropriate, an apology. Unfortunately, when they were not only offered neither but were rejected as well, they felt doubly wronged and then sought legal counsel [39].

Clinical practice guidelines (CPGs) are used by attorneys for both the defense and the plaintiff to demonstrate that a standard of care has, or has not, been met. In a malpractice trial, guidelines are weighted on the basis of the issuing body, the purpose of the guideline, and evidence of peer review of the CPG. For instance, managed care organizations' utilization-based guidelines are weighted differently than clinical medical society guidelines, which are created with reference to evidence-based medicine or expert consensus. While CPGs may be used as a reference, the jury decides how to weigh their content based on expert witnesses' testimonies. In the case of *Frakes v Cardiology Consultants, P.C.* (1997 WL 536949, Tenn Cir App), the court considered a table, "Exercise Test Parameters Associated with Poor Prognosis and/or Increased Severity of CAD," contained in American College of Cardiology and American Heart Association brochures as a consensus statement on the interpretation of an exercise treadmill test based on the fact that all the experts adopted the document as the correct standard of care. In contrast, in *Liberatore v Kaufman* (835 So2d 404, Fla. App [2003]), the Florida Court of Appeals held that the trial court had abused its discretion when it used a bulletin published by the American College of Obstetricians and Gynecologists to bolster the testimony of their expert witness. Practice guidelines have also been used to impeach expert testimony *(Roper v Blumenfeld* 309 NJ Super 219 [1998]). In general, an accepted clinical standard may be presumptive evidence of due care, but expert testimony is required to introduce the standard and to establish its source and relevancy.

The standard of proof imposed by judges in a malpractice suit is the civil court standard, namely, *a preponderance of evidence,* which is less stringent than the *beyond a reasonable doubt* standard used in criminal trials. The concept of contributory negligence is considered in awarding damages. The contribution of the patient's actions or inactions that resulted in the injury is also noted (i.e., did the patient act as a *reasonable, prudent person* would have, given his condition?). If the patient failed to follow the physician's clear and documented instructions to report a change in symptoms, or fill or take a prescription, he or she might be found partially responsible, and the final award would be lessened. Failure by the physician to provide follow-up care or to provide and document instructions may serve as proof that the physician is at least partially responsible. Handwriting legibility, evidence of adequate informed consent, and adequate delivery of specific discharge information may also have a significant impact on the outcome of litigation.

If malpractice is proven, there are two types of damages: compensatory and punitive. *Compensatory damages* compensate the patient for past and future cost, pain, anguish, and loss of income. The intent is to restore the patient to condition prior to the incident. Monetary compensation is awarded to approximate the harm caused. *Punitive damages* are a means for the judicial system to "send a message" and financially punish a defendant. Juries may award punitive damages, sometimes in the millions of dollars, as punishment for willful or malicious conduct. The Tobacco Litigation settlement, referred to as the Master Settlement Agreement, which was reached in 1998 is an example of punitive damages; in addition to limiting types of advertising, the large cigarette manufacturers agreed to pay billions of dollars up front and billions on an annual basis in perpetuity to participating states and territories [40]. A number of states have pursued *tort reform* to limit the amount of punitive damages. A Congressional Budget Office (CBO) report on common elements of tort reform attempted to quantify the financial impact of such reform:

> Several times over the past decade, CBO has estimated the effects of legislative tort reform proposals. Typical proposals have included:
>
> - a cap of $250,000 on awards for noneconomic damages;
> - a cap on awards for punitive damages of $500,000 or two times the award for economic damages, whichever is greater;
> - modification of the "collateral source" rule to allow evidence of income from such sources as health and life insurance, workers' compensation, and automobile insurance to be introduced at trials or to require that such income be subtracted from awards decided by juries;
> - a statute of limitations—one year for adults and three years for children—from the date of discovery of an injury; and,
> - replacement of joint-and-several liability with a fair-share rule, under which a defendant in a lawsuit would be liable only for the percentage of the final award that was equal to his or her share of responsibility for the injury.

...National implementation of a package of proposals similar to the preceding list would reduce total national premiums for medical liability insurance by about 10 percent... That figure reflects the fact that many states have already enacted at least some of the proposed reforms. For example, about one-third of the states have implemented caps on non-economic damages, and about two-thirds have reformed their rules regarding joint-and-several liability. CBO estimates that the direct costs that providers will incur in 2009 for medical malpractice liability—which consist of malpractice insurance premiums together with settlements, awards, and administrative costs not covered by insurance—will total approximately $35 billion, or about 2 percent of total healthcare expenditures. Therefore, lowering premiums for medical liability insurance by 10 percent would reduce total national healthcare expenditures by about 0.2 percent [41].

There are other legal pitfalls in providing medical care and overseeing quality (e.g., incorrect or inadequate informed consent prior to a surgical intervention can result in a charge of assault or battery) [5]. The physician and risk managers must be aware that if a procedure is changed without patient permission, or if additional surgery occurs without adequate informed consent, the physician may be at risk for litigation.

Cases of infectious disease require special attention. Patients must be made aware of their communicability and the actions that must be taken to prevent the spread of disease to others. Suits brought by sexual partners in various states have resulted in decisions that held physicians liable for the spread of HIV (e.g., physicians have been held responsible for not providing and documenting advice given to the patient to prevent the spread of the disease). In the case of *Reisner v Regents of University of California* (31 Cal App 4th 1195 [1995]), the court held that a sexual partner of a patient had a cause of action against the patient's physician and the hospital for failing to inform the patient that she had been contaminated with HIV-infected blood and was at risk of spreading the disease. The ruling stated that the physician and the hospital had a duty to counsel and to educate the patient on how to prevent the spread of the virus.

Facility/Organizational Risk Management Issues

Managed care organizations, hospitals, and other facilities have been held liable for harm to patients through alleged failure to use reasonable care to ensure the competency of their providers upon credentialing and recredentialing or to have an appropriate number of competent medical and support staff (*Darling v Charleston Community Memorial Hospital*, 33 Ill2d 326, 211 NE2d 253, 14 ALR3d 860 [Ill 1965]).

The doctrine of corporate negligence holds that an organization has an independent duty to the patient in credentialing its personnel. An organization may also be sued on the basis of services provided to the facility by independent contractors. For example, emergency services delivered by a contracted emergency room group may expose the facility to litigation on the basis of the legal concepts of vicarious liability and ostensible or apparent agency. In such cases, the patient came to the hospital seeking care and the institution or hospital appeared to present the contract ER physician as its employee. In a similar manner, a private anesthesiologist may appear to be an extension of the facility and thus incur liability for poor outcomes or adverse events under a legal theory of ostensible agency. Although the contract between the facility and the treatment group may allocate liability, the patient may be inclined to name all likely parties in the litigation.

Liability due to failure to exercise appropriate care is not limited to individual practitioners. It can involve the chief of clinical areas, chief medical officers, and other officers of the corporate suite. The concept of the surgeon as "captain of the ship" in the operating room holds that the physician is responsible for the actions of his or her subordinates. The legal concept of *respondeat superior* (Latin for "let the master answer") holds the employer responsible for the actions of employees. A health plan or a hospital may also be sued for the actions of their employees. This is known as *vicarious liability*.

Adequate credentialing is required through querying the NPDB and HIPDB as suggested in the HCQIA and following procedures and policies promulgated by leading healthcare accreditors. Hospitals and other facilities have been sued for failing to exercise reasonable care in credentialing participating specialists (e.g., *Harrell v Total Healthcare*, 781 SW2d 58 [MO 1989]). Pivotal cases have clearly stated that organizations are responsible for utilization review actions and their impact on the care provided (see *Wickline v State of California*, 192 Cal App 3d 1630, 239 Cal Rptr 810 [Ct App 1986] and *Fox v Health Net*, Riverside Sup Ct Case No 219692 [1993]).

Bad faith action suits can be brought against managed care organizations and their staff related to utilization management activities (i.e., for failure to promptly and adequately review requests for care, for failure to provide timely approval of care, and for failure to provide expedited reviews for cases as required in organization requirements or as imposed by state or federal law).

Medical Errors and Transparency

A number of industry groups actively encourage acknowledging medical errors, especially those that are apparent to the patient-family and those that do not result in harm. The IOM report *To Err Is Human: Building a Safer Health System* highlighted the issue of medical errors and recommended the National Quality Forum (NQF) as the entity to develop reporting standards, error reporting requirements for healthcare organizations, and nonpunitive reporting systems [6]. The NQF supports disclosure of this information as a practice that promotes safe care [42]. In 2001, the Joint Commission issued a nationwide disclosure statement requiring that patients be made aware of all outcomes of care. A number of major hospitals and health systems support acknowledging errors, providing an apology, explaining how the error could have happened, and communicating the action that will be taken to prevent a recurrence in the future.

The VA Medical Center in Lexington, Kentucky, has had a full disclosure policy since the 1980s [43, 44]. The University of Illinois Medical Center (UIC) has a well-known error disclosure program and a specific curriculum to train medical students to recognize medical errors, deal with the repercussions, and know what actions to take [43]. Since 2001, when it began to acknowledge medical mistakes and negotiate settlements with injured patients, the University of Michigan Health System has experienced a significant decrease in the number of pending malpractice claims [45]. See Table 11.2.

Medical ethics supports truth telling. A risk management approach that advocates reporting errors to patients believes that transparency will result in fewer lawsuits, early settlements, better understanding of the systemic source of errors, and the diffusing of anger through early communication. Leading clinical journals contain articles relating to disclosure to patients, and there is a growing body of knowledge in this area (e.g., a framework for apologies, how to frame the admission, and the right time and place for an apology) [45–47, 51, 52].

A number of state governments have pursued disclosure-related legislation. For example, a Pennsylvania law, "Act 13," contains time frames for disclosure and a prohibition for use of this communication as evidence of liability in litigation. The National Conference of State Legislatures lists 39 states, Washington D.C., and Guam as having apology laws in the form of a bill or statute protecting expressions of regret and apologies from being used in litigation [53]. These laws are in the process of being tested to provide a sufficient sense of safety to physicians, attorneys, and insurance companies [54]. As noted in the *New England Journal of Medicine* review article "Disclosing Harmful Medical Errors to Patients," "plaintiffs' attorneys, who must sift through dozens of prospective claims in choosing which ones to pursue, will prize information gained from disclosures, whether or not they are permitted to use that information as evidence in subsequent litigation." [44]

A national coalition of patients, attorneys, physicians, and hospital administrators—the Sorry Works! Coalition—has proposed that hospital staff review all adverse events and that hospital administrators and physicians institute a dialogue with patients and families to explain what happened, apologize for any errors committed, and offer fair compensation [43].

In contrast, the authors of a January–February 2007 *Health Affairs* article titled "Disclosure of Medical Injury to Patients: An Improbable Risk Management Strategy" have a different perspective on the financial impact of the trend toward full disclosure [52]. They suggest that any decrease in the number and the amount of claims deferred due to apologies and admitting errors may be offset by the increase in patient awareness of medical errors. Adverse outcomes once attributed to expected results of diseases or therapies are now acknowledged as medical errors and, as such, the responsibility of the clinician. There is a widespread belief that the vast majority of medical errors do not result in litigation or suits, and it remains to be seen if identifying more errors and bringing them to the patient's attention will decrease the rate or impact of malpractice litigation. Seeking to strike that balance, Studdert and colleagues conclude their paper with the following advice:

> Disclosure is the right thing to do; so is compensating patients who sustain injury as a result of substandard care. Continuing moves toward transparency about medical injuries will expose tensions between these two objectives. That severe injuries are prevalent and that most of them never trigger litigation are epidemiological facts that have long been evident.

Table 11.2 Error Disclosure programs in three different health systems

Title of program & location	Description
Extreme Honesty [46] Veteran's Administration (VA) Medical Center in Lexington, KY	In place since 1987, this policy has not caused an onslaught of litigation, and while in the top quartile for claims filed compared to 35 other VAs, the Lexington VA is in the bottom quartile for claim payments. This honest and forthright risk management approach is touted as putting the patient's interests first and is believed to be relatively inexpensive when compared to other approaches since Kraman and Hamm contend that it avoids the costs of lawsuit preparation, litigation, and court judgments [46]. Extreme honesty suggests but does not prove the financial superiority of a robust disclosure policy.
Seven pillars [47–49] University of Illinois, Chicago (UIC)	The seven pillars represent a comprehensive response to adverse events: • Reporting • Investigation • Early communication with patient • Apology with remediation (includes waiving of hospital and physician fees) • Process and performance improvement • Data tracking and analysis • Education around the entire process [47] UIC reported that over a 2-year period, the seven pillars approach led to more than 2000 incident reports and more than 100 investigations, resulting in approximately 200 specific improvements, 100 disclosure conversations, and at least 20 full disclosures of inappropriate care that caused patient harm [48]. This AHRQ demonstration project that extends to nine other medical centers has resulted in an 80% reduction in time to settle full disclosure cases and a 70% reduction in litigation-related costs, and UIC reported that no meritless suits were filed for at least 18 months. As a testament of success, in addition to the initial nine hospitals, an additional twenty hospitals have joined the initiative even though they have received no funding.
Open Disclosure with Offer [50] University of Michigan (UM) Health System	Beginning in 2001, UM Health System instituted a proactive, principle-based approach, built on a commitment to honesty and transparency called "open disclosure with offer." Three principles guided this new systematic approach to adverse events: • Compensate patients quickly and fairly when unreasonable medical care causes harm. • If the care is deemed reasonable, support caregivers and the organization vigorously. • Reduce patient injuries by learning through patients' experiences and also reduce claims (by way of improved care) [50]. Since the full implementation of this approach, UM reports a steady reduction in the number of claims filed, reduction in defense costs, reduced time between claim reporting and resolution, and reduced average settlements. The average monthly rate of new claims dropped from 7.03 to 4.52 claims per 100,000 patient encounters, and the average monthly rate of lawsuits decreased from 2.13 to 0.75 per 100,000 patient encounters [50].

The affordability of the medical malpractice system rests on this fragile foundation, and routine toward full disclosure should proceed with a realistic expectation of the financial implications and prudent planning to meet them [52].

Alternative Dispute Resolution: Arbitration and Mediation

Given the high cost and extended time frames of litigation, other forms of dispute resolution have gained popularity. Arbitration is one example of an alternative to a malpractice trial. *Arbitration* is used when the parties agree to have a third party decide the outcome of a claim based on its merits. The single arbitrator or panel allocates blame and may impose an award for damages much like a court. The process is streamlined due to the lack of a jury and expert witnesses.

Physicians generally prefer *alternative dispute* systems. There is the perception that these processes are less expensive, less time-consuming, and may result in decreasing the rate of malpractice premiums. While practicing physicians may have an office policy to request that patients sign an agreement consenting to binding arbitration if an issue arises, such documents have been challenged on the basis of whether the patient truly understood that, by signing the agreement, they had signed away their right to a jury trial.

Arbitrators are considered to be more knowledgeable of issues and less biased than a lay jury. Arbitration proceedings are more private than civil litigation. Arbitrators may act singly or as part of a panel. Deliberations are usually shorter and less stressful than a trial, and there is direct dialogue between the two parties. Some malpractice carriers offer discounts to physicians who have their patients sign arbitration agreements. Unlike malpractice trials, which may be undertaken by an attorney on contingency, the patient may be required to pay the arbitrators, the experts, a lawyer, and other fees. Rulings do not allow for appeal rights.

Arbitration can be either mandatory or voluntary. Some states mandate arbitration prior to the commencement of a malpractice suit to lessen court time and to facilitate resolution of the dispute without lengthy litigation. Benefits of arbitration include the following: may be less confrontational and less costly, may include written expert opinion without the added expense and time or witnesses, and may include an agreement to keep the hearing and the settlement confidential.

Mediation is a form of conflict resolution that brings two or more parties together to discuss their issues with the assistance of a mediator (an impartial third party), but does not involve a binding decision. Mediation usually begins as an airing of grievances after which the mediator attempts to have the parties come to a settlement with the mediator acting as an *honest broker*. The mediator has no power to require a settlement.

In 2014, CMS provided instruction to all Quality Improvement Organizations (QIOs) to implement changes related to beneficiary complaints directed at making the complaint and resolution process more customer friendly and transparent [55]. Aligned with these changes was the creation of a free, nationwide mediation program as an alternative to a quality review process initiated by a beneficiary complaint [56]. The quality review process, used as the primary investigational method for beneficiary complaints, was seen by some as a slow, time-consuming program that was confrontational rather than collaborative and that did not result in improved communications between the providers and beneficiaries, especially in the following areas:

- Complaints concerning quality of services
- Communication issues
- Quality of care issues from the beneficiaries' perspective

Participation in mediation is voluntary, and the mediation request must be initiated by the beneficiary. Mediators do not make decisions or influence the outcome of the mediation. Both the beneficiary and the physician, provider, or facility representative must agree to participate. The dialogue can be terminated by either party at any time. Mediations can be conducted in a safe, neutral environment or over the telephone. Each party has an opportunity to tell his or her story, express concerns directly to the physician (or other provider of healthcare services), and listen to the response. With the approval of both parties, the beneficiary or the physician may bring a lawyer to act in the capacity of an advisor.

A typical mediation session takes between 2 and 4 h. The key to this process is that the patient drives the system and controls how the complaint is resolved. If a mutual resolution is reached, the QIO will follow up and monitor the terms of the agreement. This process can address issues that are not contained in the medical record and facilitate explanations between patients and healthcare providers.

Some types of cases are not appropriate for mediation (e.g., gross and flagrant quality of care issues and cases already in litigation). Mediation sessions are not recorded, and any written notes taken during the mediation are destroyed at the end of the session. Parties to the mediation agree not to use information uncovered during the mediation in any future legal proceedings. If the parties reach a resolution, an agreement may be drafted and signed concluding the mediation session. Federal and state laws protect the confidentiality of mediation sessions, per the Federal Rule of Evidence (Article IV) 408. Many U.S. District Courts and Courts of Appeal have court rules providing for the confidentiality of mediation negotiations. (i.e., US Ct of App 4th Cir Rule 33), and many states specifically provide for the confidentiality of statements and documents used in mediation.

Antitrust in Medicine

Antitrust issues arise when a significant number of individuals who provide a service work together to control how the goods or services are provided or distributed (i.e., controlling reimbursement rates or access). This can present a potential risk when market players, health systems, or a number of individuals work together (even if ostensibly for the purpose of improving how care is provided) and when they create and enforce clinical guidelines that influence how providers practice medicine for a specific clinical condition. The Sherman Antitrust Act (July 2, 1890, ch 647, 26 Stat 209, 15 USC §1–7) refers to "contracts or combinations in restraint of trade" (§1). The Act includes actions taken together in a given market to engage in intended *parallel conduct* or fee setting (i.e., sharing of pricing information).

Other sections of the Act relate to unilateral actions of a single business in an attempt to monopolize a market. Cases involve hospital and managed care organizations but can occur at the medical group level. A recent case was brought against two clinics for refusing to accept new Medicaid members and possibly collaborating in this decision. The Sherman Act can be violated by agreements among provider-controlled networks and plans when competing physicians set, by majority vote, the maximum fees that they may claim in full payment for health services provided to policyholders of specified insurance plans *(Arizona v Maricopa County Medical Society*, 457 US 332 [1982]). Similar issues may arise as multiple medical groups of managed care organizations come together to write common guidelines that restrain reimbursement for certain treatments and exclude other possible treatments.

Regarding the issue of cartels and professionalism, the Federal Trade Commission (FTC) has successfully challenged provider cartels that engage in a wide variety of practices designed to raise prices, limit competition from other providers, or affect the cost containment efforts of managed care organizations. In the case of *United States v North Dakota Hospital Association* (640 F Supp 1028 [DND 1986]), the issue revolved around hospitals' joint refusal to extend discounts in bidding for contracts.

Groups and associations can run afoul of antitrust law through restrictions on advertising and dissemination of information *(California Dental Association v Federal Trade Commission*, 526 US 756 [1999]). The FTC's jurisdiction extends to associations (e.g., the California Dental Association) that provide substantial economic benefit to its for-profit members. Private accreditation and professional standard settings can risk antitrust suits for conducting or recommending boycotts or other actions that would result in the restraint of trade or for giving an unfair advantage to one group over another.

The case of *Wilk v American Medical Association* (895 F2d 352 [2d Cir 1990]) affirmed the District Court's finding that the American Medical Association violated the Sherman Act by conducting an illegal boycott in restraint of trade directed at chiropractors. When payers with market power take actions related to reimbursement, it is not always considered antitrust. In the case of *Kartell v Blue Shield of Mass.* (749 F2d 922 1st Cir [1984]), Blue Shield's ban on "balanced billing" was not considered a violation of the Sherman Act.

The crafting of clinical guidelines and the advent of pay-for-performance (P4P) programs have exposed more potential risks for running afoul of antitrust law. The AHRQ points out the risks of antitrust when crafting P4P programs in its guide, *Pay-for-Performance: A Decision Guide for Purchasers* [57]. This guide references the *Antitrust Guidelines for Collaborations Among Competitors* issued by the FTC and the U.S. Department of Justice [58]. The article suggests that antitrust counsel should be consulted if payers are considering collaborating, particularly regarding payment or provider contracting issues, and recommends the creation and adoption of uniform P4P quality or performance standards [57].

Future Trends

The increasingly complex medical and healthcare system benefits from informed government actions via laws and regulations that provide protections to those involved in quality improvement and patient safety activities. Laws and regulations provide a framework for credible, persuasive, accountable medical quality management activities. At the interface of medical quality management and the law, a balance continues to formulate among the interests of patients, practitioners, institutional providers, health plans, regulatory agencies, and the general public. Laws and regulations help establish standards that assist quality improvement and patient safety professionals bring clarity and accountability to the healthcare processes and to the entire healthcare system. The quality of care delivered by professionals working in healthcare facilities and at health plans is markedly influenced by medical quality management activities which include regulatory and accreditation compliance, provider credentialing, risk management, and clinical peer review. In the coming decade, the call for increased public data sharing and transparency will likely become louder and will likely become central to consumer as well as professional expectation around acceptable standards of care. The protection afforded to healthcare professionals and organizations via laws and regulations will continue to impact medical quality management activities and the willingness of individuals and institutions to engage in quality improvement and patient safety activities. Clearly, governmental action in the form of laws and regulation will continue to greatly affect medical quality management in the years to come. Viewing those that make laws and those who enforce regulations as partners in quality improvement and patient safety holds great promise in ensuring that governmental action in this area remains well informed and promotes the desired improvement in healthcare that is shared at the interface between quality and the law.

References

1. Dynasty of Ur (2019) Mesopotamian history. Britannica.com. www.britannica.com/topic/3rd-Dynasty-of-Ur
2. King LW (2004) The code of Hammurabi. Kessinger Publishing, Whitefish
3. Hippocrates (2019) Encyclopedia Britannica. http://www.britannica.com/EBchecked/topic/266627/Hippocrates#tab=active-checked%2Citems-checked&title=Hippocrates%20—%20Britannica%20Online%20Encyclopedia. Accessed 31 July 31 2008
4. Sarma PJ (1931) Hindu medicine and its antiquity. Ann Med Hist 3:318
5. Furrow BR, Greaney TL, Johnson SH, Jost T (2000) Health law, 2nd edn. West Group, St. Paul

6. Kohn LT, Corrigan JM, Donaldson MS (eds) (1999) Institute of Medicine. To err is human: building a safer health system. National Academies Press, Washington DC
7. Institute of Medicine (2001) Crossing the quality chasm: a new health system for the 21st century. National Academies Press, Washington DC
8. National Quality Strategy Fact Sheets (2017) Agency for Healthcare Research and Quality, Rockville. http://www.ahrq.gov/workingforquality/about/nqs-fact-sheets/index.html
9. 2015 National Healthcare Quality and Disparities Report and 5th Anniversary Update on the National Quality Strategy (2016) Content last reviewed May 2016. Agency for Healthcare Research and Quality, Rockville. http://www.ahrq.gov/research/findings/nhqrdr/nhqdr15/index.html
10. U.S. Government Accountability Office (2004) Report to congressional requestors: GAO-04-850: centers for medicare and medicaid services needs additional authority to adequately oversee patient safety in hospitals. https://www.gao.gov/products/GAO-04-850
11. Bryant, M (2017) Hospitals often retain accreditation despite safety violations. Wall Street Journal. Healthcare Dive. https://www.healthcaredive.com/news/wsj-hospitals-often-retain-accreditation-despite-safety-violations/504707/. Accessed 12 Sept 2017
12. Centers for Medicare and Medicaid (2015) Hospital acquired conditions. https://www.cms.gov/Medicare/Medicare-Fee-for-Service-Payment/HospitalAcqCond/Hospital-Acquired_Conditions.html
13. Castellucci M (2017) New data from CMS' hospital-acquired condition program have analysts questioning value. Modern Healthcare. http://www.modernhealthcare.com/article/20171221/NEWS/171229973
14. Agency for Healthcare Research and Quality (2016) How PSOs help health care organizations improve patient safety culture. https://www.pso.ahrq.gov/sites/default/files/wysiwyg/npsdpatient-safety-culture-brief.pdf. Accessed Apr 2016
15. PSO Privacy Protection Center (2019) Overview common formats. https://www.psoppc.org/psoppc_web/publicpages/commonFormatsOverview
16. Agency for Healthcare Research and Quality (n.d.) Common formats—scope and reporting. https://www.pso.ahrq.gov/common/scope
17. Wagner C, Cecchettini D, Fletcher J (2011) The safe table collaborative: a statewide experience. Jt Comm J Qual Patient Saf 37(5):206–210
18. Jaffe R, Manneh C (2015) CHPSO safe table. In: Patient safety first materials. National Health Foundation. https://www.nhfca.org/PSF/Materials3/feb15/chpso_safetable_02262015_final_2[1].pdf
19. Edwards MT, Benjamin EM (2009) The process of peer review in U.S. hospitals. J Clinical Outcomes Manage 16(10):461–467
20. Edwards MT (2013) A longitudinal study of clinical peer review's impact on quality and safety in U.S. hospitals. J Healthcare Manage 58(5):369–384
21. U.S. Department of Health & Human Services (1986) Title IV of Public Law 99–660: The Health Care Quality Improvement Act of 1986. https://www.npdb.hrsa.gov/resources/titleIv.jsp
22. Langford C (2012) Bitter feud between surgeon and hospital. Courthouse News. https://www.courthousenews.com/bitter-feud-between-surgeon-and-hospital/. Accessed 20 Sept 2012
23. Supreme Court of Texas (2015) Memorial hermann hospital system physician network; Michael Macris, MD; Michael Macris MD, PA; and Keith Alexander, Relators. NO> 14–01701. http://caselaw.findlaw.com/tx-supreme-court/1701761.html. Accessed 22 May 2015
24. Rappleye E (2017) Jury sides with heart surgeon in $6.4M defamation lawsuit against Memorial Hermann: 5 things to know. Becker's Hospital Review. https://www.beckershospitalreview.com/legal-regulatory-issues/jury-sides-with-heart-surgeon-in-6-4m-defamation-lawsuit-against-memorial-hermann-5-things-to-know.html. Accessed 30 Mar 2017
25. Sixel LM (2017) Heart surgeon wins $6.4 million verdict in defamation case against Memorial Hermann. In Houston Chronicle. https://www.houstonchronicle.com/business/article/Heart-surgeon-wins-6-4-million-verdict-in-11037414.php. Accessed 20 Mar 2017

26. Langford C (2019) Texas Doctor Keeps $6M Award in Bitter Feud With Hospital. In Courthouse News Service. https://www.courthousenews.com/texas-doctor-keeps-6m-award-in-bitter-feud-with-hospital. Accessed
27. 101st Congress (1990) Omnibus Budget Reconciliation Act of 1990, Pub. L. No. 101–508, 4401, 104 Stat. 1388–143
28. Health Resources and Services Administration, U.S. Department of Health and Human Services (2019) National Practitioner Data Bank Guidebook. https://www.npdb.hrsa.gov/resources/aboutGuidebooks.jsp
29. 104th Congress (1996) Health Insurance Portability and Accountability Act of 1996 (HIPAA). https://www.gpo.gov/fdsys/pkg/PLAW-104publ191/pdf/PLAW-104publ191.pdf
30. U.S. Department of Health & Human Services. HIPAA for Professionals (2019) Other administrative simplification rules. https://www.hhs.gov/hipaa/for-professionals/other-administration-simplification-rules/index.html
31. National Practitioner Data Bank for Adverse Information on Physicians and Other Health Care Practitioners (2008) 45 C.F.R. PART 60. http://law.justia.com/us.cfr/title45/45-1.0.1.1.28.html. Accessed 31 July 2008
32. National Practitioner Data Bank (2008) healthcare integrity and protection data bank. https://www.npdb.hrsa.gov/resources/hipdbArchive.jsp
33. DeVille KA (1990) Medical malpractice in nineteenth-century America: origins and legacy. New York University Press, New York
34. Migden D (2000) The past and future of medical malpractice litigation. JAMA 284(7):827–829
35. Bishop TF, Ryan AM, Casalino LP (2011) Paid malpractice claims for adverse events in inpatient and outpatient settings. JAMA 305(23):2427–2431
36. Hickson GB, Pichert JW (2008) Disclosure and apology. In: National Patient Safety Foundation Stand Up for Patient Safety Resource Guide. National Patient Safety Foundation, North Adams
37. Hickson GB, Clayton EW, Githens PB, Sloan FA (1992) Factors that prompted families to file medical malpractice claims following perinatal injuries. JAMA 267:1359–1363
38. Greenberg MD, Haviland AM, Ashwood JS, Main R (2010) is better patient safety associated with less malpractice activity? Rand Institute for Civil Justice. Technical Report. http://www.rand.org/pubs/technical_reports/TR824.html
39. Wu AW (1999) Handling hospital errors: is disclosure the best defense? Ann Intern Med 21:970–97246
40. Public Health Law Center (2019) Master settlement agreement. In: Tobacco Control. Public Health Law Center at Mitchell Hamline School of Law. https://www.publichealthlawcenter.org/topics/commercial-tobacco-control/tobacco-control-litigation/master-settlement-agreement
41. Congressional Budget Office (2009) Letter to Senator Orrin J. Hatch regarding the request for an updated analysis of the effects of proposals to limit costs related to medical malpractice ("tort reform"). https://www.cbo.gov/sites/default/files/111th-congress-2009-2010/reports/10-09-tort_reform.pdf
42. National Quality Forum (2019) Serious reportable events. In: Patient Safety. http://www.qualityforum.org/topics/sres/serious_reportable_events.aspx
43. Geier P (2006) Emerging med-mal strategy: "I'm sorry." Early apology concept spreads. NLJ. http://www.law.com/jsp/article.jsp?id=1153472732197. Accessed 31 July 2008
44. Gallagher T, Studdert D, Levinson W (2007) Disclosing harmful medical errors to patients. N Engl J Med 356:2713–2719
45. Tanner L (2004) Apology a tool to avoid malpractice suits: Doctors shown financial benefits. Boston Globe: National News, 12 November 2004
46. Kraman SS, Hamm G (1999) Risk management: extreme honesty may be the best policy. Annals Internal Medicine 131:963 967
47. McDonald T (2012) The "Seven Pillars" Approach: crossing the patient safety–medical liability chasm. Advancing healthcare and research. https://archive.ahrq.gov/news/events/nac/2012-04-nac/mcdonald/index.html. Published 2012. Accessed 28 Jan 2014

48. Clancy CM (2012) More hospitals begin to apply lessons from Seven Pillars Process. Agency for Healthcare Research and Quality. https://nam.edu/perspectives-2012-more-hospitals-begin-to-apply-lessons-from-seven-pillars-process/. Accessed 22 July 2014
49. Mayer D (2013) Educate the young…emerging trends in quality and safety. Paper presented at ACMQ National Conference Medical Quality 2013: Transforming quality and safety in the era of change, Phoenix, AZ, 20–23 February 2013
50. Boothman RC, Imhoff SH, Campbell DA (2012) Nurturing a culture of patient safety and achieving lower malpractice risk through disclosure: lessons learned and future directions. Front Health Serv Manag 28:13–28
51. Roberts RG (2007) The art of apology: when and how to seek forgiveness. Fam Pract Manag 14(7):44–49
52. Studdert DM, Mello MM, Gawande AA, Brennan TA, Wang YC (2007) Disclosure of medical injury to patients: an improbable risk management strategy. Health Aff 26(1):215–226
53. Morton H (2018) Medical professional apologies statutes. National Conference of State Legislatures. http://www.ncsl.org/research/financial-services-and-commerce/medical-profes-sional-apologies-statutes.aspx
54. Saitta N, Hodge S (2012) Efficacy of a physician's words of empathy: an overview of state apology laws. J Am Osteopath Assoc 112:302–306
55. Centers for Medicare and Medicaid Services (CMS) Changes in the Quality Improvement Organization (QIO) Beneficiary Complaint and General Quality of Care Review Process (2014) IPRO. https://ipro.org/medicare/centers-for-medicare-and-medicaid-services-cms-changes-in-the-quality-improvement-organization-qio-beneficiary-complaint-and-general-quality-of-care-review-process-201402
56. U.S. Centers for Medicare and Medicaid Services (n.d.) Mediation: a new option for medicare beneficiaries. https://www.cms.gov/Medicare/Fraud-and-Abuse/BeneComplaintRespProg/Downloads/3a.pdf
57. Agency for Healthcare Research and Quality, U.S. Department of Health and Human Services (2008) Pay-for-Performance: a decision guide for purchasers. https://archive.ahrq.gov/profes-sionals/quality-patient-safety/quality-resources/tools/p4p/p4pguide5.html. Accessed 26 Aug 2008
58. Federal Trade Commission and the U.S. Department of Justice (2000) Antitrust guidelines for collaborations among competitors. http://www.ftc.gov/os/2000/04/ftcdojguidelines.pdf. Accessed 17 Oct 2008

Chapter 12
Ethics and Quality Improvement

Perry Ann Reed, Eileen R. Giardino, and Angelo P. Giardino

Executive Summary

The National Center for Ethics in Healthcare defines *ethics* as "the discipline that considers what is right or what should be done in the face of uncertainty or conflict about values." [1] As applied to healthcare, biomedical ethical practice is guided by four well-recognized principles, namely, justice, autonomy, beneficence, and non-maleficence [2].

Biomedical ethics in the United States have been shaped by five important milestones including the establishment of the Nuremberg Code [3], the Tuskegee Syphilis Study [4–6], the Belmont Report [7], the Helsinki Declaration [8], and the advent of the original American Medical Association's Code of Medical Ethics in 1847 [9]. In the clinical setting, a variety of frameworks are available to guide decision-making; best practice for a particular approach depends on the characteristics of the healthcare institution in which the ethical dilemma arises. The clinical frameworks described in this chapter include:

- The "Four Box Method" described by Jonsen, Siegler, and Winslade
- "CASES" described by the Veterans Health Administration's National Center for Ethics in Healthcare
- The "Pathway Approach" developed by Texas Children's Hospital's Clinical Ethics Committee in conjunction with professionals from the Baylor College of Medicine's Center for Medical Ethics and Health Policy

P. A. Reed (✉)
WakeMed Children's Hospital, Raleigh, NC, USA

E. R. Giardino
Rush University College of Nursing, Chicago, IL, USA

University of Utah College of Nursing, Salt Lake City, UT, USA

A. P. Giardino
University of Utah School of Medicine, Salt Lake City, UT, USA

© American College of Medical Quality (ACMQ) 2021
A. P. Giardino et al. (eds.), *Medical Quality Management*,
https://doi.org/10.1007/978-3-030-48080-6_12

- The "Ethics Work-Up," Baylor College of Medicine's systematic approach to ethical decision-making which incorporates a five-step process to guide ethical reasoning

Shifting attention from the clinical to the organizational level of action in healthcare, Intermountain Healthcare's Dr. Brent James states that the same ethical principles govern our protection of the patient across the entire continuum of healthcare, spanning the clinical, operational, educational, and research activities within the industry. Systemized quality management and quality improvement (QI) efforts exist within operational activities. The characteristics of quality improvement efforts include care and treatment, considered to be usual practice, and the implementation of continual and purposeful procedures that pose minimal risk to patients which lend themselves to measurable improvements, a design that allows for ongoing local modification as the project unfolds.

Research is broader in scope than quality improvement and is defined as systematic investigation that includes testing and evaluation designed to produce generalizable knowledge. Quality improvement and research activities are distinct, though at times may overlap, depending on the risk to the patient as well as the intent for local improvement versus the production of generalizable knowledge. Typically, Institutional Review Boards (IRBs) are in place to review and provide oversight which ensures ethical standards are in place to protect the rights of humans participating in the effort. There are a number of guidelines developed to clarify whether a quality improvement initiative should be reviewed by an IRB. Guidelines and checklists help determine if the quality improvement design protocol of a quality improvement initiative intersects with a research methodology. The bottom line is that healthcare professionals must protect the patient's rights, and their rights, in both quality improvement and research endeavors.

Learning Objectives

Upon completion of this chapter, readers should be able to:

- Identify the basic concepts related to ethical issues in healthcare
- Discuss fundamental principles used in ethics discussions related to clinical dilemmas
- Discuss several frameworks used to consider the ethics of quality improvement and patient safety work at the organizational level
- Compare quality improvement to research
- Consider the need for Institutional Review Board (IRB) review of quality improvement projects

Ethics in Healthcare: Basic Concepts

Justice Potter Stewart (Associate Justice of the US Supreme Court, 1958–1981) said that *ethics is knowing the difference between what you have a right to do and what is right to do.* This chapter addresses the application of ethical principles, first in the clinical arena and then in the organizational context, specifically as applied to the quality management and quality improvement arenas. According to The National Center for Ethics, "Ethics involves making reflective judgments about the optimal decision or action among ethically justifiable options. Values are strongly held beliefs, ideals, principles, or standards that inform ethical decisions or actions." [1] Beauchamp and Childress describe four main principles of bioethics as the basic foundations for many ethical assessments and recommendations: autonomy, beneficence, nonmaleficence, and justice [2]. These principles are based on concepts such as validity, value of the research, fair patient participation, favorable risk-benefit ratio, informed consent, and independent review [2].

Respect for Autonomy

Autonomy refers to healthcare providers having a duty to protect the patient's ability to make informed decisions about care and to honor decisions made by the patient or the patient's representative. It is the supporting principle of informed consent. Key considerations associated with informed consent include the legal capacity to give consent, the ability to apply free power of choice, and an adequate understanding of risks and benefits of treatment options. Informed consent requires that the patient clearly understands the decision he or she is making and the potential risks and benefits of the decision. Asking the patient to repeat back information communicated is one method for verifying that the patient understands the intended message. A patient who does not demonstrate the ability to understand the issue may be unable to exercise autonomy, and a substitute decision-maker may need to be identified. The practical reality for healthcare professionals is that some patients make decisions that contradict the judgment of the physician. For example, patients may elect to leave the hospital against medical advice.

Beneficence

Beneficence is the principle that healthcare professionals have a duty to (1) do good, (2) act in the best interest of their patient, and (3) act in the best interest of the society overall.

Nonmaleficence

Nonmaleficence is the principle referring to the healthcare professional's duty to do no harm to the patient and do no harm to society overall. Nonmaleficence is the overriding principle for any healthcare professional who accepts the responsibility of caring for a patient. The principles of nonmaleficence and beneficence aim to improve patient care and safety by advocating the notion of *do no harm*. They focus on maximizing potential benefit while minimizing harm and risk to the patient. QI projects that incorporate the principles of beneficence and nonmaleficence should also include elements of compassion and kindness.

Justice and Fairness

The ethical principle of justice and fairness encompasses concepts such as equal access to care, provision of treatment and resources according to need, fair distribution of healthcare benefits and burdens, good stewardship of an organization's and society's resources, and accountability. For healthcare professionals in particular, this principle calls for attention to the fairest possible distribution of healthcare resources. It also demands that benefits and burdens of research participation be distributed equitably. For example, Institutional Review Boards play a key role in ensuring that subject selection is equitable.

Major Historical Milestones

Healthcare professionals benefit from understanding basic information about pivotal developments in the history of medical ethics. Five important milestones include the Nuremberg Code [3], the Tuskegee Syphilis Study [4–6], the Belmont Report [7], the Helsinki Declaration [8], and the American Medical Association (AMA) Code of Medical Ethics [9]. The Nuremberg Code was created in response to Nazi eugenic policies conducted on unwilling subjects during World War II. The risks of human experimentation came to public attention based on evidence presented at the Nuremberg trials concerning the inhumane treatment of participants in medical experiments by Nazi doctors. The 1945 Nuremberg Code was the first legal attempt to deal with ethical issues of clinical research [10]. The code encompasses the principles of informed consent, absence of coercion, adhering to scientific principles, and beneficence toward experiment participants.

The Nuremberg Code

The Nuremberg Code specifies ten standards to which physicians must conform when carrying out experiments on human subjects [3, 10].

Ten Standards of the Nuremberg Code
1. The voluntary consent of the human subject is absolutely essential.
2. The experiment should be such as to yield fruitful results for the good of society, unprocurable by other methods or means of study, and not random and unnecessary in nature.
3. The experiment should be so designed and based on the results of animal experimentation and a knowledge of the natural history of the disease or other problem under study that the anticipated results will justify the performance of the experiment
4. The experiment should be so conducted as to avoid all unnecessary physical and mental suffering and injury.
5. No experiment should be conducted where there is an a priori reason to believe that death or disabling injury will occur, except, perhaps, in those experiments where the experimental physicians also serve as subjects.
6. The degree of risk to be taken should never exceed that determined by the humanitarian importance of the problem to be solved by the experiment.
7. Proper preparations should be made and adequate facilities provided to protect the experimental subject against even remote possibilities of injury, disability, or death.
8. The experiment should be conducted only by scientifically qualified persons. The highest degree of skill and care should be required through all stages of the experiment of those who conduct or engage in the experiment.
9. During the course of the experiment, the human subject should be at liberty to bring the experiment to an end if he has reached the physical or mental state where continuation of the experiment seems to him to be impossible.
10. During the course of the experiment, the scientist in charge must be prepared to terminate the experiment at any stage, if he has probable cause to believe, in the exercise of the good faith, superior skill, and careful judgment required of him, that a continuation of the experiment is likely to result in injury, disability, or death to the experimental subject.

Adapted from "Trials of War Criminals before the Nuremberg Military Tribunals under Control Council Law No. 10," Vol. 2, pp. 181–182, by the US Government Printing Office, 1949, Washington, D.C.

The Tuskegee Syphilis Study

The *Tuskegee Study of Untreated Syphilis in the Male Negro* conducted between 1932 and 1972 was a prime example of abuse of research subjects and ignoring informed consent. The study exploited its human participants, specifically 600 black men, of whom 399 had syphilis [4–6]. The Tuskegee Syphilis Study was designed to record the natural history of syphilis in hopes of justifying treatment programs for Blacks. The study was conducted without the benefit of providing informed consent to the participants. The researchers told participants with syphilis that they would receive treatment for the disease when, in fact, all known treatments for syphilis were withheld without participant knowledge of that important fact [4–6].

The Belmont Report

Public awareness of the unethical Tuskegee Syphilis Study provided impetus for the National Research Act of 1974 and the creation of the National Commission for the Protection of Human Subjects of Biomedical and Behavioral Research which defined ethical principles for research [4]. The commission issued the Belmont Report [7] which highlighted the basic principles of respect, beneficence, and justice and summarized key ethical principles applicable to research involving human subjects [2]. These principles underscore the practices of informed consent, analysis of risk and benefits, and selecting human research subjects [7].

The Declaration of Helsinki

The 1964 Declaration of Helsinki, developed by the World Medical Association, clearly articulates a set of ethical principles for human experimentation in research [8]. The declaration's focus is on informed consent but allows surrogate consent for special situations (e.g., when a participant is incompetent or a minor). These principles also encompass risk-benefit analysis, scientific experiments, and ethics review. Many European countries are guided by the Helsinki Declaration, while the Belmont Report more commonly guides research in the United States.

The American Medical Association Code of Medical Ethics

The AMA Code of Medical Ethics articulates four elements to which physicians adhere. Those principles are ethical obligation, accompanying guidelines for the patient-physician relationship, opinions, and rationales [9].

Finally, to ensure patient autonomy, medical specialty societies, including the American College of Medical Quality (ACMQ), have developed policies related to experimental and investigational medical services and supplies. In the case of the ACMQ Policy No. 29, qualified experts must always review and approve research involving experimental and investigational treatments, and patients must sign a release to indicate that they received informed consent and understand any risks involved before enrolling in a study [9].

Clinical Frameworks for Ethical Analysis

There are a number of respected approaches for analyzing ethical situations in the clinical setting. The best choice for a particular approach depends on many factors including the characteristics of the healthcare institution in which the ethical dilemma arises. The following are four commonly used models.

Four Box Method

The Four Box Method focuses on the concrete circumstances of a clinical case and considers four areas proposed to be the essential structure of the case, namely, medical indications, patient preferences, quality of life, and contextual features [11]. Each box, representative of a core ethical principle of medicine, links an abstract principle to a concrete and specific detail of any case (see Table 12.1).

CASES

The Veterans Health Administration's National Center for Ethics in Healthcare uses a comprehensive, step-by-step approach to ethics consultations in the clinical setting aimed at resolving ethical dilemmas as they arise, identified by the acronym "CASES," which stands for Clarify, Assemble, Synthesize, Explain, and Support [12].

Table 12.1 Four Box method of ethical analysis

Medical indications	Patient preferences
The principles of beneficence and nonmaleficence	The principles of respect for autonomy
Quality of life	**Contextual features**
The principles of beneficence, nonmaleficence, and respect for autonomy	The principles of justice and fairness

From *Clinical Ethics: A Practical Approach to Ethical Decisions in Clinical Medicine 7th ed.*, by AR Jonsen, M Siegler, and WJ Winslade. 2010, New York, NY: McGraw Hill. Copyright 2010 by McGraw Hill. Reproduced with permission from McGraw Hill Education

Pathway Approach

A pathway approach developed by Texas Children's Hospital's Clinical Ethics Committee in conjunction with professionals from the Baylor College of Medicine's Center for Medical Ethics and Health Policy uses institutionally created algorithms to determine whether a particular course of action is ethically justified [13] (see Fig. 12.1). A pathway approach is particularly useful in situations where there is strong bioethics literature to support a course of action.

CASES Method of Ethical Analysis
C – Clarify the consultation request

Characterize the type of consultation request
Obtain preliminary information from the requester
Establish realistic expectations about the consultation process
Formulate the ethics question

A – Assemble the relevant information

Consider the types of information needed
Identify the appropriate sources of information
Gather information systematically from each source
Summarize the information and the ethics question

S – Synthesize the information

Determine whether a formal meeting is needed
Engage in ethical analysis
Identify the ethically appropriate decision-maker
Facilitate moral deliberation about ethically justifiable options

E – Explain the synthesis

Communicate the synthesis to key participants
Provide additional resources
Document the consultation in the health record
Document the consultation in consultation service records

S – Support the consultation process

Follow up with participants
Evaluate the consultation
Adjust the consultation process
Identify underlying systems issues

Reprinted from *Ethics Consultation: Responding to Ethics Questions in Health Care 2nd ed.*, by National Center for Ethics in Health Care, 2015, Washington, DC: US Department of Veterans Affairs. Retrieved from https://www.ethics.va.gov/docs/integratedethics/ec_primer_2nd_ed_080515.pdf.

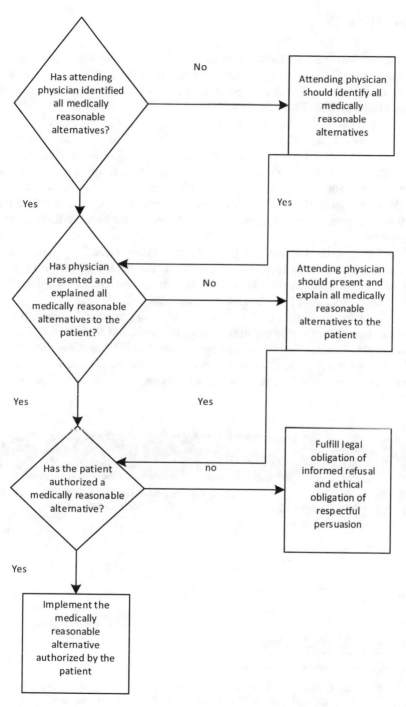

Fig. 12.1 Pathway approach to ethical analysis. Reprinted from Pathway for Informed Decision Making by Texas Children's Hospital Clinical Ethics Committee, 2017, Houston, TX

Ethics Work-Up

The Center for Medical Ethics and Health Policy at Baylor College of Medicine developed an "Ethics Work-Up" framework that provides a systematic approach to ethical decision-making and incorporates five steps to guide the ethical reasoning process [14] (see Fig. 12.2).

Since the late 1960s, healthcare ethics has undergone a shift from beneficence and professional authority to patient centeredness. The Federal Patient Self-Determination Act, an amendment to the Omnibus Budget Reconciliation Act of 1990, mandated that patients receive information about end-of-life care and their right to draft advance directives [15]. *Advance directives* are documents that express a patient's healthcare choices or name another person to make decisions regarding medical treatment in the event that the patients are unable to make these decisions themselves.

The frameworks described as methods to evaluate ethical dilemmas can be applied to the case study involving Mary Smith. The details of the case study are applied to each of the frameworks to show how the analysis occurs when applied to Mary's case. First is the Four Box Method, detailed in Table 12.2.

The Four Box Method's evaluation of the situation identified the issues of this case which center on what the patient wants. By analyzing all four boxes, we have determined the patient understands the consequence of discontinuing the ventilator, and her autonomy should be honored. The discord between the intern and attending should be addressed within the hospital system and not interfere in the patient's informed choice.

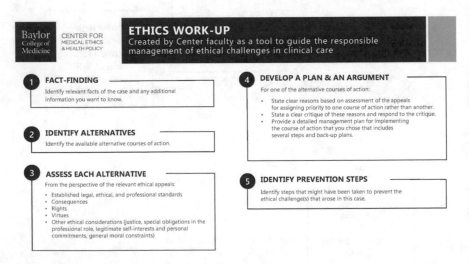

Fig. 12.2 Baylor College of Medicine Ethics Work-Up framework. Reprinted from Baylor College of Medicine Center for Medical Ethics and Health Policy Resources, 2019, Retrieved from https://www.bcm.edu/centers/medical-ethics-and-health-policy/clinical-ethics/resources. Reprinted with permission

Table 12.2 Evaluation of Case Study using the Four Box method

Medical indications	Patient preferences
Medical problems: 93-year-old female with pulmonary condition, ventilator dependent, brittle diabetes, severe rheumatoid arthritis, ischemic cardiomyopathy	Patient states she has enjoyed her long life
	Patient has outlived her family and friends
	Patient understands she will not be able to walk again or spend time with her cat
Prognosis: Fair to poor, given inability to wean off ventilator	Patient's eyesight and hearing are failing
Goal of treatment: Life extension (ventilator) versus "good death" (withdrawal of ventilator and comfort care)	Patient appears mentally competent and understands the implications of stopping the ventilator
Quality of life	**Contextual features**
Patient has severe, irreversible illness with poor prognosis	Patient's family and relatives deceased
Patient has zero mobility	Intern feels it is appropriate to discontinue ventilator
Patient has pain in her joints	Hospital risk manager concerned with liability of discontinuing ventilator and long-lost relative suing hospital
Patient unable to spend time in her apartment or with her cat	Attending physician thinks patient is "delusional" and does not understand why she wants ventilator discontinued

Case Study • • •
Clinical Quality and Patient Autonomy

QI relates not only to the quality of clinical care provided but also to patient choice and autonomy. A patient, we'll call her Mary Smith, was a lifetime smoker and had lived in a high-rise senior citizen residence for 27 years. By age 93, she had outlived her husband, her son, and all her relatives. She was brought to the ER by ambulance, mentally alert but severely short of breath. Her pulmonary condition had deteriorated, and she had been ventilator dependent for the past two months. She was a favorite on the chronic vent unit, always smiling. She kept pulling at her endotracheal tube and telling everyone that she wanted the staff to let her die. Although attempts to wean her from the ventilator failed, the staff continued to try a "slow wean."

The hospital had difficulty finding a chronic vent unit to take Mary because of her recently diagnosed brittle diabetes, severe rheumatoid arthritis, and ischemic cardiomyopathy.

The intern stated to the nursing staff, "This is a futile case. Why not shut off the ventilator and let nature take its course? The money could be better spent elsewhere."

The hospital risk manager was concerned that honoring the patient's wishes might result in a long-lost relative suing the hospital. The attending physician did not believe that anyone would choose to die. "She must be delusional...I won't obey a crazy person's wishes."

Confused about what to do, the senior resident called a member of the ethics committee for advice. Before the ethics committee met, a member of the committee met with the patient to gather information. The patient communicated the following: "I have lived a long life and liked best to walk around, watering my plants and talking to my cat. All my friends and relatives have died. My eyesight and hearing are rapidly failing and my joints hurt from being in bed so long." She stated that she expected more pain in the future, without significant improvement. She did not expect to be taken off the respirator or to walk around her apartment ever again. She had lived long enough and therefore chose to die.

The ethics committee met with the attending physician, resident, intern, and key nursing staff. The committee member who spoke with Mary provided the patient's rationale and discussed the patient's wishes and her capacity to make a decision of this magnitude. The committee reviewed the concepts of nonmaleficence, beneficence, and autonomy. Options were discussed for best serving the patient's interests.

Discussion

This case touches on a number of ethical principles. If a treatment involves pain, repeated hospital visits, lab tests, or prolonged hospitalization, the physician may still choose to preserve the patient's life. However, doing so may not have the same importance for an elderly patient who values freedom from pain and suffering or an escape from a prolonged final decline in a hospital. Compassion and understanding from the physician and practical requirements of informed consent enable patients to make decisions based on their desires and personal values.

Mary was subsequently evaluated by a psychiatrist who found no evidence of psychiatric illness that would affect her decision-making capacity. She was informed about her condition, and she demonstrated a good understanding of her current situation (i.e., it was highly unlikely that she could be weaned from the ventilator and she would be very limited in what she could do). Seeing her life as ongoing suffering without happiness, she made a rational decision about her course of care.

Advance directives, a living will, or a healthcare power of attorney would not apply in this case because the patient was capable of making her own decisions. Continuing her life would not provide happiness or satisfaction and could be seen as causing psychological and physical harm. Providing medications to relieve pain would likely cause sedation and respiratory depression. These concepts were discussed among the staff.

(continued)

One final time, the staff discussed the patient's choice of termination of life support with her, and she held to her decision. She was given a low dose of morphine as needed for her unremitting arthritis pain, and her weekly weaning began the next morning as scheduled. The staff made sure that she was kept comfortable during the weaning attempt and supported her request not to be placed back on the respirator.

Harm was prevented (i.e., nonmaleficence) by discontinuing futile care that prolonged the patient's suffering. It was the concept of beneficence that allowed the patient to exert autonomy in choosing life or death after being fully informed of her prognosis. Not returning the patient to the respirator had the highest value for her.

Evaluation of Case Study Using the Veteran's Administration CASES Model
C – Clarify the ethics consultation request

- Characterize the type of consult request:

  - The requester (senior resident) wants help resolving an ethical concern in an active case.
  - The request requires interaction with the patient and documentation of the case in the medical record.

- Obtain preliminary information from the requester:

  - Ethics committee representative should obtain preliminary information from the requestor which includes contact information, requester's title and role in the case, date and time the ethics consult request was made, urgency of request, brief description of clinical case and the ethical concern as the requester understands it, steps already taken to resolve issue, and type of assistance desired (e.g., conflict resolution, explanation of options, values clarification, policy interpretation, etc.)

- Establish realistic expectations about the consultation process:

  - Ethics consultant should provide a clear, concise description of the consultation process; goals of the consult; expected timeframe for completing the consult; and specific actions ethics consultant will take.
  - Correct any misconceptions. Ethics consultants do not conduct medical evaluation, make a treatment plan, tell the requestor what to do, or talk to patient so the provider does not have to.

- Formulate ethics question:

  - An ethics question asks which decisions or actions are ethically justifiable given a particular situation. The process for formulating an effective ethics question is outlined in Fig. 12.3.
  - In the case study, a clear, helpful ethics question might read, "Given that the patient would like to discontinue ventilator support which will produce death, but some of the clinical staff feel she is delusional and does not understand the consequences of discontinuation of ventilator support, is it ethically justifiable to allow her to choose to stop ventilator support?"

A – Assemble the relevant information

- Consider the types of information needed:

  - Medical facts: Pulmonary condition, ventilator dependent, brittle diabetes, severe rheumatoid arthritis, ischemic cardiomyopathy.
  - Psychological health: A psychological report found that the patient had sound decision-making ability.
  - Patient preferences and interests: Patient states she has enjoyed her long life, has outlived her family and friends, understands she will not be able to walk again or spend time with her cat, knows her eyesight and hearing are failing, and appears mentally competent and understands the implications of stopping the ventilator.
  - Other parties and interests: Healthcare providers disagree with care plan, risk management concerned about long-lost relative suing hospital.
  - Ethics knowledge: Ethics consultant should assemble information from code of ethics policies, guidelines of the institution, precedent cases, scholarly publications, and applicable law.

- Identify the appropriate sources of information:

  - Patient: Preferable to have a face-to-face discussion between the ethics consultant and the patient to gain understanding of their wishes.
  - Health record: Careful review of the electronic health record.
  - Staff: The ethics consultant should interview the attending physician, resident, intern, and nursing staff.
  - Family and friends: The ethics consultant should meet with family and friends to understand the patient's values and preferences. Not applicable in this case.

- Gather information systematically from each source:

  - Collect sufficient information in a thorough manner.
  - Verify accuracy of the information by collecting directly from the source rather than second-hand information.
  - Distinguish facts from value judgements.
  - Handle interactions professionally.

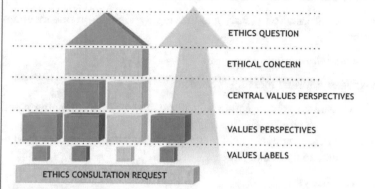

Building Blocks Description

1. Start at the bottom of the figure with the <u>ethics consultation request</u>. The requester describes the circumstances and the ethical concern as he or she understands them.

2. Moving upwards in the figure, identify the <u>values labels</u> that apply to the request. The consultant elicits value labels from the requester. Values labels are one- or two-word identifiers for strongly held beliefs, ideals, principles, or standards. Examples include "truth-telling," "equality," and "stewardship."

3. Articulate those values from the perspective of those involved. The consultant, working with the requester, describes a <u>values perspective</u>. A values perspective is a common-sense expression of how a value applies to the consultation from the perspective of one or more participants. For characteristics of a values perspective, see the inset box.

4. Determine the <u>central values perspectives</u> in the request. The consultant works with the requester to determine which values perspectives are most central to the ethical concern. Note: The requester may hold two competing values or two or more individuals may hold conflicting values. Also, sometimes both parties are conflicted about a single value (e.g., both are concerned about doing good for the patient).

5. Articulate the <u>ethical concern</u>. This step entails conjoining two central values perspectives into a single statement. The ethical concern is stated as, "[first values perspective], but [second values perspective]."

6. Formulate the <u>ethics question</u>. The ethics consultant inserts the ethical concern into the appropriate structure for the ethics question based on whether the requester is concerned about a particular decision or action, wants to know what decisions or actions would be ethically justifiable, or plans to determine if a document raises ethical concerns. (See Figure 5.)

Characteristics of a Values Perspective:

- Explicitly identifies the person or group whose perspective is being represented, i.e., who holds the perspective (e.g., the spouse or the team)

- Uses words such as "believes" or "according to…" to link the person or group to the value

- Is normative (expresses or implies how things should be as opposed to how things are)

- Explicitly expresses an underlying value (which may or may not include a values label)

- Contains enough contextual information to relate the value to the specifics of the consultation

- Does not include any names or other individual identifiers of those involved

- Uses everyday language and avoids jargon

- Is in the form of a sentence

Fig. 12.3 The building blocks of formulating an effective ethics question. Reprinted from *Ethics Consultation: Responding to Ethics Questions in Health Care. 2nd ed.*, by National Center for Ethics in Health Care, 2015, Washington, DC: US Department of Veterans Affairs. Retrieved from https://www.ethics.va.gov/docs/integratedethics/ec_primer_2nd_ed_080515.pdf

- Summarize the information and the ethics question:

  - Summarize the information clearly and thoroughly via one-on-one meetings or in writing.

  S – Synthesize the information

- Determine whether a formal meeting is needed:

  - The ethics consultant should gather all information prior to planning a full meeting as a way to be efficient and concise.
  - Introductions of care team, medical facts, and all stakeholders' views are discussed, the actual analysis can begin.

- Engage in ethical analysis:

  - Use of systematic methods of reasoning to answer the ethical argument and counter arguments by (1) generating ethical arguments and counter arguments and (2) strengthening the ethical arguments while weighing these answers for a conclusion that answers the ethical question.
  - The rationales for ethical arguments are based on:

    Credo (following guidelines that guide ethical behavior, for example, Joint Commission)
    Consequence (the action will or will not result in certain good or bad effects)
    Comparison (decision similar or different from other actions, for example, Standard of Care)

  - In our case, the arguments that the patient should have the autonomy to discontinue the ventilator after she is deemed competent is weighed against some of the clinical team that feels she should stay on the ventilator. Using the consequence rationale produces the result that the patient should be able to make her decision about her care plan.

- Identify the ethically appropriate decision-maker:

  - Confirming the patient has decision-making capacity is key to this. If the patient is not capable, finding the legal surrogate is critical.
  - In this case, the patient has the right to refuse to remain on the ventilator, and since she is deemed to have capacity and understanding of consequences, she is the ethically appropriate decision-maker.

- Facilitate moral deliberation about ethically justifiable options:

  - The process of moral deliberation should respect the rights of the ethically appropriate decision-maker within ethically justifiable limits that honor their personal values.
  - The deliberation process should produce at least one or more specific recommendations and a tangible plan of action.

- In this case, this was, again, the explanation to the patient on the consequences of discontinuing ventilator support and providing clear steps of how she would be kept comfortable.

E – Explain the synthesis

- Communicate the synthesis to key participants:

  - In this case, the summary of the consult results would be shared with all of the physicians involved in the patient's care, nurses, risk management, and possibly the service chief.

- Provide additional resources:

  - The ethics consultant should provide education to staff, patients, and families about the issue at hand, which can include articles.
  - Resources within the facility such as social work or family advocacy.

- Document the consultation in the electronic health record:

  - The ethics consultant should document the discussions in the medical record in an accurate way, should include all information gathered in the assemble section of the consult listed above, and then record in the summary of ethical analysis options considered and what the final recommendation is.

S – Support the consultation process

- Follow up with participants:

  - The ethics consultant should follow up with those who participated in the consult to see if recommendations were followed and, if not, discuss why they were not.
  - This follow-up key is to the quality analysis of the process so improvements can be made in the future if needed.

- Evaluate the consultation:

  - The ethics consultation services should evaluate their practices as a way to continually improve the ethics consult quality.
  - Formal evaluations can be solicited of those who participated for feedback for future improvement.

- Adjust the consultation process:

  - If deemed appropriate after the evaluation, changes might need to be implemented for improvement, for example, changes to the institutional policies.

- Identify underlying systems issues:

  - Evaluation of the consult service and periodic health record review can reveal issues at a system level that should be addressed by the appropriate department within the entity in which the physician practices.

Evaluation of the Case Using the Pathway Approach

- Has the attending physician identified all medically reasonable alternatives?

  - In this case, the clinical team evaluated both continuation of ventilator support and discontinuation of this support.

- Has physician presented and explained all medically reasonable alternatives to the patient?

  - In this case, yes, the physician explained on multiple occasions the resulting death that will occur if the ventilator is discontinued. The physician also explained that staying on the ventilator will not change prognosis to include the patient being able to be ambulatory and spend time in her apartment with her cat.

- Has the patient authorized a medically reasonable alternative?

  - In this case, yes, the patient is deemed competent to make decisions regarding her care, and she has authorized the discontinuation of ventilator support. This is a crucial component to the algorithm process, and if the answer had been no, then the ethics consultant and physician must fulfill the legal obligation of informed refusal and ethical obligation of respectful persuasion.

- Implement the medically reasonable alternative authorized by the patient.

  - Since evaluation of the case shows that the patient authorized a medically reasonable alternative, the next step would be to implement that alternative. In this situation, the case analysis indicates that the patient wanted discontinuation of ventilator support and comfort care through to the point of the patient's death.

Evaluation of the Case Study Using the Ethics Work-Up Model

Step 1: Identify the relevant facts which include the type of patient and medical condition.

Mary Smith's case consists of the 93-year-old woman who has a pulmonary condition, ventilator dependent, brittle diabetes, severe rheumatoid arthritis, and ischemic cardiomyopathy. Additional facts include the validity of the patient's motivation and her reasoning. The patient states she has enjoyed her long life, has outlived her family and friends, understands she will not be able to walk again or spend time with her cat, knows her eyesight and hearing are failing, appears mentally competent, and understands the implications of stopping the ventilator.

Step 2: Identify available alternative courses of action.

Continue the ventilator or discontinue it.

Step 3: Assess the case on the perspective of relevant ethical appeals:

- Appeal to established legal, ethical, and professional standards:

  - The ethical standard of autonomy and informed consent is applicable since the patient has been deemed competent.

- Appeal to consequences:

  - The ethics consultant must explain the irreversibility, probability, and severity for both courses of action.
  - Discontinuing the ventilator support will be irreversible and cause death
  - Continuing the ventilator support will not allow the patient to improve her quality of life as she will be on the support until her death from other causes.

- Appeal to rights:

  - Decisional rights and the principle of respect for persons to take actions based on their own values.
  - Rights to be protected from harm especially for vulnerable populations like the elderly or children.
  - Right to privacy and confidentiality.
  - Right to be told the truth about diagnosis and prognosis.
  - In this case, all rights were properly valued and honored.

- Appeal to virtues:

  - Compassion
  - Courage
  - Self-sacrifice

- Justice-based obligations and constraints:

  - Resource allocation: the intern in our case was concerned with improper use of the technology as a resource.
  - Special obligations in a professional role: clinicians have the obligation of beneficence and nonmaleficence by upholding their professional integrity, which was honored in this case.
  - Balancing obligations to patients against legitimate personal interests and commitments: the physician must balance his/her own personal integrity, family commitments, and personal health with that of the care of the patient. This was not a consideration in this case.

- General moral constraints:

  - These moral constraints often include religious and moral beliefs of the physician as it relates to the care of the patient. This was not a consideration in this case.

Organizational Framework for Ethics

Similar to the clinical arena, ethics and ethical principles come into play at the organizational level as well. Brent James with Intermountain Healthcare, a large Utah-based system of hospitals and clinics, provides a thoughtful, stepwise reasoning process to explain how the same ethical principles and obligations that govern patient interactions apply to each activity in the healthcare continuum, including clinical care, care provider education, and research endeavors [16]. James declares clearly that quality improvement efforts are solidly in the healthcare operations realm and that healthcare delivery organizations have legal and regulatory requirements to manage care delivery systems to maximize performance:

> HIPAA [Health Insurance Portability and Accountability Act of 1996] regulations identify both quality assurance and quality improvement activities as part of "health care operations" (a.k.a. "treatment, payment, and operations," or TPO) (§164.501). Health care delivery oversight agencies (e.g., CMS [Centers for Medicare and Medicaid Services] and the Joint Commission) require that care delivery groups put in place both quality assurance and quality improvement (process-level performance measurement and management) systems. When defects in care are found using either quality assurance or quality improvement methods, care delivery organizations are required to act to correct those defects. Appropriate corrections may include actions regarding individual health professionals (e.g., additional training; better oversight; decertification), and changes to care delivery systems (e.g., changes to policy; changes to physical layout; changes to data systems). [16]

James also describes a moral imperative for organizations to work to improve the care provided to patients:

> An extensive body of research demonstrates that (1) in terms of health benefits to patients and care-associated harms, health care delivery falls far short of its theoretic potential (the quality chasm); that (2) it is possible to close that gap; and (3) that the largest opportunities for improvement comes at the level of systems … Under the principles of beneficence and non-maleficence, health care delivery organizations have an ethical obligation to close the performance gap. [16]

Figure 12.4 graphically represents James' perspective on ethical practice that spans the entire academic health sciences center continuum of activity. James points out that organizations have two general mechanisms to oversee and manage ethical patient interactions: prevent controls and detect controls [16].

Human Subjects in Research and Quality Improvement

Institutional Review Boards

An Institutional Review Board (IRB), also known as an independent ethics committee (IEC) or ethical review board (ERB), consists of a group of expert-scientists who use a peer-review method to evaluate, approve, monitor, and review clinical, biomedical, epidemiological, and behavioral research involving humans with the goal to protect the rights and the welfare of the subjects. IRB review and oversight ensure that ethical standards are in place to protect the welfare and rights of humans participating in research initiatives that could in some way harm or place participants at risk [17, 18]. The IRB assesses research studies with regard to factors such as potential within the protocol for patient risk, testing new or nonstandard care, the intent to publish, and confidentiality requirements [19]. To that end, the IRB reviews

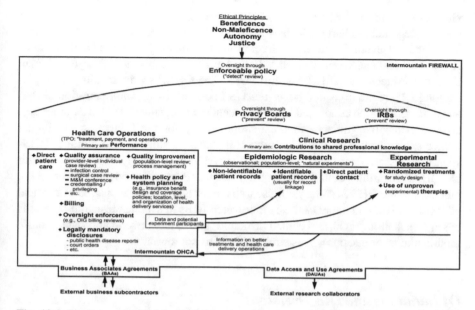

Fig. 12.4 Intermountain Healthcare's view on ethics and oversight at the organization level. Reprinted from "Healthcare Delivery Ethics of QI," by Dr. Brent James, MS, MStat, Chief Quality Officer, Intermountain Healthcare, Inc. 2007. White paper available at https://intermountainhealthcare.org/~/media/Files/Research/healthcare-delivery-ethics-of-qi.pdf. Used with permission from Intermountain Healthcare, Intermountain Healthcare Delivery Institute, Advanced Training Program www.intermountainatp.com.

research protocols and materials to include investigator brochures and informed consent documents to make certain that all parts of the research protocol are in accordance with ethical standards to protect human subjects. A research protocol is always submitted to the IRB for review to determine the level of oversight that the IRB requires to protect the subjects in the study. IRBs also focus on protecting the welfare and rights of participants in human subjects research through the use of the informed consent process that stipulates for individual participants the associated risks and benefits, including the right to refuse to participate and the right to withdraw from the research study [18]. Additionally, HIPAA privacy regulations require an IRB to protect the privacy rights of research subjects in specific ways. At some healthcare organizations, the IRB reviews all HIPAA-required authorizations and waivers of authorizations for research use of identifiable health information.

Institutional Review Boards within universities and healthcare organizations came into being in the early 1970s when the Department of Health, Education, and Welfare issued regulations that reflected the National Institute of Health's (NIH's) Policies for the Protection of Human Subjects [20]. In 1965, the NIH proposed that all human subjects research be reviewed by peers to determine if there were any ethical issues or concerns that the rights and welfare of research participants were violated [18]. In the United States, IRBs are governed by Title 45 CFR (Code of Federal Regulations) Part 46. This Research Act of 1974 defines IRBs and requires them for all research that receives direct or indirect funding from the Department of Health and Human Services (HHS). IRBs are regulated by the Office for Human Research Protections (OHRP) within HHS. The OHRP's primary duty is implementing IRB regulations that cover the US Food and Drug Administration (FDA) and clinical research conducted by pharmaceutical companies, as well as other regulations under the guidance of the Federal Policy for the Protection of Human Subjects, also known as the "Common Rule." All institutions that conduct HHS-sponsored research must have a Federal-Wide Assurance (FWA), an agreement with the OHRP regarding ethical oversight. The OHRP provides education for IRBs, guidance to the HHS Secretary on research ethics, and advises on issues of medical ethics. The HHS and the FDA have empowered IRBs to evaluate research protocols based on scientific, legal, and ethical principles and to recommend approval, require modifications, or disapprove research projects as appropriate.

QI Initiatives and IRB Oversight

Although an IRB reviews all research protocols in given institutions, the rules of engagement for IRB review do not apply to most QI initiatives. The HHS has clear guidelines for quality improvement initiatives and recognizes the independent focus and intersect of both QI and research initiatives. As such, the HHS identifies when QI initiatives do not need the oversight of the IRB. The HHS states that quality improvement initiatives limited to delivering healthcare or measuring and reporting provider performance data for clinical, practical, or administrative uses are not considered research and, therefore, do not require adherence to the HHS regulations for the protection of human subjects, review by an IRB, or provider or patient informed consent [21]. In cases where the design of a quality improvement initiative has a research purpose in conjunction with improving the quality of care, the protection of subjects in research regulations may apply [21].

The role of the IRB in the oversight of quality improvement and safety initiatives varies among healthcare institutions. Currently, many institutions throughout the United States may not have institutionally generated guidelines that direct whether a QI initiative should be submitted to the IRB, while others have developed their own guidelines for when a QI initiative should be reviewed by the IRB and make that information clear to prospective QI developers [22, 23]. Given that patient-centered QI initiatives involve patients and protocols for patient treatments, it is important that the institutions in which quality improvement initiatives take place understand the issues surrounding the protection of subjects and whether such protection is warranted through the oversight of an IRB. QI initiatives may need IRB approval when the protocol could potentially expose patients to risks and burdens, when there is a question of possible ethical conflict, and when the results of the QI initiative may expose the patient to risk [24, 25]. Some organizations suggest that it is best to submit a QI initiative to the IRB for review to determine if there are any questions or concerns as to whether a process of informed consent may be needed or if there are any questions regarding the nature of the QI protocol [21]. The institutional IRB then determines whether a QI initiative requires oversight and the protection of subjects throughout its implementation. Others suggest that since QI is not research, submitting the protocol to the IRB is excessive and may have unintended negative consequences from a resource use perspective.

Institutions often use QI initiatives to improve compliance with national patient safety benchmarks and therefore may require that its IRB be notified of the QI initiative. Usually, an IRB exempts QI initiatives from IRB oversight when participant data is de-identified or gives the QI initiative an expedited review status if the initiative tests a hypothesis, includes data with personal identifiers, or anticipates publication. Some institutions have instituted an IRB-QI subcommittee to fast-track QI proposals [19]. Of note, in many academic institutions where students and trainees may develop and implement a quality improvement initiative as part of the academic program requirements, the student is required to submit their QI project to the university and institutional IRB for review. In this situation, the submitted QI initiatives would likely receive expedited review since the protocol is not consistent with that of a research study.

Case Study • • •
Is It Research or QI?

In 2003, Johns Hopkins University coordinated with the Michigan Health and Hospital Association to implement the use of a checklist for reducing the incidence of infection during insertion of central venous lines (CVL) in 103 intensive care units (ICUs) in 67 Michigan hospitals [26, 27]. The Agency for Healthcare Research and Quality (AHRQ) funded the Keystone ICU project that was based on earlier research which showed a significant decrease in the rate of certain infections in intensive care units when a bundle of interventions including a checklist was utilized to ensure adherence to evidence-based guidelines for preventing catheter-related blood stream infections (CR-BSIs) [26–28]. The effectiveness of using the checklist was a proven intervention with its findings published in the New England Journal of Medicine [29]. The checklist identified five key behaviors that clinicians should practice every time when inserting a CVL. Those behaviors are hand-washing, cleaning the skin with chlorhexidine, avoiding the femoral site for line placement, removing unnecessary lines, and using barrier precautions [27, 30].

The Chair of the Johns Hopkins IRB and one committee member determined that the project was exempt from IRB oversight in accordance with Johns Hopkins' policy [29]. The checklist initiative did not pose a danger to patients or clinicians, nor did it involve the use of experimental drugs or processes for which informed consent would be crucial.

(continued)

After the Johns Hopkins/Michigan Hospitals initiative was implemented as a quality improvement initiative, the Office for Human Research Protections (OHRP) received a complaint about the "research study" and determined that a request for IRB review had not occurred before the research study began [30]. In February of 2007, the OHRP notified Johns Hopkins and the Michigan Health and Hospital Association that they had violated scientific ethics regulations in tracking the results of a checklist without written, informed consent from each patient and healthcare provider [30]. Furthermore, the OHRP determination letter stated that patients or surrogates should grant "legally effective informed consent" to be included in the checklist initiative [26]. The OHRP judged that because the project prospectively implemented a protocol of infection control, it was not exempt from IRB review [26].

In July of 2007, Johns Hopkins suspended the project at the Michigan hospitals, while the details of the situation were addressed [26]. The actions taken by the US Department of Health and Humans Services' Office for Human Research Protections against the checklist initiative resulted in Johns Hopkins halting the program in Michigan hospitals and their plans to extend the initiative to hospitals in New Jersey and Rhode Island [26]. Consequently, the OHRP action created grave concerns in the quality community regarding whether other QI projects might be in danger of similar actions. The need for informed consent for all participants involved in a quality initiative would hinder the ability to implement evidence-based protocols implemented to improve quality care and patient safety.

Review of the issues involved in this case showed that the quality improvement interventions were not experimental in any way. All patient-related procedures were evidence-based and standard. There were no patient risks beyond the standards of clinical care. The systematic measurement of the rate of catheter-related infections was the only part of the project that was related to research, and the patients were not subjected to any risks [26].

In December of 2007, Atul Gawande, in an op-ed article in the *New York Times*, voiced concerns regarding hospitals needing informed consent to implement the use of checklists that promote safety measures [31]. Gawande stated that the OHRPs position on the use of checklists was "bizarre and dangerous" [31] as the OHRP compared the use of a checklist to studying an experimental drug. The agency stated that a checklist may require even more stringent oversight because the data gathered could put patients at risk, and doctors as well, by exposing how poorly doctors follow infection-prevention procedures. Gawande described how checklists are an integral part of providing safety in numerous initiatives across the country and the world [31].

(continued)

There are a number of questions that this case raised that needed to be clarified [30]:

- What regulations apply when institutions are only implementing practices to improve the quality of care, as compared with the planning of research activities that look at the effectiveness of interventions to improve quality?
- Does the tracking of results of QI projects warrant oversight by the OHRP?
- Do the OHRP regulations apply when institutions are only implementing practices to improve the quality of care, even when this includes collecting information to track/monitor/confirm the results of that implementation?
- What are the distinctions between institutions planning research activities that examine the effectiveness of interventions that improve the quality of care and applying regulatory protections that protect the rights and welfare of human research subjects?

Two weeks after the publication of Gawande's op-ed article, the OHRP issued a statement acknowledging that the informed consent waiver criteria might have been satisfied [27]. In retrospect, the Johns Hopkins IRB should have completed a full or expedited review of the study protocol and articulated that the project met the four conditions for waiving informed consent, instead of deeming it exempt without specifying the details as to why it was exempt [26]. The OHRP responded to concerns that they may expect unrealistic requirements for quality improvement initiatives. The OHRP stated that any hospital or intensive care unit could implement the use of measures or checklists that would improve the quality of care provided and could do so without consideration of the requirements of the HHS regulations [30]. It would have been highly unfortunate if this OHRP investigation prompted sponsors of quality improvement initiatives to simply implement changes and forgo evaluative research, owing to concerns about the burdens of IRB review or the need for individual informed consent [26].

Determination of Research Component Within a Quality Improvement Initiative

Areas to consider when distinguishing between quality improvement and research include the purpose of the initiative, the design of the project, and the generalizability of the findings [32, 33]. When the goal of an initiative is to uncover new knowledge, test situations that go beyond current knowledge, or fill a gap in knowledge regarding a specific patient population, disease, or treatment, then the project is research and requires IRB approval [32, 34].

IRB approval is required for a quality improvement initiative when the design includes drug or device evaluation, randomization of subjects, comparison of interventions, a need to acquire protected health information, and the use of a clinical intervention that does not meet the usual standard of care or imposes burdens or risks that go beyond standard of care [32, 34, 35].

Characteristics of QI Initiatives

Quality improvement is defined as a methodical, data-guided set of activities designed to bring about positive changes in the delivery of healthcare in local settings [36]. Most urgently needed QI activity focuses on changing practices that result in suboptimal care. The characteristics of a QI initiative commonly include the use of care considered to be usual practice, the implementation of procedures that pose no greater than minimal risk to patients, a design that allows for ongoing modification as the project unfolds, and the use of personnel who routinely work at the institution [34]. Most QI initiatives involve the implementation of a protocol established through evidence-based and best practice recommendations, and therefore, there is no experimentation involved. Although the range of traditional quality improvement activities is broad, there are some characteristics that do distinguish QI initiatives from research studies. Activities with the following features are generally considered to fall under the umbrella of quality improvement [16, 34, 36]:

- Aimed at improving local systems of care
- Focused on improving the performance and outcomes of institutional practice
- Introduction of promising or evidence-based methods of care that are intended to improve outcomes over baseline outcomes
- Comparison of baseline measures to outcome measures after initiation of a new protocol, such as already developed practice guidelines or evidence-based standards of care

Characteristics of Research Initiatives

The US Department of Health and Human Services defines research as "a systematic investigation including research development, testing, and evaluation, designed to develop or contribute to generalizable knowledge." [36] This indicates that research is meant to develop new knowledge, not to implement existing knowledge.

The Hastings Center published a report that focused on distinguishing QI activities from research. The analysis determined that it is not possible to consistently identify research based on a project's stated intent, funding sources, or whether or not the project's results were published. The key rule for ethical oversight by an IRB is a potential or actual conflict of interest that might cause a health professional or care delivery organization to place some other value above an individual patient's healthcare needs (e.g., academic production for career advancement or direct or indirect financial gain) [36]. The report also specifies that there may be overlap between hospital operations, quality improvement initiatives, and research activities. Figure 12.5 depicts the areas of overlap as well as areas of distinction.

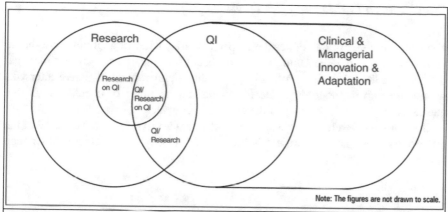

Note: The figures are not drawn to scale.

Right oval: "Clinical and Managerial Innovation and Adaptation" consists of activities designed to bring about immediate local improvements in clinical and managerial practice.
Central circle (subset of oval): "QI" consists of clinical and managerial innovation and adaptation activities designed and carried out in a systematic, data-guided way.
Left circle: "Research" consists of systematic investigations designed to develop or contribute to generalizable knowledge. Includes basic and applied medical research plus other types with a potential impact on health care quality, such as epidemiological research, health services research, management research, and educational research.
Small concentric circle within "Research" that partially overlaps with "QI": consists of systematic investigations designed to produce generalizable knowledge relevant to design and implementation of QI activities. "Research on QI" helps to answer 1) "What are the principles of change?" 2) "How do these principles work within different organizational contexts?" and 3) "How can one spread desired change across an organization or between organizations?"

Fig. 12.5 Intersects of research studies and quality improvement initiatives. Reprinted from "The ethics of using QI methods to improve health care quality and safety," by MA Baily, M Bottrell, et al., 2006, *A Hastings Center Special Report*, p. S12

An example of an intersect between quality improvement and research is a QI project that introduces an untested clinical intervention to both improve the quality of care and to collect data on patient outcomes to determine how well the intervention achieves its intended results. In this case, the HHS regulations say that the QI initiative is subject to the status of nonexempt human subjects research [21]. HHS provides excellent information on situations to consider when developing and evaluating the nature of the QI initiatives [21]. The chapter appendix shows the questions that the HHS addresses regarding the need for protection of human subjects in QI and whether an IRB review is warranted. The HHS guidelines are the ones that institutions look to for guidance. Many of the subsequent checklists that institutions have developed to guide quality improvement initiatives come from the HHS guidelines.

Checklists to Guide the IRB Review of QI Initiatives

There are a number of guidelines developed to clarify whether a QI initiative should be reviewed by an IRB. Guidelines and checklists help the QI project manager determine if the QI design protocol of a quality improvement initiative intersects with a research methodology. The following are examples of checklists and the questions they include for project developers to consider.

Hockenberry developed a question checklist that asserts if the answer to all of the questions is yes, then the project is most likely quality improvement rather than research [37]:

Questions to Determine If a Project Should Be Considered Quality Improvement

If answer to all of the questions is yes, then the project is most likely quality improvement.

1. Is the project anticipated to improve care delivery while decreasing inadequacies within a specific healthcare setting?
2. Is the project focused on evaluating current practice or attempting to improve it based upon existing evidence?
3. Is there sufficient existing evidence to support implementing the project to create practice change?
4. Are the methods for the project flexible and include approaches to evaluate rapid and incremental changes?
5. Are clinicians and staff who provide care or are responsible for practice change in the institutions where the activity will occur implementing the project?
6. Will the project involve a sample of the population (patients or participants) normally seen in the institution where the activity will take place?
7. Will the project only require consent that is already obtained in clinical practice, and could the proposed activity be considered part of usual care?
8. Will future participants at the institution where the planned activity is implemented potentially benefit from the project?
9. Is the risk to participants no greater than what is involved in the care they are already receiving?

Reprinted from "Quality improvement and evidence-based practice change projects and the Institutional Review Board: Is approval necessary?" by M. Hockenberry, 2014, *Worldviews on Evidence-Based Nursing, 11*(4), pp 217-218. Copyright 2014 by Sigma Theta Tau International. Reprinted with permission.

The Children's Hospital of Philadelphia (CHOP) developed guidelines to help determine if a QI initiative has design characteristics that might warrant IRB review [23].

When Is IRB Approval Needed for QI Activities?
- Seeks to develop new knowledge or validate new treatments rather than assess the implementation of existing knowledge
- When the methodology employs a standard research design, such as randomization
- When the protocol is fixed with a rigid goal, methodology, population, time period, etc.
- When the funding for the activity comes from the outside organizations such as the NIH or those with a commercial interest in the results
- When there will be a delay in the implementation of results
- When the risks from the intervention to participants are greater than minimal

Reprinted from *Quality Improvement vs Research*, by MS Shreiner, 2015, Retrieved from https://irb.research.chop.edu/quality-improvement-vs-research. Copyright 2019 by Children's Hospital of Philadelphia. Reprinted with permission.

CHOP's IRB website also directs readers to a document entitled *Quality Improvement or Research Worksheet* to help investigators determine when the IRB should be consulted regarding a study or initiative [23] (see Fig. 12.6).

Quality Improvement or Research Worksheet
Rachel Nosowsky, Esq.

SEQ	Issue and Guidance	Rating
1	Are patients randomized into different intervention groups in order to enhance confidence in differences that might be obscured by nonrandom selection? *Randomization done to achieve equitable allocation of a scarce resource need not be considered and would not result in a "yes" here.*	☐ Yes ☐ No
2	Does the project seek to test issues that are beyond current science and experience, such as new treatments (*i.e.*, is there much controversy about whether the intervention will be beneficial to actual patients – or is it designed simply to move existing evidence into practice?). *If the project is performed to implement existing knowledge to improve care – rather than to develop new knowledge – answer "no".*	☐ Yes ☐ No
3	Are researchers who have no ongoing commitment to improvement of the local care situation (and who may well have conflicts of interest with the patients involved) involved in key project roles? *Generally answer "yes" even if others on the team do have professional commitments. However, where the project leaders with no clinical commitment are unaffiliated with the project site, it may be that the project site is not engaged – and does not require IRB approval/oversight – even if the project leaders' roles do require IRB oversight at their institutions.*	☐ Yes ☐ No
4	Is the protocol fixed with a fixed goal, methodology, population, and time period? *If frequent adjustments are made in the intervention, the measurement, and even the goal over time as experience accumulates, the answer is more likely "no."*	☐ Yes ☐ No
5	Will there be delayed or ineffective feedback of data from monitoring the implementation of changes? *Answer "yes" especially if feedback is delayed or altered in order to avoid biasing the interpretation of data.*	☐ Yes ☐ No
6	Is the project funded by an outside organization with a commercial interest in the use of the results? Is the sponsor a manufacturer with an interest in the outcome of the project relevant to its products? Is it a non-profit foundation that typically funds research, or internal research accounts? *If the project is funded by third-party payors through clinical reimbursement incentives, or through internal clinical/operations funds vs. research funds, the answer to this question is more likely to be "no."*	☐ Yes ☐ No

Adapted from Hastings Center, "The Ethics of Using Quality Improvement Methods to Improve Health Care Quality and Safety" (June 2006)

If the weight of the answers tends toward "yes" overall, the project should be considered "research" and approved by an IRB prior to implementation. If the weight of the answers tends toward "no," the project is not "research" and is not subject to IRB oversight unless local institutional policies differ. Answering "yes" to sequence #1 or #2 – even if all other answers are "no" – typically will result in a finding that the project constitutes research. *It is important to consult with your local IRB if you are unsure how they would handle a particular case, as the analysis of the above issues cannot always be entirely objective and IRB policies and approaches vary significantly.*

Fig. 12.6 Worksheet to determine if a project is quality improvement or research. Developed by Rachel Nosowsky, Esq., based on The Hastings Center Report "The Ethics of Using QI Methods to Improve Health Care Quality and Safety." Reprinted from Quality Improvement vs Research, by Children's Hospital of Philadelphia Research Institute, Retrieved from https://irb.research.chop.edu/quality-improvement-vs-research

Institutional Approaches to Quality Improvement Initiatives

Institutions throughout the United States provide guidance for their employees to protect human subjects and follow the legal requirements of state and federal agencies that protect human rights. The sophistication of institutional guidelines varies as to what the institution documents on websites, expectations of their employees, and, specifically, the required approach to QI initiatives. For healthcare organizations to be successful in QI endeavors, the system in which QI initiatives are conducted should provide ethical oversight, have an accountability system in place for professional responsibility, and provide proper supervision and management of clinical care, even if IRB review is not required [36]. Taylor et al. found that there are a number of internal mechanisms within institutions that review QI initiatives prior to implementation without going to the IRB for initial review or oversight. The three most common mechanisms are review by the QI management team/office, clinical leadership conducting QI, and an advisory board (or equivalent) created for the purpose of reviewing QI [22]. The rigor of supervisory procedures for QI activities should include the expected impact of the initiative and any additional risks when compared to usual care and must diligently observe the resources and methods used [38]. James proposes that the most consistent way for a QI team to be certain of appropriate oversight for QI initiatives is to view every initiative in a framework of risk for conflict of interest [16].

Future Trends

The principles of bioethics which include respect for autonomy, beneficence, non-maleficence, and justice are the basic foundations for clinical care, biomedical research, and organizational QI initiatives. Healthcare professionals benefit from understanding the pivotal developments in the history of medical ethics so they, in turn, can apply those principles in all aspects of their clinical, research, and quality responsibilities.

The increased attention on quality improvement and patient safety initiatives has sparked an intense focus on the protection of patients who are involved in QI initiatives. Institutions in which quality improvement initiatives take place increasingly grapple with the issues surrounding the protection of patients and determinations of when IRB protection is warranted. A number of guidelines and tools applicable to quality improvement initiatives identify when QI initiatives do and do not need the oversight of the IRB, and QI professionals increasingly understand the characteristics of situations where a quality improvement initiative may intersect with a research purpose. Ethical principles in healthcare extend across the entire continuum and informed dialogue and action will best ensure that all patients who participate in quality improvement and research endeavors are best protected from undue risk and harm.

Appendix

HHS.gov   US Department of Health & Human Services

Office for Human Research Protections

Quality Improvement Activities FAQs

How does HHS view quality improvement activities in relation to the regulations for human research subject protections?

Protecting human subjects during research activities is critical and has been at the forefront of HHS activities for decades. In addition, HHS is committed to taking every appropriate opportunity to measure and improve the quality of care for patients. These two important goals typically do not intersect, since most quality improvement efforts are not research subject to the HHS protection of human subjects regulations. However, in some cases quality improvement activities are designed to accomplish a research purpose as well as the purpose of improving the quality of care, and in these cases, the regulations for the protection of subjects in research (45 CFR part 46) may apply.

To determine whether these regulations apply to a particular quality improvement activity, the following questions should be addressed in order:

1. Does the activity involve research *(45 CFR 46.102(d))?*
2. Does the research activity involve human subjects *(45 CFR 46.102(f))?*
3. Does the human subjects research qualify for an exemption *(45 CFR 46.101(b))?*
4. Is the nonexempt human subjects research conducted or supported by HHS or otherwise covered by an applicable FWA approved by OHRP?

For those quality improvement activities that are subject to these regulations, the regulations provide great flexibility in how the regulated community can comply. Other laws or regulations may apply to quality improvement activities independent of whether the HHS regulations for the protection of human subjects in research apply.

Do the HHS regulations for the protection of human subjects in research (45 CFR part 46) apply to quality improvement activities conducted by one or more institutions whose purposes are limited to (a) implementing a practice to improve the quality of patient care and (b) collecting patient or provider data regarding the implementation of the practice for clinical, practical, or administrative purposes?

No, such activities do not satisfy the definition of "research" under *45 CFR 46.102(d)* which is "…a systematic investigation, including research development, testing and evaluation, designed to develop or contribute to generalizable knowledge…" Therefore the HHS regulations for the protection of human subjects do not apply to such quality improvement activities, and there is no requirement under these regulations for such activities to undergo review by an IRB or for these activities to be conducted with provider or patient informed consent.

Examples of implementing a practice and collecting patient or provider data for non-research clinical or administrative purposes include:

A radiology clinic uses a database to help monitor and forecast radiation dosimetry. This practice has been demonstrated to reduce overexposure incidents in patients having multiple procedures. Patient data are collected from medical records and entered into the database. The database is later analyzed to determine if overexposures have decreased as expected.

A group of affiliated hospitals implements a procedure known to reduce pharmacy prescription error rates and collects prescription information from medical charts to assess adherence to the procedure and determine whether medication error rates have decreased as expected.

A clinic increasingly utilized by geriatric patients implements a widely accepted capacity assessment as part of routine standard of care in order to identify patients requiring special services and staff expertise. The clinic expects to audit patient charts in order to see if the assessments are performed with appropriate patients and will implement additional in-service training of clinic staff regarding the use of the capacity assessment in geriatric patients if it finds that the assessments are not being administered routinely.

Do quality improvement activities fall under the HHS regulations for the protection of human subjects in research (45 CFR part 46) if their purposes are limited to (a) delivering healthcare and (b) measuring and reporting provider performance data for clinical, practical, or administrative uses?

No, such quality improvement activities do not satisfy the definition of "research" under 45 CFR 46.102(d), which is "…a systematic investigation, including research development, testing and evaluation, designed to develop or contribute to generalizable knowledge…" Therefore the HHS regulations for the protection of human subjects do not apply to such quality improvement activities, and there is no requirement under these regulations for such activities to undergo review by an IRB or for these activities to be conducted with provider or patient informed consent.

The clinical, practical, or administrative uses for such performance measurements and reporting could include, for example, helping the public make more informed choices regarding healthcare providers by communicating data regarding physician-specific surgical recovery data or infection rates. Other practical or administrative uses of such data might be to enable insurance companies or health maintenance organizations to make higher performing sites preferred providers or to allow other third parties to create incentives rewarding better performance.

Can I analyze data that are not individually identifiable, such as medication databases stripped of individual patient identifiers, for research purposes without having to apply the HHS protection of human subjects regulations?

Yes, whether or not these activities are research, they do not involve "human subjects." The regulation defines a "human subject" as "a living individual about whom an investigator conducting research obtains (1) data through intervention or interaction with the individual, or (2) identifiable private information... Private information must be individually identifiable (i.e., the identity of the subject is or may readily be ascertained by the investigator or associated with the information) in order for obtaining the information to constitute research involving human subjects." Thus, if the research project includes the analysis of data for which the investigators cannot readily ascertain the identity of the subjects and the investigators did not obtain the data through an interaction or intervention with living individuals for the purposes of the research, the analyses do not involve human subjects and do not have to comply with the HHS protection of human subjects regulations.

(See *OHRP Guidance on Research Involving Coded Private Information or Biological Specimens.* October 2008: available at http://www.hhs.gov/ohrp/sites/default/files/ohrp/policy/cdebiol.pdf - PDF.)

Are there types of quality improvement efforts that are considered to be research that are subject to HHS human subjects regulations?

Yes, in certain cases, a quality improvement project may constitute nonexempt human subjects research conducted or supported by HHS or otherwise covered by an applicable FWA. For example, if a project involves introducing an untested clinical intervention for purposes which include not only improving the quality of care but also collecting information about patient outcomes for the purpose of establishing scientific evidence to determine how well the intervention achieves its intended results, that quality improvement project may also constitute nonexempt human subjects research under the HHS regulations.

If I plan to carry out a quality improvement project and publish the results, does the intent to publish make my quality improvement project fit the regulatory definition of research?

No, the intent to publish is an insufficient criterion for determining whether a quality improvement activity involves research. The regulatory definition under 45 CFR 46.102(d) is "*Research* means a systematic investigation, including research development, testing and evaluation, designed to develop or contribute to generalizable knowledge." Planning to publish an account of a quality improvement project does not necessarily mean that the project fits the definition of research; people seek to publish descriptions of non-research activities for a variety of reasons, if they believe others may be interested in learning about those activities. Conversely, a quality improvement project may involve research even if there is no intent to publish the results.

Does a quality improvement project that involves research need to be reviewed by an IRB?

Yes, in some cases. IRB review is needed if the research involves human subjects, is not exempt, and is conducted or supported by HHS or otherwise covered by an applicable FWA.

For more information see *exempt categories*.

Does IRB review of a quality improvement project that is also nonexempt human subjects research always need to be carried out at a convened IRB meeting?

No, if the human subjects research activity involves no more than minimal risk and fits one or more of the categories of research eligible for expedited review, the IRB chair or another member designated by the IRB chair may conduct the review.

The categories of research eligible for expedited review are available at: http://www.hhs.gov/ohrp/regulations-and-policy/guidance/cateqories-ofresearch-expedited-review-procedure-1998/index.html.

If a quality improvement project involves nonexempt research with human subjects, do I always need to obtain informed consent from all subjects (patients and/or providers) involved in the research?

No, the HHS regulations protecting human subjects allow an IRB to waive the requirements for obtaining informed consent of the subjects of the research when:

(a) The risk to the subjects is minimal
(b) Subjects' rights and welfare will not be adversely affected by the waiver
(c) Conducting the research without the waiver is not practicable
(d) If appropriate, subjects are provided with additional pertinent information after their participation *(45 CFR 46.116(d))*

Other applicable regulations or laws may require the informed consent of individuals in such projects independent of the HHS regulations for the protection of human subjects in research.

If a quality improvement project is human subjects research requiring IRB review, do I need to obtain separate IRB approval from every institution engaged in the project?

No, not if certain conditions are met. The HHS protection of human subjects regulations allows one IRB to review and approve research that will be conducted at multiple institutions. An institution has the option of relying upon IRB review from another institution by designating that IRB on its FWA and submitting the revised FWA to OHRP and having an IRB Authorization Agreement with the other institution.

Reproduced from US Department of Health and Human Services. Quality improvement activities FAQs, n.d., Retrieved from https://www.hhs.gov/ohrp/regulations-and-policy/guidance/faq/quality-improvement-activities/#

References

1. National Center for Ethics in Health Care (2015) Ethics consultation: responding to ethics questions in health care, 2nd edn. National Center for Ethics in Health Care, Washington, DC. https://www.ethics.va.gov/docs/integratedethics/ec_primer_2nd_ed_080515.pdf
2. Beauchamp TL, Childress J (2001) Principles in biomedical ethics, 5th edn. Oxford University Press, Oxford/New York
3. National Institutes of Health Office of History (2009) Laws related to the protection of human subjects: the Nuremberg code. https://history.nih.gov/research/downloads/nuremberg.pdf
4. Gray Fred D (1998) The Tuskegee syphilis study. New South Books, Montgomery. http://www.history.ucsb.edu/faculty/marcuse/classes/33d/projects/medicine/The%20Tuskegee%20Syphilis%20Study.htm
5. Centers for Disease Control and Prevention (2015) The Tuskegee timeline. In: U.S. public health service syphilis study at Tuskegee. http://www.cdc.gov/tuskegee/timeline.htm
6. U.S. Public Health Service Division of Venereal Diseases (1932) The Tuskegee study of untreated syphilis in the male negro. U.S. Public Health Service Division of Venereal Diseases, Washington, DC
7. The National Commission for the Protection of Human Subjects of Biomedical and Behavioral Research (1979) The Belmont report. https://www.hhs.gov/ohrp/regulations-and-policy/belmont-report/index.html
8. World Medical Association (WMA) (2018) WMA declaration of Helsinki – ethical principles for medical research involving human subjects. https://www.wma.net/policies-post/wma-declaration-of-helsinki-ethical-principles-for-medical-research-involving-human-subjects/
9. American Medical Association (AMA) (n.d.) Code of medical ethics overview. https://www.ama-assn.org/delivering-care/ethics/code-medical-ethics-overview
10. Shuster E (1997) Fifty years later: the significance of the Nuremberg Code. N Engl J Med 337:1436–1440. https://doi.org/10.1056/nejm199711133372006
11. Jonsen AR, Siegler M, Winslade WJ (2010) Clinical ethics: a practical approach to ethical decisions in clinical medicine, 7th edn. New York, McGraw Hill
12. National Center for Ethics in Health Care (2015) Ethics consultation: responding to ethics questions in health care, 2nd edn. U.S. Department of Veterans Affairs, Washington DC. https://www.ethics.va.gov/docs/integratedethics/ec_primer_2nd_ed_080515.pdf
13. Texas Children's Hospital Clinical Ethics Committee (2017) Pathway for informed decision making. Texas Children's Hospital, Houston
14. Bruce CR, Majumder MA, Bibler T et al (2015) A practical guide to developing & sustaining a clinical ethics consultation service. Baylor College of Medicine Center for Medical Ethics and Health Policy, Houston
15. U.S. General Accounting Office (1995) Report to the ranking minority member, subcommittee on health, committee on ways and means, house of representatives: patient self-determination act. https://www.gpo.gov/fdsys/pkg/GAOREPORTS-HEHS-95-135/pdf/GAOREPORTS-HEHS-95-135.pdf
16. James B (2007) Healthcare delivery ethics of QI white paper. https://intermountainhealthcare.org/-/media/files/research/healthcare-delivery-ethics-of-qi.pdf?la=en
17. American Psychological Association (2019) Frequently asked questions about institutional review boards. https://www.apa.org/advocacy/research/defending-research/review-boards
18. U.S. Food & Drug Administration (1998) Institutional review boards frequently asked questions. https://www.fda.gov/regulatory-information/search-fda-guidance-documents/institutional-review-boards-frequently-asked-questions
19. Weiserbs KF, Lyutic L, Weinberg J (2009) Should quality improvement projects require IRB approval? Acad Med 84(2):153. https://doi.org/10.1097/ACM.0b013e3181939881
20. Grady C (2015) Institutional review boards: purpose and challenges. Chest 148(5):1148–1155. https://doi.org/10.1378/chest.15-0706

21. U.S. Department of Health and Human Services (n.d.) Quality improvement activities FAQs. https://www.hhs.gov/ohrp/regulations-and-policy/guidance/faq/quality-improvement-activities/#
22. Taylor HA, Pronovost PJ, Faden RR et al (2010) The ethical review of health care quality improvement initiatives: findings from the field. Commonw Fund 95:1–10. https://www.commonwealthfund.org/sites/default/files/documents/___media_files_publications_issue_brief_2010_aug_1436_taylor_ethical_review_hlt_care_qual_improve_ib_v4.pdf
23. Schreiner MS (2019) Quality improvement vs research. In: Children's Hospital of Philadelphia Research Institute Institutional Review Board. https://irb.research.chop.edu/quality-improvement-vs-research
24. Lynn J (2004) When does quality improvement count as research? Human subject protection and theories of knowledge. Qual Saf Health Care 13:67–70. https://doi.org/10.1136/qshc.2002.002436
25. Shirey MR, Hauck SL, Embree JL et al (2011) Showcasing differences between quality improvement, evidence-based practice, and research. J Contin Educ Nurs 42(2):57–68. https://doi.org/10.3928/00220124-20100701-01
26. Miller FG, Emanuel EJ (2008) Quality-improvement research and informed consent. N Engl J Med 358(8):765–767. https://doi.org/10.1056/NEJMp0800136
27. Berenholtz SM, Pronovost PJ, Lipsett PA et al (2004) Eliminating catheter-related bloodstream infections in the intensive care unit. Crit Care Med 32(10):2014–2020
28. Savel RH, Goldstein EB, Gropper MA (2009) Critical care checklists, the keystone project, and the Office for Human Research Protections: a case for streamlining the approval process in quality-improvement research. Crit Care Med 37(2):725–728. https://doi.org/10.1097/CCM.0b013e31819541f8
29. Pronovost P, Needham D, Berenholtz S et al (2006) An intervention to decrease catheter-related bloodstream infections in the ICU. New Engl J Med 355(26):2725–2732. https://doi.org/10.1056/NEJMoa061115
30. Healthcare Benchmarks and Quality Improvement (2008) OHRP action shuts down quality improvement research in Michigan. Healthcare Benchmarks Qual Improv 15(3):25–2831
31. Gawande A (2007) A lifesaving checklist. New York Times. https://www.nytimes.com/2007/12/30/opinion/30gawande.html
32. McNett M, Lawry K (2009) Research and quality improvement activities: when is institutional review board review needed? J Neurosci Nurs 41(6):344–347. https://doi.org/10.1097/JNN.0b013e3181b7052e
33. Cacchione PZ (2011) When is institutional review board approval necessary for quality improvement projects? Clin Nurs Res 20(1):3–6. https://doi.org/10.1177/1054773810395692
34. Platteborze LS, Young-McCaughan S, King-Letzkus I et al (2010) Performance improvement/research advisory panel: a model for determining whether a project is a performance or quality improvement activity or research. Mil Med 175(4):289–291. https://doi.org/10.7205/milmed-d-09-00087
35. Wagner RM (2003) Ethical review of research involving human subjects: when and why is IRB review necessary? Muscle Nerve 28(1):27–39. https://doi.org/10.1002/mus.10398
36. Baily MA, Bottrell M, Lynn J et al (2006) The ethics of using QI methods to improve health care quality and safety. Hastings Center Report. https://www.thehastingscenter.org/publications-resources/special-reports-2/the-ethics-of-using-qi-methods-to-improve-health-care-quality-safety/
37. Hockenberry M (2014) Quality improvement and evidence-based practice change projects and the institutional review board: is approval necessary? Worldviews Evid-Based Nurs 11(4):217–218. https://doi.org/10.1111/wvn.12049
38. Jennings B, Baily MA, Bottrell M et al (2007) Health care quality improvement: ethical and regulatory issues. Hastings Center Report. http://www.thehastingscenter.org/wp-content/uploads/Health-Care-Quality-Improvement.pdf

Additional Resources-Further Reading

Lynn J, Baily MA, Bottrell M et al (2007) The ethics of using quality improvement methods in health care. Annals of Internal Medicine 146(9):666–673

Schumann JH, Alfandre D (2008) Clinical ethical decision making: the four topics approach. Semin Med Pract 11:36–39

Tarzian AJ, Wocial LD ASBH Clinical Ethics Consultation Affairs Committee (2015) A code of ethics for health care ethics consultants: journey to the present and implications for the field. The American Journal of Bioethics 15(5):38–51. https://doi.org/10.1080/15265161.2015.1021966

Index

A

AAFP, *see* American Academy of Family Physicians

AAAHC, *see* American Association of Ambulatory Health Care

AAP, *see* American Academy of Pediatrics

ABMS, *see* American Board of Medical Specialties

ACO, *see* Accountable care organization

Absenteeism, 200, 221, 229

Academic detailing, 25

Accountable care organization (ACO), 126, 156, 185, 246, 250, 252, 254

Accounting
generally accepted accounting principles (GAAP), 210–211
reporting tools, 207–210
skills needed, 231–214
statutory accounting standards, 211
types of accounting systems, 210–213

Accounting basis
accrual-based accounting, 209
cash-basis accounting, 208

Accreditation
agencies, 220, 221, 233, 262, 283, 288, 313
financial impact, 132, 222
government mandates, 219
and utilization management, 158–160

Accreditation Council on Graduate Medical Education (ACGME), 59, 273–275

Accrual-based accounting, 209

ACGME, *see* Accreditation Council on Graduate Medical Education

Achievable Benchmark of Care (ABC), 40, 208, 210

ACMQ, *see* American College of Medical Quality

Active failures, 55–58, 80

Activity-based cost accounting, 213

Administration errors, medication, 62, 63, 67

Administration phase, *see* Medication loop

Advance directives, 326, 328

Adverse drug event (ADE), 60, 61, 105

Adverse drug reaction, 61

Adverse events, 10, 44, 54–55, 61, 74–76, 78, 80, 82–84, 86, 108, 109, 292, 293, 307–309
See also Errors, medical

Advocacy, 126, 155, 159, 162, 188, 193, 333

Affinity diagrams, 12–15

Affordable Care Act, *see* Patient Protection and Affordable Care Act

Agency for Healthcare Research and Quality (AHRQ), xi, 3, 35, 45, 46, 73, 76, 151, 152, 154–157, 186, 254–256, 285–287, 292, 308, 312, 339
Hospital Survey on Patient Safety Culture, 73

AHRQ, *see* Agency for Healthcare Research and Quality

AICPA, *see* American Institute of Certified Public Accountants

Alarms, 54, 60, 66, 128

Alert fatigue, 37, 92, 108–109

Alerts, 37, 65–67, 74, 80–82, 95, 104, 106–109, 123, 129, 327

Allergic reactions, 60, 67

Allocation strategy, 214

All Patient Refined Diagnosis-Related Groups (APR-DRGs), 104

Alternative dispute systems, 310

Printed in the United States
by Baker & Taylor Publisher Services